T0380292

F*CK THE SYSTEM, MAKE LOVE

(R)EVOLUTION OF CONSCIOUSNESS.

LIANA LAGA

All bible versions from NIV

www.mandalaslovensko.sk

Balboa Press books may be ordered through booksellers or by contacting:

Balboa Press
A Division of Hay House
1663 Liberty Drive
Bloomington, IN 47403
www.balboapress.com
1 (877) 407-4847

Contact / Author: LianaLaga.com
Translation: Profipreklady.cz
Cover: PatriKelemen.com
Mandala of the book: mandalaslovensko.sk

Print information available on the last page.

ISBN: 978-1-9822-1554-5 (sc)
ISBN: 978-1-9822-1555-2 (e)

Balboa Press rev. date: 12/06/2018

"TOTUS MUNDUS AGIT HISTRIONEM"

"ALL THE WORLD'S A STAGE"

Motto of William Shakespeare's Globe Theatre

CONTENTS

INTRODUCTION

Everyone would like to take a ***magic pill*** *that would (immediately, if possible) solve all his problems. Best of all, those offering the pill promise you the fastest results! "I have just the right medicine for you (whatever your problem is). I have a magic solution to open your eyes! I have the guaranteed recipe for happiness! Listen and pay for it! I will save you!"*

Sorry, but I have bad news for you – such a pill does not really exist.

But I have good news, too: ***You are the pill.***

I observe the world around me, and I don't like it. And now, I am not talking about my own personal reality as much as I am referring to our global reality. Honestly - if it was only about me, I would never bring myself to spend so much time in front of the computer.

There are a lot of books written about life, and the only differences are in the personalities of the authors who interpret the same truth in different ways. **But for the first time you have the chance to see the whole picture – the holistic view.** Each chapter describes the main ideas of a topic, but in each topic you can go deeper. And that is left to you in your individual development. The things that are happening on planet Earth these days are more than unbearable. Everyone is aware of it, but no one knows what to do about it. **This**

change needs to be individual. It is up to each of us, and it is our responsibility to make this world a better place.

"So many people say they want to save the world. Just try your block, will you?"
Rev. C. Williams

Everyone's fighting for freedom, but the "fight for freedom" is a contradiction in itself. It is not possible to fight for freedom – freedom simply is - in all of us. Only genuine people have the courage to go their own way. The others usually walk with the crowd. And that is just because they haven't found themselves yet…

"We are not going to achieve freedom by searching for freedom, but by searching for the truth." L. N. Tolstoy

Truth is a relative term, just because it has many forms. You do not need to agree with my truth, but if you at least start thinking about it, that will be the first step. If we were not in the period in which we currently are, I would most likely postpone this writing for at least twenty years to gain more experience. So that it would have weight, so that everyone would know that this was written by an older person (with gray hair, if possible) who has the right to comment on life. That's how we see it. Or am I wrong? Social conventions – they control us.

The truth is always relative in parallel with the present moment.

Life is change - a process. It is the only God that exists. Life.

So, I decided to explore it. I began to study at the "school of life" on my own, in practice. This is actually my "thesis" on life. Nothing more, nothing less. Or let's just say, that I am full of important information which is of no use to me if I keep it to myself and don't share it. Because **life is a game, but it is hard to play with people who don't know the rules.** Just as each machine has its own instructions for use; it is the same with life and people. And they are actually very simple instructions! And my greatest desire is to be surrounded by **happy people.** Because why else would we be here?! Today is that exceptional time in terms of space cycles for which we have all been waiting - when miracles can happen. The vibrations of the Earth have increased, and everything is accelerated. Ideas are materialized more quickly, and therefore it is very important to understand how our minds work, how we work. If **everyone goes down the right path** (to ourselves), we will **all join together in a wonderful flow of synchronicity, where everything happens in accordance with what we manifest** (no one on Earth has the mission to "destroy", rather, everyone should create something). **When each of us starts working individually, it will join us all together.**

"The person we know the least is our own self."
Cicero

This book is too esoteric for consumerist people and too consumerist for esoteric people. But I say that only one chapter in the book is about esotericism. The state of knowing how one functions has nothing to do with the esoteric. It is very important to find the middle ground (unity) in everything. Connect the two imaginary worlds – East and West – the heart and the head. This is not about some unique literary achievement. T**his book was not written to be liked - it should be, above all, understood.**

This book is "alive" so each person will get something different out of it, as each person is in a different stage of development. If you are ready, you will find that reading these lines is like balm for the soul. Basically, I will just put into words all the feelings and thoughts which you have already been having for a long time. If you are still not ready, you will easily get angry and think: That girl has some nerve to say that! Alternatively, you will not like what you read, but you will know that it is the truth and you have to overcome yourself - for your own good. People who are interested in the "study of life" will not find much new, I'll just offer them a so-called summary. If, however, you get the feeling that it does not offer you anything new and you already know everything, but you are still not unconditionally happy (you still fight at some level), then there is only one option – let's finally put your knowledge into practice! That's all.

"The shortest answer is to act."
E. Hemingway

Many truths are repeated here because it is important that they become commonplace, just as you brush your teeth every morning, only it will be happening inside of you. Of course, the truth depends on the circumstances, and it's up to you to accept it and interpret it. If you feel that you do not understand something or you do not agree with something, do not stop reading, do not judge, do not worry about it at the moment. As you continue, you will gradually get the answers to most of your questions. And if you do not find them in this book, believe me, they are inside of you – when you start to ask, you will start to get answers - that is the law of the Universe. Sometimes in the text I intentionally provoke you so that you can see what things you assign undue importance to and you will be able to work with them. Moreover, there is a lot of information here, and I would advise you to read this book twice. The first time, just read informatively - to comprehend it in its entirety, and the second time, go deep, thinking about the details. Originally, even the chapters in this book were arranged differently, so their order is unimportant. However, you can also read through it in a so-called tarot way, which means that you open to any page and start reading. And while my main goal is to awaken people on the level of consciousness, it is important to "see" the bare reality which we are all part of. These topics are not pleasant because our history has been manipulated in the wrong direction for thousands of years. Today, however, it is necessary to change the course of this world which is actually based on exploitative principles. There are many solutions that depend only on us - ordinary people. Therefore, don't be intimidated by these topics and if something provokes doubts in you, please, start to do your own research regarding anything which seems doubtful to you.

"If liberty means anything at all, it means the right to tell people what they do not want to hear."
G. Orwell

This book includes many quotes that I mostly chose after writing my own text. I added them especially for you, to help you understand that "the truth" is always the same and that it has come to the minds of many people in the past. You will notice that it is dominated by the quotes of the Indian mystic Osho. That's because he is my big inspiration and this book is no exception. To a large extent, it was written in the Osho meditation resort in India, so it has certainly been influenced by this master. But this mostly concerns the universal truths that cannot belong to a specific author. In this text, you will also find sentences that you often say to yourself. Quotes also give us the opportunity to reflect on the main idea. Later you will understand that it is best to meditate on it. Meditation leads to understanding. Do not judge or criticize, just focus on the context and freely receive what you like. Only after that, comes the most important part, and that's your only task - to put it all into practice. **In this day and age there are a lot of spiritual posers in the world who can speak for hours on these topics and they still understand nothing. They have been overwhelmed by their own spiritual pride, which is oftentimes worse than any atheist stance. It's just a superficial image, like everything nowadays.**

"Now that we have learned to fly the air like birds, swim under water like fish, we lack one thing – to learn to live on earth as human beings."
G. B. Shaw

Almost everyone would like to be someone other than who they are. However, they are many times ignorant of the fundamental fact that they have no idea who they really are. The irony of this situation is that people basically do not want to change at all (in terms of what is inside). They revel in their worlds, and they are used to just complaining about everything. They live in a world of ego (mind) and know nothing about it. Ego does not want to change. It wants to gain new information and knowledge (so-called fictitious intellect), but it believes it is perfect. Only a stupid person believes that there is nothing for them to improve. Did that impact you or hurt you? Try for a moment to separate from your mind - watch it… It is only some kind of program which you are accustomed to. There is nothing more to it. Your mind will be talking to you the whole time you are reading this book and will try to convince you of the opposite of what you are reading. Never mind, relax, do not worry about it, let it flow… as if it was happening to someone else. Everything is changing; nothing stands still. Life is change. Nothing is "still" - not even you. There is always something going on inside you. Whether it is in the physical body or in your head, there is always something going on. Our goal is to find ourselves in the first place, and then "only" the silence. Because your own "hell" is created solely by you - in your head. Also, if you don't love yourself, you are unable to truly love others. Love is not something we should seek or obtain. Unconditional love must first exist towards oneself. Has anyone ever defined the true nature of love? Can you define laughter, joy or beauty? It is not possible. **The noblest and most beautiful things can be lived and learned, but not truly defined**. That`s why writing about all these things is such a difficult task. Because the real point of being is indescribable. Nothing significant can be expressed by words. Speech not only divides us as nations, but also as people. Speech is the source of confusion, and therefore the "secret of life" lies in silence, in survival…

"You can always find something to defend. You can defend your foolishness, you can defend your disease, you can defend your neurosis. You can go on defending the state in which you are. You can defend your suffering, your misery. People defend their hell so passionately – they don't want to get out of it. The moment you say 'Yes, I'm wrong' you will immediately feel better. You don't have to defend yourself anymore and you can be completely open."
Osho

I am honest and so is this book. Maybe you are not always able to accept new views, but open your heart. **The truth will set you free.** In what aspects is this book therefore different from the others? I live in the everyday world. I face the same reality as everyone else – I have lived in Europe, Australia, India, and the USA. I am quite an "ordinary" girl and I write so that everyone can understand, so that every reader can apply this to his or her life. My expressive approach is necessary in this case because, once again, we find ourselves in a very problematic time. If we do not change something, we will destroy ourselves. I have chosen a point from some great teachers, although **it is YOU who will always be (and who has always been) the best teacher for yourself**. It is not important whether you believe me or not, **after all, you still need to live through everything.** Also, I still have a lot of "work" to do on myself, but that's why I am here… We all are! But most importantly, we should enjoy it all!

You do not need to believe me. Check everything out for yourself and find your own truth. I try to do that myself every day, and the fact that I know the context gives me an incredible feeling of happiness. Suddenly, everything is completely different. Everything has its purpose. If you want to live in a sensible world, welcome! Only your ego will initially fight these lines because it is used to living a life as before. Ego is afraid of change, and actually, a change in thinking is the best thing you can do for yourself. This sounds very simple, but it is tough work. Work with yourself. **Do you really want to be responsible for your own life?**

"Try to work as much as possible, to truly live!"
W. Saroyan

Let this book be your personal meditation, which will make you listen… not to me, but to yourself.

(I would like to thank all those whose quotes have helped me put together this book. I believe that it is also your purpose to spread these ideas supporting what we all seek to promote. I believe that our overall objective is the same and that we will not go against it (ourselves). THANK YOU! Truth and love will win… PEACE :)

(R)EVOLUTION OF CONSCIOUSNESS

"I know that I know nothing."
Socrates

This Socrates quotation contains more truth than you would think. It includes paradox, duality, and life. If you start looking for the truth, you will never stop. The further you dig, the more you realize that you actually know nothing.

It is said that man is inherently evil, greedy, egotistical, combative – in short, that he has many negative traits. No one, however, is looking at our society as a real whole. Maybe you feel that events on the other side of the world do not relate to you at all. You are right; they do not. But the people who live and die there are people exactly like you are. Aren't chance our education, culture, and religion the culprits, being built on foundations that are absolutely poor and have been unable to meet human needs for thousands of years?

"Cruising the sea and changing cities have no value! If you want to escape what's bothering you, do not change places – change yourself!"
Seneca

Our packaging is constantly changing and our technology is expanding. Our outer appearance seems to signal our incredible advancement, but the opposite is true. In their essence, humans have not changed at all. This can be most easily seen in literature or theatre, which has mirrored society for centuries. If you read Shakespeare, Molière or Dostoevsky and compare their characters with people today, you will understand that humans are still the same ignorant creatures living in their gardens, convinced of their insurmountability, and longing for power, recognition, sex, and last but not least, always for love. On the other hand, we feel that more and more things are changing from day to day. Yes, they do – every moment.

Nothing is certain except change – no other constant exists.

Therefore, if you think you are perfect, it's time to realize that no one is, was, or will ever be "perfect". Nevertheless, everything is perfect as it is. The dichotomy of life is in everything. Man is not bad or good. He is only what you make of him. Therefore, it is time to take responsibility for the whole world – that is the only way to invite real transformation. All of us are responsible for where we are just now. If we don't critically approach the issue, the humans of tomorrow will be exactly the same as they were a hundred or a thousand years ago. **This world is far from being OK, and there is no evidence more convincing than today's human.**

"It is essential that a person can read not only books but also real life."
N. K. Krupskaya

Humans are the latest creation of unconscious evolution. (Despite the fact that all evolution is led by consciousness. In any case, this does not mean that everything is predetermined. Consciousness itself is free and unpredictable.) At the moment when there is consciousness, there is no return. Consciousness is the target of the unconscious evolution we all know as the creation of the world. **Humans can only freely decide whether to continue their development on the conscious level or not.**

"We all want to do good, but only seem to create evil. We all want peace, but are constantly fighting each other. We all want love, yet there is so much hatred. Everything has its light and shadow, every single thing in this world. One example for all: Every intelligent and informed person must stand against nuclear power. You really have to question the state of mind and spirit of the people who support nuclear energy. It shows suppression of the shadow. People are ignorant, not aware - and that is their shadow. Consciousness is light."

Dr. R. Dahlke

Consciousness has been a mystery to mankind since time immemorial. It belongs in the same indefinable category as love. People have tried to expand their consciousness in many ways. The most common ways include drugs from the outside and meditation from within. Nevertheless, clinical death can lead to expanded consciousness, too. After such an experience, your consciousness will never vibrate at the same frequency as it did before. Therefore, people who have experienced clinical death may seem to be a bit different (being much closer to the overall essence of being). However, only few people are aware that such conditions also bring responsibility. You should learn how you can consciously work with such conditions (so-called spiritual pride seems to be a simpler solution in this case). Therefore, people like, for example, recovered addicts should be able to quickly understand those, who have gone through clinical death. But how you function in the future is influenced by the very experiences through which that state came upon you. In practice, therefore, recovered addicts feel that nobody can really understand them, unless they have had a similar experience. But since they received those substances from the outside, they ultimately affect their egos and false feelings of importance. Even their recovery essentially supports mainly their particular ego so that their perception and knowledge move in an entirely new direction. However, in the latter case (meditation, clinical death) the experiences come from within, i.e., they are mostly based on humility.

Extended consciousness allows us to perceive the whole. It simply means that if, for example, you find yourself in conflict with ten people, in the same moment you are able to see/feel the consciousness of each specific person, i.e., you will be aware of the facts rather than your emotional associations. And this is the way to embrace the whole world and to be part of the Earth and the Universe. In any case, rational justification is not easy.

"Research on human consciousness is a great mystery even today, in the 21st century. We have explored the oceans, the Earth, the Moon… but the depth of human consciousness is like a jungle that the first pioneers are trying to penetrate."
E. Pales, cybernetic and sophiologic

Scientists jointly agree that our research on consciousness is still in its infancy. The same consensus exists regarding research on the Universe, where they are just confirming the initial idea that the more they know, the more mysterious the Universe is to them. Indeed, even in the late 19th century they were convinced that the Universe does not change (not to mention the conviction that we are the only beings in the Universe). What they can say with certainty is that we are constantly being bombed by cosmic rays – particles of the Universe (caused by cosmic explosions) that affect us and that are primarily responsible for the evolution, i.e., genetic fluctuations (which have been much more intensive since December 21, 2012). Nowadays, opinions that genetics is immutable are considered obsolete by biologists and neuroscientists.

"A lot of people think that hyperactivity of children, or schizophrenia are genetically determined, but the opposite is true. Nothing is genetically programmed. There are rare diseases that are actually caused genetically, but they are very scarce and only a small percentage of the population suffers from them. Outbreaks of many serious diseases may be subject to a genetic predisposition, but the

predisposition is not the same as predestination. All the research aiming to find the cause of disease in the human genome was doomed to failure even before it's started, because most diseases are not genetically predetermined. Heart disease, stroke, cancer, rheumatic diseases, autoimmune diseases, mental disorders in general, addictions - none of these diseases are genetically predetermined."
Dr. G. Maté (from film *Zeitgeist – Moving Forward*)

Everything in the universe works as a vibration, having its own rhythm, which influences the events around us. In his research titled DNA Phantom, quantum physicist Vladimir Poponin proved that particles of light that vibrate very quickly (the emotion of love) naturally bind to DNA structures and maintain their form even after the removal of the DNA. On the other hand, fear has a very low frequency and does not bind to DNA. As a result, **people who are influenced by fear have a much smaller impact on the changes in life. Emotions are thus triggers between these two poles. Moreover, they also directly affect genetics, i.e., the structure of our DNA, which shapes the physical world around us. Means that matter at its micro level is subjective to observer's awareness.**

"In quantum physics, objects are not precisely defined subjects, objects are rather defined as options. What options? Options for human consciousness to choose."
A.Goswami, physicist

In my opinion, if we could precisely define, understand, and activate the functionality of the overall structure of DNA, we would be able to explain consciousness as such from a scientific perspective. Modern humans fail to use as much as 91.8% of our total information memory (DNA). For comparison, plants fail to use about 75% of their DNA and other animal species approximately 90% - which means that they are more in harmony with nature than us humans. Although when it comes to animals, it depends on the species and level of perception. For example, chimpanzee DNA matches up with almost 99% of human DNA and more than 98% of that of mice – therefore, they are each used for different kinds of research. I also think that there must have been a reason why until 1998 (!) scientists from the West were forbidden to examine the other 90 percent of DNA that humans don't seem to use. As a result, it is just now that researchers around the world are exploring in depth that which they should have started their research with. Thankfully, since 2012 we have gradually (based on the level of awareness) begun to actuate the remaining strings of DNA, and there is even a generation of "new kids" who naturally make use of more of their DNA, allowing them to use so-called supernatural powers such as telepathy, clairvoyance, etc. What surprises me even more is that the researchers did not differentiate between DNA and the brain, when they say that we are using only about 10% of the brain. The brain, however, is only a tool that allows us to process what we send to it. Therefore, if we were able to activate new strings of DNA, the brain would naturally adapt - that is to the living intelligence that we are unable to define yet at the current stage of development.

"The mystery of consciousness" is also hidden in the pineal gland also known as "the third eye". Images illustrating it can be found in almost all hieroglyphics derived from Ancient Egypt, where highly intelligent creatures experimented with genetics. On the 49th day of life the human fetus' newly created pineal secretes a substance called dimethyltryptamine (abbreviated as DMT) into the bloodstream, and at that moment - according to ancient Vedas - the soul enters the body. It penetrates into the heart, rises along the spinal cord, and settles in a small gland in the center of the brain - the pineal gland (through Kundalini energy). Therefore, the DMT molecule opens our consciousness in a way similar to the effects of LSD, as well as causes dreaming processes, and that is why these mind-altering substances have been made illegal. Adults, according to X-ray images, already have a calcium precipitate in this miraculous spot, which naturally blocks its development. This is mainly the result of using fluoride. Not coincidentally, after the Second World War nations all over the world began adding fluoride to water, presenting it as the best way of preventing tooth decay. Applying this toxic element to the misled population is more than perfect.

"In a point of fact, fluoride causes more human cancer death, and causes it faster then any other chemical."
Dr. D. Burk, Phd. (34 years at the National cancer institute)

Scientists have also discovered a "consciousness turn off switch" in the brain, so they believe that consciousness is a property of the brain. Forgive me, but what you have discovered can easily be achieved with a liter of vodka. An excellent example is the television - the fact that you can turn it off does not mean that you know where the program or the broadcast comes from. It is as if you thought the TV set itself creates what you watch on it, and you would disassemble the box to the very last part and still not be able to understand that the signal originates somewhere else...

Unconscious evolution is collective. That`s why there are no individuals in it, but species. From the moment the creature becomes a "consciousness", it cannot return to the state of unconsciousness, but it becomes an individual with its own free will. Despite this fact, scientists say that man has no free will because according to Libet's experiments, the brain makes a decision 500 milliseconds before we perceive something as our decision. This is only a confirmation for me – that consciousness is not a property of the brain or the mind. The "new idea" arises only on the basis of a conscious decision which does not accompany thoughts. The idea is, in a way, given to us from above, which means that all perceptions are formed through consciousness as such, which we are able to adopt within the human body through DNA. It then sends this information to the brain, the brain ONLY processes it and creates a thought - in other words, gives the idea a shape (based on previously learned individual parameters). So for me, it is mainly proof that thoughts are material and formed on the basis of perceptions that consciousness creates for us. The fact that we were never taught about meditation, i.e., turning off the flow of ideas, "we think" it is the mind that determines our reality. **The mind is only a tool for the expression of consciousness.** If you need an example, take a drunken state for instance - you do not change your mind, but the consciousness (and that reveals the unconscious which you unconsciously suppress by rationalization, i.e., by thinking). For this reason it is important to become a fully conscious person - that is to consciously connect to the cosmic stream of consciousness that reflects our highest potential and is in harmony with our personal plan.

"My brain is only a receiver, in the Universe there is a core from which we obtain knowledge, strength and inspiration. I have not penetrated into the secrets of this core, but I know that it exists."
N.Tesla

In 1909, the scientist Ernest Rutherford shocked us by his discovery that the atom is an empty space, after which naturally followed the question: How can empty atoms form a solid world around us? It is therefore not possible even to prove, for example, non-physical communication that takes place through consciousness – not through the mind. Respectively, we can talk about the universal mind, but we are still talking about the consciousness itself. Only through the adoption of this fact can we understand paranormal powers, telepathy, astral traveling, and predicting the future. As a matter of fact, everything exists in a single moment and any specific person is able to connect to the universal consciousness (intuition) which is not affected by his own mind. Later, in the last hundred years, we indeed "split the atom", but one can't really say that we found something "new" (that is, with the exception of protons, neutrons, electrons and quarks). The fact remains that the atom is an indivisible unit that makes up the material world. However, if we look at the whole thing in layman's terms, we find that the atom contains positive and negative charges which hold it together, i.e., it is itself the bearer of a dual existence just as well as it is a principle of sacred geometry. The atom alone as well as its particles are representatives of Metatron's cube, which is the essence of all living things. It also contains the so-called pentagram, whose magical power was kept secret for centuries. The pentagram has always been used / is used mainly in various rituals and magic because it represents eternity. Its characteristic is that it can reproduce itself (also in the geometric sense), thus creating a spiral - vortex - that is representative of life. Today it has also been proved that the universe is not static and that the planets do not orbit around the sun, but this whole system is in constant motion, which is represented by a vortex.

Consciousness also causes inherent hereditary knowledge of certain patterns of behavior that need not be learned by people (e.g. maternity) and others which we should work with throughout our lives (they cause hereditary diseases unless we start to address them on the conscious level). Recently, some research was done, which was performed independently in the Netherlands and in Australia. Both agree on the fact that the immune system can be controlled by consciousness in many ways. This means that **our thoughts, beliefs and mood can affect our body on a physical level - scientifically confirmed.**

This whole process called life is possible mainly thanks to the sacred geometry (Metatron's cube = Golden Ratio, Fibonacci spiral, Flower of Life...) that forms this world. **Everything has been "designed" with absolute precision, especially since the force behind it is pure intelligence that synchronously adapts to the present moment in time.**

(If you have never addressed these issues before, it is possible that you will not understand after the first reading, so only freely accept them. Later on you will return to this issue, once you understand some other contexts. Please do not be discouraged.)

"Our brain is a believing device. We are set to believe an emotional explanation and the rationalization that it could be otherwise comes only afterwards. It is often emotionally uncomfortable that the rationalization is possible only through science which uses some tools for it and then fights against our own emotional barriers that make us believe in interesting results, although they are often false. Thus, for example, it is very difficult to explain to some believers that it could be otherwise."
The document – *Consciousness* by V. Cakanyova

Our biggest problem is that after the appearance of self-awareness, also uncertainty – duality entered the development. We have decided to experience the most material reality and try its extremes. It is the most popular sport of our minds – to move from extreme to extreme - it's easier. **"The golden mean" is about an attitude, not about acting.** But a conscious person always has a free choice, even if society says something else, even if he decides to do nothing, that was his choice. (Therefore, to promise "certainty" to anybody is the biggest nonsense.) Existence is essentially mechanical - things take place according to the law of action and reaction. Our conscious being, however, depends only on us - it is our responsibility, our deeds, our words, our choice. Society is always looking for reasons outside itself and mind represents society, therefore always sees problems elsewhere but not within itself.

Evolution has been here and is still present. It is in progress whether you want it to be or not. Therefore, it is high time to make a **revolution of consciousness.**

"It is our duty to make the world better than we found it."
J. Taylor

But this can happen only in individuals. So far we have tried to solve everything collectively. It is convenient for us to hide behind many different structures and customary "isms". It is easier to be a part of something than to take absolute responsibility for ourselves. One functions as part of a structure while admiring individuality. He is, however, afraid. Freedom goes hand in hand with responsibility, and therefore only strong individuals seek a kind of freedom. The others are very pleased to be part of a team because in the case of failure, they can blame it on someone else. It's so comfortable, and most people live like that. And the few brave individuals who choose to take responsibility for themselves, experience the feeling of power or the feeling of artistic freedom. However, we remain on one point.

When it suits us, we turn to "God" or nature. However, understand that we are part of both these units. We are part of nature, but unlike animals, we are a conscious species (in terms of awareness). So we cannot go back. We are part of the deity we can become. We are all on this journey, whether we like it or not - willingly. It is silly to blame nature or compare animals with humans. Although we bear a resemblance to monkeys, we have a consciousness that is self-aware. Why are today's monkeys not becoming people?

"Nature is a tremendous individualist. Everything it creates is presented with a personality."
K. Capek

It is not possible for us to turn back, once we have lived as man (respectively, this is possible only in very rare situations). The conscious decision to develop further is the greatest and only adventure for us. It's not the easy way, because we have a choice - always and everywhere. This means that we suffer from doubt, the fear of making decisions and of responsibility. These feelings often lead us to destructive thoughts. Depression has become the most widespread disease and often leads to suicide. It is also the evidence of conscious and unconscious existence. Animals cannot commit suicide; it is a purely human phenomenon (except for dolphins who are more intelligent than men on the level of consciousness). Although nowadays, we are faced with different mutations of animals and subsequent mental illnesses. In any case, it is a human responsibility. If, for example, a dog "commits suicide", it's a matter of instinctive survival instinct. He feels that he is in danger, so he will choose any of several other ways to survive – he does not think about it. In comparison, the dolphin can consciously decide to stop breathing. Birth and death are unconscious. They are of animal nature because we do not make a decision for them to happen (although on a higher level it is we who have chosen this life, this place, this family, this time to go through what our soul needs to experience in order to reach the higher levels of being - it's a so-called pyramid game). But again, **this does not mean that everything is predetermined in advance. There are always more possible scenarios for our lives that match our actions. However, the possibility that is the closest to our hearts and is also in harmony with what we really want, leads us along the path that was pre-determined by US to be the path of our experiences in this present life. They are thus those decisions which fulfill us and create natural joy and growth in us. Then we find ourselves in the divine synchronicity of our original plan.**

An important fact is that language (which we invented) is very limited. The word "consciousness" has two completely different meanings which at the same time have a lot in common. We are conscious beings in terms of the mind - consciousness. But consciousness itself, from a holistic point of view, is innate to everyone and everything, whether it is an animal or a stone. Consciousness, seen from this point of view, contains the information on the whole being – everything is alive. Therefore, from this perspective, animals do not have a "mind", but this does not mean that they do not have consciousness – a soul. We can even communicate at the level of consciousness, if we begin to consciously perceive others. So if a man does not choose conscious evolution, it is very likely that he will commit suicide. Not necessarily suicide according to its literal meaning, it is often a state of mind. Most people, paradoxically, choose it consciously - unconsciously. The slow and tedious process, in which we are still waiting for Godot.

"Nature never violates its laws. Gracious nature always ensures that wherever we go, we discover something we can learn from."
L. N. Tolstoy

When you realize that you're the one who bears the responsibility for your being, you will stop running to the unconscious (drugs, alcohol, sex, any addiction - any form of "escape"). Everything is up to you. Even your "God" has been born only in your imagination. If you realize that everything is connected with everything, you will understand that you are a part of everyone and everything, your consciousness will naturally expanding and many questions will be explained to you.

We are alone, but at the same time we are part of a whole. Duality is in everything, in all of existence, in every thought. Male – female, day – night, warm – cold, little – big, etc., so called yin and yang. The (rather paradoxical) fact remains that they are always just two sides of one coin. Therefore, our goal is to find unity in the paradox. It's ironic, isn't it? With growing consciousness comes also the growing recognition of the fact that we are alone – absolutely alone. You escape from this fact elsewhere – to your family, friends, romantic relationships, various groups, religions, and even material items. But the "enlightenment", which we all slowly walk towards, can be achieved only in solitude. A state of unconditional bliss, gratuitous joy – simply our absolutely natural state which we had experienced when we were children.

"There is no need to worry about anything in life.
The only need is to understand everything."
M. C. Sklodowska

However, there is a difference between being alone and feeling lonely. You have to grow up to understand solitude. If you do not take solitude as a fact, it will really make you feel lonely. You will search for company or for some drugs, just to forget yourself, just to not have to deal with yourself. You are afraid to be alone because society does not want to nurture individuality and therefore is afraid of all those who embrace freedom. Society is a social ego which does not want to (and even does not know how to) be alone. Just like your ego. Ego really needs society – to be recognized and admired, even though the opposite is often true, but this illusion is known only to the creator of the illusion. Whenever you are alone, ego gets weaker. It has no one to whom it can prove its strength. If you find the courage to be yourself, you will gradually become less and less selfish. You will start doing things for the joy of sharing and not for ego fulfillment (admiration). Man feels a natural joy when he becomes more and more aware. However, it is necessary to discover the path of meditation, to learn how to calm your own mind which constantly supports you as you proceed based on your learned programs. Otherwise your ego can begin to play the game of internal monologue telling you how wonderfully you can be alone and you will start acting superior towards others. Many people live like that - they are alone because their ego is so strong that it paradoxically does not allow anyone to come closer. Not to be hurt, to be safe from anyone taking their fictional freedom from them - the freedom of which they are the only masters, to have everything under control, to be safe from accidentally opening their hearts. Once again, we have two extreme positions. As in everything, it is necessary to find/understand the harmony between these two poles. Be humble and patient, mostly with yourself.

"Even the greatest mystery of life is something a man has to walk through alone. Who are all the people standing at a man's deathbed? Only supernumeraries. Different from those who were there at his birth."
J. Vrchlicky

Being alone is a true revolution. Learn to be independent of relationships – all relationships (this goes for family as well). You need a lot of courage for it. Jesus and Buddha were alone. This does not mean, however, that they left their families, that they left the world. It may seem so, but it's not so. The path of solitude does not lead through a secluded retreat. You also need to find balance in solitude and take responsibility for your actions. You will not find your solitude - silence, if you move to a cave or somewhere to the Himalayas. Your mind will always be with you.

Loneliness is not a matter of place or time, but of an understanding.

If you can live by yourself, you become responsible, which automatically comes with internal discipline and a real awakening of consciousness. The ability to live with the fact of your own solitude gives you the ability to experience the solitude of the others. Understanding that everyone is essentially alone will awaken a sincere compassion in you. If you're brave enough to live with reality as it is, you become innocent. Innocence cannot be learned, cannot be controlled. Innocence simply is. It is in us at the moment of our birth and also at the moment of our death. In essence, we are innocent, divine, blessed - enlightened. We just need to go back to the state where we are completely natural, the state which seems to be forgotten. Glimpses of this state are experienced whenever you do something that truly brings you joy. The real goal is to make this state a part of your daily life. Then you will understand the old saying - the path is the goal. If you live in the present and experience the present in all its beauty and you trust the existence, then you can get rid of all the "unnecessary" desires and fears. Awareness of unity will provide you with the understanding that everything is always as it should be and the flow of synchronicity will guide you along your way completely naturally. Joy is HERE and NOW, it has been and always will be, in everything and forever. Presence is the only thing which actually exists and only you will determine how it will continue...

Now it begins: **The individual transformation of consciousness.**

"So much has been told, maligned, gossiped, prevaricated, excused... The thing that will eventually kill this generation won't be the huge heap of plastic waste, but the rubbish created by our empty talking - as that cannot be recycled. If only all those words were empty... but they are not, they are full of poison, malice and also hatred... everyone is commenting on everything, everyone understands everything, everyone feels like spitting hatefully just to add some fuel to the flames. All those story tellers, fortune tellers and preachers are gradually abandoning their craft... Why should they be telling their stories in the country where everyone talks and nobody listens to anything! That's why we all should shut up and take silence as our witness, and this silence could stand against our blabber, so only our echo could be heard in this country of the deaf."

D. Hevier

(If you want to step deeper into the understanding of consciousness, I recommend reading, for example, Drunvalo Melchizedek, the author of numerous publications.)

GOD VERSUS RELIGION

"Existence is something that is. God is something that is not. Existence is reality; God is fiction. Existence is available for meditative people who can share the silence. God is a comfort for sick minds, sick psychology. Existence is not our production - God is. Therefore, there is only one existence and thousands of Gods."
Osho

Sorry, I'm just going to "take away" your most precious "truths". But if you open your heart to life, you will understand… My attitude to **man** is most wonderfully expressed by this quote:

"I have always believed in one thing. That God made us all the same. One is white and one is black. One is beautiful and one has a spotted face. But we all feel cold when it's freezing outside, and we all sweat when the sun shines. And we all need to breathe, if we don't want to suffocate. And all of us will eventually be taken and carried away. In other words, we are all mortal. And immortal. But we do not have to make slaves of the others. Everyone, whether his father was a president or a tinker, must have an equal opportunity to live a full life. No one may think that they are something more or better than the others. Maybe they are cleverer, maybe they are wearing a better shirt, maybe they are better with their hands or have bigger biceps. But all this only commits them to do more for those with smaller

biceps and worse shirts. This can only be believed and understood by those who like people. To like people and love people, that's the whole secret and the only recipe for happiness, and this is true for everyone. For me, for you, for Stalin and Truman, for the whole world."

J. Werich (1966)

This is what Metapedia says about God:

Atheism is the belief that God does not exist.

Deism is the belief that there is a God, while refusing any detailed religions. This word also indicates that God is the first cause - the Creator of the world who defined its basic principles, but does not interfere with further events.

Theism is the belief that there is a God or gods who created the world. They are omnipotent and active, and intervene in world events according to their own will.

Theism can come in more forms:

Monotheism is a parallel of theism – it is the belief that there is just one God who is omnipotent, who created the world, and who actively interferes with world affairs. The most well-known monotheistic religions are Christianity, Islam, and Judaism.

Monotheism most commonly takes the form of **eutheism** – this kind of monotheism declares that God is good. On the other hand, **dystheism** says that God does not have to be good, and he can even be bad.

Polytheism is similar to theism. It is the belief that there are multiple gods who are omnipotent (each god freely manages his or her own sphere of influence), created the world (either one of them, or together), and actively, according to their own will, intervene in world events.

Henotheism is sometimes seen as a parallel to polytheism and sometimes as an independent belief system. It is the belief that although there are multiple gods, one of them has primary status (a classic example is the worship of the sun disk Aten, introduced by Pharaoh Akhenaten IV. around 1340 BC. He still recognized the other Egyptian gods, but this one was the most important for him).

Pantheism is the belief that God is impersonal, and it is identified with the universe and the world.

Otiosus Deus (from Latin, meaning: "Resting God") is the belief that God created the world, but as soon as this work was finished, he stopped interfering with it. However, it is possible that some other gods did it for him.

National Socialism is not an atheist ideology. It includes some ideas about God. In general, National Socialism does not recognize any extensive religious teachings, but speaks only about "God", who is associated with nature or natural laws. God is seen as the primary cause, source, and main mover. He is, however, not described any further. This position is similar to deism and partly similar to pantheism.

Religion - in many languages, especially Indo-European languages (Italian, French, English, German, Spanish, Russian...), is a derivative of the Latin word *religio*. **The origin of the Latin word is NOT entirely clear.**

"A believer is someone who professes a religion; he who believes in unverifiable claims about things which cannot be seen, heard, felt or be touched. And he believes to such a

degree that he worships an unverifiable God, subordinates his behavior to certain rules, just stands by while people are being killed or lets others kill. The fact is, many people labeling others or themselves as believers did not come to the faith concerning their religion by themselves. It is only an idea with which they have grown up since childhood, and so they automatically adopted it, just as the others around them."

Metapedia

"The study of theology is the study of nothing; it is founded on nothing; it rests on no principles; it proceeds by no authorities; it has no data; it can demonstrate nothing; and it admits of no conclusion."

T. Paine, an English-American political philosopher from the 17th Century

"God must be lived, not talked about. You have to taste him. The process of narrating is theology. It only talks and never reaches the heart of the matter. It moves in a vicious circle. Theology is a policy that divides people. And if you can divide people, you can control them."

Osho

It is imperative that we change our relationship with God.

Forget the "old God" and find the new one in yourself. As you can see, this chapter will be very provocative, but open your heart and receive it without prejudice. You do not need to agree, but better yet - start asking questions.

"The God of the Old Testament is probably the most outrageous literary figure: jealous and proud of it, petty, unjust and ruthless, obsessed with control, vindictive, bloodthirsty, an ethnic cleanser, racist, hating women and homosexuals, murdering children,

relatives and entire nations, prejudiced, megalomaniacal, sadomasochistic, capricious and a malevolent bully."
R. Dawkins, scientist

God - a word like any other, and yet, the most controversial of all the words that we, the human race, have created. Religions took it as their own, and that's the problem. We all pretend that there is only one God, but in fact every religion has its own. All Western religions are based on the book of Genesis, although they are in constant conflict with each other. Does this sound logical?! Or is it that logic has no place in religion? Anyhow, something is not right here.

God is a process. Life is a process.

God = Life = Man

Just replace these words and everything will suddenly make much more sense.

There has been so much evil committed in the name of "some god" that it amazes me how he can still be considered the icon of religions. We should learn from the past. What is your opinion about the Crusades? Fought in the name of God, of course. How could "God permit" Hitler to exterminate the Jews?! Was it God who was acting, or a man?! Currently, the so-called terrorist attacks in the name of Allah… was it He who sat on a plane and crashed into the WTC?! No! It was a man! You ask then, how could He permit it? Now which "God" was it? Whose god?!

Religion is the biggest scam perpetrated on mankind. Paradoxically, **it was fabricated by people. Not God - people!** They are easily controlled, and those in higher places abuse it as much as they can. Till when?! Please understand that as we know it, religion is an illusion that we have invented ourselves. Those in power needed to control us and we needed to believe something, to join somebody, to define inexplicable things. However, if you really start to search for the origins of all the religions that currently exist in the world, you will find yourself going in a circle. Whenever you feel that you have arrived at the beginning, there is always new and more recent information that disputes the previous information. Finally, you will find that if there is something that is inconvenient, an entirely "new truth" will be created in the course of time (overwritten Old Testament, etc.). So ultimately, just using religion as an example, we could prove that everything is changeable. There has just been no change in this for a long time.

All religions are basically the same – they are about a man looking for the kingdom of heaven. All western religions (Christianity, Judaism, Islam) promise it. But there is a small catch that appears - after death. "Redemption" in each of these religions, which affects how the entire planet is run, is based on what actually is not. Because if they could answer with certainty: What is death? What exactly happens when a person dies? - then they (the religions) would not need to exist. Everyone physically dies, so we have the greatest common denominator that allows religions to exist - death. There is no man who would not be interested in this question, who would not, at least once, think about it. So the fact is that religion - whether you like it or not - concerns absolutely everyone. They just replaced the word *death* with the word *truth.* This is the entire know-how of this business plan. Because what **we have in ourselves as some kind of program, is an unquenchable thirst for truth and eternity.**

"Religion is what I call the art of life. It should not become instructions on how to defeat life, but it has to become a means to delve deeply into the mysteries of existence. Religion does not mean turning away from life, it means standing up face to face with

life. Religion is not an escape from life, but rather – it embraces life to the fullest. Religion is a full implementation of life."
Osho

So in today's materialistic world, we can say that religion is actually the product for which there is the greatest demand. We have three large manufacturers – competitors here. Of course, each of them claims that their way is the right one, and you can go "to heaven" only if you strictly follow the rules they sell. We have been buying them for thousands of years because it's easier than looking for our own truth. And in thousands of disguises we have been looking for the best manufacturer - today it is Christianity, tomorrow you'll find solace in Islam, and maybe Judaism will appeal to you the day after tomorrow. Who will have the best advertisement today? Who will promise me more? You can convert from one manufacturer to another, depending on what you want. But of course, every business has its own terms and conditions and this transaction is not without a "lucrative" sales contract. At that moment, you will encounter for the first time what our merchants call "the golden rules", which are basically only traditions of the past. Rituals from "the beginning", our own beliefs and words – this is your ticket to a competitive God. In this case, Christianity is the most peaceful religion because, for example, in Judaism you will only be taken "seriously" after several generations, and in Islam you will never really be treated as equal – especially if you're a woman. Of course, most businesses do not like to lose their lambs, so if you were "born" (successfully represented the company from the cradle) into one of these religions, it will not be so easy to convert to a different one. The conditions do not change, of course; you just risk a complete "disinheritance" from the former company. Suddenly, all that eternal love, with which they all pay so peacefully, will be lost. You will never be able to return to your home-company, and you'll be probably rejected by all the "employees", who suffer from a false image of the perfect company.

When I look around, I do not feel that society is founded on the so-called religious principles, which are, in fact, love, truth, and freedom. Sadly, these are the slogans the well-known companies present all the time, despite the fact that all their actions say something completely different.

Let's look at the most famous companies - religions, which, whether you like it or not, govern this world. But not only do they control it, they are continually destroying it. And not only are they destroying Earth, killing people, and fighting against each other, they still think that it is them, and no one else, who has a monopoly on Earth and man, and that it is only their company that will eventually buy out the whole world! Only one company is the chosen and right one! Isn't it ironic that all three of these companies have a common base - Jerusalem?! The holy place where people from all these companies come to pray. How could some prophet have come up with the idea that his vision is the most accurate?! Don't we all have the same "boss"?! Is it not, by chance, just an interpretation by clever manipulators?!

Jesus - a man like any other. He knew the alchemy of life and reached so-called enlightenment, which in his case is called Christ. This condition, however, was not known to the others. And what we do not know, we are mostly either afraid of or admire. In any case, we cannot decide how we feel about it. If we do not know how to explain something, we will try to interpret it our own way. We can call it religion. There was a man we believed in, he performed miracles! Oh, it's God! Sorry, the Son of God! Never mind that God did not tell us that himself; it is enough that he just presented himself that way. Let's believe in him (?), preserve him forever and for all! Wait, but actually Jesus was a Jew, and Jews do not allow Christians in their temples. I do not understand! Don't worry, we can ask Allah, or no, no - ask Buddha, we saw him as well, he knows everything and he is also "in"! Wait, but Buddha is only a state of mind again… **so what do we actually "believe" in?**

If all three of the aforementioned religions come from the same country, all of us who grew up in one of these three companies, I cannot help myself, but it means that we have absolutely equal backgrounds! Therefore, the **only real difference is race.**

Yes, there are different races. We are all part of some race that has been around for thousands of years. Each of us is different - that's a fact. Not only as individuals, but also physically. If we take collective consciousness into account, we can divide ourselves racially as well. But note that racial intolerance has been created only by man. In anthropology (the science of human beings), race is defined as*: a group of people with a set of similar, hereditary characteristics which make them different from other races.* This means that we share common characteristics and particular genetic predispositions with a certain type of people. They have, however, developed under the influences of the environment in which the group of people has lived. This means each race is different and each race is exceptional in some way. This does not mean that one race is better than the other races! It just means that everyone has been given certain abilities and if we combined them, we would get a perfect being, i.e., God – in his wonderful glory. It is our absolute stupidity to think that someone is more chosen and someone else less.

> *"The differences between races can be seen in everything from the intricate musical melodies of Mozart as compared to the elemental beat of rap, from quiet fashion to flashy dress, from thoughtful and considerate speech, to a loud and boisterous nature. In the cold north, as the European was more restrained and less aggressive, so the European had to develop an intense sense of community and social justice. In an African tribe of gatherers everyone can provision themselves. They can eat and indulge themselves while they gather*

and no one will be the wiser. They have no vital need to share or develop higher systems of social justice or common welfare. On the other hand, an individual hunter may not have luck bringing home any animal for weeks, but one hunter's reindeer kill might fend off starvation for the whole group. Pressures for community created group altruism, the social conscience and ethics of Europe."
D. Duke: My Awakening

This is only a fraction of the comparison of the two races. In reality, it can be seen using the example of the north, where they have the best developed social system (which has paradoxically changed into extreme abuse), and in the south they have incomparably freer lives. What we need to realize is the fact that we will never have the same predisposition as Africans and Africans will never have the same predisposition as Europeans. Therefore, we should take advantage of it, instead of humiliating and hating each other. The world is naturally being mixed, together we are creating unity, races are being founded on the basis of love, and brand new mixes are being created. So it is entirely primitive that even now there is still racism. Eventually, all the races will be so mixed that will not be possible to condemn someone on this basis. So the sooner you accept this fact, the better for you. We all know the visible racism too well. Black - white - yellow… it is the one that is the easiest to see. But the fact is that there is also another racism, which is not so often talked about, and that is religious racism. Unfortunately, it is based on races again. Several studies have shown that there are also some differences between races. For example, Jews dominate in verbal skills, Europeans in visual and spatial skills. If we go East, in Asia, we find again some exceptional abilities in each race, although it seems to us that they all look the same. Each ethnic group is dominant in something special. You can see it plain and clear - no one has athletes like Africa does, Jews are always the best businesspeople, Europeans have created the most beautiful monuments and works of art, etc. This is also true for the Romani (Gypsies or Indians?), who present a problem for several countries. It is like nobody realizes that they are just different based on their race (they have a dominant right hemisphere). For example, they are such great musicians (and nomads). So many of them have incredible talents. They just cannot exist in conditions that are not natural for them. How can you fully mature on the margin of society?! And we could go on like this. I do not really understand why do we keep fighting?! **If we instead initiated a global project in which we highlighted the strengths of every race, without prejudice, can you imagine how splendid it could be!?** Instead we do the exact opposite.

And in particular, let us realize one important fact: **If we were to do DNA testing today to trace our ancestry, we would find that we are part of almost every race on Earth. A group of seven million people is more genetically homogenous than a single tribe of chimpanzees in Africa. From the scientific point of view, all humans have the same neurons - the same genes.**

"Religion is offered to simple people as the truth, to the educated as a lie and to the ruling class as a utility."
Seneca Jr.

All religions are based on the completely wrong thing (death?!). Power and money have become their motivation. They forgot about man a long time ago, or maybe they never really found him in the first place.

Christianity - the most widespread religion on Earth. It has spread mostly in Europe, but it has followers all over the world. If you think it does not concern you, let me remind you that we are all using the Christian calendar – we distinguish the time before the birth of Christ and after the birth of Christ. It seems a bit strange to me. If I wanted to explain it to my child, I would have to confess that if someone has the power, they can change anything, even such a thing as a calendar. They even did it again later, when the Julian calendar was changed to the Gregorian. As for the calendar, it is a nice example of the variability of this world. In short: a calendar was created in the time of ancient Egypt by observing the phases of the Moon and the Sun. At the time when Roman emperor Julius Caesar conquered Egypt, he (as is usually the case) took all the best things from them. In this case, he took the predecessor of the calendar (inter alia). The word calendar in fact has a Latin origin, and it means the first day of the month. Of course, they used a calendar in Rome before this, but it was rather inaccurate when compared with the Egyptian calendar. However, there were some errors, so the mathematicians had quite a lot of work to do if they wanted to determine the actual course of Earth, which was considered the center of the universe at that time. The final version of the calendar was created 46 years before the birth of Jesus, i.e., the year 46 "BC". This version – the Julian calendar was used until the 16th century, when Pope Gregory XIII decided to improve it. Thus, the Gregorian calendar came into existence, and we have been using it ever since. (By the way, at that time the church did not recognize any science and Galileo was declared a heretic. After the arrival of the priest – astrologer, they started recognizing new ideas and admitted to the existence of a "science" that might know more than God himself, who had already put down everything he knew). What I'm missing here is the exact information about how the year 0 or the year 1 A.D. (Anno Domini, from Latin – the Year of the Lord) came to exist. This system was invented by the monk Dionysius Exiguus, who calculated the accuracy of Easter in 525 AD. This novelty, just as the Gregorian calendar, took a long time, taking root in several countries. Try as you might, you won't be able to find the exact numbers and facts because all the information preserved is very misleading. And that was the time when early mass manipulation began.

So now it is clear to us that this is indeed the Christian calendar. The Jews, who allegedly count from the date of the creation of the world, celebrated the year 5772 on the 29th of September 2011. The Muslims began to count their years on the date when the Prophet Muhammad fled from Mecca to the Arabian city of Medina, which happened about 622 years after Christ's birth. Therefore, on the 15th of November 2012 they celebrated the year 1434. In China, they celebrated the year 4709 in 2012. Thus, we would be able to go on and celebrate the Tibetan New Year, Hindu, Persian, Assyrian, Bengali, Sinhalese, Nepali, etc. **Do we really live on several different planets?!**

"Love thy neighbor..." Do you think you can really love someone if you do not like yourself? No. *"As thyself"* - this is the point that is absolutely forgotten by all. Today you are just mistaking your dependence for loving your neighbor. You need to feel loved and you do anything to satisfy this need. You are neglecting the fact that the foundations are false – in any case, the world is a great example. First, you must learn to truly love yourself, only then can you love the whole world (others). It is not possible to love your neighbor if you do not value yourself. None of the Western religions teach you to love yourself, to truly know yourself. They want you to sacrifice yourself to God, to follow Muhammad, Jesus, or Moses, to do this, to do that – rituals, prayers, sacrifices... They are continuously employing you with something that is absolutely unnatural for you. No one says: ***You're perfect as you are! Paradise is here on Earth, just look around! Look in the mirror, that's me - God! You have everything you need here and now! But you're blind... you are asleep. You still want to be someone else. You restrain your nature at the expense of revelations which happened thousands of years ago. You have everything, and you keep wasting it...***

Why have we come to this stage? Because we do not listen to ourselves; because we have not even learned to love ourselves. Since our childhood, programs have been put into our heads, telling us that we are not sufficient, that we are not good enough, that we should be like "them". On your deathbed you will realize that you have wasted your own life and pinned your hopes on your children. ***Wake up, please, and realize that there is no greater miracle than you!***

I do not mean to offend anyone, but if we really look into history, we find that every one of these western religions can be replaced with the word *murderers*. Look through the history of Christianity again - wherever they went in the world, they wanted to control the masses. Endless crusades - look at the expansion of Christianity in the world and realize the power. Poor Jesus, if only he knew what his followers have done… and of course, it was all done in the name of God. Maybe he wrote them a letter telling them what they should do. We can dissemble that everything is fine, but the deeper we dig into history, the more dirt we find there. Actually, Catholic Church destroyed many world cultures, whether in Africa, America, India, or Asia.

"In 1095, Pope Urban II declared the first so-called crusade against the infidels in the East. He promised eternal salvation and forgiveness of all sins to anybody who accepted the sign of the cross. Absolution was given to murderers, thieves, rapists, et al., not only notionally, but really. At that time, people of Christian, Jewish, and Muslim faiths lived in peace in Jerusalem, which was the target of the expedition. In 1099 the Crusaders conquered the place killing everybody regardless of religion, because God knows his people. Catholics behaved similarly upon the discovery of America – murders, burnings, torture, forced baptisms, destruction of indigenous cultures, and the burning of valuable codes of pre-Columbian civilizations describing events much older than Christianity itself. As early as the 4th century, St. Augustine came up with the idea and a defense of holy war, which allowed the violent spread of the true faith. As a matter of fact, there is no other organization in known history, which is as stained with blood and destruction as the Catholic Church.

It began with the destruction of monuments, ancient cultures, and ancient files that contained important ideas of mathematicians, philosophers, geographers, physicists, architects, and writers. By the way, only the Catholics and the Nazis burned books en masse."
J. Hrdina, historian

And there is so much of it that it would fill more than one Bible, Torah, Talmud, or Qur'an. In fact, we do not have to go to the distant past. It is enough to look at some current cases concerning priests. Christianity has declared war on sex, too. It is impossible to avoid deviations if you suppress your absolute nature! We are sexual beings and we're only against our own selves if we preach anything else.

Look at an exemplary (contemporary) public response of a priest to a young person who wanted to kiss someone for the first time:

"Many kisses and long kisses are mortal sins because they can easily arouse sexual pleasure and sexual passion which can lead a person to commit fornication or adultery. This is particularly true of open-mouthed kisses, where the participants' tongues touch. This kind of kissing is definitely a precursor to a sexual relationship and it is a mortal sin for those who are not married, even if in that situation it does not lead to sexual intercourse. The same is true about petting - touching the sensitive parts of the body of another person. Sex before marriage is a sin!

This is also a prelude to sexual intercourse, and it's definitely forbidden for those who are not married. This is also true for long or excessive hugging, although it may seem that this is only a very subtle kind of sexual pleasure which is not very exciting. Even dancing, when you keep touching the body of another person, is a mortal sin because it is nothing more than prolonged intimate embrace, and it has the incentive of rhythm, music and movement added to it. One might say that it gives them just a 'romantic feeling', but this 'romantic feeling' can easily develop into sexual pleasure. Furthermore, what may seem 'romantic' to one dance partner, for the other may be a serious sin. Dancing itself is not a sin, but this kind of dancing is. Here again, let's recall the warning of Holy Scripture: 'He who loves danger shall perish in it.' (Sir 3:27). Even prolonged hand holding can be a mortal sin, depending on whether it excites those who are doing it."

Because I grew up as a Christian, I can honestly say that this kind of "good advice" can evoke reproach and chaos in a young person. But what can we expect from a religion where a virgin has a baby?! However, even if there is such an attitude towards the most natural act in the world, do not be surprised by the scandals involving pedophile priests. I do not want to judge anybody unfairly, there are certainly exceptions who feel their mission, but those who are primarily "people" are really rare. As I mentioned, I was brought up as a Christian and in school, in religion classes, I was lucky enough to have a good priest, wonderful and exemplary, who was "man" above all. And even then, I encountered the fact that these people do not last long. He was honest and told the truth, so they sent him somewhere to the country, where he would not have so much influence on the masses. Practices of power are filthy, and the desire to get all the sheep under the roof is even filthier.

"The Christian God seems to be gay - the whole trio is composed of three men. How do they manage, no one knows - not even one woman among them! Only the Holy Spirit is a bit suspicious - maybe bisexual?! Spirits are capable of many different things. How else can you imagine the Father, Son and Holy Spirit - what is this trio? It's very homosexual. They did not let one woman among them and that is only because they wanted to avoid problems. The one woman would destroy this trio; it would become a real triangle." Osho

Christianity also does not recognize women as authorities. As a matter of fact, it does not even recognize them as equal humans.

From the beginning, they were considered inferior to man and they basically had no rights. Hatred against women escalated during the "witch hunt", where thousands of women were tortured, raped, and burned. Until the 1950s, the only skirts in the Vatican were cassocks. To date, the Vatican is the only state in the world where women do not have the right to vote.

"I believe that woman is the origin of evil,
and lies began through her, too."
St. Ambrosius

"A woman should learn in quietness and full
submission. I do not permit a woman to teach or to
have authority over a man; she must be quiet."
(Timothy 2:11-12)

"Submit to one another out of reverence for Christ. Wives, submit to your husbands as to the Lord. For the husband is the head of the wife as Christ is the head of the Church, his body, of which he is the Savior. Now as the church submits to Christ, so also wives should submit to their husbands in everything. …women should remain silent in the churches. They are not allowed to speak, but must be in submission, as the Law says. If they want to inquire about something, they should ask their own husbands at home; for it is disgraceful for a woman to speak in the church."
St. Paul

"I will make your pains in childbearing very severe; with
painful labor you will give birth to children. Your desire
will be for your husband, and he will rule over you."
Genesis 3:16

"A man ought not to cover his head, since he is the image and glory of God; but the woman is the glory of man. For man

did not come from woman, but woman from man; neither was man created for woman, but woman for man."
St. Paul

"A woman is a quickly growing plant; she is an imperfect human whose body grows faster because it is inferior..."
St. Thomas Aquinas

Having read these quotations, we could say that Christianity actually supports homosexuality without realizing it - isn't it all ridiculous?!

Jesus, if we believe what sacred scripture tells us, lived for only 33 years. Who today would actually follow a 33-year-old man?! It is also said that Jesus did not die on the cross. It took at least 48 hours or longer for a person to die on the Jewish cross. They crucified him on Friday afternoon and, as we all know, Jews have Sabbath on Saturday, so they couldn't do anything then. Therefore, they had to take him down on Friday before sunset. Jesus was carried away after about six hours, so at that time most likly he was not dead, although he could have been unconscious. They carried him to the cave where he was liberated by his followers as quickly as possible and fled to safety. When he recovered, he went to India and lived there for 120 years a peaceful enlightened life in humility - as a Jew, respectively Buddhist monks. He had never heard of Christianity. It was his followers who created the cult of Christianity. If he had really risen from the dead, how would he have evaporated?!

"When we read the stories of the resurrection of Jesus Christ, it is like reading four different sports reports about one football match in four different newspapers."
T. Wright (Canon of Westminster London)

By the way, a 1500-year-old Bible was found in Turkey in 2000, which denied the crucifixion of Jesus. The Vatican, however, intervened as they were strongly against it, so it has not been disclosed. As an example, in 1960 an Italian priest, Pellegrino Maria Ernetti, invented the chronovisor that made it possible to see the past or future based on increased vibrations. He argued that it made it possible to watch the crucifixion of Christ, or any event in history. The Chronovisor disappeared and reportedly it is owned by the Vatican.

"Christianity has depended on Jesus' miracles for two thousand years. These have become the basis for the claim that this religion is superior to other religions – because Gautama Buddha did not walk on water, Mahavira did not revive the dead, Krishna did not cure sick people by mere touch and Mohamed did not turn water into wine."
Osho

One way or another, it basically does not matter now. I am even willing to admit that many of these "miracles" really happened, because everything is just a substance and if you know the true alchemy of life – you can do miracles. I'm just asking, why didn't any of those chosen Popes ever have such abilities?! The highest representatives and no miracles?! Therefore, I say that there are many "Jesuses" walking around these days, and their number is constantly increasing. Today, any esoteric literature could be "Scripture". And what about the book *Conversations with God* by N. D. Walsch? According to ancient tradition, we could declare Ashland, Oregon a holy place! After all, a conversation with God took place there! But if we have a lot of something, we do not value it. Therefore, this book carries no weight, while we appreciate a text that was written thousands of years ago. Even though it was only one – the chosen one! Because we did not have the media, internet?!

"The first and the last Christian died two thousand years ago on the cross. There have been no other Christians since then."
F. Nietzsche

It is easy to build a cult (and business) around a person who is no longer alive. The Jews are, after all, the masters of the trade. Jesus, while he lived, was filled with love, health, happiness, but our businesspeople portray him as a serious, unhappy sufferer who is only rarely depicted as blissful. He knew what it was to live in ecstasy and that was what people admired about him. He dispensed joy everywhere he went. Christian ideology, however, made him a sad man who found his redemption only after death (although he was resurrected). Anyway, if you are really interested in Jesus – in Christ's energy – I recommend the book *Jeshua Channelings* by Pamela Kribbe or "channeling" (receiving information from the higher consciousness, other entities, angels, or masters, as originally "communicated" by our well-known boys) with Pamela Aaralyn, who has already confirmed that Jesus did not die on the cross, was married to Mary Magdalene, and they even had children. (Btw, we might prefer to create a sculpture of a dancing Jesus to have place where we could go dancing ☺)

"Spirituality is a rebellion and it cannot be different, because spirituality contradicts tradition, because there cannot be only one of these: either there is a mass of people – an unintelligent mob - the mind creating a tradition; or there is a man like Jesus or Buddha, and they are alone. God had never been as rich as he became after the Christ. He had never been as rich as he was after the Buddha. And He will be richer than ever before when you meet Him, because you will join Him. God is also evolving, God is not static."

Osho

Osho used to tell a funny story: For centuries, it has been a custom in Vatican that one day a year the Pope meets with the principal Rabbi. All Christians and Jews gather in the square to see this meeting, although no one knows what is going on between them. The Rabbi gives a rolled-up document to the Pope; the Pope bows and that's it. The next day this document is sent back to the Rabbi, where it remains for the rest of the year. For two thousand years no pope had bothered to open that document, but this one was curious, so he decided to look at it. Do you know what he found there? It was a bill for the Last Supper! Jesus died before he got a chance to pay ☺

So Jews, or **Judaism** actually, but 85 percent of Jews are not believers (they "only" honor the traditions that exist on the basis of religion).

I have a consciousness that allows me to perceive things holistically. That`s why it is a big problem for me to actually grasp this question in its entirety. It is mainly because their (the Jew's) intelligence enabled them to devise such a dirty trick against the world that we would hardly find a match for it in history. But I devote more attention to this issue in the chapter *MORALITY* because it is not about religion anymore, although paradoxically, it is all fabricated on the basis of religion. However, to help you understand the impact and power of this religion or race, let me quote here at least a couple of verses from the Talmud, which a Gentile - which I am for them – should never read (though I do not know why, for example, such a Bible is available to everyone).

But first, Herman Wouk, a very popular Jewish writer, describes the impact of the Talmud as follows:

> *"The Talmud is to this day the circulating blood of the Jewish religion. Whatever laws, customs or ceremonies we honor, whether we are Orthodox, Conservative, Reform or convulsively sentimentalists - we follow the Talmud. It is our common law."*

And now again, as examples, a few quotations from the "Holy Scriptures" follow:

> *"A heathen* [gentile] *who studies the Torah* [and other Jewish Scriptures], *deserves death, for it is our inheritance, not theirs."*
> (Sanhedrin 59a)

"You [Jews] *are invited people, but the world's nations* [Gentiles] *are called animals* [cattle]*."*
(Baba Mezia, 114b)

"Even the best of the Gentiles should be killed."
(Babylonian Talmud)

"If a heathen [Gentile] *hits a Jew, he must be killed. To strike a Jew is like slapping God."*
(Sanhedrin 58b)

"What a Jew obtains by theft from cutheana [Gentiles], *he can keep."*
(Sanhedrin 57a)

"Those who read the non-canonical books [New Testament] *will not share in anything from the new world to come."*
(Sanhedrin 90a)

"The best of the Gentiles: kill him; the best of the snakes: smash his skull; the best of the women: is full of sorcery."
(Kiddushin 66c)

I do not know about you, but I was pretty sick when I read these lines, and this is only a small selection of these "revelations" which again influence how the entire planet is run. It does not matter whether we take the Old or the New Testament, the principle remains the same. It changed only in a populist way, not in reality. Every Jew is programmed to think this way, whether consciously or unconsciously (as Christians or Muslims have their own beliefs). Even children are brought up to believe that they are something different than everyone else. I have personally witnessed more than absurd racist scenes, whether it was in a synagogue or during an ordinary dinner. Also, I would like to point out that in addition to the serious racism on which this religion is based, we encounter here again the abuse and suppression of women. It is no wonder that the most famous feminists were, and are, Jewish women. Based on this, the emancipation crossed all boundaries of genuine femininity, and therefore you would have great difficulty dating a woman without an engagement in Israel. Probably, you would totally fail. Compulsory military service for women is also an example of the perverse values of the nation, which is always ready for war. Why? Young people who refuse to undertake compulsory military service, or even join Israel Defense Forces (IDF), are imprisoned.

"She who was the descendant of princesses and governors [the Virgin Mary] *was a prostitute to a carpenter."*
(Sanhedrin 106a)

"If a Jew has coitus [sexual intercourse] *with a non-Jewish woman, whether it be a three-year-old child or an adult, a married or single woman, even if she is less than nine years and one day old - if it was intentional coitus, she should be killed, as it is with animals, because she got a Jew into trouble."*
(The Talmudic Encyclopedia)

"When a grown-up man has intercourse with a little girl it is nothing, for when the girl is less than three years old, it is as if one puts the finger into the eye and a tear comes out."
(Kethuboth 11b)

"A maiden three years and a day may be acquired in marriage by coition."
(Sanhedrin 55b and 69a-69b)

So if you are a Jew, please acknowledge that also your faith is built on absolutely terrible foundations. Even if it assumes many alchemical truths, they are suppressed by more manipulative arguments which are a part of you whether you admit it or not. And most importantly – **no race is the chosen one, more or less**. Today, there are also many rabbis who provoke/promote soldiers to their "divine mission". In the current global military conflicts, it is they who give them mental strength and reinforce their persuasion that the extermination of alien races in the Middle East is correct. It does not sound exactly pleasant, but in fact it is again mainly religion that gives them the courage to do the "work of God" as they call it.

"All rabbis study the Talmud. How would Jews react if Christian preachers studied Mein Kampf as part of their holy writ, but excused it by saying that the book has no effect on their current attitudes? Any open-minded reader who reads both Mein Kampf and the Talmud would find the Talmud to be the more wrathful of the two.»
D.Duke, My Awakening

Islam?

"And kill them [disbelievers] *wherever you find them and expel them from wherever they have expelled you, and fitnah* [Turning away from faith] *is worse than killing. And do not fight them at al-Masjid al- Haram until they fight you there. But if they fight you, then kill them. Such is the recompense of the disbelievers."*
(Qur'an 2:191)

Hence, we have the third peculiar nation full of hate. Verse 29 already specifies the fight against Christians and Jews, if they do not submit to Muslims according to Islamic law. "Holy Scripture" again very clearly encourages the members of this religion to fight everyone. Traditional Islamic law clearly prohibits the peaceful coexistence of believers and non-believers as equals in one society. Mohamed "clearly told everyone" that Islam must be dominant! Also, if someone converts to another religion, they should be killed; of course, it does not matter whether it is a family member or a stranger.

"I am with you, so strengthen those who believed. I will cast in the hearts of those who disbelieved the terror, so strike above the necks and strike from them every fingertips. That is because they opposed Allah and His Messenger. And whoever opposes Allah and his messengers, then indeed, Allah will severe penalty. And that, for the disbelievers is the punishment on the Fire."
(Qur'an 8:12)

Jihad = holy war (!) of Islam against all infidels.

"Jihad is the highest and most sacred duty that a Muslim can do according to the God of the Quran. Every Muslim believes that if he sacrifices his life, by committing a suicide attack on innocent people (unbelievers), he will go to heaven. It's a promise of the highest authority in Muslim society that if you die for the glory of the God of the Quran, you will go to heaven where 72 virgins will await you. They all grow up believing it, it's everywhere - on the street, in the family, at school - you have no choice. They believe that the Quran was sent down by God Himself."
Mosab Hassan Yousef, the author of *Son of Hamas*

(I wonder what awaits them if they are gay ☺)

Sharia = Islamic law, which (again) does not recognize the equality of people and women.

On the other hand, the whole issue has reached such extreme forms that, for example, today Kurdish women specialize in killing men in combat, because if a man is killed by a woman, he will not be received by the 72 virgins. Paradoxically, this is the thing they are afraid of. Sick.

So the irony is that all three religious groups essentially are coping with the same main problem of suppressed sexuality - of course, especially as far as women, since all the laws are fully adapted to men on the basis of historical primitive assumptions that every woman should be subordinated to a man (though, women did not have the right to express to all these "homophobic revelations"). So, for example, a man – a Muslim – certainly does not feel that his sexuality is being repressed anyway because the law allows him to have several wives or official mistresses. It has even come to such an extreme that women – lovers – have been enacted so as to pay taxes or the status "mistress" was their regular job.

"Allah honored women by clarifying the punishment by beating. Muhammad said: do not hit a woman in the face; you should not cripple her with the beating. And when you beat her, you may not curse her. Beat her for educational reasons! Moreover, he may not hit her more than ten times, break the bones, or hurt her too much, smash her teeth or jab the eyes. These are the rules for beating women. She needs the beating as guidance. Hitting is allowed if a woman refuses sex."
Egyptian Islamic Spiritual (!) Sa`d Arafat

Muhammad said: "Compare yourself to the man, he is your paradise, while you're hell", recorded by Imam Ahmad

"There is no minimum age for entering marriage. You can marry a one year old girl. But is the girl ready for sex? What is the appropriate age for first sex? It depends on the environment and traditions. Prophet Mohamed showed us a model to follow. He took his wife Aisha when she was six years old, but had first sex with her when she was nine."
Dr. A. Al-Mu`bi

"If a woman exposes even a small area of skin on her legs by wearing ripped jeans, she is inviting men to harass her. Men should have a national duty to rape such women."
N. al-Wahsh, an Egyptian lawyer (2017)

Does that seem normal to anyone?! And these are official statements! What do you think it is like in real, everyday life?! If we look at today's Dubai, we can get the feeling that it is a very developed city. But even there the harsh Sharia law is in control. In recent years, several women from the West have been sentenced because they were drugged and raped by men! According to Islamic law they would consider this rape only if four grown men – Muslims - testified. That will never happen of course. And so a man may divorce his wife if he sends her three texts. A woman definitely has a much harder time getting a divorce, if it is at all possible. (Not to mention the embargo or blocking of several foreign sites and social networks.)

"Online chatting between men and women, who are not relatives, is religiously unacceptable because it is a tool of the devil and a method of spreading conflict and corruption." Institution Dār al-Iftā' in Egypt

This is the present exemplary logic of Islam – it's a publicly available definition. Think about it.

"Islam is not a religion, not a cult. Islam has religious, juristic, political, economic, social and military components. The religious component is the foundation for all other components."

Traditions at the expense of humanity?! According to today's supporters, Islam is not a religion or cult, but a lifestyle. I'm starting to get the feeling that there was some prophet (chosen informant) who said that religions will be eradicated and thus the most aggressive of them (which have a strong need to dominate the world) very quickly said: Ok, but this is not a religion - we are a race! This is not a religion - it is a lifestyle! Do you really not see that the only thing that affects us is the past, the sick clinging to traditions and especially an illusion of religion based on absolutely utopian foundations?!

However, I would like to remind you of the following fact, which is kind of ironic:

"The religion {Islam} *was influenced by Judaism and Christianity, with which it shares most of the prophets and* ***it adheres to the same God.****"*
Wikipedia

In particular, do you know what is the most ironic? Jesus was a Jew. He is the central figure of Christianity and Muslims also consider him the highest authority. So please think again: Wasn't, by chance, Jesus' mission the very thing that absolutely does not resonate with those morbid verses in the "holy books", which only ever condemn, command, or prohibit things?! Wasn't the state of his enlightenment the very thing which inspired us to want to live in love?! Is it a coincidence that it is joy that should lead us?!

Also, Moses – it is precisely his visions that became the basis for all three aforementioned religions and are the basis of all "holy books." The prophet who lived more than three thousand years ago still affects the operation of the whole planet, and paradoxically, he is the main liaison between these competing groups. So simply put, his ideas (visions) were the source that was used by the three races (or one?) to create competitive products. And as I mentioned before, they are the products most in demand because no one can really prove where we came from and where we are heading. We gave authority to those who trade in chimeras. For a while, all of us believed this false act, although that was certainly not its original intention. Please understand that this whole thing has a common denominator (the mission) from which a group created a business – the biggest, bloodiest, and most ridiculous one. For comparison, the visionary prophet Nostradamus, who lived in different times, around two thousand five hundred years later, was for the same ideas and visions persecuted, imprisoned, banned… And especially by whom? Well, unexpectedly, by the Church. And he was an educated doctor who surpassed his professors in thought and action.

But if we don't take the reality we live in as proof, we can discuss a different story, which can only be confirmed by the Vatican, or more precisely its exclusive members – the Jesuits. At the end of his life, former Jesuit agent Dr. Rivera spoke out and his testimony is more than shocking. He argues that the creator of the worldwide "religious farce" was the ancient Roman Empire in its arrogance and lust to dominate the world. It was its rulers who felt afraid of the booming faith of Christ's followers as well as the growing Jewish community and that of Israel, which has always been a respected place mainly because of its strategic position and spiritual significance. (Among other things, for example, the communications chakra of the Earth is located there, which has allowed "channeling" from higher spheres.)

"The creation of a religious monster has begun. Statues of Jupiter have been renamed St. Peter, statues of Venus became the Virgin Mary and other statues became the other saints. It was necessary to invent and add the missing number of ecclesiastic authorities starting with St. Peter as well as the first pope. Rome is a city on seven hilltops, of which one named Vaticanus was chosen as the site of a new religion. This is where Satan's temple called John's (Jupiter's?) once stood. The new religious system was named Roman universal – a common religion led by the Roman - universal Church (lat. Catholicus = general, universal). The Roman evangelistic block was created to kill Christ's true followers, introduce false religion, start wars where Christians would not bow to Rome, keep Jews under close watch and force all nations to convert to the Roman empire's occult teachings."

Dr. A. Rivera

Dr. Alberto Rivera also admitted that the Vatican is actually the founder of Islam:

"When the Roman Catholic Pontiff and his helpers observed numerous Arab nations in Northern Africa, they saw these crowds as a source to perform their unclean, abominable work. So they put together another tool – an underground spy network that was used for the transmission of information for the execution of a masterpiece - a plan to control large numbers of Arabs who rejected Roman Catholicism. Thus the Vatican attempted to help Arabs find their own 'Messiah', one who would rise up as their great leader. It had to be a person with skills that they themselves could teach and finally, through him, bring all non-Catholic Arabs together in one huge mass - in one army, which would then take Jerusalem for the Pope."

Dr. A. Rivera

"These writings are closely guarded because they contain information on how the Vatican created Islam. Both sides have so much information about each other that if it were made public, it would create a scandal that would bring shame and destruction to both religions."

Cardinal A. Bea

An example of manipulation in the last century:

"In 1910, Portugal became a socialist country. Red flags were everywhere. The Roman Catholic Church faced a serious problem. Everywhere sounded: 'Down with the Church.' It was time for a religious miracle. The Jesuit elites arranged with the dark spiritual mafia for an apparition of the Virgin Mary. Such a miracle should have a much greater impact than just the return of Portugal to the iron yoke of the Vatican. It was agreed that this should occur at Fatima. The Jesuits wanted to involve Russia, plus the location for the apparition of the Virgin Mary at Fatima should also play an important role in including Islam under the 'Holy Church'. So in 1917, there came Our Lady's apparition at

> *Fatima. The performance of the 'Holy Mother' became a huge success, resulting in the defeat of the Portuguese Socialists."*

And a bonus of course:

> *"Our apparitions of the Virgin Mary in Fatima meant, in terms of conversions to Christianity, a turning point in the lives of 347 million Muslims, i.e. a turn in the most problematic of all religions."*
> The Jesuit bishop Sheen

I think if the Vatican could talk, we would find out the real truth. Today it is just theory, however, I am convinced that history is repeating itself in the worst possible sense and, therefore, we are witnessing live broadcasts of the same process with the "Islamic fighters" as it was (planned) in the past. To address these issues in detail, there are currently many books on the market that describe the history (not only religious) from a completely different angle. However, let us once again use "common sense" and realize that if it was in fact exactly as it is written in these last quotations, the Vatican would have long ago withdrawn these statements. This game is of much higher interest than would appear at first sight. We will come back to this theme in the chapter called *Morality.*

I really love all people and I honestly do not care what their religion or race is. But do you think this is all right? The more I learned about these religions, the worse I felt. Honestly, I cannot believe that what I'm writing is actually happening. Of course, I recognize that so-called civilized Christians, Jews, and Muslims do exist, who absolutely do not identify with these statements. And there are even more of them than those extremist psychopaths. But where are you, please? Why don't you comment on the fact that a couple of fools are making a murder weapon out of your faith?! **Have**

you ever wondered what you actually believe in? Why should one nation be more peculiar than any other? How could we let all this shit happen? For what or whom? Because of Jesus, Allah, Mohammed, Moses?! "Human" should be the ultimate goal. **Note that any organized religion is only a black tape over your eyes that was actually stuck there by someone else – it is not a given. It is not a natural part of you; you were not born with it – it is paradoxically your weakness.** It is something you are addicted to, something that seemingly makes sense in your life because you are too lazy to look for your own way. That's the whole joke. And the eternal fear of death – why? Do you need official consolation that someone specific will be waiting for you? **You will not take your VIP status to the next world. ONLY your actions will determine your "place". And those will not be forgiven, not by anyone on Earth or by anyone specific "up there". It is a perfect system of life – the existence which operates on the basis of karma, and you will not avoid it even if you pray a hundred times a day.** If you hurt someone and that person forgives you, your act is inscribed in the "book of life" and you will have to live through it one way or another, to understand the pain that you have caused. You will not lie your way out of it by confessing to any "peculiar" person, even if it were God himself. **Action – reaction, no magic**. Return to Earth and live fully every day. Death is a part of us from birth, reconcile with it as soon as possible, otherwise you will never live your integral life – life in the present.

There are many other various religions (mostly with dominant gods), but they all contain a huge BUT. With all due respect, of course. Some ideas are not bad. In some cases we can say that most are good, but people started abusing them over the course of the years. In practice, we have long forgotten the true religious essence of man, respectively, it was found only by a few individuals – never by groups. Although the mission - final understanding - is still the same. (We could also preferably create a project in which we unite the useful alchemical rituals of each religion.)

It is not pleasant to read about this, but open your eyes, please. Maybe I have just "offended" your religion, but it is important to start thinking about it. It is easy to criticize. There is good in everything, even in the most ridiculous religion, but realize that it affects us more than we would like. In everything. In everyday life. We need some rules - laws - because we are afraid that otherwise anarchy would prevail. And we have given this power, if we don't take politicians into account, especially to God. Currently, the basis of all laws and moral principles are religious views. To add authority to the moral law, we call it "God's law". As a matter of fact, God is morality in today's world, a morality disguised as "facts". It is neither life itself nor the so much mentioned love (which it actually is). According to these three main religions, it is a fanatical leader who alone knows what is good and bad, what we should do and what he absolutely condemns. He even quite frequently requires us to kill somebody! Once again, I ask: **God or man???** We treat each other according to doctrines which arose an extremely long time ago with completely evil intent. Does it seem to you that today's daily life is the same as it was 2017 years ago? How can we live by something that no one can really substantiate when we live in such a "highly rational time"?! Yes, now the so-called atheists agree with me, but even you do not live "without God", no matter how much you would like to… he is in everything.

Let's look at an extreme. You're gay, and your sexual orientation is frowned upon. You cannot get married or raise a child (obviously I'm not talking about the one percent of countries where it is accepted). Why?! Because your politicians don't allow it, not God! Because morality does not allow it, and in this case that is represented by God. Oh, so suddenly "God's law" suits the atheist politicians?! On each dollar is written "In God We Trust". And who does not use money? God and money - does it go together?! Curiously, we mention God only when it suits us. How many people in the world live precisely according to their religion?! One percent, two percent, three percent? However, it hypocritically affects one hundred percent of the population.

Religion itself is not bad, but from generation to generation it has been deformed. The Bible that is currently available has so many translations and copies that it is absurd to believe in everything that anyone has ever added there over the last 2,000 years. In spite of that, there are many wise words and facts in the book. But keep in mind that everything can be interpreted in many different ways. It is like the children's game called "the phone", where one person in a group says one sentence which the others whisper to each other one by one and the last one says it out loud. Isn't it true that we mainly play it for fun because the sentence at the end will be quite different from the sentence we started with in the beginning? Think about it.

Who ever said that our relationship to God is untouchable - unchangeable?! Why does everything make some progress but we insist on the "perfect vision" in religion?!

Therefore, we should burn any psychic or fortune-teller now, because they are witches! Or are we no longer afraid because we know they are in the minority? But if I said that even Jesus or Moses or any personality from the past that affects our present was just exactly a man like this. Or take Jews for example – actually they do not have it devised half badly. They integrate the great alchemy of life into their rituals. If we took just the good thoughts from each religion, imagine all the beauty that would come of it!

> ***"Christ is just another word for Buddha - this is the ultimate state of awareness.*** *You will never be like Gautama or Jesus. Believers live like that. They try to follow*

someone else, imitate him. An imitator can never be simple. He is still merely adapting to someone."
Osho

The biggest advantage of today's world is that, thanks to the Internet, we are entirely connected for the first time in history. We know almost everything about everything, and if not, we use Google. If there had been an internet at that time, maybe we would have discovered several Messiahs in the world (not to mention old shamans from the native Americans, Asian masters, monks from India, etc.). We would have been able to discuss it, and we would have realized that we all can have the same opportunities he had. Because we all have it in ourselves whether we believe it or not. All of us will discover it sooner or later. We just have one huge "problem" here – the present.

BEING AWARE OF THE PRESENT TIME IN ITS INTEGRITY IS A MUST TODAY. To admit the true reality of your awareness with all the absurdities we live with – to see the unity in this clumsily made separation.

The word "devil" (Diablo) is a synonym for division - two horns are a symbol of that. We have made a threat out of everything. Regarding general handling, they all try to divide us because then we do not have as much strength. Power is in unity - we know it, but again only on the level of sayings.

We cannot delete history, but let us learn from it. That`s the only thing it is good for. We are just going back even though we have come an incredibly long way. Today, however, "officially" it is not the Christian God who is killing people, it is the Arabic God. Although we send the Christian God to fight against him. Or is he Jewish?! Since it says that a few "Jews" control the world… Unfortunately, our senses are so weakened due to modern times that we perceive mostly through our eyes. What we see, we believe. That`s why we have state-controlled media. A couple of the "peculiars" want to control the world. How? Using God, the media, and of course, fear.

When a person is born, he is naked. He has nothing. No faith, no belief, no opinions on what is right and what is not. Everything is instilled by society. Everything. From the first word, first meal, the first person we begin to perceive. Everything is created by society and the environment in which we grow up. We learn to accept a faith that affects us for the rest of our lives. When you are born, you do not choose whether you want to be a Christian or a Jew or a Muslim. They just make you one. Many times we do not even have a choice. You can talk about the race, blood, and similar "genetic nonsense" (in this case), and even though you are basically right, it's all just the "program" that must be seen as it is. Stop taking it so dead seriously. **Here on Earth, we are all first and foremost part of a single race and that is the race of Man**. We come naked into this world, and when we leave, we are naked as well. If we are lucky, we have two arms, two legs, two eyes… And the fact is, all of us only need love – nothing more, nothing less. It is not you, it is your education and it is up to you how strongly it will affect you. Will you start looking for your true self or will you accept your social self?! We are brought up to compare. Our education is based on it and so is our culture. So we are still trying to be someone other than who we really are. I'm probably not going to change your opinion, if you are a steadfast Christian or Muslim, but it is not about me at all, it is particularly about you… and also about preserving this world, because once again we find ourselves in a crisis, which is probably best described using the words of Hamlet: "*To be, or not to be?*" We are looking for all kinds of "Gods" in order to get rid of the responsibility for what is happening, and in particular, the responsibility for ourselves.

Our reality is made up of our thoughts. Out of these thoughts, a future is formed. Opinions form behavior, and that produces experiences. Therefore, what you believe in is the most important

thing. We live in a time when we believe only what we see. But it should be the other way around. We have to start believing, and then we will see the results.

If you believe that the way life manifests itself is through God – believe it. But find Him in you first, and then you will see Him in everyone.

The word *God* is totally interchangeable with the word *life* or *love.*

All religions want you to believe them.

Do you believe in life? Do you believe in love? You do not need to because they are here whether you believe in them or not.

First, believe in yourself. You are God, you are love, you are life, whether you want it or not. Now, it is just about how quickly you start understanding it and accept this truth. We are all one. We are all interlinked. This is the most revolutionary idea to be accepted. I am neither the first nor the last to say it. Therefore, I am actually trying to prove it on the basis of facts. (Whether it is the law of karma or a mirror.) We are, in reality, one energy fragmented into many parts. That is the beauty which we have changed into a fight – an absolutely useless fight. We fight everywhere - at home, at work, in relationships, in the world… everywhere! WHY?!

Religions do the exact opposite of what is natural for us - they divide us. They want us to follow others and not ourselves. So, in whom or in what do we really believe? Always in someone other than ourselves. But how can you believe in others if you do not believe in yourself? It is simply impossible! As a matter of fact, you want to believe, but only in what suits you at the moment. In these Western religions it is not about man, but it is a game about their social ego, which wants to possess the widest audience possible and control the world, nothing more. It has always been like that. And if you do not understand, it will continue to be like that. How does religion really help you when you are starving? You start praying and hope God will help you. But in the end you will have to help yourself. Then you'll get angry - obviously at God: How could he let this happen?! What an injustice! But you forget that it is not some "He" who lives your life, but you… all the time it is you and only you.

Organized religions have completed their mission and they no longer make any sense. Accept it, please. **With their wealth we could immediately save the whole world, if love were their actual mission, as all of them say it is.** It is not like that – and our history, and our present are just direct evidence of it. Open your eyes, you do not need to belong anywhere. Just learn to be yourself – that is really the whole miracle.

"All the mythologies of the world are much closer to the truth than the so-called history."
Osho

Fortunately, there are Eastern religions which are like sweet nectar when compared to these three. I have to mention them because "logically" people start heading in this direction.

Buddhism is currently the most prevalent religion, although it should be seen rather as a philosophic course. This teaching is based on love and the biggest difference, compared to the previous, is that it leads us to ourselves. So here, finally, there is no vindictive, asexual, omnipotent male God, but man. It has a beautiful philosophy, but it is not perfect. For example, Buddhism claims that our mission on Earth is to suffer. It should be noted, however, that suffering is created particularly by us and in us, it is not "given". The suffering we go through happens just because we are cleaning the karma that we cause ourselves. If we have caused pain to someone in the past (or in our past lives), we will simply have to go through it - there are no exceptions. Pain teaches us humility, through pain we are growing - but it's the only way. Buddhism was born in the East, and so it is mostly adapted to the "eastern" man and does not understand "the western man". We can pretend that this division doesn't exist, but the fact is that the world operates on the principle of the West and the East. In any case, it lacks life. Generally, it focuses on the unearthly delights instead of leading us to an actual real life here on Earth. No wonder; it arose in a time that vastly differs from today. Therefore, it should not be the aim of contemporary man, even though it may be a beautiful way. Again, it was not Gautama Buddha who founded the "religion", but his followers.

Buddha was born a prince. He lived in immense wealth. And yet he lacked something. When he was born, his astrologers predicted that he would give up this world when he saw a beggar. His father was very afraid of the prophecy, so he made sure that nothing like that would happen. In their kingdom you could not find a single sick person or dead leaves. Legend says that the Gods were so desperate that they themselves took on the form of beggars. When the young prince was celebrating his 29th birthday, he went to visit the city, but the guards did not watch him well enough, and so Siddhartha saw beggars for the first time in his life. He was very shocked. This powerful experience forced him to start looking for a higher meaning of life – for himself. Six years passed before he became enlightened, before he understood it all. The news of the enlightened young prince spread quickly, and people began to feel that it was not good to live in wealth. This led to the misconception that enlightenment can only be achieved in poverty. That's not the correct attitude, because Siddhartha - Buddha - formerly filled his material needs. He came from great wealth; he escaped from the palace. He was not afraid he would not survive, so he could happily look for a higher sense of existence. (The principle remains that one must learn to prove to move away from the material world, but do not curse it.

On the contrary, begin to use it purposefully, not be dependent on it, because our inner happiness does not depend on it.)

"Existentially we are all Buddhas, but psychologically we live in different private worlds."
Osho

The Western religions - Christianity, Judaism and Islam - arose from poverty. Thus, they started longing for riches, they did not have a relationship to material wealth. Therefore, it is important to accept the idea that the image of a spiritual man living a poor is just a devise for religious leaders to accumulate all the wealth available - nothing more. Therefore, today's West is "rich" while the East is "poor". Therefore, the West idolizes money, social status, prestige and power. Look at the churches, mosque and synagogues - wealth rules everywhere. Do you want a good business? Create your own religion! Paradoxically, beggars are worshiped in the East, if they pretend to be spiritual seekers, and people willingly give them gifts because they believe in their salvation – they worship simple beings. Today, however, as in the West, the situation has become extreme, and this is, unfortunately, a particular kind of (evil) habit which is widely abused. **Western religions were born in poverty, and so they have nothing to offer today's rich man. They do not satisfy him. Eastern religions were born in wealth, and therefore they have started to interest Western people. Buddha's religion has the greatest resonance. Why? Because it was born in wealth. The West is in the same state of mind as Buddha was when he became interested in meditation - being.** It was the quest of a wealthy man. That is the point of Jainism and Hinduism as well. These three great religions were born in abundance. Therefore, India is losing connection with its own religions. Many people there have converted to Christianity or Islam. They are not interested in meditation. They need to eat or at least to have a home. So when Christians come, open a hospital, give them food, give them some clothing, they make a very good impression (although it was them who literally destroyed these original cultures).

"The mafia of your religious leaders is still preaching the same thing - that poverty is something spiritual. Poverty is the greatest crime because all other crimes are born out of poverty; it is a source."
Osho

We have reached a critical point where we must begin to understand the whole as such. The need to satisfy both parts – Zorba and Buddha is an integral part of man. You will hardly look for meditation and enlightenment if you have nothing to eat and nowhere to sleep. Therefore, it is wrong to think that the "true" spiritual man should be poor. It also does not mean that enlightenment is only for the rich. It is not easy to take one's eyes off of "wealth", but believe me, no rich man has ever reached fulfillment and happiness thanks to his riches. Those who have "everything" will sooner or later see that it cannot buy joy. But it is not necessary to attain great material wealth to find yourself - you just need to want it badly enough (and later do not fall out of spiritual pride). What is happening in the West is an accurate reflection of what is happening in the East. We must find balance not only in ourselves, but also worldwide. East and West will be joined, whether we like it or not. They need to come together. The West has begun to overflow with wealth. Apparently, it has everything it ever wanted, and yet it's not enough. It has lost the essence - man. The hunt for power has lost its soul. A large imbalance has come to exist. The West developed science, the East meditation. The West was focused on the material world, while the East was focused on the inner world. And these should be combined today.

The good news is that Zen has already done it. It is the only one that is at the same time earthly and unearthly. Zen is the culmination and transcendence of Indian and Chinese thinking. The Indians are represented by Buddha and the Chinese by Lao Tzu. Today we cannot say what comes from what; it is a harmony of what should be achieved.

"To call Zen `Zen Buddhism` is not right because it is far more. Buddha is not so earthly as Zen is. Lao Tzu is tremendously earthly, but Zen is not only earthly: its vision transforms the earth into heaven. Lao Tzu is earthly, Buddha is heavenly. It is integration rather than synthesis. Zen is neither Buddhist-like, nor Taoist-like. Zen is both. As a result, it has become the most extraordinary phenomenon."
Osho

Zen is a real religion - because it is not theology. But I don't like to call it a religion because this word has been misused many times. Zen is Zen. It lives in the present and its "object" is man. It does not know the concept of God because God is in every one of us.

"If you meet the Buddha, kill him."
Zen proverb

This means that you should seek your own self and not somebody else, even if it is Buddha himself, it's just an illusion on our way. These "Zen slaps" are exactly the thing that each of us needs to wake up (this book is something similar to many). Masters often don't hesitate to use physical power, if it helps the student move to a higher level of consciousness. So-called shock therapy will lead you to find yourself through your own experience. Zen is ungraspable and full of paradoxes. Zen transforms everything secular to sacred, dissolves the boundaries between the world and God. It teaches you how to get out of the vicious circle of words in which you constantly wander, it teaches you absolute straightforwardness, it teaches you to live. Again, however, **you do not have to go anywhere to find such a master because everyone you meet is such a man. This world is really a perfect place if you start to consciously perceive it…**

"Truth has nothing to do with authority, truth has nothing to do with tradition, truth has nothing to do with the past – truth is a radical, personal realization. You have to come to it..." says Zen.

Today's religions have the masculine principle in themselves - philosophy, logic – they analyze and separate. Zen has mostly the feminine principle, it is like poetry, it synthesizes and unifies. It doesn't want to prove anything, it doesn't propose anything, it doesn't insist on anything... it simply is. It deals with beauty rather than with truth. Because truth is ultimately the product of the mind, but beauty is truly indescribable. You have to experience it, perceive it, and discover it – survive it. Zen knows the harmony between the two poles - the heart and the head. **The mystery of life cannot be solved because it is impossible to solve it. The life must be lived, loved, and celebrated!**

"Zen has no theory. It is a non-theoretical approach to reality. It has no doctrine and no dogma - hence it has no church, no priest, no pope. The moment you start talking about Zen theory, Zen is no more Zen. Theories are very limited; Zen is unlimited experience. Zen is primarily existential, not theoretical. It does not talk about truth, it presents the truth as it is. Zen is just waking you up. It is shocking you, screaming at you to wake up - but will not impose any theory, doctrine, or sacred books. Zen is the only religion that is able to burn its sacred texts, the only religion that is able to destroy its idols and ideals. Zen is like love - you cannot define it."

Osho

However, you can discover this beauty only by yourself. Using your own spirituality, your own truth... Because the man who seeks truth and makes mistakes will be forgiven. This is the law of the very essence of being, and the truth will always find you.

Spirituality forces us to look for our own experience. Religion wants us to learn from the opinions of others. Spirituality requires us to get rid of all thoughts and feel reality.

"Spirituality requires a certain amount of humor to make it more humane. If spiritual doctrine lacks humor, it is too intellectual, mathematical, logical, but it lacks the touch of humanity. It becomes a scientific object. But a man is not an object of scientific inquiry. There is something beyond scientific research in man. Trees don't laugh, animals don't laugh, only man has a sense of humor."

Osho

On Earth we just play a party game called Man. All of us are playing it. It has its rules; it has its unwritten laws. This game was here long before us and will be here after we are gone. We just find ourselves on some "level" where we left off. That's it. (By the way, this understanding is abused by Scientology which is only the so-called "spiritual pyramid game" = business.) **The soul is eternal, whether you believe it or not. Life is eternal, whether you believe it or not. It is not possible to destroy it - life just changes its form. We are climbing up the ladder of life values - according to our deeds.** What is a win for you if you're alone? The most beautiful joy is the joy that is shared. Paradoxically, our happiness depends on nothing else but ourselves and that is our win: a state of unconditional bliss as a permanent condition. That's it. We are one being.

"Become crazy like Buddha, Christ and Muhammad. Become freaks like me. And it will be an extremely beautiful madness, because everything beautiful is born of madness, and all that is romantic stems from the madness. The most amazing life experiences and coolest ecstasy are based on insanity."

Osho

Who would not want to live in a state of permanent joy, peace, love, celebration, humor, dance? That is the life… It is the only God… and it is in us… nowhere else… in YOU!

You have the possibility to create…

You have the possibility to create your world by your thoughts…

You have the option to create a new life…

What more do you want as proof?!

YOU ARE THE CREATOR!

YOU ARE "GOD"

Believe mainly in yourself, please… nobody wants any more from you… if so, only because you believed it… it's all just our social game… if you understand the absolutely simple rules of existence, you will become a winner… we are all one… we are all interlinked… we are all part of everyone, but also of ourselves… know yourself and you will know the entire universe…

"You are God having a human experience. Anything less is a compromise." D. Chopra

MORALITY

"Think of how much intellect and energy is spent on showing people how evil they are. And imagine what would happen if all this energy was used to show people what is good in them." M. Gorky

Morale should be primarily about how society functions. Do you think that we function "normally"?

Morality is not really defined by anything, and if you try to look it up, you will get to ethics. This word comes from the Latin *ethos*, which means *custom, opinion, character, way of thinking* - that is something changeable. If you investigate further, you will find that it is actually a philosophical discipline. Few people realize that ethics, and thus morality, is currently based mainly on religious principles. Although it was not originally so, adherents of these groups have infiltrated society more than enough, and even if you are an atheist, in essence you are influenced by many religious views without realizing it. Philosophers also agree with the fact that it IS about "observance of divine laws". Again, we rely mainly on "God's law". Whose God?!

In some languages, the word *etiquette* bears a wonderful ambiguity of meaning – an advertising label and the rules of polite behavior. The fact is that all morality is merely a label that hides us. It is our biggest official mask. But again it has gone into such an extreme that "labeling" others has become a tool of the society. The term "marketing" is based on the word "mark", which means a brand, a label. Without it, you won't be able to sell anything. Marketing has taken on a whole new meaning in the media era, which is mainly understood by those in power. When you think of the World War II, it has had the best marketing in history that has been aided by many well-known companies that are still thriving today. The most visible example of brand abuse is the "hooked cross", better known as swastika. People will automatically associate it with Nazism; however, if you were to visit India, you would find this symbol on almost all altars. So don't identify yourself with labels of any kind; by the same token - don't label others, as you will then never feel completely free. You only identify yourself with something that is absolutely not a part of you as it is someone else's problem instead. Likewise the so-called mockery has become an absurd PR (public relations) tool. If you don't understand something and you don't have enough information about the subject, it is much easier to join a group of people who rather mock others instead of looking what is and isn't true themselves and admitting that they don't know the answer.

We are in a crisis that we have created. There is a lot of evidence that the world does not work according to this pattern of conduct. Every day there are so many disasters happening around us that it is really incredible how we can allow them to happen (and I am not talking about those natural disasters that have always been here and always will be). We see it all and we think we cannot influence it… but we can. It is necessary to change the way this world functions. And change in the way this world functions is even inevitable. The important thing is whether something works or not. Life works - based on adaptability. Our moral principles, however, only depend on what brings us profit in the present.

"Morale is the same as magic. It keeps talking about the perfect man without knowing what it actually means - what is the real man. It created an image of a perfect man who is in fact only an illusion, a dream. Morale uses an image of a perfect man just to condemn a real man who will never reach its ideal."

Osho

We have been trying to solve this problem through politics for thousands of years now and let's face it - we have not resolved anything substantial. The fact is that our society is managed by people with good verbal skills. They do not need to be smart at all, or humane or good. They can do just one thing – speak convincingly. The game of words has a greater impact than one would expect. Politicians, priests, philosophers… they like to listen to themselves and they would be even happier if the greatest possible number of "sheep" agreed with them. They pretend to care about us, but it is just an act. In reality, they have never helped us resolve anything substantial.

"The more you say - the less people remember."

F. Fenelon

Every creator of any system uses logic only to distort the truth and to prove their opinion. It is very easy to invent a system. Everything has gaps and those are easily filled with visions and ideas. The system must be logical, the being however is not. For example, man has formed theories that clarify the creation of this world. However, there are so many of them that no one can say with certainty which one is correct. And it is actually completely useless to try to find the truth, as it is just a mind game at present. If you believe a theory, it will become the truth for you. If you do not believe it, you will only see its shortcomings.

First, we need to realize that **we - people - determine the rules.** We need to be mature enough to start taking responsibility for this world. Not only for our own lawn but for Earth as a whole. We can work together whenever there is a disaster: suddenly everyone feels compassion and they feel the need to help. But there is a disaster happening somewhere every day. However, we also unite if we experience a victory. Have you ever felt the power of an optimistic, cheerful crowd? Think of the atmosphere – do you feel what power can be reached by an upbeat crowd? **A change in consciousness can indeed only occur individually, but the intention that we as humans operate naturally, should be a common goal.**

"The law is bunch of words written on paper by people who are generally considered to be liars and thieves. So let's try figure out what's right rather then whats legal."
J. Rogan

If we changed our moral principles, we would change our opinions. And then we would see what hypocrites people actually are. Basically, they have no opinions of their own, they just want to believe they have some. Almost all of their opinions are based on the past, their education, religion, or comparison. And that is sad. You want to be honest, but basically you are still hiding something. We believe that everyone is hiding something, so we do it as well. We are not able to accept ourselves as we really are. We are constantly comparing ourselves with someone, whether it is a comparison with a neighbor or a multicultural comparison with another country. Because we do not even know who we really are. Our ideas and opinions are mostly only something that has been copied over and over again for years. They are not our truths experienced by us.

"You cannot believe everything you hear, but you can, unfortunately, repeat it."
G. B. Shaw

Every day about 30 thousand people die just because they do not have access to basic necessities. Every day (!) about 400 children die of hunger! And this is nothing compared to how many people die daily "completely unnecessarily" because of some international conflict, war, etc. If we do not take responsibility for the world and for every day, nothing will change. The fact that we can pull together when it comes to the worst can be compared with if you were on your deathbed and began to shout that you actually meant it very differently... But what now? Not enough time? Is it really necessary for a man to struggle for life on a planet where there is more than enough for everyone?! It is not about making people identical, we have heard such chimeras already. But everyone's basic needs for survival should be met. Only then can humans develop as individuals. It is difficult to work on yourself if you have no place to sleep and no food to eat. Every day the restaurants of the world throw out enough food to feed the whole starving Africa. Every day so many empty houses and buildings are built that we could accommodate all those who have no home. In spite of this, there are millions of homeless people all around the world who are struggling for survival every single day. And the fact is that they have been brought to this situation by this "wonderfully functioning" system. The latest statistics even specifically say that there are more than 11 million empty houses in the European Union at present and "only" about 4 million homeless people. So, who truly wants to settle any social issues? Yes, everyone grows up in entirely different circumstances. Does that mean that we should end up on the streets as beggars for any failure? So excuses like "even I had nothing and see what I reached" should stop. Although we do not all have the same conditions, **we have the same foundation, which is called MAN, who is, paradoxically, lacking in humanity.**

When a child is born, he has no idea whether he is white, yellow, or black. Parents, friends, society put some opinions in him that make him, in the worst case, a racist beast. He should be treated, not locked up in a prison where he will learn many more "deformed guidelines for life". (Unfortunately, today the fact is that "white European atheist heterosexuals" have the fewest rights.) In the USA (and not only there) prisons are owned by corporations, so that means: the more people in jail, the better it is for the economy. A recent study even found that in the United States there are more than 356,000 people with mental illnesses in prisons, compared with only about 35 thousand mentally ill people who are being treated in public hospitals. This finding highlights the desperate state of the national system of psychiatric care. Since 1970, the proportion of prisoners with mental disabilities in each state increased by an average of 5 to 20 percent. And these people are not being treated, but after some time they are again released into society – it is a tragedy. 96 (!) people are shot and killed in an avarage day in U.S. (statistics from 2012-2016). The United States was actually the largest experiment in "uniting nations". However, it has totally failed as a result of greed and competition. Can cooperation and competition co-exist? Perhaps in Slovakia where everyone knows everyone, and therefore it seems to be so. In other societies where there are millions of people, it's impossible. Or not? This world must be managed by someone, and it is... and exactly according to this formula - it's a scam. The whole basis of morality, the whole economy, the whole financial system... the world is governed by a certain group of people.

"Mankind will not remain on earth forever... Our planet is the cradle of sense, but we cannot live in the cradle forever."
K. E. Tsiolkovsky

The biggest problem today can actually be defined in one word: ignorance. Even those who are in power today have realized this, so on the other side they are giving us a lot of misleading information. I will try to summarize the essentials which you need to understand as a whole. Do not to judge it; take it as fact. However, we will focus more or less on the past century, because today it is not so important to study a lengthy history of nations because if your consciousness can holistically grasp the following information, you will realize what the game which we all play now is about - here and now. (We are currently at the forefront of questioning the sources we get information from, but in a number of cases I do not mention them here since, frankly, I am unable to put together all the articles, insights, inspiration, interviews, books, etc. that have helped me compose this "story". I repeat that it depends on you and how you grasp the truth in the overall assumption - **you do not have to believe me - look for your own sources, we will definitely meet in the end, because today many thoughts and people are condemned merely because of the source or the name. Disinformation, manipulation through official media, or hidden propaganda are created. What matters to me are thoughts and words - the point.)**

Today it says everywhere that the Jews control the world, so let's start with this controversial issue. And because winners write history, the reality is always different…

"Identify with your race, your religion, with politics…
Why?! It is just a vehicle for your consciousness."
D. Icke

(Despite these information, I truly love and admire many personalities and mainly artists of Jewish origin, as are many of my friends too. I've totally depersonalized this "program" which I am pointing to. In this case, the word "Jew" is the only common denominator among one group of people – a name, nothing more nothing less. It is similar with Christians and Muslims. I am generalizing in order to make it easier for you to understand what game we are in. Any personification regarding this problem can bring us back to "Hitler's idea", so please try to depersonalize all this in spite of your religion or race, but consider the facts. Thank you.)

"In the last decade of the 20th century, to criticize the Jewish people, religion, or the nation of Israel is considered the worst of moral crimes. Jews are the most sacred of sacred cows, and anyone with a negative word about them finds himself labeled an 'anti-Semite'. Once a man acquires that label, true or not, nothing can redeem him from what the mass media views as the ultimate sin."
D.Duke, My Awakening

Unfortunately, it is so. I really do not know of another group of people who have created better marketing than this "company". I do not know of an expression to protect any other race or the adherents of any other group or religion. So if we think about it again, a little bit rationally, we might be aware of the worldwide "brand protection" that is historically unparalleled. It is also interesting that they founded a multi-million-dollar global organization, ADL (Anti-Defamation League), whose only goal is to discredit and blame those who will tell the facts about Jewish racism. So you can calmly insult the whole world, just not the most untouchable… because no one else in history has ever suffered more than "them". Excuse me for the sarcasm, but it is necessary to first understand this absurdity in its overall context. Once again here we have a great paradox, because in reality they are the only Semitic nation are Arabs - so the term "antisemitism" is in fact "anti-Arab" and not "anti-Jew." So if we consider the current situation, the only "anti-Semites" are the Jews themselves. In their rhetoric, the "anti-Khazari" should be used instead. Following this mindset, Africans or Asians should be entitled to these same rights, even more so Europeans. Freedom of speech is once again becoming a crime.

"The present day Jews are no longer of Semitic origin, but they are ethnic Khazari."
A. Koestler (1976, Jew)

There are thousands of depictions of persecuted Jews where they are portrayed as innocent, noble, and heroic, while their opponents are portrayed as pure evil. No other group has created better rapport with the public than the Jews. We all believe their story as they teach it to us in schools, as they present it in the media. It would be impossible to count all the Holocaust-oriented films, documentaries, and books.

"The Holocaust is written with a big H – it has become a trademark."
D. Irving

You probably will not believe me when I tell you that the Russian revolution was not as much "Russian" as it was the Jews being renamed communists. From the beginning, they financed communism and they also dominated the communist movement in the United States. The first to begin pointing it out publicly was Winston Churchill who published an article in the *Illustrated Sunday Herald* called *Zionism versus Bolshevism: A struggle for the soul of the Jewish people.* Of course, he was immediately denounced by the "public" as anti-Semite.

"There is no need to exaggerate the part played in the creation of Bolshevism and in the actual bringing about of the Russian Revolution by these international and for the most part atheistical Jews."
Winston S. Churchill

For most of you this will be new information which you did not learn at school. You will sense a conspiracy (which is a recent means of fighting against the truth) mainly because you will not believe that you could have been so deceived. This applies to all of us, however, and even more than we would like. Therefore, I decided to put this "story" together, more or less using quotes (that can be verified), to help you put the pieces together.

"It is probably unwise to say this loudly in the United States, but the Bolshevik movement is and has been since its beginning guided and controlled by Russian Jews of the most dastardly type."
Cpt. Schuyler, an American intelligence officer in Russia during the revolution (in his official report)

"The Bolshevik leaders, of which 90 percent are displaced returnees, do not care about Russia or any other country. They are internationalists and try to start a world social revolution."
D. Francis, U.S. Ambassador to Russia at the time of the revolution

"We have definite evidence that Bolshevism is an international movement controlled by the Jews."
Instruments from the report of the Director of British Intelligence, U.S. Department of State.

"Trotsky's book, Stalin, written in exile, attempted to show that Stalin had played only an insignificant role in the early days of the Communist takeover. Trotsky attempted to illustrate this point by reproducing a postcard widely circulated in the months following the revolution. The postcard depicted the six leaders of the revolution. Shown are Lenin (who was at least one-quarter Jewish, spoke Yiddish in his home, and was married to a Jewess), Trotsky (real Jewish name: Lev Bronstein), Zinoviev (real Jewish name: Hirsch Apfelbaum), Lunacharsky (a Gentile), Kamenev (real Jewish name: Rosenfeld), and Sverdlov (Jewish). Not only does the postcard show the Jewish domination of the revolution; it also illustrates the fact the Jewish Communist leaders shown had changed their names just as reported in the Encyclopedia Judaica."
D. Duke, My awakening

"Without Jews there would never have been Bolshevism. For a Jew nothing is more insulting then the truth.

The bloodthirsty Jewish terrorists have murdered sixty six million in Russia from 1918 to 1957."
A. Solzhenitsyn (Nobel Peace Prize winner)

"The Communist secret police, which underwent many name changes, including Cheka, OGPU, GPU, NKVD, NKGB, MGB, and KGB, was the most feared police agency in the history of the world. They imprisoned, tortured, or murdered more than 40 million Russians and Eastern Europeans. Even the more conservative Soviet historians of the 1960s were placing the number of murdered at about 35 to 40 million — figures that do not include the millions more who were dispossessed, imprisoned, exiled, tortured, and displaced." D.Duke, My awakening

"Until I looked into the foundations of Communism, I had always thought Karl Marx was a German. In fact, I had read that Marx's father was a Christian. It turns out that his father, a successful lawyer, was a Jew who had converted to Christianity after an edict prohibited Jews from practicing law. Much later, in 1977, I read an article from the Chicago Jewish Sentinel that revealed Marx as the grandson of a rabbi and 'the descendant of Talmudic scholars for many generations'. *I looked up Karl Marx in the Jewish encyclopedias, and I found to my amazement that the man who taught him many of the principles of Communism was Moses Hess. As incredible as it might seem, contemporary Zionist leaders venerate Moses Hess as the 'forerunner of modern Zionism'."* D.Duke, My awakening

"Communism is as Jewish as the Mafia is Italian. It's a fact that almost all of the convicted spies for communism have been atheist Jew like the Rosenbergs. And international communism was invented by the Jew Karl Marx and has since been led mostly by Jews - like Trotsky."
G.L. Rockwell

"The Jews will never forget that the Soviet Union was the first and the only country in the world where anti-Semitism was a crime."
The magazine Jewish Voice, 1942

The reflections of a popular Jewish intellectual, living in France in the 19th Century, who examined the status of the nation in its eternal conflict:

"If this hostility, this repugnance had been shown towards the Jews at one time or in one country only, it would be easy to account for the local causes of this sentiment. But this race has been the object of hatred with all the nations amidst whom it ever settled. In as much as the enemies of the Jews belonged to diverse races, it must be that the general causes of Anti-Semitism have always resided in Israel itself, and not in those who antagonized it."
B. Lazare

"The question then remains is why they have been persecuted so many times in history: Mainz year 1012, France yr. 1182, Bavaria y. 1276, England y. 1290, France y. 1306, France y. 1322, Saxony yr. 1349, Hungary r. 1360, Belgium r. 1370, Slovakia r. 1380, France r. 1394, Austria r. 1420, Lyon r. 1420, Cologne r. 1424, Mainz r. 1438, Augsburg r. 1438, Bavaria r. 1442, Netherlands r. 1444, Brandenburg r. 1446, Mainz r. 1462, Mainz r. 1483, Warsaw r. 1483, Spain r. 1492, Italy r. 1492, Latvia r. 1495, Portugal r. 1496, Naples r. 1496, Navarre r. 1498, Nuremberg r. 1498, Brandenburg r. 1510, Prussia 1510, Genoa r. 1515, Naples r. 1533, Italy r. 1540, Naples r. 1541, Prague r. 1541, Geneva r. 1550, Bavaria r. 1551, Prague r. 1557, Papal States r. 1569, Hungary r. 1582, Hamburg r. 1649, Vienna r. 1669, Slovakia r. 1744, Moravia r. 1744, Bohemia (Czech Republic) r. 1744, Moscow r. 1891." S. Anderson, Baptist Pastor

And what came next? Era of mass media followed by World War 1. and World War 2. These wars had the best marketing in the history of mankind. Just think about it, please.

"The movie industry, sugar industry, tobacco industry, over 50% of the meat industry, more than 60% of footwear producers; the music industry, jewelry; grain, cotton, oil, steel; distribution of newspapers and magazines; alcohol distribution; loans; this is all in the hands of the Jews often from the US alone, sometimes together with Jews from other countries."
H. Ford, 1921

Jews are even the founders of the interest rate, the so-called usury, as it was called in the past. They even have it in their holy scriptures that it is their "duty" to charge gentiles interest. And here lies the beginning of the so-called financial crisis - the interest that does not really exist, and yet affects the operation of the whole world. And there is always someone who will prosper from this fictional money.

"'You may charge a foreigner interest, but not a brother Israelite…' (Deut. 23:20) - to your brother it is forbidden, but to the rest of the world it is allowed. Charging gentiles interest is a positive commandment."
Maimonides - Europe's greatest Jewish teacher
(Code of Maimonides, Book 13)

"A heathen may not raise an allegation of fraud, because it is said `to one of your countrymen' (Leviticus 25:14). However, when a pagan fools an Israelite, he must repay the overpayment in accordance with our laws, because pagan law may not exceed Israelite law."
(Code of Maimonides, Book 12)

"The Jews should not be allowed to keep what they have obtained from others by usury; it were best that they were

compelled to work so that they could earn their living instead of doing nothing but becoming avaricious."
St. T. Aquinas, scholastic philosopher of the 13th century

It is no secret that the most important family in banking is, and has been for 200 years, the Rothschild family. Their most famous financial move dates back to the Battle of Waterloo where Mayer Amschel Rothschild feared Napoleon's victory. He knew that if Napoleon won, the stock market would collapse, and if France lost, business would grow. Therefore, he devised a system which helped him get information about the state of the battle earlier than anyone else. Using pigeons and signal lamps from the ships, he was the first to find out about Napoleon's defeat. He released a false report about Napoleon's victory that caused the fall of the London Stock Exchange. Then he very quickly bought up shares for a trifle. When bankers in England heard about the British victory, the share prices increased incredibly. The Rothschilds are proud of this move. But this scam was paid for at a high price by hundreds of thousands of people. I think the follow-up of this story is more or less logical. For example, in Berlin in 1923 there were 150 Jewish banks and only 11 non-Jewish. These practices have merrily continued and are still here today. It is the same on Wall Street today, only the quantities are incomparably larger. If you, as a minority in a multicultural society, stick together, you have won.

"Give me the power to issue a nation's money, then I do not care who makes the law."
M. A. Rothschild (1744 - 1812)

"Money is the God of our times, and Rothschild is his prophet..."
H. Heine (1841)

The biggest problem, however, is the "holy land".

"I checked the figures compiled by the British Census in 1922. At that time, Jews accounted for only about 10 percent of the population. In the last such census, taken the year before the establishment of Israel, Jews had made up only about half of the population within the area that subsequently became Israel. The Palestinians then owned 93.5 percent of the land. The facts were inescapable and damning: Zionist immigrants had forced their way into Palestine against the wishes of the inhabitants and then, through the weight of arms and terror, had driven the residents from their homes, robbing them of their land and possessions. The facts could not be plainer. The Zionists, with help from their cohorts all over the world, had stolen a whole nation: the nation called Israel. No equivocation, no mountain of pro-Israeli propaganda, no playing of 'Exodus' on the radio, and no replay of millions of feet of Hollywood films."
D.Duke, My Awakening

Perhaps the original inhabitants of this area thousands of years ago were Jews, but that changed over time. I cannot imagine this idea taken up by any nation in Europe where borders changed quite often in the past. Therefore, it is absolute nonsense to occupy any land, create borders (just for checking!) or claim a land just because someone was there first and by force. In ancient times, ancient cultures, and indigenous tribes, it is basically unthinkable. It is precisely the path that leads to slavery and to the "official enslavement" which has been happening more than ever before in the last millennium. Just as one cannot own air, sun, and water (although thanks to huge corporations, business with water is taking place right at this moment and we just sit and watch indifferently!). Many problems would disappear if people could understand this without the need to own and control.

"The establishment of Israel three years after the defeat of Germany was the secondary effect of the Holocaust."

Encarta Encyclopedia, article on the Holocaust from Raul Hilberg, a leading historian of the Jewish Holocaust

"We took their land; we must do everything to ensure that they will never return... We must use terror, assassination, intimidation, land classification and the severing of social services, in order to rid Galilee of its Arab population."
D. Ben-Gurion (ex-Isreali Prime Minister in 1948)

"Our race is a gentleman's race, we are the gods of this planet, we differ from the other inferior races, as they differ from insects, and indeed, in comparison with our race, all other races are beasts and animals, in the best case cattle. We will rule our earthly kingdom with an iron hand, the masses will kiss our feet and serve us slavishly."
M. Begin, ex-Prime Minister of Israel (before the emergence of Israel he was the leader of the Israeli terrorist group Irgun)

"The Zionist dream of Israel needed a 'Holocaust' – the worst Holocaust imaginable - to support its goals."
D. Duke

"The Israeli government is in the U.S. placed on a pedestal and its criticism is immediately called anti-Semitism. People in the U.S. are afraid to say that evil is evil, because the Jewish lobby is very powerful."
Bishop D. Tutu (South Africa)

"We have to appreciate the success of Israeli propaganda, which has turned what actually happened backwards. The first is the reputation of Israel, and its government is also adapting reality to it. Of course, an ordinary person, on the basis of television reports, is of the opinion that Israel only defends itself. Israel is basically only able to talk about terrorism and its own security."
P. Hart, National Censorship Association

"We are actually fighting to get the Americans to stop believing the fairy tales the media presents to them. The more Americans there are who know the truth about the Israeli occupation of the Palestinian Territory, the more they see the images of violence, oppression and humiliation that will never get to the mainstream, the more questions will be asked as to whether Israel is really the little David who resists Arab Goliath, and they will begin to wonder if David's team is a coincidence in Palestine. And the more Americans are told the truth, the quicker the real image of Israeli terrorism will come to the forefront. US support for Israel can only change public support, which will start seeing this event through different eyes. The US government will support Israel as long as the Americans tolerate it."
N. Chomsky - Jew (Occupation or Media War on US Public Opinion)

"I want to tell you something very clear: Do not worry about American pressure on Israel. We, the Jewish people, control America, and the Americans know it."
A.Sharon (ex-Isreali Prime Minister in 2001)

"No country in peacetime - not even the Soviets or the Red Chinese in the heyday of their gulags - has held as many prisoners per capita as the nation of Israel. It is one of the few nations that will not officially renounce the use of torture. The inescapable fact is that Israel was born and built by invasion, murder, and theft. Such injustice requires the use of force and terror to maintain its power. Israel exists in its functioning as a living testimony of an absolutely racist nature of Judaism and its secular son - Zionism. ***The Israeli claim that God gave them the land of Israel is ludicrous when one considers that at least three-quarters of Israelis don't believe in God in the first place.*** *Far from being a religious promise, Israel's creation came not from divine intervention, but from Zionist intrigue that began during the First World War.*

Those who wear the six-pointed star and who bomb United Nations shelters, ambulances, civilian refugee camps and civilian automobiles are never described as terrorists. They are simply referred to as "commandos" or simply "military forces." In contrast, Palestinian fighters outside the borders of Israel are, of course, routinely described as terrorists."

A Palestinian who was born in the boundaries of what is now Israel, and whose family lived there for thousands of years before being forced out by the Israeli army, cannot return to his homeland and become a citizen of Israel. In contrast, an atheist Jew born in New York City and who speaks no Hebrew, can immigrate to Israel and be given instant citizenship. In addition, the Israeli government offers him help in housing, living expenses, education, and numerous other benefits to immigrate. The president of the Israeli Human Rights League, Doctor Israel Shahak, a professor at the Hebrew University of Jerusalem, in his book, The Racism of the State of Israel, tells us that there are in Israel whole towns (Carmel, Nazareth, Illith, Hatzor, Arad, Mitzphen-Ramen, and others) where non-Jews are forbidden by law to live."

D.Duke, My Awakening

I would like to see what the reactions would be if there was a city where Christians, for example, would not allow Jews to live.

"The bitter irony of fate decreed that the same biological and racist argument extended by the Nazis, and which inspired the inflammatory laws of Nuremberg, serve as the basis for the official definition of Jewishness in the bosom of the state of Israel."

H. Cohen, a former judge of the Supreme Court in Israel

"The story of the Holocaust centers on the concentration camp Auschwitz in Poland. For several years it was presented as a death camp where the Nazis had gassed three to four million Jews and millions of non-Jews. Half a million tourists every year see what is passed off as the real gas chambers where millions of Jews were murdered. Boards at the main gate in the years 1945 - 1989 proclaimed in many languages that 4.1 million victims died there. During a 1979 visit to the camp, Pope John Paul II stood before this memorial and blessed the four million victims. Then it became clear that at least three million of the murdered were a figment of the imagination. Soon after the Pope's visit, without fanfare or publicity, camp historians removed the board and replaced it with a new one, reflecting the new official number: 1,2 mil."
D. Duke, My Awakening

I was trying to find some scientific evidence that would confirm the gassing of the victims, but I did not succeed. Although a number of autopsies were performed by Russian doctors, their findings were never presented in Nuremberg.

"If there were gas chambers in the camps, they were for disinfection. Most of the victims died because of inhumane treatment, medical experiments, or various diseases or they were shot. Please think: Why would they have people cut, disinfected, deodorized, dressed, or even tattooed if they were going to kill them?!"
S. Anderson, Baptist Pastor

I suppose that they were inspired by Gulags - Russian labor camps that gathered people for obligatory state work in incomparably larger numbers. Unfortunately, there is no interest in creating similar PR for these "work prisons", despite the fact that many more innocent victims were killed there than in concentration camps during World War II. The principles of these camps were the same, the difference was that the Gulags were in operation for thirty years and, in many ways, they were even more cruel. Nobel Prizewinner Aleksandr Solzhenitsyn in his opus, The Gulag Archipelago, using the research of a Soviet statistician who had access to secret government files, I. A. Kurganov, estimated that between 1918 and 1959, at least 66 million died at the hands of the Communist rulers of Russia. (We could also recall a similar story from history about the British and the Irish. Why aren't there thousands of movies about this?)

Fred Leuchter, an apolitical man, perhaps the greatest authority in the United States on the construction of equipment for executions, which are carried out in many American prisons, was approached in 1988 to do chemical research in Auschwitz. They wanted to refute accusations raised by Ernest Zundel on the basis of his research (and he was prosecuted for it).

"In his investigation, Leuchter surveyed the construction of the alleged gas chambers and researched the chemical properties of the Zyklon B fumigant. He found that Zyklon B is a compound that, when exposed to air, releases deadly hydrogen cyanide gas. It clings to surfaces and has a tendency to react chemically with materials containing iron (ferric compounds), creating a ferricyanide. If Zyklon B is used in iron chambers or in red brick structures, it reacts with ferrous (iron) material to produce a distinctive blue color. Not only did Leuchter find that the supposed homicidal gas chambers at Auschwitz were structurally unsuitable for gassing, he also took samples from the walls and had them chemically analyzed. Independent laboratories in the United States found no evidence of the ferricyanide compounds. Yet, when Leuchter examined the rooms used as disinfestation chambers for clothes and luggage, he readily observed the distinctive blue coloring associated with ferricyanide. Leuchter also pointed out that the disinfestation chambers used for delousing clothes were well made, airtight, and designed for safety. On the other hand, the supposed human gas chambers were shoddily constructed."

D. Duke, My awakening

He was even imprisoned for six weeks. For his translation and commentary on Leuchter's report, Günter Deckert, a former college professor, was also given a suspended sentence. The 87-year-old grandmother Ursula Haverbeck was also imprisoned for ten months for her statement that Auschwitz was a labor camp rather then an extermination camp. The questioning of the Holocaust became a crime.

"I've been working on your case for seven years, and I know that Holocaust is such a scam that it has to be evident even to a High school student. Every chemist knows that it is impossible to gas poison one to two thousand people at once using hydrogen cyanide - this is well known. Even the best known American Jewish newspaper in their annual almanac claimed that in 1942 the number of Jews in the occupied Europe was 3 million. So I have no idea how the claimed amount of Jews killed could be 6 million."
R. Dommergue (French Jewish professor
in an interview with E. Zundel)

If someone feels that it is impossible for us to be so deceived (after those years of excellent propaganda), I would be very grateful if that person can truly prove how it really was. **I would be extremely happy if this case were re-opened and investigated. The content of quotations does not represent my personal opinion - I want to know the truth - nothing more, nothing less.**

"To call anyone who questions the dogma of the Holocaust a 'Holocaust denier' means to imply that he is a stupid and evil anti-Semitic lunatic. How can he deny, they ask, the 'authority' of the Holocaust, something that was seen with our very own eyes - photos and film footage, piles of Jewish bodies? In fact, I found that no responsible revisionist denies that many innocent people, including many Jews were killed by the Germans and their allies during World War II. No one denies that the Germans gathered

Jews from all over occupied Europe and put them in concentration camps. Revisionists do not deny that the Nazis perpetrated atrocities against Jews, they however claim that the number of those who were murdered is greatly exaggerated. And more importantly, they claim that there was no central plan, policy, or command of the German government to exterminate the entire Jewish nation. The revisionists declare that the Nazis established concentration camps as prisons for Jews because they considered them a security risk, just as the U.S. government massed and interned Japanese for security reasons.

Instead of describing the mere suffering of the Jews, it would be more appropriate to describe the whole Second World War as a holocaust. The bombing and burning of the most beautiful cities of Europe and works of art, the death of tens of millions of the bravest and best young men, ruthless exploitation, starvation, rape and murder of tens of millions of innocent civilians of all nations and ethnic groups of Europe - it was the greatest holocaust the world has ever known.

It's not a conspiracy. There are just two groups - Jews and gentiles - in a state of ethnic war. Of course, most Jews and non-Jews do not even realize that we are at war. ***Although we know the racist nature of Judaism, as well as Zionism, we recognize that there are individual Jews who do not accept any of these doctrines, and they are not involved in any activities on the disruption and destruction of non-Jewish societies, of course."***

D. Duke, My Awakening

(If, within this context, you have reservations against David Duke's personality, study the work of the French professor of Jewish origin Dr. Dommergue, or another French professor Robert Faurisson, for example.)

Despite the fact that we have specified the group of "culprits", the designation "Jews" might simply be called US and Israeli policy today. Even though they won their dream of Israel, it is not enough for them. For instance, still today they cannot accept the so-called liberation of Europe by the Russian army, their power and influence. And while the European Union is only their extended hand, they are the co-creators of the current conflict in Ukraine, too. Although the given intrigue created cooperation between the two superpowers, after moving the main power components to the USA, Russia (ZSSR) fell to its knees and it seems that only now - when the situation is unbearable and it influences them directly - fortunately, they have started to act. And so we can watch media cases all over the world against Russia, whatever the arguments, the Russians are always portrayed as "the bad guys".

"We thought the Cold War was over. We had peaceful, transparent relations with the world, with Europe and the US. We decided to count on support, but instead we were witnesses as US intelligence services supported terrorists. And I will now say something very important: then we firmly believed that our US partners were talking about Russia's support, the need for cooperation, including the fight against terrorism. In fact, these terrorists used to destabilize the intra-political situation in Russia."
V. Putin (*Interview with Putin* by Oliver Stone)

"The US and EU aim to force Russia to provoke a war with Ukraine at all costs, and it seems that there will be no peace in Ukraine until they reach their goal. US consultants are advising the Ukrainian government and especially the army.

"The US agreed with Kiev that the Ukrainian National Guard will be financially subsidized and trained by US professionals. The question is, why and for what purpose will the US train soldiers in Ukraine – of course, the reason is concealed. As you can see, neither the media nor politicians have any objections and you will never hear that conflicts with separatists are supported directly by the US and EU.

"The US and the EU cause permanent military conflicts and spread hatred between nations and states as well as between social groups in their own countries. Hatred is an essential tool for controlling nations and waging wars, in addition to misleading propaganda and censorship. This situation has now reached the highest possible level. The criminal massacres of civilians in southeastern Ukraine are proof of the seriousness of the situation, which has alarmed neither top politicians nor so-called global humanitarian organizations. The evil is going on, civilians are being bombed and killed, and basically everybody is silent about it. Of course, the church is silent as well!!! In any case, citizens should not be quiet because they are the ones who will pay all the costs."
S. Chrtkova, journalist (2014)

"The Russian market was fully open to imports from Ukraine. So far, the zero duty rate has been reached. For 17 years, we have discussed with the EU the conditions for Russia's accession to the WTO (World Trade Organization). *And suddenly we learn that Ukraine has signed an association agreement with the EU. The Ukrainian market opens. The EU team actually gets their goods onto our territory without any bargaining, notwithstanding the previous agreements reached during the 17-year WTO accession negotiations. We then had to respond because it happened to the detriment of our*

citizens. We have proposed to the European partners that we will conduct trialogue negotiations. They have refused it vigorously."
V. Putin (Interview with Putin, Oliver Stone)

The following important fact should be emphasized: the European Union was established by the Nazis to dominate Europe and Russia (please google the following names: Walter Hallstein, Fritz Teer Meer, Carl Wurster, et al.) And since the US-like, attractive independent life arrived in post-war Europe, it was not hard to believe this propaganda. However, we believed in chimera, while we did not notice that Europe was very discreetly occupied in a much more refined way. At present, NATO bases are being established across Europe, and if we look at the map, we see that all of Russia is encircled, as the media-headline enemy of the US and Israel. The Russians are one of the few who do not share their policy, are resource independent (also financially very soon), and that does not suit those who want to control the whole world. The fact is that many in Europe do not have good memories of the Russian army, but another fact is that it is they who have overlooked how this overall situation as well as the fabled phoenix has risen from ashes. Even they are not proud of their past actions, but today the situation is diametrically different. It must be remembered that everything is changeable and nothing is the way it is officially presented to us...

"What kind of peace do we seek? Not a Pax Americana enforced on the world by American weapons of war. We need to reexamine our attitude toward the Soviet Union. Our most basic common link is that we all inhabit this small planet, we all breathe the same air, we all cherish our children's future, and we are all mortal."
J.F. Kennedy, former President of the United States

(Remember that at present, about 80% of the ruling class has no children.)

"It seems to me that in order for NATO to justify its existence, it needs the external enemy it is constantly looking for or is inciting provocation to name someone. Today, NATO is only an instrument of American foreign policy - it has no allies, only vassals. Once a country becomes a member, it then can hardly resist the pressure of the US. Suddenly, they can place anything on their territory. An anti-missile umbrella, a new military base, and new attack systems if needed."
V. Putin (Interview with Putin, Oliver Stone)

During the Clinton administration, Russia even wanted to join NATO, but everyone was nervous - they would lose an enemy.

"After the Second World War a bipolar world emerged. The Soviet Union made a strategic mistake, and honestly behaved quite primitively, which gave the West, including the USA, a pretext for the founding of NATO and the dissolution of the Cold War. The US felt that it was at the helm of the civilized world, and when the Soviet Union collapsed, Americans began to live in the illusion that they could afford everything, with no impunity. But it is always a trap, because in such a situation, people or groups begin to make mistakes. The country becomes ineffective and one error leads to another."
V. Putin (*Interview with Putin* by Oliver Stone)

"The United States can achieve a united pro-American Europe and NATO only if it has an external enemy like Russia."
O. Stone

Although I do not want to believe it, it all fits together. Our current society is the most misled society ever. Power, money, weapons, and media have been used and abused to perfection. This is exactly how destructive creativity and the world based on the left hemisphere, thus masculine principles, operates. Of course, **from a holistic perspective it is about offset energy, because the Jews were oppressed and abuse in many societies. However, dear ones,**

please be aware that in the last century it is your race, which is literally the only breed. You have the best educational resources, information, conditions, etc., you even love to teach others. So it is you who can greatly help this world today. We all could learn from you as for cooperation. And in particular, based on personal experience, I know that today's young people do not even recognize the atrocities committed by their states, and it does not matter whether it is Israel or Germany. It is not people who are fascist, but states. The fact is that every western nation has done so much evil in the world that there is nothing to condemn now. In particular, it is imperative to learn from it and accept the facts. Just note that in Europe we are now on the direct path to repeating the formula of the "Holocaust" with Muslims, or they will do it to us... Or will we wake up?

"Jews have to stand up even when — especially when — the wrongdoing is BY Jews/the Israeli government"
S. Silverman (Tweet of Jewish actress)

A certain group of people actually controls, or would like to control, the whole world, and whoever wants to become and stay successful must cooperate. Those who understood this happily joined the game, and so they established the Bilderberg Group for example, whose members are probably the ones who know how it really is with this planet and the slaves. This group wants to basically create one world company that would be superior to all governments on Earth. The name of this group, however, thanks to investigative journalists, began to appear more often in public, and so it was for appearances' sake officially dissolved in 2010. Another such group is the CFR (Council on Foreign Relations), which is funded by Rockefeller. This institution controls the nations of the Western world via institutions such as the World Bank, in which they have power over the board. Basically, it is a private organization that gives instructions to governments (officially they make suggestions). The group has "affiliates" around the world, of course. A very important player is the Committee of 300, which was founded in 1729 by the high nobility, together with financial leaders. The BEIMC (British East India Merchant Company) was established to control international banking and trade, mainly the opium trade.

"The only things of value in Afghanistan are Afghani carpets and drugs, and I do not think that NATO is there because of the carpets. They are there to make sure that the drugs make their way to Wall Street. The drug business is the most important business in the world. Drug money is laundered through Wall Street, and if you do not have drug money laundered through Wall Street, you do not have a world economy - it collapses in on itself." D. Estulin (for Czech TV, 2011)

"Russia and China are the biggest enemies of the Bilderberg Group, who is manipulating both of them. For example: in 2005 at the Bilderberg conference they talked about manipulating oil prices. First it should go up to 150 USD per barrel and then it should drop to 30 USD per barrel, and this is exactly what happened. If you push the price to 150 USD, you will destroy China's economy, and if you push it down to 30, you will do the same, but to Russia. So they have different ways of influencing these strong countries. Russia is their arch enemy and military enemy, and China is their economic enemy. So that is why there are 70 secret military bases in Afghanistan whose only objective is to attack Russia in case of war. They are not against Iran."
D. Estulin (for Czech TV, 2011)

"This financial meltdown was orchestrated by the Bilderberg Group, because we are living on a planet inhabited by 7 billion people and we have limited natural resources. If we have 20-30 billion people, we will not have enough resources for everyone. And the people who want to control the world want to make sure that they will have enough resources for themselves - like food and water. And to do that you need

to destroy the population base and the world economy. When you have progress, you have growth and population expansion. If you don't have any economic growth, you have zero progress and population destruction. So this is what they are doing right now. It is very well engineered and orchestrated. The same situation/meltdown occurred in 1345 when the Bardi-Peruzzi banks collapsed causing the black plague epidemic and the destruction of half the population of Europe."
D. Estulin (for Czech TV, 2011)

The Committee of 300 is a secret society led by the Black Nobility, the British Crown, and, of course, by our "favorite" family clans. **The Black Nobility is a real atrocity and they are fully responsible for this world farce.** It is they who turned the Jews into their "servants" and they would do anything for power and money. Their name is no accident. Most of these families gained their wealth and power through incredible brutality. Their favorite hobbies are Satanism and black magic. Then we also have the Club of Rome, which has nothing to do with Rome or the Vatican. The club consists of Black Nobility and the 13 families of the Illuminati in America. Their goal is to educate a new generation of those "faithful to the regime" through their own schools, with a vision of creating a global society and government of the 21st century. Finally, we can mention the Trilateral Commission (TC), whose founder is none other than David Rockefeller. While the "Bilderbergers" are a connection between the American and European elite, TC deals with Asia and the Far East. Members include the heads of the biggest concerns, senior politicians, and editors of major media groups.

"The Trilateral Commission was founded in 1973 and is nothing but a world government in a state of expectation. During their meetings, current global issues are discussed and appropriate decisions (such as the 1991 collapse of Yugoslavia) are made. I acquired a total of 51 protocols from TC meetings and used them for my book 'Trilateral Komisja'. The Bilderberg Group is

another association, for the most part. However, it has the same members. Its establishment was prompted by the Vatican."

Said Belgrade expert on international law Smilja Avramov in an interview with J. Elsasser in 2009. When he asked her what precedes important decisions of the International Monetary Fund or the World Bank, or G8 top members, she replied:

"They decide here only for effect, everything must be agreed upon in advance. And that is what the Trilateral Commission is for."
S. Avramov *(What you should NOT know* - M. Morris - to add to this "puzzle", read, for instance, this book.)

Thanks to the above examples, you can see how easy it is to manipulate everything and that it really is governed by the same group of people. This is not something "given". At present, these are mainly artificially contrived wars in the Middle East and various terrorist attacks. This contemporary game with terrorists was "officially" started with the attacks on the WTC on September 11, 2001 (the day when probably even the laws of physics did not work). It had to be something the whole world would notice. There are many documents that prove that this whole atrocity was fabricated by the abovementioned group. It is up to you whether you want to know and see the truth, or if you are satisfied with the information you are being fed. (Please, see the true story of this event – there are many videos on the internet.) Also, if we look closely at each area where fighting is going on today, we find that each of those countries has some mineral wealth the world is interested in. These wars will go on forever in those same areas, if we do not wake up.

"It was a senseless war that put us down economically and morally. We went to war against a man who had nothing to do with September 11. It was just an excuse! It's inexcusable and Bush,

Cheney and Jewish neoconservatives who wanted to reshape the world are to be blamed. Maybe I can say that, because I am a Jew."
C. Bernstein, journalist

"Watch the flow of money. To see who is behind something, just watch the flow of money. Check out the stores closed just before 9/11. These guys knew something was coming. Sons of CIA agents, government officials, close relatives of the most powerful men in America. Cheney, Rumsfeld, etc., they all got rich. And it was not just the contracts they had made with their friends in the construction industry, in the shops, not just the wars and bribes. It was 'insider trading' (trading on the basis of non-public information). As early as 9/11, many countries, including Britain, France, Germany, Italy, Japan and Monaco, began investigating possible insider trading in the hope that if al-Qaeda operators had gained profits on the stock exchange, it could be proven that this organization actually stood behind the attacks. But all the evidence showed intense 'insider trading' around September 11. Italian Foreign Minister Antonio Martino said: 'I think terrorist states and organizations are speculators on international markets.' The head of the German central bank, Ernst Welteke, said his investigators had found 'almost irrefutable proofs of insider trading.'"
M. Howard, retired CIA agent

Today, these men are basically hiding behind the flags of corporations - but they have names! In this century, no one really significant was persecuted or prosecuted. There were some victims who were not useful or were inconvenient, but the vast majority just change coats. And it is like this worldwide. If by any chance someone comes along who wants to make a change, they are very quickly and systematically silenced.

"Fascism should more accurately be called corporatism because it combines state and corporate power."
B. Mussolini

Judaism has actually slowly turned to Zionism - the Jewish racial nationalism. But to get away from this "title" we can use a different expression that covers all these family clans and their loyal friends – the "Elite". And unfortunately, if you already have everything in the physical world (and it is not as much as one might think), then comes a natural desire to go further - to have more... You really don't want to know how these, mostly gentleman, "kill time". Various rituals take place which are worse than the worst horror and fantasy films combined. The bloody sacrifices of small children on altars are just a small example of the atrocities of the society that manages us. David Icke, a former British journalist and "light worker", made the effort and found that in the world you can check statistics on really anything, just not on lost children. The biggest atrocities are actually happening behind closed doors. Our "elites" also know the ancient alchemy of life, but they are definitely more excited by the black magic. And if you are "consecrated" once, then you are on the direct path to what we call hell. So, to make matters worse, our elites also desire eternal life, and so according to black magic, it is the blood of children that will best serve them. Yes, you read that right – the blood of children.

Fortunately, the International Tribunal of Crimes of Church and State (ITCCS.org) was founded in 2010 and is the first organization to deal with the ritual killing of children by the "elite". It was founded by Canadian Reverend Kevin Annett, along with the survivors of the mass murders of children, as well as other victims of violence against children. As an extension of the ITCCS, the International Common Law Court of Justice (ICLCJ), i.e. The International Court, was established in Brussels on September 15, 2012 and actually serves people where other state branches have failed. They actively cooperate with the witnesses of these rituals.

"The first case in the ICLCJ file began on November 6, 2012 and addressed the deliberate genocide of the original children in

Canada, incited by the Vatican, the British Crown, and other parties. In its final verdict on February 25, 2013, the court and its fifty-five civil judges successfully accused and prosecuted thirty defendants for committing and forgiving the genocide. These accused victims included: then Pope Benedict - Joseph Ratzinger, former Cardinal Tarcisio Bertone, Elizabeth Windsor 'The Queen of England,' and Canadian Prime Minister Stephen Harper." www.ITCCS.org

Pope Ratzinger announced his resignation in February 2013 after a court decision in which he was convicted of crimes against humanity and personal involvement in ritual murders on February 25, 2013 - all of which is evidence. He resigned on February 28, 2013.

"The case in Oudergem, Belgium, has been as follows. Near the place was a forest in which naked children were hunted and shot down. The perpetrators cut off their penises and raised them over their heads like trophies and rejoiced. Soldiers were stationed around the forest to guard the whole event. Among the perpetrators were Prince Johann Friso, King Albert, Prime Minister Mark Rutte, and George Soros. The children were provided by the Octopus Syndicate, which is a branch of the largest Italian mafia group, Ndrangheta. The children were from children's homes or institutions, all at the request of Queen Beatrix. Our witness is the wife of a high-ranking member of the mafia, so she knows. She was often forced to take part in these rituals." A. Endriss, ITCCS.org

"I'm here to make money. I cannot, nor will I take into account the social consequences of what I do." G. Soros

The ICLCJ has been working exclusively with the evidence since its inception, so it is not a matter of presumption or conspiracy. The situation is that, according to their findings, almost every trace leads to the Vatican and the Jesuits. But there our vicious circle ends once again, because the Vatican stands above the law - it is extraterritorial. This sovereignty was granted in 1929 by the Italian government. So, as ordinary citizens, we are legally helpless because they have their own canon law. For this reason, former Pope Benedict also hides there. So we are back to the beginning, and as I mentioned in the previous chapter - if the Vatican could speak, we would have learned the real truth. However, at the moment it is very important for such independent investigative committees to be set up around the world.

"Fighting for peace is like fucking for virginity."
G. Carlin

Of course, Islam is another problem today. Although the whole "terrorist war" is just the propaganda of the above groups, they also plan to dominate the world. The Arabic god is very angry, and I'm actually not surprised by this. In spite of this, the men in "the highest positions" shake hands over contracts we would never dream of. Oil – that is their common language. If war – then mainly for oil and for Israel.

If we sabotaged the financial system and changed the "oil economy" to the source economy, this whole sad story might have a happy ending.

But this is definitely not in the interests of the "powerful". On the contrary, their destructive creativity really has no limits. They are trying to divide the world as much as possible, at any cost, including innocent lives, a lot of money, controlling the media, threats, intimidation... Creating conflict is actually much easier than dealing with peace.

ISIS (or ISIL as it was renamed by the media in the USA - while ISIS represents only Iraq and Syria, the "L" indicates the larger "Levant" region), so the Islamic State – this is the name of the latest propaganda of Islam in practice.

"In fact, the United States created ISIS. Nothing like this existed before the American occupation. We created it – it's ours and now we are trying to deal with consequences."
M. Danner, American author and journalist (He predicted the establishment of ISIS as early as 2003.)

"It began during the Soviet war in Afghanistan (1979–1989) when US intelligence services provided support to various Islamic fundamentalists to fight Soviet troops. So the Americans alienated Al-Qaeda and bin Laden themselves, and then it got out of control as always. Our American partners should know better. It's their fault."
V. Putin, President of the Russian Federation

The CIA is quietly withdrawing the terrorist group Al-Qaeda, which they created and sponsored themselves in the eighties, from public scrutiny and is gradually supplying power to the new bogeyman named ISIS (ISIL). The irony of the situation is that the weapons and training of these quasi enemies even comes directly from the office of the US President.

"The creation of an Islamic state is not the ultimate aim of ISIS. This is only the first phase of the area cleansed of 'undesirable elements' such as Christians and radical Muslims. When the ethnic and religious cleansing in Iraq and Syria is complete, ISIS will be 'heroically defeated' and puppet regimes set up by the United States and Israel will arise throughout the territory, similar to how it is for instance in Kurdistan. However, Bashar Assad and Syria are the main targets of the attacks. The liquidation of Assad's regime is crucial for the United States, who aim mainly to suppress the Russian influence in the area. Great Israel should arise as a result.

According to sources reportedly coming from Edward Snowden, ISIS is again the work of Western secret services. It is led by Abu Bakr al-Baghdadi, an agent of the Israeli Mossad, the so-called Caliph – the head of ISIS. In fact, his name is Shimon Elliot, and he is an operative agent of Israel. He was reportedly recruited and trained by Mossad for Psychological War, and he has previously worked with the American and British secret services to establish an organization that would be able to attract 'scattered' terrorist extremists from around the world. Still today, the information has only been confirmed by some media outlets in Iran, but the Iranian secret service disclosed the identity of Abu Bakr Al Baghdadi as well: Elliot Shimon."

source http://www.veteranstoday.com

(Incidentally, if you have conspiratorial suspicions, take a look at, for example, the movie ***Snowden***, which was filmed by a man who is not only a director but also a great activist, Oliver Stone.)

This is not really the idea of Arab rebels, the most dangerous band in the world has been consciously artificially created today, because they literally believe everything the Caliph commands. It is a society without education, culture, real information, intelligence, or any empathy. They are killing machines, which actively lead even children to this blind faith. The irony of the situation is the fact that both religious groups read the same "motivational texts" from their own "holy" books to accomplish this "divine work".

"I have met many extremist groups in the world, but ISIS is the strongest one because they have an enthusiasm which is incredible and they feel that they are part of the historic mission of the destruction of all other religions and non-conforming Muslims. And they do not feel they are doing anything wrong, but rather that it is absolutely essential to fulfill the plan of God."

J. Todenhöfer, a German reporter who spent 10 days in ISIS

However, as history has already shown, if someone starts to talk too much, the name and tactics will change and information chaos will arise. But, unfortunately, this conflict is not just about the so-called terrorists. According to the Arab League, settlers on the West Bank in 2015 attacked the territory of Palestine more than 11,000 times. If you wanted to share anything about these attacks on social media, you would immediately go to jail. These attacks are launched repeatedly on a daily basis and are not a coincidence or defense as it is presented everywhere. If you are interested in getting a realistic view of this situation, again there are many activists who have visited the area and spoken about it based on their own experiences. One activist who addresses this issue is the journalist Abby Martin, who has already created several documentaries on the subject. So if you are really interested in getting a realistic view of the Israel versus Palestine situation, you can find it.

"40% of Palestinian men on the West Bank of Jordan and in Jerusalem have already been in Israeli jails. 'The only democracy in the Middle East' criminalizes a large part of its population through its judicial system. What kind of crimes have led to such a high proportion of prisoners? On the West Bank, no one has the right to protest. All political parties are banned because Palestinians on the West Bank are under Israeli military law. All their political and civil rights are dictated by the occupying army. This occupation has been in effect since the Israeli occupation in 1967. And since this attack, which aimed to conquer all of Palestine, the Israeli military regime has used extreme violence and their dictatorial legal system to punish any Palestinians who have defended their rights."

A. Martin (*The Empire Files*—YouTube channel)

"Palestinian are not human beings, they do not deserve to live and they are nothing but animals."

E.B.Dahan, Deputy minister of religious zionist

"I realized that my job was actually to maintain the apartheid system. I quickly realized that the rights of the Jewish settlers were not like those of the Palestinians. I understood that I could not touch the Jewish settlement when attacking the Palestinians, so these Jewish settlers living in Hebron had the same rights as I do in Jerusalem, but the Palestinians next to them in a secondary house, sometimes in a neighboring apartment, lived according to my military rules. And I could do whatever I wanted with them. I could take someone's house and use it as a temporary base. I could decide to arrest the people in the house, give the order to blow up their house, lock their door and not let them into their own house or on the street where their home is. I did not feel like I was blocking someone, but on the contrary, I felt like I was terrorizing people."
E. Efrati, a former Israeli army soldier

"Israel isn't a democracy but rather an apartheid state par excellence. Two peoples and two systems of rights. That's what apartheid looks like, even if it hides behind excuses ranging from temporariness to security grounds, from the right to the land to the concept of the chosen people, including the divine promise and messianic redemption." G. Levy (Haaretz, April 15, 2018)

"You cannot fight terrorism while you are directly supporting the terrorists with an army, weapons and have connections to the biggest supporters of terrorism in the world, which is the Saudi Kingdom. This is a contradiction - ***you cannot be the police and the thief at the same time****."*
B. Al-Assad, president of Syria / From the interview for Czech TV, December 1, 2015 (Besides, neither Asad nor Putin in the interviews have any problem answering any question and they are open to dialog with anyone - think about it.)

This game basically uses the same formula that proved effective in World War II. And unfortunately, again particularly Europe is suffering because they pose a real threat to the system. They are intelligent informed citizens who know their identity and are unable to tolerate the present. Today, Europe is suffering immensely, mainly because of its ambition to help the weak, since it has a vivid recollection of the Second World War. Karma determines who is "affected", and therefore Germany has the most Muslims. You also constantly feel guilty, so today you have some kind of savior syndrome. Unfortunately, your nation has also been badly misused. Because of the past, which you cannot change, you have become the victims of this global farce. Please wake up, because today you are actually helping to destroy Europe. Also, to the French and British - Do you really not see it at all? Do you think these refugees really want to adapt? Or do they behave like you did when you occupied their territory? Do you feel like they want to assimilate and help us create global peace? Or are they mostly just causing problems? Instead of being grateful for everything that they have received, they turn their backs to their saviors and, on the contrary, they want you to conquer that which does not belong to them. They, instead of being grateful for everything that they have received, turn their backs to their saviors, and on the contrary, they want you to conquer that which does not belong them. According to this formula, it should be namely Israel who should offer help first. Rhetorical question: Whose borders are closer to Syria - Israeli or European?

> *"If you destroy the Europe economically it affects development on the whole planet. So if u destroy epicentrum, which is Europe, means that u will not have progress in the third world too."* D. Estulin (for Czech national Tv, 2011)

In this case, it is useful to remember that the cultures of those desert peoples have entirely different ideas about how the world functions overall and their information only comes from resources that are actually very limited. Of course, they mostly just have historical and religious roots. So once again we return to the initial problem, which is in fact primarily the unavailability of real information.

"Historically, we are confronted with a certain mentality that is older than Islam, and in many respects it is common to all nations that live in semi-desert areas of the Middle East and North Africa. It is this common base formed by the desert that enabled the subsequent rapid expansion of Islam. Control of resources is the essence of this life, i.e., initially the water and fertile land. Semideserts are as such that they can only feed a certain number of people, and therefore it is necessary to establish a relatively stable 'ecological' model in which the population does not grow further.

The Old Testament was compiled during the harsh war conditions of the Iron Age, including the initial invasion of the sea people among whom we distinguish the people of Cyprus and the Greek islands, otherwise called the Philistines, which is also the basis of the word Palestine or Palestinians. Even the Qur'an is bound to an environment of constantly warring tribes that is more recent, but still similar.

Desert areas have given us a lot of good ideas about discipline, justice, and the existence of one God, but they certainly did not give us humanism, which is the basis of modern democracy. European humanism arose in cities. Basically, it says that there are enough resources, they just need to be fairly distributed because each is worthy of them. In the desert, this approach would not work.

The West essentially does not need God because it has health and social insurances and supermarkets full of food. The attitude of poor communities to religion is different. They have few things, but a lot of relationships whose depth they carefully protect and consider. Often, they live in a chaotic environment where a decent life is provided by the idea of fate and God. When you take their God away from them or you defame or ridicule Him, you are taking away a huge psychological support."
V. Cílek, PhD., geologist, climatologist, writer, philosopher

So why is radical Islam so attractive for today's people?

"Because nothing else left them. Muslim societies were colonized, madrasas (spiritual schools) closed. In Algeria, French Republican schools opened. It was a good idea - for everyone to have free access to quality education. But the Algerians began to teach that their ancestors were Galoreans. In some African countries, French organizations are still setting up schools and using the same textbooks, even for blacks. It's schizophrenic. There was nothing left of our history, we suffered a complete amnesia. The only part of our culture that they did not take from us was Islam. But it was abused by our generals, the army, and the oligarchs to justify totalitarianism, the taking over of power, the army and the money of big companies. Something similar then happened in some form in some areas of France. I do not justify terrorism, jihadism or fundamentalism. But I worked for ten years in a poor neighborhood in northeastern Paris. Only Blacks, Indians, and Arabs lived there. Among the young, 50% was unemployed. Very many diseases, violence, drug trafficking. But no education and perspectives. These people left nothing but Islam, which they heard most from their illiterate parents. The construction and operation of their mosques allowed foreign donations - from Turkey, Algeria, Morocco, Saudi Arabia. People who seek spirituality, of course, do not find anything but hell, fascism, and politics."

L. M. Zahed (gay imam) for Czech Newspapers
Lidové noviny (February 2017)

A Danish child psychologist who has been confronted with a number of juvenile delinquents - Muslims, characterizes these differences as follows:

"There are four essential differences. The first is anger. In the west, we see anger as a sign of weakness, but in Muslim culture, and at the same time in the Koran, anger is seen as a strength. They even have a day of wrath. It is the holy day each week when they go to the mosque - every Friday. The second difference is confidence. Islam essentially does not tolerate criticism. Even if it concerns completely absurd things that Muslims have great difficulty absorbing. And when someone is criticized and does not get angry, it is perceived as dishonest conduct. If someone is unable to perceive the logic of arguments, their second line of defense is aggression. The third difference is accountability. In the West we make decisions about our lives ourselves, and if we have a problem, we look first to ourselves and seek to arrive at a solution. In Islam, everything is the will of Allah in the name of Allah. Most things are decided on the basis of male authors, and there is very, very little space for personal freedom. Muslims have developed a culture where one's life is controlled by external authorities. The fourth difference concerns tolerance. In the West, we believe that to be tolerant and open is correct. But Islam preaches hatred and violence against non-believers. It's straightforward. It is not possible for there to be friendship between believers and non-believers. There must always be a distance."

N. Sennels, a psychologist who works with Muslims

So, regarding the above mentioned facts, let us realize that everything has much deeper foundations than it first appears. The living conditions of these people simply destroys the increase of intelligence. On the contrary, their system is what they consider to be correct, and thanks to this the whole current conflict is actually based on absolutely primitive foundations (such as the Western religions). Today, for example, Muslims understand that their power is also in their quick proliferation and the settlement of foreign countries. Jihad (Holy War against all infidels) is already underway, so now they have realized that if they continue to give birth as they do today, they should be able to win and master any continent, even without war. Today the Muslim birth rate is 50 percent higher than that of other religions. According to these statistics, Germany should become a Muslim state by 2050. To compare: in the USA in 1970, there were 100,000 Muslims. In 2008, there were already nine million of them. Their greatest desire is to get Turkey into the European Union, and the reason is simple – to have 50 million more Muslims in the EU.

"There are signs that Allah will grant victory to Islam in Europe without swords, without guns, without conquest. We don't need terrorists; we don't need homicide bombs. The 50+ million Muslims in Europe will turn it into a Muslim continent within a few decades."
M. al-Gaddafi, the leader of Libya

Despite the fact that everyone should have absolute freedom to live anywhere in the world, I want to point out the following statistics which show the positions of Muslims in several countries:

up to 2 percent – they remain peaceful (USA, Norway...)

more than 5 percent – they start asking the government to allow them to apply Sharia law (UK, Spain...)

over 10 percent – they start demonstrations and looting (France...)

over 20 percent - the burning of Jewish and Christian places of worship (Ethiopia...)

over 40 percent - extensive massacres and periodic terrorist attacks (Bosnia, Lebanon...)

over 60 percent - endless persecution and harassment of the non-Muslim population, including non-conforming Muslims (Albania, Sudan...)

80 percent or more - planned mass cleansing and genocide to expel the infidels (Iran, Iraq, Pakistan...)

100 percent - DAR - EL - SALAM ("Islamic Peace") they kill only non-conforming Muslims (Afghanistan, Saudi Arabia...)

These statistics are freely available on the internet because it is in nobody's interest to conceal them, quite the contrary. What our media did not show us were, for example, incredible numbers of Arabs reacting sympathetically to September 11, 2001. Not everyone feels the need to control the world. It is just a few individuals who make the whole nation suffer. Again, we could first start to behave like people and show respect for other cultures. What do you really know about Arab culture? Do you realize how much it has influenced the world? Science, technology, astronomy, literature, architecture, etc. - everything is connected and all of us have learned from them. For example, the whole world uses Arabic numbers! Or, let's recall the folk tales of One Thousand and One Nights - they are totally intertwined with female sexuality! (Even though this collection was altered at the end of the 16th century.) But where did it all get lost? Compare Arabic or Russian culture with American culture, and be critical. Which nation has contributed more to the development of man? Where does more wisdom and beauty come from? **Please, let's start to show interest in the true values and honesty of people.**

Shalom / Salam = PEACE

It is imperative to understand the absurdity of everything that is happening here in its ENTIRETY. Do not just believe me. Feel free to check everything, investigate, look around. Just wake up and open your eyes! The world really needs a massive reboot. This is not about Jews, Christians, Muslims, et al., but about MAN! Understand this, please. Do not lose time with some "anti" approach. Do not judge me, this book, politics, or anyone - accept reality as a whole. For the first time, look beyond the threshold of your own house. Be aware of these facts, but do not add unnecessary (negative) force to them with your attention.

If you can put together what I'm trying to say here, you will understand the whole situation with the so-called refugees. Several volunteers were in refugee camps themselves, and it is their living testimony that these people are introduced to something completely different from their "rescue before the war" as it is officially presented to us. These people are rejecting real help and have really come to destroy European culture. Many have been provided with even better conditions than some of our retirees. Creating new mosques in Europe is like creating new military bases for them. We're digging our own graves... This is not a solution to the problem but the conscious creation of a new one. It would be very easy if these "fictitious" wars were to end and the money used in the arms industry was used to restore that country. All of these people would like to go home if they were allowed to do so. However, that is not in the interest of "elites" because as often happens, this "refugee game", once again, has its roots somewhere deeper. The public actually found out about the so-called Kalergi plan. In his book *Practical Idealism*, Kalergi declared that citizens of the future "United States of Europe" would no longer be the indigenous peoples of the Old Continent, but a kind of animal mutt as a result of the mixing of races. He maintained that it was necessary to "mix" European nations with Asians and blacks in order to create a multi-ethnic herd without specific features, easily manageable by the elites in power. Kalergi stated that it was necessary to void the nations' right of self-determination and gradually eliminate the nations using ethnic separatist movements or foreign mass immigration. For the elites to dominate Europe, he required that homogeneous nations be converted into mixed groups of people. To these hybrid nations he ascribed characteristics such as cruelty, infidelity, etc. These new hybrid people had to be created so they would be inferior to the superior elite. Ironically, the creator of this plan was an Austrian politician of Japanese ancestry with Czechoslovak citizenship. (Count Richard Nicolaus Coudenhove-Kalergi 1894-1972 / original title of the book - *Das Europäische Pan-Manifest*)

"Depopulation should be the highest priority of foreign policy."
H. Kissinger, 1974

Again, it's especially a case of very unsuccessful approach, where they play with the most precious thing - real life. They consciously involved us in this massive game, and it's up to us to decide whether we will let ourselves be fooled. **We can only help locally, if we are personally confronted with it. Then we cannot pretend that it does not concern us. But on the same level, we should also help our neighbors if necessary. Otherwise, it's an unsolvable problem for the ordinary citizen, and again it is a must to understand the general situation, which in this case is very alarming.**

In 2012, the Committee of 300 even published its plans, including: reducing the population of the Earth to one "golden billion"; the destruction of the Slavs; the creation of a single financial and religious system (the destruction of Christianity); the destruction of any national pride; a conscious increase in unemployment; halting progress in industrialization; the spread of drugs; turning pornography into an art form; demoralizing people; making up crises; spreading viruses; taking control

of the education system; the collapse of world economies; and political chaos. Noble, huh?

I would love to move the emphasis of this book deeper into the history of the earth and its ancient civilizations, but after several confrontations, I have come to understand that in order for one to accept and understand all this, a person needs true awareness and to know at least the "irrational basis". Because this world is built on the patriarchal principle = the left hemisphere, it is of utmost importance to begin actively developing the right hemisphere and the opening of the third eye, e.g., epiphysis. Only then will it be possible for us to understand history as offered to us by Drunvalo Melchizedek or David Icke. Today, however, we must realize that there is a certain group of people - the same one that was here many times before and which caused the collapse of advanced societies such as Atlantis, Ancient Egypt, Babylon, and the Roman Empire. I am personally convinced that even Christianity is purely just a business plan from the same group of people for world domination. Only recently the so-called secret files of the Vatican began to circulate on the internet, but if we were to plunge deeper we would find that this story about how the Vatican created Islam is already among us, and even in a comics version for dummies. There are also indications that Christians, i.e., The Vatican, created both the Nazi Party as well as the Communist Party. If it were so "clear-cut", someone would have stood up against it long ago. However, this was not the intention - the main intention is in fact to stir up the Christians and Muslims against each other until they slaughter one another. This intrigue has roots in the Roman Empire where "shadow advisers" existed, even advisers to the Caesar, and therefore, he was betrayed by the one closest to him. However, no one has been able to reverse this plot ever since, quite the contrary. (Compare history of the Roman Empire with US history - common characters are not random.) The Vatican today is the greatest center of wealth (gold, antiques, documents, etc.) on Earth, including the strictest military that guards it all. Communism was the one that wanted to abolish the "Catholic game", but unfortunately it failed because its original planners did not count on the fact that the teaching of Jesus actually works. Just as they did not expect that the internet, which they want use to get us under their control again, would be a double-edged sword that we are slowly but surely using to unite. Just as I believe that Kabbalah is an inheritance stolen from the original Atlantis and that this situation must have repeated itself again in ancient Egypt. Kabbalah hides in it the reason for existence, sacred geometry, as well as original rituals. The Tree of Life, which is also part of Metatron's cube, is the basic structure of all living things. However, as this knowledge can be used, it can also be misused, and then it is converted into black magic, which this group has been using for ages.

The issue at hand is that **humanity as a whole has been involved in an age-old struggle within itself, where the warring parties can very simply be divided into those that represent good and those that stand for evil, respectively on mature and immature ones.** Then we can divide people who have a dominant left hemisphere of the brain and those with a dominant right hemisphere. Our goal is to find unity in ourselves, otherwise we will not see it even in the world. I would be extremely happy if we could all understand it as such, where **every human being is capable of transformation since what is really at stake is our bare existence and survival on our planet Earth. Please, let us not repeat the past. In the present days the manipulation of consciousness has reached its peak, and it is solely up to us how far we will let them go.**

"It makes no sense to fight corruption, famine or stupidity, because that which we fight against will still remain. Only when I heal myself and I am happy - and conscious - can I start a snowball effect around me. All it takes is the courage to begin the journey - chasing your shadow is the most intense adventure you can take. Once you

take the first step, it will be more and more enjoyable - little by little bringing light into your own darkness, increasing your consciousness and becoming friendlier - to others and above all to yourself."
Dr. R. Dahlke

Boys and men in particular, please do not go to war unless you have to. Do not support this stupid game with your participation. No amount of money is worth turning yourself into the wreck you will be when you come back, if you ever return. You will never be the same as before, you will never fit in with society as you would like, you will never understand common people. Your own psyche will torture you and no amount of money can replace what you have lost.

"If people are blissful you cannot lead them to war — to Vietnam, or to Egypt, or to Israel. No. Someone who is blissful will just laugh and say: This is nonsense! If people are blissful you cannot make them obsessed with money. They will not waste their whole lives just accumulating money. They will not miss their lives accumulating wealth. They deem unreasonable to destroy your life and your being and to sacrifice them to dead things."
Osho

Slovakia - Slovaks are a very nice example of the absurdity of "nationalism". Our country has had several names. It belonged to the Germans, Hungarians, Czechs, Russians... and succumbed to several absurd regimes. In the years 1989 - 1993 we lived in three countries! First, in the Czechoslovak Socialist Republic, then in the Czech and Slovak Federal Republic, and finally, in the Slovak Republic. Over the last 15O years we have had four different capitals - Vienna, Budapest, Prague, and Bratislava. Do we want Vienna or Budapest again, or maybe some other city?!

"Czechoslovakia" is currently a bridge between East and West. We separated absolutely peacefully, which is actually unique in

today's world. Since then our relationship has improved, and we cooperate much better in many areas. We are like yin and yang. We wouldn't actually exist without one another. It is a beautiful example of our culture, which cannot be separated. Our nations are a beautiful example of how if we start to work individually, it will connect us in the end.

"Alternately, one and then another branch of nations take over the baton and become the focal point of spiritual formation, each with its own special talents which will eventually transform and create its culture, thereby contributing on an additional level to the common temple of humanity. Once, there was an ancient Indian and Persian epoch; later on, the Sumerians and the Egyptians were the ones who were the leaders and the others learned from them. And after them, the time of the Greeks and Romans came. Latin culture was replaced by Anglo Saxon-Germanic, which still dominates today. Eventually, a time will come when Germans will be replaced by Slavs and they will move us to a whole new, higher cultural level."
E. Páleš, sophiologist

We can all overcome this manipulative schism if we start to actively solve our very own personal problems first. However, this planet and we with it are faced with even more serious problems that we, as a matter of fact, know how to solve. Let's look at the most prominent of them.

How many of you know, for example, that we have Himalayas of water under our feet?! (In Slovakia) Under which regime were we informed about it by our dear politicians? Their only concern is to exploit as much as possible and to sell it! Regardless of human rights and behind our backs. Such areas in the world can be counted on one hand. Which is better: water or oil?! There are about 30 billion cubic meters of water under Slovakia and the amount continues to grow. The interesting thing is that our corporations have known this for a long time and, without our knowledge, have long benefited from it by making various nonsensical transactions with foreign countries.

The government = corporations = profit (all around the world)

The best-known current proponent of this business with water is Nestlé, which is also one of the largest customers when it comes to water.

"That every human being should have the right to water is an extreme view. Water is a foodstuff like any other and should be charged for."
B. Brabeck, CEO of Nestlé

It is only a matter of time before someone will benefit from the most basic needs. (It's a wonder that we still do not pay for the sun.) Currently, 11 percent of the world population has no access to drinking water, which is about 783 million people. "Thanks" to this approach, in the last 10 years more children have died of diarrheal disease than the number of casualties in armed conflicts since the end of World War II. Half the beds in hospitals around the world are occupied by patients who suffer from diseases associated with poor water quality. However, again the main problem lies somewhere different than it would seem. In this case, I thank the creators of the documentary *Cowspiracy* who helped me again supplement this puzzle.

Animal agriculture is the leading cause of deforestation, water consumption, and pollution. It is responsible for more greenhouse gases than the transportation industry and is a primary driver of rainforest destruction, species extinction, habitat loss, topsoil erosion, ocean "dead zones," and virtually every other environmental ill. Yet it goes on almost entirely unchallenged.

Raising livestock produces more greenhouse gases than the emissions of the entire transportation sector. This means that the meat and dairy industry produces more greenhouse gases than the exhaust of all cars, trucks, trains, boats, and planes combined. Cows and other farmed animals produce a substantial amount of methane during digestion. Methane gas from livestock is 86 times more destructive than carbon dioxide from vehicles.

Hydraulic fracturing for natural gas uses an incredible amount of water. A staggering 100 billion gallons of water is used every year in the United States. But when we compared this with animal agriculture, in the US alone, raising livestock consumes 34 trillion gallons of water. And it turns out that the methane emissions from both industries are nearly equal.

One quarter-pound hamburger requires over 660 gallons of water to produce. This means that eating one hamburger is the equivalent of two entire months of showering.

So much attention is given to lowering our home water use, but domestic water use makes up only 5% of water consumption in the US versus 55% for animal agriculture. That is because it takes upwards of 2,500 gallons of water to produce one pound of beef.

The transportation and energy sectors are understandably given a lot of attention because of the terrible impact carbon dioxide is having on our climate. But animal agriculture produces 65% of the world's nitrous oxide, a gas with a global warming potential 296 times greater than CO2 per pound. Energy-related CO2

emissions are expected to increase 20% by the year 2040. Yet emissions from agriculture are predicted to increase 80% by 2050.

Two environmental specialists at the World Bank Group, using the global standard for measuring greenhouse gases, concluded that animal agriculture was responsible for 51% of human-caused climate change, when the loss of carbon sinks, respiration, and methane are properly accounted for, which the UN study failed to address. And not only that, animal agriculture is responsible for 30% of world water consumption, occupies up to 45% of Earth's land, is responsible for up to 91% of Brazilian Amazon destruction, and is a leading cause of ocean dead zones, habitat destruction, and species extinction.

"10,000 years ago, wild animals made up 99% of the biomass. Today, only 10,000 years later, which is really just a short period of time, we human beings and the animals that we raise as food make up 98% of the biomass. And wild, free animals make up only 2%. ***We have basically completely stolen the world - Earth - from the wild animals to use for ourselves, and our cows and pigs and chicken and factory-farmed fish, and the oceans have been even more devastated. We are in the middle of the largest mass extinction of species in 65 million years."***

Dr. Will Tuttle, an environmental ethics writer

Palm Oil *plantations are causing tremendous deforestation in the Indonesian rainforest. It is estimated that palm oil is responsible for 26 million acres being cleared. But this does not seem like much compared to livestock and their feedcrops, which are responsible for 136 million acres of rainforest loss to date.*

Over 1,100 activists have been killed in Brazil over the last 20 years.

Methane produced by cows and other livestock is a major contributor. Global warming is mostly due to deforestation and the waste they produce, which is 130 times more waste than the entire human population.

It takes upwards of 1,000 gallons of water to produce one gallon of milk.

(By the way, drinking milk in adulthood is not suitable at all- this is a fact that I believe will be soon confirmed by more experts and not just by doctors - vegetarians.)

Some people would say that the problem is not animal agriculture, but human overpopulation. Let's look at some facts: 216,000 humans are born every day on this planet.

In the year 1812 there were 1 billion people on planet Earth, in 1912 there were 1.9 billion, and in 2012 there were 7 billion people.

For comparison, we had 70,000,000,000 farm animals.

Every day the human population drinks 5.2 billion gallons of water and eats 21 billion pounds of food.

1.5 billion cows drink 45 billion gallons of water and eat 135 billion pounds of food.

The UN has reported that three-quarters of the world's fisheries are overexploited, fully exploited, or significantly depleted due to overfishing.

> *"The oceans are under siege like never before, marine environments are in trouble, and if we do not wake up and do something about it, we are going to see fishless oceans by the year 2048. That's the prediction from scientists."*
> Lisa Agabian, Sea Shepherd Conservation Society

(Information taken from the documentary *Cowspiracy* - www.cowspiracy.com)

Today there is truly a need to stop consuming such enormous quantities of meat and become at least "partially vegetarian". If not because of yourself, let us do it for our planet which is our home. It is important to realize that **climate change**, to the greatest extent, is caused by us. Rainforests can serve as an example here. The more we destroy them, the more we increase the risk of climate change. This subsequently changes the ecosystem and causes so-called desertification (the spreading of deserts and drying up of extended areas). Each day the planet loses about 30 species. A UN study shows that 17,000 kinds of plants, animals, and microorganisms are endangered. This is not just a natural, but also an economic disaster. The destruction of "natural capital" costs us up to 50 billion euros a year. However, the global investment in biodiversity conservation is only about 3 billion euros, so there is a huge gap which increases every year. Also, due to the mishandling of water, large areas dry up daily on Earth. They would not, if people knew what they are doing. (Again, however, there are ways to help it realistically).

The so often talked about **chemtrails**, i.e., discharges of chemicals into the air from aircraft, are also a cause of so-called global warming. And not only that, but it is also the reason why so many people have begun to suffer from various allergies. If we did an analysis of the air we breathe, we would be surprised that we are even alive. There is some footage presenting and pointing to the evidence but, of course, on the level of conspiracy theories.

"It is believed that barium salt, polymer fibers and other chemicals in the atmosphere are the physical irritants that are either directly or indirectly responsible for the recent epidemic increase in cases of nose bleeds, asthma, allergies, pneumonia, upper respiratory symptoms and noticeable increases in arthritis symptoms recently reported nationwide. Chemicals illegally sprayed into the atmosphere are producing atmospheric and ground conditions detrimental to human and animal health but favorable to the growth of harmful molds and fungi. These conditions are not conducive to good health. The soluble salts of barium, an earth metal, are toxic to mammalian systems. They are absorbed rapidly through the gastrointestinal tract and are deposited in the muscles, lungs, and bones. No case data is available from the medical community on the long-term effects of barium on the human body."

Dr. Stephen D. McKay

The latest fact is being made public, for the first time, by the Swedish politician Pernilla Hagberg – Chairman of the Green Party. She claims that the spray is a joint venture of the US Central Intelligence Agency (CIA), the US National Security Agency (NSA), and the Swedish Government. They aim to change the atmosphere by the deliberate spraying of aerosols.

An American biochemist who used to produce mixtures for chemtrails also acknowledged this. Although he is now retired, he of course published the information anonymously. In his statements, he said that he used to work for US biochemical laboratories from 1980 to 2010 and that they were actually producing different mixtures that were always delivered on order with different characteristics, therefore always for a different purpose:

"90% of what we were producing was aimed at changing moods, emotions, modifying the weather, environment, influenza syndromes, etc. They only rarely required us to prepare mixtures causing anger or violent behavior. Rather, I felt that it was always intended for different specific markets, i.e., states. As for the spread, some mixtures were made so as to be dispersed at such a low level of concentration that only one billionth fell to the earth. Others were designed to be able to last up to a year, even in the rain or snow, and the like. Despite the fact that we had to ensure the non-toxicity of our products, many of them evoked so-called symptoms, but which were not lethal. Of course, no official patent exists for these mixtures as these are public. I know that North America is not the only continent that uses ADC (Aerially Dispersed Chemicals) without their population knowing about it. But I also know that the chemical technologies of other countries are about ten years behind those owned by USA. 99% of commercial pilots are not aware that their aircraft can spray chemtrails. After some time I realized that whoever handles the 'backstage organization' behind it all, they are very good at being able to deal with as few people as possible."

Have you ever seen violence in the universe? There is a big difference between natural phenomena and the results of deliberate action. There is a big difference between the instinctive reaction of some animal species and human conscious reaction.

Politicians do not really help us. They bend the system, patch things, but they still care mostly about their egos and about maintaining power.

Take for example the three most controversial topics: **tobacco, alcohol, and cannabis.** In Europe alone, more than 5 million people and 79,000 passive smokers die every year from smoking related illnesses. And that's okay. Let's put a giant sign on every cigarette pack: Smoking kills! And supremely hypocritically get rid of any responsibility. Owners of tobacco companies, however, are in power and shake hands with the most influential politicians. Why should they ban it if they make such a huge profit off it? (The "ugly pictures" campaign only leads people to switch to a different type of cigarette produced by the same corporation. Do not imagine that smoking an aluminum spiral will be much healthier, on the contrary.) Each year around 2.5 million people die because of alcohol. That is also okay. Not to mention that almost every fifth person is basically an untreated alcoholic. How much violence is perpetrated by intoxicated people every day?! Just like the saying goes – Alcohol: the scourge of humankind; but it is used by the select few who don't care at all. But let's be honest, it's mainly because our socio-economic system, thanks to which we are slaves, not people, is "forcing" us to act this way. We need to switch off, and unfortunately this is the easiest way, because we do not know another way. Prohibition, however, leads only to an unhealthy attitude and, just as everything that is repressed, produces precisely the opposite effect. In countries where alcohol is banned, it is produced mostly at home and because of these experiments, several thousand people die each year. However, if all drugs were legalized/decriminalized, such as they are in Portugal, the number of users would drop rapidly as well as crime. But that is not the elites' intention. As we already know, it is a very necessary business for them, and not just for the money. For example, it was only through alcohol that the original inhabitants of America were "destroyed", out of whom they eventually created gamblers, as they "allowed" them to have casinos on their reservations without paying taxes. The situation with drugs in Czechoslovakia since 1989 has been similar. One generation has been affected very badly by the Albanians being trafficked with drugs since the borders have opened, and many young people have died. Something similar is currently happening in Europe with refugees who do not plan to work legally.

"The stricter the society, the more rebels we find in it. The more liberal the rules are, the fewer rebels and the less resistance is required. I consider the society free if it doesn't prohibit anything." Osho

In spite of this, marijuana, which has not been the cause of a single case of death or domestic violence, is officially prohibited. The Netherlands is the only country where it was tolerated for many years (although now they have made the laws stricter in an absurd way because of "forced" smoke-tourism). Fortunately, however, governments of various countries are waking up, although their actual motivations are still not sufficient, since today it concerns, in my opinion, mainly taxes. So this "trend" started exactly where we would least expect it, since they are the ones who initially forbade it, in the United States. In 1999, they suddenly patented "medical marijuana" and in 2000 it was already tested in Colorado. As a result, paradoxically, marijuana for recreational use is now legal in the States of Colorado, Washington and California. They collect many millions of dollars in taxes monthly. Today, medical marijuana is legal in 29. US states and it is readily available, indeed. On the other hand, it reminds me of the game where you give a child a piece of candy while continuously reminding him that candy is not healthy. Again, a schism is deliberately generated, because in most cases consumers have absolutely no idea what the plant does and how it should be handled. Again, this is primarily about business, to the detriment of man. The absolute underdevelopment of contemporary man is the problem rather than the marijuana itself. For thousands of years, people expanded their consciousnesses using hemp, but never in the past did they have such superficial lives. Personally, I would prescribe marijuana in the USA based on psychological tests, because at this rate people tend to quickly become even more irresponsible, apathetic, or paranoid. (Currently congratulations to

Canada on legalizing marijuana for recreational purposes - they paid the state debt in 24 hours.)

"What the US Patent 6630507 says:

The patent clearly states that cannabinoids are powerful antioxidants which have the potential to treat a myriad of ischemic, age-related, inflammatory, and auto-immune disorders. The patent goes on to say cannabinoids are also a natural neuroprotectant which could help treat neurological damage caused by stroke and trauma, as well as, other neurological disorders like Alzheimer's, Parkinson's Disease, and Multiple Sclerosis. Essentially, US Patent 6630507 means certain departments of the US Government are at odds with how to approach marijuana, medicinally or otherwise. On one side, you have the US Department of Health and Human Services maintaining a patent for a medical miracle; and on the other you have the Drug Enforcement Agency fighting to keep it illegal."
https://internationalhighlife.com/us-patent-6630507

However, I will not defend this plant in terms of its use because the problem is somewhere else. Indeed, if people were allowed to grow it without restrictions (it is one of the easiest crops to grow), most of the farmers who grow cotton and the businesses involved in forestry would go bankrupt. (One acre of hemp, which is about 4,000 square meters, equals 4.1 acres of trees.) Hemp is one of the most useful, strongest, and most durable materials on the planet. We would not have to cut down a single tree to produce paper. In the past this fact was clear to everyone – in 1820 approximately 80% of all textiles were made of hemp. The history of industrial hemp dates back to ancient Egypt. And it's not just paper and textiles, but also various lacquers, paints, cosmetics, batteries, building materials, and even cars. The first car, the Model-T by Henry Ford, was made entirely of hemp. It had hemp plastic panels whose impact resistance is 10 times greater than that of steel. And to make matters worse, it even used hemp gasoline. There was also a hemp plane flying on cannabis oil at that time. But in 1937 Mr. Dupont, who was at that time behind the largest investors and government support, patented the production of plastics from petroleum. And this is also a fundamental pillar of our "oil economy". Around this period, these gentlemen also discovered the magic of media manipulation, and suddenly hemp was presented as an "aggressive narcotic".

"Plant a lot of hamp in the land of Fukushima. Hemp's vibration has the same potentiality to purify the contaminated environment made by radiation."
Dr. M. Emoto

Hemp seed is a perfect food. Its nutritional value surpasses even high quality meat. It contains a perfect ratio of omega 3 and 6 fatty acids - 20 amino acids including the eight essential fatty acids that the human body is not able to synthesize in normal conditions. It also contains chlorophyll and lecithin. The seeds are rich in vitamins A, B, B1, B2, B3, B6, C, E, PP, and F. They are rich in minerals such as magnesium, iron, phosphorus, potassium, calcium, zinc, iodine, chromium, silver, lithium, sulfur, etc. As we all know, this miraculous plant is also needed for countless medical interventions (where it is gradually starting to be used, but here too it is accompanied by heated debate and multiple constraints). Again, this is primarily about business and not about man at all, as we all naively think. It is medically proven, for example, that it regulates cholesterol (which is one of the most common medical problems of our time) and strengthens the immune system. Arthritis, Alzheimer's, cancer, cardiovascular disease, sclerosis, AIDS, premenstrual syndrome, indigestion problems, skin problems, problems with nails and hair, acne, etc. One handful of these seeds feeds an adult, as far as the necessary nutrients. So then why is the world starving? Only for profit - from oil. Of all the drugs such as tobacco, caffeine, and alcohol, cannabis is the least harmful plant. **Marijuana can cause**

only psychological dependence, not physical dependence. A psychological dependence is something we create every day - whether it's a dependence on relationships, food, objects - on anything. Marijuana users are never aggressive, quite the contrary. So, this also does not appeal to the government, which needs to control people. That is why it must inspire fear - not joy and peace - fear. If you are happy and calm, you don't let anyone manipulate you. The problem is that we are totally immature. We do not use such substances occasionally for fun. Instead, we use them as a solution, an escape from reality. Because the conditions in which we currently exist are not human. And anyway, how can it be that in one country I can be healed with this plant and in another I will go to jail?! Are we not all people?!

Not to mention the so-called officially approved drugs, which can be used without restriction. After all, they support the largest business – **the pharmaceutical murderers**. For instance, namely in the USA, ca 14,800 people died in 2008 as a result of using so-called painkillers. That is statistically more than all the victims of heroin and cocaine combined (annually). This is currently the most rapidly growing drug addiction in the world, which is even officially supported. Daily we have the opportunity to observe hundreds of ads for these products. Over the past 27 years, from the date when these statistics started to be recorded, more than 3,000,000 people have died due to prescription drugs! The latest analysis has found that in recent years pharmaceutical drugs have caused more deaths than all the road traffic accidents in the USA. There are also, for example, nasal drops which lots of people are addicted to. But this is "normal".

"The third leading cause of death is prescription drugs. In this regard, I advise you to seek medical attention only in really urgent situations."
Dr. R. Dahlke

Fortunately, Dr. Mathias Rath has filed a lawsuit against the pharmaceutical industry (i.e., against the familiar corporations owned and controlled by our famous family clans) at the European Court in The Haag. The defendants are accused of deliberate harm and the deaths of millions of people due to this "disease business", war crimes, and crimes against humanity.

"It is no surprise that the two largest exporters of pharmaceutical products – the United States and the United Kingdom - are in the forefront of the current international crisis and incitement of war against Iraq. To citizens in America, in the UK and to the rest of the world the alleged necessity of this war was presented under the false pretenses of a global fight against `terrorism', the elimination of `bad governments' and a crusade against the proliferation of weapons of mass destruction."
MUDr. M. Rath

In his allegations, he even claims that medicines for cancer and HIV have been invented, but it has not been officially admitted. On the contrary, the information is classified, because it is really about the "disease business". The last thing these companies want are healthy people. Cancer is making them a gazillion dollars a year and chemotherapy encourages further diseases, and so it creates more "potential clients". Annually, about 15 million people pay for this with their lives! And this is how vast quantities of information is kept secret from ordinary people.

"Withholding vital information on unpatented natural alternatives used to prevent and fight against infectious diseases not only leads to the unnecessary deaths of millions of people, but also to the collapse of the economies of many developing countries. A direct consequence is the further dramatic deterioration of the already existing imbalance in the current global economy. These countries are deliberately driven into conflicts which they can only lose.

Aspirin is collectively sold under the false pretense that it prevents heart attacks and strokes, although it is known that the long-term use of this drug causes the destruction of collagen and therefore gradually increases the risk of heart attacks and strokes as well as other conditions such as stomach ulcers and gastrointestinal bleeding.

Estrogen (found for example in almost all contraceptives) and other hormonal drugs are mass-marketed under the false pretense that they prevent bone loss (osteoporosis) and heart disease, although it is known that the long-term use of these products causes cancer in more than 30 percent of women who take them. The forms of cancer most frequently caused by these drugs are hormone-dependent cancers such as breast and uterine cancer.

Tranquillizers and antidepressants. Another mechanism by which the defendants systematically develop their markets is the deliberate induction of habituation to increase the sale of drugs. It is known that many tranquillizers and anti-depressants, including the widely-used diazepam (valium), cause addiction. To further expand global sales of these drugs, the defendants have even advertised in commercials worldwide and in non-professional magazines."
MUDr. Mathias Rath (www.dr-rath-foundation.org)

"For example, vaccination against cervical cancer is completely absurd, yet it is in place. We also have plenty of research backed studies that confirm that mammography itself causes breast cancer. I'm rather embarrassed to say this, because I am also a doctor, but it is true. When male gynecologists at a lecture

were asked whether any of them would send their wives or partners to get a mammogram, not one stepped forward."
Dr. R. Dahlke

A few months before his death, even the acclaimed American psychiatrist Dr. Leon Eisenberg confessed to the "business" and confirmed that the American Psychiatric Association (APA) invents diseases. He himself was the "father" of ADHD (attention deficit hyperactivity disorder) and he confirmed that "ADHD is a first-class example of a fictitious disease." Of course, the goal was to promote a new drug, currently known as Ritalin, which caused the drugging of millions of children, because it is a substance similar to cocaine which also causes serious damage to the brain and addiction.

"The average age for a childhood cancer diagnosis in the US is age 6. Children in the US recieve 50 doses of vaccines by age 6. To publicly say that these vaccines are good, it's like saying that getting heroin is healthy. Childhood asthma rose 300% in 40 years. Childhood leukemia and brain cancer rose 40% in 40 years. American couples struggling with fertility issues rose 20% in 10 years." Holistic Health magazine

The investment bank *Goldman Sachs* published a market analysis (April 4, 2018) in which it discourages the pharmaceutical industry from healing its customers. In its report, the bank literally recommends: *saving lives and taking care of patients is a very bad business model.* In particular, the study looked at a new model of gene therapy which could completely cure patients, but the "system" does not like it. So we are once again at a stage where there are solutions to many health problems, but instead of using science in a positive way, we are more likely to witness its abuse.

"Today we have a real chance to get into and manipulate the human genetic code. What consequences could that bring? It means

that man can create a person with certain characteristics not only in theory, but also in practice. He could be a mathematical genius, a brilliant musician, or a soldier - a man who could fight without fear, compassion, sorrow, or pain. As you see, humanity could, and it most likely will in the near future, enter into a very difficult and very responsible period of existence. And what I have just described might be worse than a nuclear bomb."

V. Putin, President of the Russian Federation

Again, it should be noted that there are a lot of professionals among us who are able to set the medical system "right" with regard to the person as a whole.

Also, another very important topic is the food industry, which these days exceeds the critical bounds of humanity. **GMOs (genetically modified organisms** - genetically modified foods) are mentioned more and more these days. "Chemically" modified foods grow way faster and look much better than those from the garden. I will not waste time with the fairy tales which are presented to the public and will move on to the point. Each independent study concerned with the impact of these foods on humans has come to the same several major findings. GMOs cause failure of the immune system, infertility, holes in the digestive system, and multiple organ system failure. They also have a significant impact on the ecosystem, which can very quickly get into disharmony, and this can cause many natural disasters.

The most "visible advocate" of these foods is Bill Gates, who bought shares of *Monsanto* (an American multinational agricultural biotechnology corporation) worth $23 billion. All around the world he is promoting this to starving people as the best "solution for the world". He was, however, recorded while admitting that this "solution" is actually the reduction of the world population.

"There are over 6.8 billion people on this planet today, and we are approaching nine billion. This number can be reduced by about 50%."
B. Gates

Gates also suggests the so-called "Death Commissions" because he sees no reason to invest in someone who only has three more months to live and is no longer of any benefit. The head of *Goldman Sachs* naturally agrees with him, and he adds that together they perform "God's work". Thanks to the deregulation and removal of "restrictions on trade", GS started buying and holding enormous amounts of the most important foods (wheat, rice, corn, etc.). Their prices are reaching, thanks to "God's work", the critical maximum.

"Cotton seed used to cost only 5-7 INR/kg. Since Monsanto came on the market with their GMO cotton, prices have shot up to 3,600 INR/kg! The seeds thus became the property of one corporation - Monsanto."
V. Shiva, Indian environmental scientist

In the USA, more than 90% of basic crops such as corn, is genetically modified, as well as 94% soy beans and 94% cotton. *Monsanto* has publicly declared that they want to control 100% of the world food supply. (In 2012 it was 80%.)

"The Epicyte corporation patented the Epicyte gene that causes infertility in men and in women. Dupont and Monsanto have created a joint venture, purchased the Company Epicyte and commercialized the Epicyte gene. Do you want to know which foods contain this gene? The FDA (Food and Drug Administration), the office of deception and death, has made sure that it is illegal to get this information."
R. E. Laibow, Medical Director of the Natural Solutions Foundation *(www.RT.com)*

This information caught the interest of investigative journalist A. Gucciardi, and he asked the head of GMO Monsanto about it. The answer was more than shocking:

"If this shit causes infertility – great! The planet is overpopulated. This is the reason why GMOs are actually saving the planet. We are doing humankind a fucking favor! Sincerely, Ed."

"Monsanto should not assess the safety of these foods. Our interest is to sell as many as possible."
P. Angell, Monsanto - Head of Corporate Communications *(www.RT.com)*

"The most recent data from the International Agro-Biotechnology Application Service shows that more than 18 million farmers in 26 countries - including 19 developing nations - planted over 185 million hectares (457 million acres) of GMO crops in 2016. This represents a 3% increase over 2015 and the highest area of biotechnological crop adoption since cultivation began in 1996.

The countries growing GM crops are: Brazil, the United States, Canada, South Africa, Australia, Bolivia, the Philippines, Spain, Vietnam, Bangladesh, Colombia, Honduras, Chile, Sudan, Slovakia, Costa Rica, China, India, Argentina, Paraguay, Uruguay, Mexico, Portugal, the Czech Republic, Pakistan, and Myanmar."
https://gmo.geneticliteracyproject.org/FAQ/where-are-gmos-grown-and-banned

At present, many countries have banned GMO crops but are allowed to import them. The only countries that have banned cultivation and imports are: Algeria, Bhutan, Kenya, Kyrgyzstan, Madagascar, Peru, Venezuela, Zimbabwe, and Russia (!).

"If Americans like to eat GMO products, let them eat them. We do not need to do that; we have enough space and opportunity to produce organic food." D. Medvedev, Prime Minister of Russia

Worse is the fact that even if we avoid these foods in shops, they are fed to many livestock.

"Hypocrisy rules: Europe imports over 30 million tons of corn and soy-based animal feeds per year, the vast majority of which are genetically modified, for its livestock industry." M. Lynas, Political Director of the Cornell Science Alliance

The biggest march against Monsanto was held on May 25, 2013, when more than 20 million people protested in 45 countries around the world. These marches have been going on since then, but as we can see, in reality nothing changes, just the opposite. On June 7, 2018, even a huge merger took place when *Buyer* purchased *Monsanto* - so now the same company that sprayed carcinogens on our food will sell us the expansive drugs needed to treat our cancer.

"The number of U.S. lawsuits brought against Bayer's (BAYGn. DE) newly acquired Monsanto has jumped to about 8,000, as the German drugmaker braces for years of legal wrangling over alleged cancer risks of glyphosate-based weedkillers." Reuters

Food irradiation has also begun to be used in great numbers. This means that food given to you will stay "fresh" for more than a year. In the 20th century these technologies were used purely on food given to soldiers, but today it is a common practice.

"It is not possible for an individual to ecologically help the whole Earth. But each of us can help a specific place on Earth, provided

that we have an emotional attachment to the land and we are equipped with the appropriate knowledge, tools and skills."
J. Slinský (www.agrokruh.sk)

Again, there is a solution and it even comes from Slovakia (and certainly there are many more). Ján Slinský has been searching for ways to create sustainable agriculture without the use of artificial additives or chemicals. The solution is the Agro-circle, which ensures a balance between the three pillars: environmental, ecological, and social. Also, in this respect we will find more in it, because as he says, the circle unites and harmonizes.

*"**In nature, everything is in balance.** The moment an organism starts to dominate, a reaction is elicited: a sufficient population of its natural predators appears. In practice this means that if there are lots of aphids on peppers, it is a sign to ladybugs that they have enough food and can reproduce. **Chemicals are really not necessary.**"*
J. Slinský

The real threat of *Monsanto* may also be mycologist Paul Stamets. He recently patented a technology he calls "smart pesticides". These organic pesticides can supposedly resist nearly 200,000 insect species, all thanks to the active ingredient - mushroom. So again, it is only up to us whether we want to use or abuse progress.

Another issue that concerns every country is **waste.** Popular campaigns for recycling are mostly business which mainly supports prosperous corporations and does not really benefit Earth. Despite the fact that this "idea" was implemented with good intentions, it is about three times more expensive than storing the waste in a dump as usual; and as for the organization and transfer, it is oftentimes environmentally unbearable.

"Recycling is used as a short-term benefit for a small group of people – politicians, who want to please the masses and environmental consultants, and recycling companies, which use state financial support. In the long run, it can have a more negative impact."
H. Hazlitt, economist (*Magnus magazine)*

In the years 2002–2007, world trade in waste increased by 67%. According to statistics available from the OSN, in 2007 around 191 million tons of waste moved between countries, which is about four times more than the weight of passenger cars sold in international trade. So just imagine the sum of money we are looking at. The media have often pointed out that developed countries frequently remove toxic waste to poor countries – illegally. (This toxic waste is often stored in places where people live, and the waste dumps, therefore, often become a source of plague.) The real data shows that up to 80% of waste changes owners in accordance with the applicable OECD (*Organization for Economic Co-operation and Development*) regulations. The garbage business is among the most lucrative in the world because there is no country that is free of this problem. Presently, there are over 35 million tons of plastics only in the Pacific Ocean, in an area of about 6 million square kilometers, which is about 10% of the total area of the Pacific Ocean. It takes 600 years for a plastic bottle to degrade in nature. But even this issue has a solution today - ocean cleaners and the Swedish Recycling Program should be an example for every country.

"*The laws of nature have nothing to do with morality: gravity is neither fair nor equitable.*" A. Schopenhauer

Technology should set us free. It makes our life easier in many ways. It is only up to us to what extent it helps us. Using technology, we could eliminate the enormous number of alarming problems we have these days. We should use it to our advantage and not just adapt to it. Just as we are slaves of this age, we are somehow slaves to technology.

And officially, we do not know what exactly this "unconscious" use of technology may cause.

In the seventies, the Russians found that electromagnetic radiation is very dangerous and causes countless diseases. Today, each of us has mobile phone, microwave, cordless phone, or is exposed to constant Wi-Fi radiation. In the past, all these devices would have been examined for years before anyone would have been permitted to produce them. In capitalist societies, however, we do not even think about it.

"Electromagnetic pollution (EMF) may be the most significant form of pollution human activity has produced in this century, all the more dangerous because it is an invisible and insensible 'toxin'." Dr. A. Weil

"Existing safety standards for cell phone towers are completely inadequate. Quite justifiably, the public remains skeptical of attempts by governments and industry to reassure them that all is well, particularly given the unethical way in which they often operate symbiotically so as to promote their own vested interests."
Dr. G. Hyland, a physicist

"If there are risks, and we think that maybe there are, then the people most likely to be affected are children, and the younger the children, the greater the danger. No child under the age of nine should use a cell phone, and anyone under sixteen should use one only for emergency calls."
Sir W. Stewart, chairman of the British Health Protection Agency

"Turn off your cell phone and never turn it on again. It reduces the efficiency of the immune system and causes brain tumors. That's a fact. But you will most likely realize it only after it happens to someone you know. According to a study conducted at the Hospital

in Örebro, Sweden, ten years of mobile phone use results in an average of 290% higher risk of developing a brain tumor."
Dr. R. Dahlke

I don't want to scare you with all the side effects caused by cell phones, but again, I would rather leave you to find the whole truth yourself. The above quotations are used in the documentary *Poison by Mobile Phone*. You can also learn more at www.cellphoneradiationusa.blogspot.com. In any case, use mobile phones as little as possible or use hands-free and at least turn them off for the night. The same goes for Wi-Fi. When it is not in use - turn it off. (And microwave ovens could also end up.)

The good news is that, once again, we have a technology that can replace Wi-Fi which is a alternative called Li-Fi. With Li-Fi the information is transmitted using VLC (Visible Light Communication). It was invented by professor Harald Haas from the University of Edinburgh. In comparison with Wi-Fi it has a number of advantages, and it should be noted that it is also much safer.

This is only a selection of the most important issues, because if I were to write down everything that is currently happening, I would need a couple of years to do that. All over the world, whether it is Africa, Asia, or the Middle East, daily fights go on because of absolutely "absurd" conflicts for the sole purpose of profit. Whether it's **Syria** (a conflict artificially provoked by the media), **Afghanistan's opium paradise** (it is not a secret that about 50% of the population is supplied with drugs), "**the communist prison" North Korea**, **occupied Tibet, slave-owning China, starving Africa**, **destroyed South America, etc. These are genuine genocides!**

Daily, in several countries, whether it's South America or Africa, children under 15 years of age deal drugs or are involved in prostitution. They are addicted to drugs of the worst quality, just to numb the reality in which they exist. In Nigeria, there are even "baby factories" where girls from 15 to 18 years of age give birth to children who are then sold. Who buys them and to what end - nobody cares. Every day in Paraguay two girls between the ages of 10 and 14 give birth to children conceived as a result of rape. It is an epidemic. In the Middle East and Africa there are generations of children who have been brought up to really fight and kill! "Holy" India raised generations of children to be professional beggars and thieves. Mafia groups who enslave children exist all over the world, and this fact is completely ignored. **No one is really interested in saving working, fighting, and begging children!** According to recent statistics, there are now 1.5 million (!) homeless children only in the USA and about 217 million working children in the world. Annually, 16 million adolescent girls give birth to a child, mainly because they do not have essential health care. What do you think will become of them?

Statistics say that the world spent 1.735 billion dollars financing war in 2012. To eradicate poverty, we would need about 135 billion dollars.

Please start to take a real interest in the world you live in, and in particular, admit that it can be changed. Now I have revealed many truths, however, try to take them in. Do not "fight" them unnecessarily. Young people are still trying to fight for a better world, but they are not heard, and so they become the same. This has been happening for thousands of years! This current "game" is only about power and money. It has nothing to do with the nature of man; it has nothing humane in it! How much longer are we going to tolerate this?!

"Thanks to civilization man is so human he cannot kill anything without remorse - except man."
G. B. Shaw

Today's older people have experienced several different regimes, so I am not surprised they are so negative. They have been deceived so many times, they were hurt many times, and now they are at an age when they are old and not "useful" any more. They may seem "useless" because of their views and opinions, which were formed and reformed several times, and because of advancements in technology, for which they were not ready. Of course, it is up to them whether they want to or are able to adapt. But the fact remains that they have contributed to society more than enough and now they feel like outcasts. We pay this government our whole life and then we have to save money for our own funeral. What do we pay for? For the process of turning to dust? How many generations will come to water flowers on our grave?! Two, maybe three... and that's only because they will be forced to do so by their parents. Why do we have so many cemeteries?! The one who left you will remain in your heart forever. He doesn't need to have a rock! Again, this is mainly business, and currently quite a prosperous one. Sometimes people actually reserve a place in the cemetery. There are advertisements in the media and they even have a funeral magazine. Do you think that after you die you will feel like a VIP if you have a good place, or that it will force your survivors to think about you more?!

All religions are oriented on death, not on the man who is here today. Celebrate being, forget about death! It's just a transition to another world, a world where we will not care if somebody lit a candle on our grave or stole a vase. It is only a need of the ego when we are here on Earth. Furthermore, it makes absolutely no sense. Tradition, respect?! Cherish and celebrate man while he is alive, not when he does not care anymore. Therefore, in countries where they celebrate life, they also celebrate death - otherwise it cannot work.

However, you must first fall in love with life to stop being afraid of death. Again, we as humans added this whole unnecessary pathos to it. Death is only a transition to another level of consciousness and being. One day we will all meet again, and for those who have left us it will only be a moment, but for those of us here on Earth it will seem like an eternity. Before coming here, we fell into "oblivion", because if it were not so, we would immediately want to go back. It is (the pyramid) game that all of us "planned" in advance to learn what needs to be experienced in the densest and heaviest material reality. Death is birth to another level of consciousness. A person who is not afraid of life is not afraid of death.

"If we want our nations to mean something, then it must happen with deeds which will permanently incite life."
A. Dubcek

It has somehow slipped our minds that we ALL have one common home - the Earth. It offers us absolutely everything we need to survive, but we scoff at it. We discovered oil and we established the whole world on it! Oil, which was formed over millions of years, will be exhausted in just a few years in comparison. And it's in everything! Our economy is based on limited resources! Thanks to poor people, i.e., ordinary consumers dependent on oil, the "rich boys" are building their own islands and truly incredible nonsense. No example is more relevant and visible than Dubai. Till when?! Until they find, or devise, a way to replace this business with another business which will be, of course, profitable only for them? In this system it would be naive to expect that someone else will come to power.

"Who controls the past, controls the future. Who controls the present, controls the past." G. Orwell

The only solution is to switch to a resource based economy. Solar, wind, geothermal, and tidal energy and so on. It is up to us which we would like to use. Or maybe we can use all of them! (There are even many other options.) But who will get rich? That is the only question as long as we live in a world of money. Thanks to these resources we would no longer need oil. All of these resources are **freely available**! They do not destroy the planet, but are in symbiosis with it. But there is the poetic question once again: Who will profit from it?!

In 1775, the Paris Academy of Sciences adopted the decision to no longer evaluate proposals for the creation of perpetual motion machines. This date became the turning point when all countries and nations started systematically blocking the possibilities for humanity to obtain such energy sources that could incite a new leap in the development of mankind and, basically, get humanity out of subordination.

Nikola **Tesla** was the first to warn us about all this, and not only that. He even provided solutions. These and many other documents of this nature have been destroyed or are still unavailable.

"In the FBI files it is emphasized that any action must be carried out in complete secrecy, so there is no public interest in Tesla's inventions."
(From the book: *The Fantastic Inventions of Nikola Tesla* / D. Childress)

To make matters worse, when the Second World War was brewing, Tesla came up with a revolutionary solution when he introduced the real weapon of mass destruction which was originally created for defense. The weapon produced so-called death rays, which functioned according to the energetic principle. They were able to destroy 10,000 combat aircraft at a distance of 400 km. When he tried to promote it among the leaders, he was not heard out and the documents were made strictly confidential. Logically, then we would not need any war, which of course did not appeal to those who earned incredible money during wars, gained power, and divided this earth. And not only that, he even introduced a free-energy car that was driving 180km per hour at that time.

In any case, once again, a second side of the coin exists. Fortunately, a number of Tesla patents finally got to production, and Tesla was established in California.

> *"The fossil fuel industry is the largest in the world. They have more money and more influence than any other sector. However, the scientific fact remains that we are on a direct path to seriously harming the planet, and the sooner we start acting the better the result. We have calculated how much it would cost if the whole world wanted to convert to free energy. We would only need one hundred such gigatarists. One hundred in the world!"*
>
> E. Musk, CEO, Tesla and Spacex

(One such factory is the size of a football field, and the world needs only one hundred. This is a fact. I would also like to remind you of the fact that the first Tesla factories were founded in Czechoslovakia and resisted until - guess when - 1989.)

At the moment, it is again Russia which could be disconnected from this cycle of stupidity, and as usual, this does not appeal to anyone in the West. As President Putin himself has said, they have developed a nuclear battery that is a hundred times smaller than a submarine reactor and two hundred times more powerful. Do you understand what that means? It means trains powered by eternal fuel, electromobiles that don't need to be charged, and so on. And the main thing - aircraft without aviation fuel. That means the oil that the Americans are fighting for around the world.

We need to start taking care of our Mother Earth (heart). It gives us life, and we destroy it daily. If you find a few good souls who take care of her, they are considered freaks. Society has become a tool of technology instead of technology being a tool of society. Most of us worked successfully without cell phones in the past, and maybe we were even happier. Today, people cannot imagine switching off their phone for a day. The same goes for internet, portables, iPad, etc. Unfortunately, even our work is largely adapted to this trend. Instead of using the possibility to be connected as an option, we abuse it. We "have to" sit at work for 8.5 hours, although we have work for just 3 hours. We do not make use of these technical achievements just out of principle – because of a poorly configured system. But as managers we do not have a problem with "abusing" staff when they are on holiday, "spoiling" their holiday just because we can.

"Not from consent but from doubt is progress born."
J. A. Comenius

We need to start using progress rationally! Science is not here to be liked - it has to work! (Although now we have to be careful when it comes to scientists who may cleverly, manipulatively abuse it.)

"Why does this magnificent applied science which saves work and makes life easier bring us so little happiness? The simple answer runs: Because we have not yet learned to make sensible use of it."
A. Einstein

Each person is an individual. Each person functions differently, has completely different ideas, different (luxury) needs, regime, a different way of thinking. And he spends his whole life comparing and adapting to the majority. In the past, people provided food for themselves, that is why they were working. It was a completely natural activity. It was the industrial age that made us slaves to the system. **We have endless possibilities how to reconfigure this system.**

For example, I personally have had a reversed regime since birth. I wept at night and slept through the day. Likewise, I studied for school in the evenings and used almost every break at school to sleep for a while. I am writing this book in the evenings. I have the highest energy in the evening and the lowest in the morning. It's a fact. Of course, I can adjust, but not for long. Recently, I had over two months of getting up early in the morning without sleeping in on the weekends, and the only thing that came out of it was that I was tired and "useless" the whole day. It is just not my nature, however hard I try. It may seem strange to the "ordinary worker" who is satisfied working from eight to five because that is "normal".

"During the 8-hour shift, the average worker is actually working only 2 hours and 53 minutes." Fakty.cz.sk

There are two types of people - early birds and night owls. We all know it very well, but nobody actually accepts it. In nature, everything is balanced, and if we tried to do the statistics, it would be 1:1. But as it usually is, we have to adapt. It is beyond my power to understand why I can work enthusiastically with joy at 11 p.m., but if I do the same work at 8 a.m. I am tired and unfocused. You may argue that if everything was adapted to suit everyone's needs, nothing would work. You would be surprised, however, how everything would change if we paid attention to individuality. The division of the week is also very absurd when everyone works at the same time. Endless traffic jams during the same hours every day, and on the weekends you cannot find peace because there are lots of people everywhere. You look forward to the weekends instead of enjoying each day. Everything could be set up so that everyone could take time off whenever they wanted and work when it suited them. With awareness comes internal discipline. Of course, you do not have it if you're in the position of a slave. Of course, we search for every possible way to fool the system, to not go somewhere where we "must" go.

> "It does not matter what we do, if we do not take ourselves as we are. *Once we accept ourselves, it does not matter what we do.*"
> H. Heavenrich

Believe me, people would be more satisfied and would perform better. There are jobs which need to keep the "from – to" system, and there are people who like it. They need structure and system. Others need freedom for creativity. We are all different, but like everything in nature, this division also exists in harmony. If we set the system according to it, we would avoid a lot of misunderstandings and even traffic jams… Most jobs (statistically as many as 75%) could be automated leaving people with much more time for themselves!

> *"When we work merely for material gain, we build our own prison. We enclose ourselves in isolation; our coins turn to ashes and buy nothing worth living for."*
> A. de S. Exupéry

Monotonous work has not been needed for a long time. Our system does not admit it, even though it does not work anymore, and despite the fact that it is somehow paradoxically happening. For our system, it just means that unemployment rate is rising. Unfortunately, in practice it seems that more of the unemployed are even poorer than before. Their basic needs are not automatically met. They live off the dole and the government treats them as if they were incompetent. Indeed, it is impossible that the unemployment rate would do anything but get worse and worse. Today unemployment has exceeded the critical threshold in almost all countries, and no one comes to any real solutions. Tell such a person (who is not getting his basic needs met) to start meditating. I can vividly imagine the ridicule. A person cannot develop if society treats him as an outsider. It takes a really strong personality to be able to live up to some standards if one has nothing. Of course, a weak man will turn to alcohol or depression. What should motivate him in this kind of society?

"Nicer to me is freedom fraught with danger than peaceful slavery."
P. Holbach

Does this current system support health, good interpersonal relationships, or creativity? Are you afraid that if people worked much less they would become lazy? This is not true. It is this system that forces us to be lazy! Because we are not doing things that we really enjoy and that fulfill us, but quite the contrary. Most things we do because we "have" to do them. That's the main reason why you think that if you suddenly did nothing, you would become lazy. But if you did not have to sit at a boring job and you could have a vacation any time you wanted, you would love to do something! Man has an internal longing to do (create) something all the time. More time produces more creativity. It does not have to be artistic creativity. It is found in everything, really! If you could do what you have always wanted to do, what you really enjoy, you would not have a reason to get lazy. On the contrary, it would launch a flow of energy in you which you did not even know you had! And finally, you would start to live life fully!

"Laziness created more philosophers than wisdom."
G. B. Shaw

If a person finds himself, he is not able to understand how he existed before. We do not think the same way, we do not like the same things, we do not have the same (luxury) needs, we do not have the same regime, we do not like the same people, etc. We are individuals! And the world should start adapting to it. It is only this system that makes us really lazy. You do not have time to devote to what you really like. When you finally have some free time, you are happy to do nothing, and usually you do not even have the money to do what you would really like. That is why we may seem lazy. If you had more time (and money at present) to do the things you wanted to do, believe me, laziness would disappear immediately. "Thanks" to the workload, you do not have time to devote to yourself or even to your own children.

Let's review one very important fact:

WE - PEOPLE - DETERMINE THE RULES…

Who would you govern if you did not have people?

"We live in a time when the higher calling of man is not only to explain the world, but to change it, make it a better and more interesting place corresponding to the needs of mankind." I. V. Mitchurin (1911)

Let's look at the Icelandic revolution as an example. An information embargo was imposed on the whole situation so only a few people who are really interested in the situation in this world have heard or read about it. People in Iceland refused any form of government, big banks were nationalized, and they decided that the people will not pay the liabilities which politicians have created, because they are the result of poor financial policies, not the people. A new constitution was codified in which it stated that the main political protagonists will no longer be the politicians, but the citizens. The censorship of these events is the best proof of how information harmful to the economic and political elite is handled. Facts about this revolution were not seen either on television or in the newspapers. That is because the last thing the elite want is for people to realize that it's actually in their hands.

"There will always be disagreements between nations, because these are manifestations of individuality. Violent solutions, however, are a manifestation of immaturity."
Osho

Everything is individual, yet also interdependent. We are one unit, while each of us stands alone. Over the millennia of separation, we have only promoted our egos. We look for communities, we feel that we cannot exist on our own (which is true in some ways), and so we kill individuality in favor of groups. We have added artificial value to nations and religions. We forget that man is first of all a human being. We all have blood in our veins, and we are all equally vulnerable. Everyone needs to eat, sleep, and love. You can argue - no, we are different – and it may even be true. Each of us have grown up in completely different conditions (individual and historical) that have shaped us. They are not only individual, but also historical. I'm not saying that we should not keep our traditions, just the opposite – just let us stop clinging to them. Everything would have much nicer energy if we did not "have to" stick to our habits. Suddenly we would want them to survive and we would support them with joy! It's nice to keep the poetics of the nation, but not at the expense of other people. We have made everything commercial, thus paradoxically it has lost its true value. All prejudice, laws, and even boundaries are created by man - not by God.

Human is our race and Earth is our home - that is true for everyone.

Let's recall, for example, the story of the Tower of Babel. According to the myths, the people of Babel tried to build a tower high enough to touch the skies - to be closer to God. God, however, did not like this idea, and so he confused their languages to prevent them from finishing the tower. But the fact is that at that time King Nebuchadnezzar I. was trying to build a variety of gigantic buildings.

He was unsuccessful most of the time and had to endure mocking from his people. To build this tower he brought many prisoners and slaves from various parts of the world into Babylon. The people didn't actually speak the same language. It was just used as a metaphor to say that society was at peace and in social harmony. However, the opposite was true. Babylon was one of the world's ancient capitals, a center of religion and science, a symbol of wealth and fame. The streets there were built with geometric precision just like in cities today. It was the period called the Golden Age. People could have it all, and so they wanted more. Human pride, power struggles, politics... It all caused the destruction of an advanced society. It was not God, but again only people who ruined everything. For ages we have been fighting only with ourselves. The same situation occurred in the "fabled" Atlantis. Repeated again and again.

I cannot help but return for just a moment to the most controversial topic, and I will use two quotes from the book *My Awakening.*

> *"In the Middle East (and later throughout the world) the Jews mingled with many peoples, and yet they preserved their heritage and their essential customs. They are the only ethnic minority in Western nations that has not assimilated after thousands of years. In Babylon, they lived under slavery and then under domination for hundreds of years and developed a code that enabled them not only to survive, but to prosper while living as a minority in an alien society. When they emerged from their Babylonian sojourn, they were stronger, more organized, and more ethnocentric than ever before.*

> *Perhaps more importantly, a Babylon-like, multiracial America suits Jewish interests. In a divided land, the most unified group exercises the greatest power. In a jumbled, kaleidoscope society, the exercise of alien power is less apparent to the majority elements,*

for if a tiny minority has an agenda hostile to the majority, that minority needs to be as unobtrusive as possible. Multiracialism makes it invisible. Jews will always thrive in such a Babylon." D. Duke

Life is a circle. This is the Golden Age or currently profaned "New Age". Think about real contexts. We are in the same situation. We can have everything (and we do) and yet we waste it. We cannot handle ourselves yet we want to rule the world. There are only two ways - either we destroy ourselves, or we realize that we could move in another direction, away from the vicious cycle of human stupidity and greed. Or maybe one day, thousands of years from now, our descendants will read or watch how stupid and especially incorrigible we were. It is not human nature; we are forced into it by social conditions and so-called historical facts, nowadays mainly governed by those whom it suits. Even wars have never been anything but a huge business. But what do the kids learn at school? History should uncover the facts. However, politics excuses them and supplies the version that suits those in power. Current politics will never solve anything substantial. The world protests, but nothing has actually changed. For millennia, the coats have turned, but the rotten core remains.

This change must occur first at the level of consciousness of every man, otherwise we will not move an inch. It is imperative to understand that we can function differently and the fact is that we have everything we need for it. What we don't have is the advanced consciousness (awareness), thanks to which we could function on entirely new principles. If you are not drawn to a certain kind of service, do not worry about the world, and worry about yourself first. **If enough critical people who are willing to really change things get together, you must be prepared only at the level of your consciousness. We have to go through this change without the feelings of fear and insecurity.** Thus, work on yourself first and then you will know exactly what to do.

"Once you get to know your essence, you will discover the source of infinite power, a source of absolute power. The desire for power disappears, because you realize that you have always been kings, only you thought that you were beggars."
Osho

To "leave the system" is not the solution. As long as we are on Earth, there will always be some system. And the more the system is streamlined to the target, the less effort is required to reach it. We just need to have "normal" targets. The system itself is not bad, quite the contrary. Every freedom requires discipline, that is the paradox. However, returning back to nature is again only an extreme - we have lived like that many times. Going back is not the right way, rather it is probably the easiest one. Do not be afraid of things that teach you something. You can try to "impress" others with departures and transitions, but if you do not grasp what is HERE and NOW, you will not understand it anyway. It will become only food for your ego and you will not be able to function "everywhere". You will fight and condemn everything that is different. Give it up, please, surrender to what is… and in particular, be yourself - nothing more is required from you. And if so, it is just because you believe it. Clean that particular level of your consciousness. Dissolve all your fears (old programs) and be brave! Do what you enjoy! Take a risk and it will lead you in the right direction as a kind of thank you for listening to your heart. A lot of people fly in space, but they forget that they came to Earth. Let's learn to live here first.

"Zen is not morality, it is aesthetics. It does not impose a code of morality, it does not give you any commandments: It simply makes you more sensitive towards the beautiful, and that very sensitivity becomes your morality. But then it arises out of you, out of your consciousness. Zen does not give you any conscience as against consciousness; it simply gives you 'wide consciousness' and that becomes your conscience. Then it is not that Moses gives you a commandment, it is not that

it comes from the Bible or Koran or Vedas… it does not come from outside. It comes from your innermost core. And when it comes from there it is not slavery, it is freedom. It becomes your love."
Osho

Morality should come forth from everyone individually. **If you treat others the way you would treat yourself, you do not need any written rules.**

Do not do to others what you do not want them to do to you – this is the only law of morality.

"If people wanted to simply live, there would be surplus, joy, harmony and peace everywhere."
F. Fenelon

MONEY

"When it comes to money, everybody is of the same religion."
Voltaire

Money is the absolute and only common religion of our time. Regardless of the currency, its energy is still the same. In every country, in every home, in every relationship... everywhere! Anywhere!

Since **humans invented money**, there has always been a problem with it. It is about power and ownership. Money allows everything. Are you aware of this? We are totally dependent on money. Of course, if we don't move somewhere to the countryside where we bio-farm. But still, who would give you the land? You have to buy it. Who ever decided who owns some land, country, or water!? The wars?! They have always been about power and money. In the past, goods were exchanged. Today, money makes money. In the past, money was covered by precious metals. Today, it is just numbers in computers. Who decides how much money will be in circulation? A man. It does not matter if it is a group of people or an individual. The essence remains the same. It is man who invented this game called Money. It's not God, it's not a supernatural power, it is not anything that cannot be examined in terms of facts and history. We have created this game and yet half of the world is going bankrupt and half of the world is starving. Is this really okay? Of course, it is okay for about one percent of the population in each country that has understood this game, but not for anyone else. However, if you understand this game, your ego is your driving force. Ego has a constant need to own something, to control something. That is why, for instance, a truly spiritual person would never enter into politics (only if they wanted to start a revolution). All these are mere poses, in which the "chosen" primarily think of themselves. Everything is for sale! Politics is the most expensive business and religions are a close second.

"Money often costs too much."
R. W. Emerson.

If we counted how much money is spent each year to support different political parties, not to mention the election period, we could probably feed one African state. If all the money spent during the First or Second World War had been used for a good purpose, we would be somewhere else.

"Last year, the United States sold weapons worth a total of USD 66.3 billion to foreign countries, accounting for more than ¾ of the world arms market, which in 2011 reached 85.3 billion USD. Well behind the USA, second place was taken by Russia, which sold weapons worth 4.8 billion USD."
Source - *Magnus* magazine (2013)

"3% of U.S. military spending could end the starvation on earth."
worldbeyondwar.org

"In 2012, the world's ten richest people earned so much money that they could eradicate world poverty four times." Fakty.cz.sk

Check the numbers again and try thinking about it: Who has a real interest in peace?

And why is this happening?! Because a few people are playing Gods. Because some people want to control the whole world. And then what?! What if they take over the world? Oh yes, then they will go to the Moon! Indeed, they have already started selling land there, despite the absolutely unsuitable conditions for living. Doesn't this sound absurd to you?! And why? Only because of the obsession with property and power. This is a time of an absolute shattering of values – the richest are the most influential, and those who have contributed the most to society are forgotten. Because they are not prestigious? They do not have the right image? They are not for sale?! These rules were made by the rich for the rich. They get richer and the poor get poorer. It is impossible to reverse. After all, who has bank accounts in "tax havens"? Those who would benefit from it or those who get even richer than they already are? How is it possible that there are tax havens? How is it possible that the world fights against corruption and, for example, Switzerland does not have this problem? Isn't this an example that things could be different if only a few adjustments were made?

"The oldest curse of humanity is money."
Sophocles

We live in times of money, whether we like it or not. Never in history has there been a situation similar to what we are experiencing today. This is because never in history has there been so many people on Earth and, paradoxically, so much material abundance. It is society that forces us to accept this **new God - money**. When we look at all this from a distance, we find that everyone - the whole planet - is living in debt. There is no country that is not indebted. (Indebted people will not rebel!) Slowly but surely the whole world is collapsing. And because of who?! Because of us. We can create another war, another epidemic, anything... Our creativity has no boundaries! However, we use it absolutely destructively. All the world's conflicts are only about power and money. War is the greatest political business. There is nothing more to it. The fact remains that a demolished country is something like a paradise for various corporations and there are in fact billion-dollar contracts being signed. What difference does it make that thousands or millions of people were killed? The planet is still overpopulated and any possible family members are always well informed and protected.

"Mankind must put an end to war - or war will put an end to mankind."
J. F. Kennedy

This society is built on competition and exploitation - because of profit. Money was created by us, and now it is us who is being destroyed by it. There is nothing other than debt. I therefore ask: **Is it even possible for a financial crisis to exist?! It is NOT!** It was Adam Smith who defined the financial system as the "invisible hand of the market that was given by God." On all dollar bills it is written: "In God We Trust." Religion and money? Exactly. Every religion is politics, and politics is just another kind of religion. Basically, they both want the same things – power, control, and the greatest number of adherents. And, of course, contributions, a lot of contributions, taxes, and fees! This world is sick.

"All paper currency is on the brink of complete collapse, as world leaders are scrambling to make the transition to a new currency as smoothly and quickly as possible. ***Those who control the money are trying to start World War III, because bankers always thrive during times of war. However, a major player in this whole thing is the Vatican, particularly the Jesuits."***
K. Hudes, an ex-lawyer for the World Bank

Money is created out of debt. But who repays this debt? Paradoxically, it is the poor part of the population. The lower class actually pays the interest of the upper class. And they can happily trade on the stock market, but again only with debt. The cycle of stupidity. The biggest irony is that all this money does not even exist. It is all just numbers in computers. Today, only 7% of tangible money exists, so if one day we had the revolutionary idea of withdrawing all the money from the bank, we would actually have nothing to withdraw.

And this is the latest plan of our favorite groups – to dispose of cash, under the false pretenses of crime, terrorism, and other fictitious reasons. Because, in fact, the main goal is to ensure that we are under their full control and that there is no tax evasion. Of course, right-wing Israel is the biggest supporter of the recent financial policy. However, in practice, Sweden is on top, where only 3% of transactions are made in cash. However, at present, for example, the financial institution HSBC in the United Kingdom has limited the withdrawal of customer funds to a minimum. When withdrawing any significant amount, you need to prove and document its purpose. This is a huge interference with individual liberty.

"If the government can monitor all our financial transactions, they can actually monitor every action of ours. If you do not believe it, try to operate without money for a while. In short, the cashless economy is an extremely powerful tool that executives can use to track people."
Source www.infowars.com

This is also the principle behind the current conscious indebtedness. Indeed, the entire US economy forces its citizens to buy using money they do not actually have, thus creating so-called credit. And without it, nobody will sell you anything (except food). So the larger the credit, the more promising the client = the most heavily indebted citizen. For example, if you pay with a hundred-dollar bill in America, basically you are suspect. And also, paradoxically, even if you have several million dollars in your account, you are forced to pay in installments – otherwise you would not create the fictitious credit which is required from you by all. The country simply forces you to be in eternal debt, and thus you are firmly bound so you can be blackmailed anytime and you are under absolute control. A free country? Maybe in Army advertisements.

Although the financial system is essentially one, such economies as China and Japan have their own currencies that are covered by gold and they are independent from Wall Street. Starting in approximately 2007, Putin tried to establish a similar system in Russia, too. The irony of the situation is that he succeeded as late as in 2014, when the country found itself in conflict with Ukraine (USA?). So again, the unwritten rule is being confirmed here, i.e., banks benefit from war the most.

"Bank robbery is for amateurs. The real pros will establish a bank."
B. Brecht

People are currently the cheapest labor force. Slaves for generating money. There is nothing more to it. In the past, slaves were at least provided with the essentials for life. They were given food and accommodation. Today's slavery is unprecedented in history. And what do the economists do? Actually, they just watch the circulation of money. What more can they do? Create an incredible number of theories and analyses. But how does that help us to survive?! Obviously, something is not working!

It is interesting that people with brain damage perform much better in the economic sector. Because they have no empathy, they are good investors. So whether we like it or not, this world is, according to the facts, controlled by selfish brain-damaged people. In most cases, they are even addicted to drugs, mostly cocaine, which "helps" them immensely in this animal-like behavior. Also, sleep is gradually becoming the enemy of their time. As a result, they are usually not able to have any full-fledged private life, but quite the contrary. Their daily earnings exceed the annual income of ordinary citizens.

And that is quite constant in this game because they must document at least 10% profit annually, and their bosses don't care how they achieve it.

"At the end of my career, I had to work a tenfold number of lawyers compared with the 90s. The threat of potential losses from pending litigations increases. It's because the quest for ever higher returns shifts business towards illegality."
R. Voss, a former banker, businessman

"Traders, who are currently doing well, behave as if they were under the influence of drugs and their personality is changing. They enhance the position and in a euphoric mood they ignore the negatives. More and more they are convinced of their own infallibility and predestination to success."
J. Coates, an ex-trader on Wall Street

"A new discipline – neuroeconomics - shows that traders on the stock market are controlled by the same emotions as were prehistoric hunters when standing face to face with ferocious beasts."
Source - *Magnus* magazine

All the "boys" admit that they gradually begin to feel like masters of the universe. What more can I say…

"From this point, the crisis will be scientifically created."
Ch. A. Lindbergh Sr. 1913

1929 marked the beginning of a large economic crisis (the Great Depression). And this situation will be repeated over and over as long as we continue to use money. If you think about it, it is actually comical that money is being lent to regressive economies such as Greece, Spain, and Portugal while the financial system is still the same. The USA, meaning the World Bank, has a strong interest in causing European countries to turn against each other, to make us their vassals. Europe has actually been their vassal for some time now. It is just less noticeable "thanks" to the European Union.

"There are people who are interested in preventing the fall of the euro. There is huge profit potential in banks. Such amounts of money can conquer whole countries. You can start with Greece and continue with Portugal, Spain, and Italy. France could be the next one, as they also have economic problems. Just one step towards their neighbor Germany and the game is over. I do not think there will be a happy ending."
R. Voss, a former banker, businessman

Let's look at Europe today after the adoption of the euro, and let's admit the present situation, which is more than dire in every country. Money has lost value, more and more people have only enough for the most basic needs. People are actually surviving rather than living.

"The belief in the inevitability of poverty is the worst gossip of the world."
O. S. Marden

Gandhi said that poverty is the deadliest disease. And it is true. If you are poor, you cannot eat healthy, you do not have the right conditions for life, you don't develop, you don't even have access to health care. Over the last 30 years, the poverty rate has doubled. The stress of poverty, of course, causes health problems. The more sick people there are, the better it is for the economy. Yes, we have come this far. The pharmaceutical industry is, after the firearms industry, the largest grossing one. So if we simplify it a bit, our economy needs sick and dead people. That does not sound very nice, does it? But the one percent that owns 80 percent of the wealth on earth does not mind. And we are not thinking about it… because it is a "given"!?

"The luxury of the rich is paid for by the misery of the poor."
F. Kafka

And what about unemployment? It is part of life these days, although people really want to work. It is not even possible for it not to get worse in this system. We could replace 75 percent of the human workforce with machines and computers at this moment. If one could really do what he liked and what was fulfilling, this problem would not even exist. We do not permit progress so that we do not have to redo our "great" economy. But again, in some sectors it suits us, so there we permit it. In other sectors we prefer to artificially create work so that we can have jobs, because we "must" work. It was probably invented by God, so it's a given. But after a while there will be no money for unemployment benefits – then what? Fewer and fewer people have the money to buy much of anything other than food. Will we become farmers once again? But we need some land for that as well. Every third person on the planet lives from less than $2 a day. Eighty percent of the population live for less than $10 a day. In particular, the European Union spends over EUR 2 billion every year on self-promotion. And what about pensions? Life expectancy is growing, yet nobody is really prepared for this. On the other hand there is still a generation that ages faster and it has not had the opportunities that today's young people have now. So at the present date it is almost impossible to design a pension system that would benefit most of the people. Again it's just a "fictitious" game of the economists to demonstrate some activity and for the politicians to gain their electoral votes.

"There are more and more millionaires since the crisis in 2008. In the last year, the number of millionaires worldwide rose again. Their property expanded, too, totaling ca $38 billion. The report High Net Worth Individuals (HNWI) lists people who hold financial assets worth more than a million dollars. In 2009 there were more than ten million millionaires – hence the increase amounts to 17 percent."

J. Morris, What You Can (Not) Know

Economic crisis? The crisis of debility!

"People do not understand our banking and monetary system, for if they did, I believe there would be a revolution before tomorrow morning."
H. Ford

Today everything is based on image - advertising. Brands even determine your status in society. Advertising is one of our "favorite" sectors. Companies use it to get new clients - new profit. In the current system, more money is spent on advertising than on production. It is no wonder. Progress is incredibly fast. It is so fast that we encounter the concept of the planned obsolescence of products. (Not to mention the "fictitious" campaigns of monopolies or state contracts which need to be "documented" in all directions.) For cyclical production, i.e., the economy to work, we need everything (money) circulating. So they manufacture products that don't last long, preferably no longer than two years. Even though we could produce goods with a longevity of approximately 20 years, that is the last thing our economy needs. The waste we produce daily because of this system is full of precious metals and even reusable parts. How many phones have you had? How many computers, cars, or televisions...? (Everything that is cyclical is eternal, so life is "eternal".) Who gave the value to precious metals? Again, it was man. A diamond is just coal! Just as a lotus grows from mud, coal becomes a diamond. If we lived in a rational society, we would use these mineral resources in science and technology, which would create the highest quality products. No, instead we hang them on ourselves and what is more – we want to prove our social status with them. Not to mention the inhumane practices that are tolerated during the extraction or the possibly deliberate destruction to prevent the market price from declining.

"Wealth is like sea water - the more we drink the thirstier we are."
A. Schopenhauer

Science is developing every day. Science has no ego - either something works or it does not, just as it is in life. There are no good or bad cars. They only have more or fewer functions. It is a fact (the thing) that makes our life easier. But do we really need 100,000 types of cars? We are incredibly spoiled, which is bad for life itself. The achievements of science are artificially suppressed just to keep the existing brands on the market. There is a project that could help by constructing a vacuum tube train which would move so fast that we could get to the other side of the planet in a few hours! However, it has not been approved because then air transportation, hence the use of oil, would no longer be necessary. It is the same with cars. Eco-friendly cars have already been developed - cars which do not need oil! Of course, some people (who profit from oil) do not like it (even though they use them in private). In the past, some companies actually produced electric cars which were subsequently ordered destroyed! What do you think, which oil company owns the patents? So now we must wait and watch as these "novelties" are gradually incorporated into existing companies (and their cars) while the companies pretend they really want to help us all. Also, cars could be controlled by satellite allowing us to avoid accidents. After all, today we drive only on the basis of trust. Have you ever thought about it at all? If some psychopath who has decided to end his life drives towards you, he can easily take your life as well. And we could go on and on – anti-gravity cars are a reality. We could avoid intervening in nature when building highways as well.

Science has an incredible number of solutions for everything, but their success depends only on who will profit from them. If it is found that "only" our planet, the environment, and common people will benefit, that's actually a very small, irrelevant reason – it is actually not a reason at all… I would recommend you look online, for example, at the Venus Project. I am not idealizing it, but here we can find an impressive number of ideas that an experienced scientist has been trying to promote to society for many years. Unfortunately, to no avail. I also suggest you watch the internet film Zeitgeist (Moving Forward), which describes the entire financial system in great detail. This documentary already has three parts and is developing. We should not, therefore, feel that everything in the film is the unchanging truth and it should be "like this and not otherwise". Let's learn to be more open-minded.

"Capitalism ends – we need to look for something else."
Prof. K. Schwab, the most authoritative advocate of capitalism

If you expected that in this chapter I would write about how to get money and how it's a special energy, I am sorry. When it comes to money, it is completely unnecessary to give it any spiritual significance. Of course, it is energy - neither good nor bad. It's up to you what kind of relationship you have with it and how it affects your reality. Your current situation is merely a reflection of your past thoughts. How many times have you said that you do not have money? That money is bad, dangerous, and so on...? With money it is like it is with anything else. You can have or get it, but never idealize it unnecessarily (there are an overabundance of books about money and our erroneous programs). However, please admit that you know how to enjoy life without money too. Although it is difficult in the current system, you will be at ease and prepared when it all comes to an end. Only society is forcing us to believe in this religion. Money is only a thing that we invented and to which we assign value. Money is, in its essence, divine as is each of us. While it is, it is imperative to begin to love and enjoy it! And if you just do not have it, in spite of following all the good advice and reading all the right books, you may be in that period of life when you need to experience some things that you would otherwise never experience. Observe all the hidden meanings that lurk in everyday life. There is nothing wrong with money as such. Only certain powers (religions) have been inducing guilt in us for many centuries (even though they live in magnificent wealth). Try to forget about them for a moment. Live for the present and it will come, it always comes. It is only our social system that does not allow us to think like that…

"The hardest art in life is to get rid of greed."
T. Gulbranssen

The financial system will collapse sooner or later – across the whole world. It is not possible for it to survive - even if it seems like science fiction at the moment. If the planet were struck by a global disaster, we would not know how to survive. We would need water and food. What would we have banks for?!

There are potentially three options:

Make the financial system totally transparent. Imagine you knew how much everyone earned, how much goes to interest, fees, how it really works. That would be a lot of surprises! This would be a real threat. Suddenly, the whole system would "have to" be set fairly. Let's make it visible. Everywhere and in everything - totally. (By using Blockchain technology and a common currency for all.)

We could also press restart and return to our original currencies that would be covered again. Each country would be entirely independently responsible for its own economy – independent of the others. That means that each country would have to set up a fair system again, because any discrepancies would be felt by its citizens and there would be no other culprits. Each country even has some mineral resources, their own funds, and/or other negotiable items. As a result, we would have to start behaving in a mature way towards ourselves, our neighbors, and other countries. Cooperation on an entirely new level – smart, creative, humanistic, non-static, and adaptable to the given time, situation, and demand.

Cancel the financial system and switch to a resource based economy. However, access to input information must be accessible to all without restriction. Only in that way it can become righteous. The natural resources that we have are more than enough.

However, for the abolition of money we need a large amount of money so we could take care of the whole world, although the funds are more than sufficient. Even the number of people with money who feel the emptiness and do not know where to continue is sufficient. My advice is: **begin to form a new world!** Maybe a catastrophe will make us do it, if the fact that the whole world is collapsing is no longer enough. It is completely useless for some sheik to provide for his offspring when they will not have fresh water.

Money is not evil. It helped us get where we are now. It has helped us many times, but we have paradoxically become its slaves. All of us. Even the richest man in the world is a mere slave. Although money gives us freedom, it is very limited. What will you do after you have traveled round the world, tasted the best food, made love to the most beautiful women, when you own 100 cars and 50 airplanes, after you have tried everything you have ever wanted to experience… Then what???

If money did not exist, would you still chase the same dream?

You will find that it was not money that made you enjoy music, dancing, love, and laughter. It is simply a means to achieve an absolutely natural part of ourselves. Is it not sad? In the present system we need money for everything. It is a game we have fallen for to the extent where we no longer realize what really pleases us, what makes us happy. Is that okay? You will never buy true love (if you do not buy a dog), you will never buy joy or laughter. You can pay for them, that is what you know, but it will never be sincere. We have gotten used to it. It's comfortable.

What would it be like without money?
WHO would I be without money?

Yes, **you would have to be yourself. And that's what you're afraid of?!** Of being yourself without any artificial values?!

Suddenly we would meet completely new people. Real people. In my opinion, this is really worth the experiment.

"The real measure of your wealth is how much you'd be worth if you lost all your money."
Anonymous

(MASS) MEDIA

"Media is the most powerful entity on Earth. They have the power to make innocent guilty and to make the guilty innocent. And that's power, because it controls the minds of the masses."
Malcolm X

The issue of today's media covers only the last century, yet it already exceeds the critical level of stupidity. The world media is overgrown, and that's a fact. Whether we talk about television, newspapers, magazines, radio, the official internet news - the same information is repeated basically everywhere, and we accept it without question. All of these media repeat themselves – they must, because not so much happens every day. Actually, there is always something going on, but in most cases it is not so significant that we should have to immediately hear about it. Several times a day is best, and most importantly – it should be negative! It is a "must" for the state to make us afraid because when we are afraid, we are controllable. When there is someone who tells us how bad and dangerous everything is, but on the other hand, he assures us that we should not be afraid because "they" really want to help us – what can we do? We are in a deliberately generated schism. And then, immediately after such news, we go and watch the 859th episode or so of our favorite series to avoid any opportunity to think about it.

"Conservative rulers were not only afraid of liberal and socialist thinking, they were afraid of every kind of thinking, even reactionary thinking. The idea was to instill mindless discipline in the masses. And that's the point: any thinking is dangerous for the survival of the system. Today's strategy is similar, although it cannot be so obvious.

In the age of information, it is most important for the elite to distract the masses from the real issues and overwhelm them with the entertainment industry. The bottom line is the same - people should not think, they should obey."
L. Blaha (Member of the National Council of the SR "The media do not want us to think" / czechfreepress.cz).

The whole thing is basically one huge game; people just take it too seriously. The media are our new gods and the same goes for the people who work there. While in reality, if you looked closely at the life of any one of these people you look up to, all your illusions would dissipate very quickly. I personally have been a part of almost all the media in our country (Slovakia), so it is not a presumption, but a fact. 80% of the people in the media are pitiable wretches longing for attention and power. Thus, they particularly long for attention and recognition out of a subconscious desire for love. Therefore, in the media you find mostly people from broken families, those who are mentally unstable, malicious, forever underrated = sick. Of course, there are the other 20% who do the job because they enjoy or even understand it, and they are the real creators. But the people in power belong to the first, bigger group, and so here again is a vicious circle and therefore it is not possible to move from this place. And if in this "dreamed of industry" you have a so-called backbone, be sure you will not get far.

But let's go back in time for a while and identify the facts. The newspaper, i.e., print is considered the first means of public communication. The World Association of Newspapers (WAN) refers to the newspaper *Acta diurna* (Daily Events) as the predecessor of the modern newspaper. It was carved in stone (by order of Julius Caesar) in ancient Rome. His nephew Augustus already understood the power of manipulation and began using it to deceive people. He became an inspiration for many dictators, and he is also proof that human nature has not changed at all. The first handwritten "newspaper" was created in 713 at the imperial court in Beijing. But as many of you know, the real beginning of print is connected with Johann Guttenberg's invention of the printing press, which happened around the year 1450. In the 16th century, reports about various battles, natural disasters, and the like were published periodically. The origin of mass printing, however, dates back only to the 19th century, when the first rotary machines were created and hence the ability to print huge numbers of newspapers for the general public.

That would have been all right, if we had not moved on to tabloids (gutter press), which has now become mainstream and also affected other forms of contemporary media (TV, radio). Gutter press is called "boulevard journalism" in some languages. The French word "boulevard" means "big street". At the beginning of the 19th century, newsboys sold the first newspapers which were focused on the general public, i.e., the working class. As it was a "lower class" means of expression, it had to be adjusted accordingly.

"Tabloids contain large headlines and pictures, abbreviated articles, the language can be vulgar, works well with emotive syllables and cries, simple sentence structure and limited vocabulary. It mediates instinctive emotions (sex and violence) rather than information. It moves at the border of ethical rules. Financially, it lives from the advertising of large networks and huge circulation. This model is so expensive because editors use photographers – paparazzi – who often fake reports, feign them or construct them together with the celebrity."

Wikipedia

"Tabloids are a means of mass communication in which emotions (blood, sex) and novelty (the importance of which decreases with time) play a key role. Its content is characterized, among other things, by parochialism, scaremongering, scandals, personalization, populism, shallowness, negativity, simplicity, clarity, creating celebrities and working with them, pretending authoritativeness and closeness with consumers. It shows and interprets phenomena on the basis of background information and gossip."

Wikipedia

"It just satisfies the masses who need the information hidden among ladies tits and soccer balls. Readers do not require journalism; they just want abridged and entertaining information."

P. Novotny, general editor of a weekly tabloid

I think these definitions completely describe what currently has the most influence on us and really just show that about 90% of media outlets today can safely be called tabloids. Of course, as from time immemorial, people have been watched and controlled by the state (or by the church before). Newspapers have always been subject to such control as well, to prevent them from releasing information that could compromise someone. For that reason, we now have people who work in PR (public relations), who provide information to newspapers according to their interests, i.e., depending on with whom and for whom they work. Where appropriate, they can distract the public's attention from what is really going on, because not everything that goes on "behind the scenes", whether it is in politics, economics, or show business, is for the general public. So, we must first of all understand that the term "objective reporting" is nonsense. Therefore, if you find an investigative journalist who puts his heart into this business and has good intentions, he generally doesn't last long.

"There is no such thing as a free press. You know it, I know it. None of you would dare to write your honest opinion, and even if you did, nobody would print it. Every day I was paid not to interfere in the news with my own opinion. The same applies to all of you, too. Whoever stands out will find himself on the street, and he can look for a new job. The role of a journalist is to undermine the truth, tell lies, fudge the facts, and sell out himself, his country, and his race for his daily bread. You know it, I know it. So what is this nonsense about toasting a free press? We are instruments and puppets in the hands of the rich who pull the strings behind the scenes. We dance to their tune. Our talents, potential, and lives are owned by strangers. We are nothing more than intellectual prostitutes."
J. Swinton, publisher of the New York Times, in his farewell speech for the New York Press Club, 1953

"The fear of the press forestalls far greater crimes and incidents of corruption and immorality than the law."
J. Pulitzer

The creation of radio, television, and the first sound films date back to the 1920s and 1930s. Thus, we can speak about a relatively young industry. Movies were the first of these three most significant forms of media (if we do not count the radio as such). Already in the twenties, major film companies that are still prosperous today were established. Despite their good cinematographic base, war-torn Europe had to abandon this business, which suited the large studios in the USA, and so thanks to World War I they "won" this very competitive struggle. As we have mentioned in previous chapters, the Jewish community was already prosperous at that time. They were successful mainly in banking, which made it possible for them to finance films. Everyone realized that a new era of expression was beginning. A new era of shaping and influencing people. So, of course, those who were in power realized it, too. Since films are very difficult to produce, especially in terms of finances, it is totally logical that it was the Jews who seized this opportunity. And if they finance something, they have their conditions.

"Jewish power is so great that they can make a coward of even the greatest Hollywood icon. During an appearance on the Larry King television show, actor Marlon Brando said that `Hollywood is run by Jews. It is owned by Jews.' Brando contended that Jews are always depicted as humorous, kind, loving, and generous while they slander every other racial group and are ever so careful to ensure that there is never any negative image of them. Jewish groups came down hard on Brando, stating in their press releases that they would see to it that `he would never work again`. No one in the Jewish press seemed to notice that the threat simply validated Brando's observation of their unchallenged media power. Brando was so intimidated that he had to arrange an audience with Wiesenthal himself. Brando cried and got on his knees and kissed Wiesenthal's hands, begging for forgiveness for telling the truth. Wiesenthal absolved him of his sin and Brando has said nothing but positive things about Jews ever since."

D. Duke

"Barely a month goes by without a new television program, film, drama, book, poem, or prose dealing with this issue, and this is escalating rather than receding."

Prof. Y. Bauer (Hebrew University, Jerusalem)

"Show-business is an extension of jewish religion."

J. Lennon (The Beatles)

Since I started taking notice of it, I can only confirm it. In almost every American movie where Hanukkah or a similar feast is celebrated, Jewish actors are featured or they just somehow mention this "topic". When I asked during a premiere whether his film could at least be nominated for an Oscar, a prominent Czech director (Oscar winner) replied: *"I did not make a movie about the Second*

World War, so I know it will not be." Of course, there are other movies that win awards, but with the topic of the Holocaust you simply play it safe. The following example, however, speaks in more detail about the impact of media on public opinion.

"The public image of the man who called himself 'Martin Luther King' (his legal name was Michael King) is a textbook illustration of the power of the media. Most people still do not know about King's involvement in communism, especially since the media ignore that part of his life. King openly admitted that he was a Marxist and he said to his friends that his efforts were part of the class struggle. His personal secretary, Bayard Rustin, was a Communist. When King was forced to replace him in 1961, he chose another Communist - Jack O`Della. His main advisor was the Jewish Communist Stanley Levison, who edited and probably wrote a good deal of King's book Stride Toward Freedom. *Levison filed his tax returns, audited financial activities and was responsible for the transfer of Soviet money to the Communist Party in the United States. The media always presented King as a good, Christian, family-based man. But King had dozens of liaisons with prostitutes, white and black, used church money to pay them and commonly beat them — all documented by the FBI and admitted by King's associates. King even spent the night before his assassination copulating with and beating white prostitutes. In the FBI video recording he screams during sexual intercourse: 'Today I fuck for God' and 'Tonight I'm not a nigger.' These videos are so demonstrable that the FBI sealed them for 50 years. Despite these facts, King's Jewish handlers and their allies in the media were steadfast in their laudatory portrayal of King."* D. Duke

"The Western press kept mostly silent on the Soviet mass murders even while millions still suffered in Communist concentration camps. Millions more died in Red China during the 'Cultural Revolution,' in many nations of Africa, in the jails of Cuba, in the killing fields of Cambodia, and in the 're-education camps' of Vietnam. Yet, during a

period when Marxists liquidated millions, all we seemed to see was the endless parade of stories about the Jewish suffering of decades before." D. Duke

And to be honest, when we were taught about communism in school, we talked about some of the horrors it caused, but I do not remember seeing any pictures, heartbreaking films, or documentaries about the victims of communism. These are incomparably higher numbers if we compare them with all the victims of the Second World War. Or why not make a movie about the murder of 75 million Native Americans or the indigenous peoples of Australia - this was the real genocide! Not to mention that almost all of these natives live in their countries on the edge of society! British, French, or Spanish colonies have destroyed the culture of many countries. While US inhabitants celebrate Thanksgiving, indigenous peoples – Native Americans – "celebrate" a day of mourning.

"Controlling the world's sources of news, Jews can always prepare the minds of people for their next move. The greatest exposure yet to be made is the way that news is manufactured and the way in which the mind of whole nations is molded for a purpose. When the powerful Jew is at last traced and his hand revealed, then comes the ready cry of persecution and it echoes through the world press. The real causes of persecution (which is the oppression of the people by the financial practices of the Jews) are never given publicity." H. Ford, 1920

Watch, for example, the film *Wag the Dog* by Barry Levinson to see how it is all "cooked" - with humorous detachment, but unfortunately, honesty. I returned a little to these difficult issues because in these examples you can see that public opinion really is being manipulated. So once again, I dare to say that the Western media is actually a dictator's mouthpiece controlled by one social group with a greater interest than it would appear at first glance. The media is in fact their latest "weapon".

"Practically all states have retained the right to decide on the allocation of frequencies, not only to private, but also to public service broadcasters. In this context, it is important to recognize that the technical nature of radio brought the first level of state interference. Hertz frequency, as a precious national treasure, has become a part of the public sphere which has to be used in accordance with the public interest."
Wikipedia

Thus, the fact remains that we have either public broadcasters, which broadcast only in accordance with the interests of the state (i.e., regularly changing employees after elections) or private broadcasters, owned by corporate bodies, i.e., corporations. And because corporations are essentially states within a state, we once again find ourselves in a vicious circle from which there is no escape. Private television can choose independently with whom they will or will not cooperate. Public television does the same thing, only under the patronage of the state. But in both of these institutions, there are lists of companies and people who will never appear on the television screen. As for the criticism of systemic rules, each television station has its own interests and offers you what you want to hear. It is so-called fictional choice, because it is limited by what they want you to say. Ultimately, there is advice for retransmission, which is the official censorship. So where is the objectivity?! Again, this is primarily a business. Everything else is far less important. The license fees that we pay would be meaningful only if they could help preserve the structure of the original idea of public television, which should be to inform, educate, entertain… and especially to be another pillar of democracy. In today's capitalist world, however, these values are long forgotten and what dictates the conditions to the media is particularly advertising and the ridiculous positioning of people meters. It is ridiculous, especially since, for example, in a country with 5 million citizens there are about 2,500 of them, and only those viewers actually determine the audience rating according to which advertising time is sold and the life of various programs is determined. Only those people decide "everything". (To put it simply.)

"The state is becoming weaker nowadays, since political parties privatized multinational corporations and the wealthiest segments of society. Therefore, the same media owners who are chasing profits also de facto control the state institutions that should be controlling them. The methods of media manipulation were probably best documented by the famous American philosopher Noam Chomsky. He claims that major media groups are big corporations, owned and linked to even larger cartels. He demonstrates that in the '90s, in an era of mega-merger corporations, the global media were seized by nine mega-corporations such as Time Warner (CNN), Disney (ABC) and News Corporation (FOX). This trend continues. And, of course, the image of the world that the media present represents the narrow interests and values of the media owners and the purchasers of their advertising services. So - the richest segments of society. However, it is not a conspiracy. Chomsky clearly points out that manipulation is not projected by the collusive agreements concluded in smoky rooms. It springs from the fact that the thinking of many of those who make decisions independently is based on the same belief, the same values and pursues the same goal - to gain profit for their own parent corporation. This is how it is set. To expect from today's media, which are under the control of the greatest capitalists in the country, that they will support objective information about the economic theft in which these capitalists are involved is about as naive as to expect the media which were in the former regime controlled by the communist party to objectively inform people about the dark side of the former regime. One need not be a lumen to understand a very basic fact, that the media serve someone, and it is not the people they serve. They are referred to as the guard dogs of democracy. Someone forgot to add, however, that the guard dogs do not bite their masters. Otherwise, the simile of guard dogs is

relatively accurate. The media really guard the system so that it is not endangered by excessive thinking. The media prevent people from realizing that this system is upside down and that they have been running around their whole lives just to make a few people rich."
L. Blaha, politician

"In the 1990s, there were over 100 media holding companies in the West. Today it is the seven that own most media companies in the world. The owners of these companies are Jews or Zionists."
N. Chomsky (Jew)

"The freedom of journalists is now becoming, in most cases, a very relative thing: it ends where the interests of the business begin."
H. Camara

So who are the ones to whom the bohemian qualities are attributed? What do we allow to get into our homes each day – who?

"The press is manipulating everything that's been happening... They do not tell the truth. They are lying. They manipulate our history books. The history books are not true. It's lie. The history books are lying. You need to know that, you must know that."
M. Jackson

We invented the media. But instead of using this connection with the whole world for good, we misuse it. We play with fire, in everything. The above-mentioned facts are only a brief synopsis of the principle on which they work. But what I find to be more important in this case is the psychology behind it.

Film was created to be fun, just like the original theater, which is the great origin of these "toys". It's a game which from time immemorial reflects society and its shortcomings. The basis of Commedia dell'arte, which originated in 16th century Italy, is masks and the exact types of people (Arlecchino – a clown, servant; Dottore – a cartoon doctor or lawyer; Pantalone - a miser, usurer; Capitano – a soldier, braggart, et al.) I mention this only because it is nice evidence that the types of people have not changed even after thousands of years. Only the costumes and settings change, the characters remain the same. It is mostly artists who see this, and therefore they are the ones who want to change the conventions, the broken and repetitive rules. It is so in every society, in every nation. Subconsciously people know that they are right, and therefore they look up to them. Thanks to art the human consciousness can expand. That is why good actors have consciousnesses that are expanded further than those of ordinary people – they experience every character in each new play. They must understand the character, i.e., live their lives and that expands their consciousness with each new character. As a matter of fact, **consciousness is a live intelligence – it has nothing in common with intellectual knowledge**. There are also real musicians, painters, designers, writers, simply artists, who thus expand their consciousnesses (without even realizing it). This does not mean that they have "grasped life" or are somehow better. They just perceive more thanks to their mission. For example, during a certain period of my life I was a cultural reporter on TV. I did hundreds of interviews with real people (Czech and Slovak celebrities), and I could ask them whatever I wanted. This expanded my consciousness each time I met someone new. The art-form simply expands consciousness, mostly because it is not based on facts but on experiences, whether on your own or someone else's. To some degree, the internet has this function as well today. For this reason, today's young people have much broader consciousnesses than their parents did at their age. There are also other things that can help such as traveling, books, theater, movies, and people, meaning anything that intermediates you some experience not more facts. Arts constitute the feminine principle, i.e., they work mainly with the right hemisphere. For this reason, artists are more emotional and, on the contrary, they have difficulty grasping daily reality that is represented by the left hemisphere.

But let's get back to the media. At first there were movies. (If I do not count the radio which has a smaller impact on us, unlike visual expression. Therefore, I do not devote such attention to it. Although, if we consider the example of the radio, the older generation may realize that until recently they could not even freely listen the radio.) Man is naturally playful – it is a natural and integral part of us. Therefore, theater and film were, first of all, a game for people; they were a way of escaping reality. However, **games have their rules, but art has none. On the contrary, it changes them and introduces innovations**. That is why it has become an attractive form of entertainment for people. Since we are talking about the early 20th century, the films at that time were phenomenally successful, because what else would people do during the war? They fled from reality into a dream world.

> *"The '30s were a great era of classic Hollywood, when many new genres were created and it gradually became a `dream factory`. Exciting and funny short films allowed people to escape from the depressing reality of their everyday lives. Almost all genres reproduced the myth of the land of unlimited possibilities and vowed to endless variations of the 'American Dream' – a big career 'from a dishwasher to a millionaire'."*
>
> Wikipedia

In the beginning, film was meant to be funny and entertaining, and therefore many slapstick and other comedies were created. Only later did people realize the power of film and begin to knowingly influence public opinion. During the Second World War, Hollywood produced more than 1,500 films to prepare people for the war (both psychologically and physically). Gradually, television was added. Suddenly, people could have fun at home, and thus the above mentioned groups could reach every single household. It is totally logical that this creation started in "free" America (at that time). Everyone else was, in terms of television production, (at least) one step behind at that moment.

Television also can expand our consciousnesses; it provides new information that forms our opinions concerning the matters we follow, i.e., personality. For the first time, we actually began to look at ourselves. Therefore, if we look at the programs from the beginning of this era, people act artificially and unnaturally in them. People learned from it - what looked good or bad. There was some pathos in that which looked unnatural. People began to notice that and gradually changed it. In those days, thanks to film and television, the first celebrities appeared. Their success will never be surpassed because they were the first ones and there was no competition like today. Such personalities are valued above average and a cult of unattainability was created around them. It is precisely the same illusion that is consciously generated among people to give them something to dream about. Just as rich people knowingly create a cult of poverty. (The state still needs their sheep who will have to "work hard" dreaming of a better future and with a raised finger pointing to the "third world". The present system is not set up like this by accident. "The rich" even have their own media where you would not find any of the "shit" they feed us. They have accurate information. Actually, they have their own world in our world.) Famous people should first realize that an incredible number of people look up to them and that they have the power to affect their views. There's a tremendous responsibility which is, unfortunately, only made use of by advertising agencies.

However, the film industry today, in addition to their specific problems, does not present any threat to mankind. Rather, thanks to it we can watch our own decline. This is seen in the topics. The majority of films are either action or catastrophe movies. As for the stories, the quality has plummeted since the late nineties. Although we have improved the technology and have been increasingly creating spectacular works, they often lack a good script. The stories are based precisely on the "formulas" that the screenwriters are taught at present, and these mainly include the well-established draws on viewers. And the main draw has become mainly profit, which always leads to the tried-and-tested combination of actors and directors. Young artists are having a difficult time today because every company is afraid to risk failure. However, if you decide to create a celebrity out of someone, it's only a question of money, i.e., a good campaign and you can become famous overnight throughout the whole world! (I would like to remind directors that there are countless books of high quality in the world which are just waiting to be filmed. Just start reading again, huh?)

"All kinds of technology have already been created - it's time to create!"
J. Jakubisko, director

Magazines and tabloids support the same cult of stupidity. In the beginning it was interesting because it was new, but now everything just repeats itself. And it cannot be different. We are invited to deal with everything and everyone, just to have no time to deal with ourselves. Every year the same topics are repeated (in all media) - spring (Easter, spring trends, detox…), summer (vacation, cellulite, salads…), autumn (depression, school, Halloween…), and "Christmas" (everywhere and a lot!). And you're buying it again and again. We are lucky that every year someone creates "summer hits" - changes the colors, gives it a new cover, a different title and you feel that something is actually happening - there are new trends! You even adapt your life to this artificially generated cult which influences your values: "Oh God, you do not have these purple Louis Vuitton shoes, you are totally out!" Values which don't matter are artificially generated and the real values are suppressed by external image. This "sick cult" arose already in the sixties thanks to models.

Skinny Twiggy was the inspiration of many girls who ended up in the hospital with anorexia or bulimia. Gradually this trend changed, but the principle remains the same.

"If people believe that their main aim is to be constantly entertained, to shop, enjoy and consume – you will get, as an entrepreneur, millions of avid followers of all your nonsense and users of all the useless things that you produce. The media today have a dual function in this - they create an artificial world where the reality is transformed to their needs and then they struggle to maximize their influence in this artificial world, dragging it towards the moral bottom. No, there are no charitable institutions. They are only ordinary commercial subjects chasing profit."
L. Blaha, politician

This is the real illusion – the media.

In the '60s, thanks to television, magazines, and movies in general, the consciousness of mankind expanded (also with some help from drugs, which are particularly about the desire to escape reality and get to know the universe, i.e., oneself). This was again caused by the post-war period and also due to the war in Vietnam which hurt the Americans more than previous conflicts. The hippy movement started as well as a cult of musical bands fighting for freedom. It was a period of great changes in the cycles of the Universe and a consciousness of unity began to emerge. What few people know is that this was also the period which gave us the greatest media miracle - the internet. It was developed by government agencies and gradually integrated into the public sphere. The original idea was, however, to have everyone under control. It turned against them though, because no one thought we could also use it to our benefit. Naturally, they thought of that, but based on their definition of human nature, they felt that this could never happen. But it is slowly happening, and therefore the negative reality and so-called conspiracy theories are foisted on us more and more intensely. It is precisely Project ACTA which tries to limit the freedom of this means of expression. Today it is perhaps obvious to everyone that everything you have ever written on your computer, it is as if you wrote it to some secret control organization. (It's also important to remember that the entire cyberspace has its roots in the US.) This, however, is our salvation.

"I firmly believe that the internet is a tool that can help the development of human consciousness. This relates to the consciousness of unity. The internet was given to humanity as a sacred organ of consciousness."
R. Kuchinskij, internet mystic

A kind of freedom came to us thanks to the Internet. Until then, we only had the information that came from someone. Therefore, people in the past created and gathered in various secret societies to exchange information and discuss it. Otherwise, they officially did not have access to it. There's also a cult of artists who met with the high-ranking personalities and so had the relevant information which was oftentimes more interesting than, for example, the information a group of peasants in a tavern had. The essence was (is) basically the same, but the level of knowledgeableness is different. **The lack of access to real information is the main cause of the state our world is in today.**

The internet today gives us the freedom to find what we are interested in and gives us a chance to create our own opinion about things. Man as such was not prepared for such a rapid expansion of technology, particularly in terms of communication. Our communication was made easier, and paradoxically we are getting worse and worse at communicating "normally". The internet has enabled us to change our identities and, paradoxically, to hide even more than before. The effect should be the opposite, however, but our low level of consciousness caused this problem. Many arguments arise only due to a misinterpretation of the intonation of a text. Time is accelerated so that we have "no time" to go for a two-hour chat over a cup of coffee when we can skype, send SMSs, write a rather informative status update, or send a picture without a comment. So, on the other hand, it makes us distrustful paranoid psychopaths who still need to check on someone, whether it is an actual relationship or someone on a social network.

Facebook is so successful mainly because we have finally begun to speak for ourselves. In particular, we can be in touch with the people we want to be in touch with. In a way, we have begun to open up. But again, this is just a beginning. People have found their new dream world to which they have become addicted and which they have not yet learned to "use". They do not realize that Facebook is their own medium which they can use to create an image for themselves. On the other hand, many people believe that everything that a person has on Facebook is really "him", not realizing that the other person may just be playing with others, creating an image he wants to create, regardless of reality. Thanks to Facebook, I personally have "met" an enormous number of people that I would never have met otherwise, have received several job offers, we organize regular meetings with friends that we would never have been able to agree on via landline, and since I am surrounded by smart and informed people, it has even fully replaced mainstream media for me. I can also promote this book and communicate with supporters while playing with what I want to share and then expect the reactions of people who write to me which is very helpful. I create an image I want you to see, but I also provide space for your analogy. Others are stupid enough to think that I put all the events in my life there and that my Facebook profile says everything about me. (This is how social media works.) And just using this example we could do research on how the human mind works. One post can create thousands of different opinions, no matter what I wanted to say initially. People are suddenly no longer hidden, they are more open than in the past when they were worried about what others would think of them. So there is a new way for us to present ourselves which we actually do not know anything about. The fact is, that those working in the media are of course way ahead in understanding this "miracle". People are still just learning how to use these amenities. However, Facebook is our direct mirror. You can see that negative status updates always get more "likes" than positive ones (as in the first case it is compassion and in the second envy), that short status updates are more popular than long reflections (the principle tabloids are built on), that you care whether your contribution will have more "likes" than a friend's post (otherwise you would not put it there, even though you would love to shout it from the rooftops), and so on. On the other hand, we can move straight to the things that interest us, even with someone we haven't seen for many years, instead of asking questions like: What's new? What are you doing now? Do you have any children? You can share your joys, heartaches, life moments, or get support for some projects - the possibilities are endless! Joy is truly meaningful only when we have someone to share it with. We can observe here that the greatest event (the one with most likes) is the birth of a child or the beginning of a new relationship or marriage. Creation and love really resonate with us most. The other side of the same coin is that people have started judging others instead of dealing with their own issues. The informational war is in full swing and censorship on facebook is enormous. Therefore, handle information with care. Everything you upload there can be used against you - as we already know. The glory of Facebook has been replaced by Instagram, which is also a novelty in this media world. As it is primarily about (nice) photography, people are less burdensome. However, in this case, we all have a direct connection to the whole world, which is the greatest advantage of this medium (same for Twitter). It is also the best platform for celebrities to present the truth about themselves - we have never been closer to them, as they have the opportunity to communicate directly with their fans, deny the tabloids, and at the same time they get a real indicator of their popularity.

"Facebook makes their money by exploiting and selling intimate details about the private lives of millions, far beyond the scant details you voluntarily post. They are not victims. They are accomplices."
E. Snowden

"Arguing that you do not care about the right to privacy because you have nothing to hide is no different then saying you do not care about free speech because you have nothing to say." E. Snowden

All of these companies are of course interconnected. Many new independent internet television providers have been established recently. Although they are a step ahead, the fact remains that the major media will remain dominant. It can be overcome only with difficulty (if they don't begin to broadcast under the program structure, in which case they would fall to the level of classic television). People have always been happy to be entertained and it is the same with these programs. They cannot find what they like themselves, and they are certainly not willing to sacrifice their free time to this. Of course, today's young generation is doing a little better, although at the same time becoming unsuspecting slaves to their computers. Since we exist in the principle of duality, it is reflected also in this direction. **Whether it is television or computer, people go from one extreme to another. They "do not know" how to turn off these devices, so they turn to a radical solution – throw it out! As if there were no OFF button.** Many people are in the habit of turning on the television, radio, or computer when they come home, just to avoid feeling alone…

"The TV viewer is really a strange spectator - he has succumbed to the fixed idea that he bought his own TV, which he installed in his own apartment and now believes that everything that is happening

on the screen was created for and addressed to him personally. And he is tired of it - and there are so many viewers like that! He could think: `Hmm, others are having fun, what's wrong with me?` But no, he thinks otherwise: `What are those people laughing at today...?` But he does not read the program: `On Monday I won't be at home, Tuesday – that bores me, Wednesday – I do not understand the topic, Thursday - that's it!` No! He turns it on every day and watches it, thinking that it cannot be so stupid! All the while he considers himself the best judge nationwide of what is and is not good."

M. Hornicek, 1976

And once again we come to our favorite topic - the golden mean. It is not about what we do, but about the approach. If you do something, do it 100%, but stop approaching everything with the idea of "all or nothing". Learn to be alone, in silence, and that will remove the need to be dependent on external circumstances, whether they are tech toys, drugs, or people. The principle is unfortunately still the same. Studies show that a regular kid growing up in the Western world absorbs 10.45 hours of media. Since most of the information is negative, we should not be surprised by what becomes of them. According to what they see, they hide behind various identities and "hate" everything that comes their way. Their parents do not have time for them and so the virtual world becomes their reality. Countless computer games only dumb their senses and create essentially a new generation of apathetic gamblers. These are new worlds to which millions of children around the world escape, to learn how to fight and kill. Today this business has surpassed even the film industry. Also, there is a new addiction to series which already has a large number of victims who are even being treated. At this time the world is overflowing with media, and it is as if people have stopped dreaming. They have everything, and the more they have, the less they value it. It can also be seen in the fact that they no longer create fairy tales (compared to the past), apart from the special animated movies from the most famous companies.

Everything is mainly about profit, not about man and his natural needs. Therefore, today's fairy tales are manufactured to interest adults as well. More viewers mean more profit.

If you wanted, you could have all the information available, but since there is so much of it, you don't have the time and energy to look for it. Interactive documentaries showing mostly the truth are called conspiracies today. I wonder why they cannot be shown on normal television when every day they show us all sorts of sci-fi movies. Not to confuse us? Oh, all right! Manipulation has gone so far that we do not even know how to distinguish the truth from propaganda.

"It is only ideology that has turned all of us into an artificial, selfish, ambitious society whose only value is so-called pleonexia, which means we want to have as much money, power, sex, food, admiration, etc. as possible. The media support the consumerist market society and all the political ideologies that help maintain it. The aim is to indoctrinate educated groups and to stupefy the masses. The point is that anyone who expresses a different point of view should be seen as "eccentric". Maybe there are a few more "eccentrics" presently who refuse to play the media's game, but the media still have enough power to present them to the rest of the public as fools and outcasts."

L. Blaha, politician

All information is measured out as if for complete fools. You can see for yourself that the whole world is protesting and you hear or see almost nothing about it. If they decide to air something, it is something negative about the aggressive troublemakers and not the real substance of the protest. The refugee theme is a textbook example of the manipulation done by the media. They filmed a couple of families who they showed to the whole world, but the fact is that mostly single men who were promised the "American Dream" immigrated to Europe. But that was not what awaited them, quite the opposite. So do not be surprised by the aggression that stirred up in them. Later, under the pretense of a "rescue", they will call the army and create a "European" army fighting against the "Russian enemy." No one cares about real Europeans, their values, morality, culture and Europe as such. These people really do not respect any living thing; their only driving force is the desire for power. They create a story exactly about what they want to believe. It has nothing to do with the truth or the facts. It's a game - the most dangerous one now.

Countless laws are adapted only to those who are in power. They do not want us to think. They want us to believe their version of reality. Thanks to this, we are distracted by everything and forget to deal with our own selves. You have compassion for various ill fates and close your eyes to your own reality. Time has accelerated so much that you prefer experiencing emotions on the screen rather than in reality. It is clearly demonstrated by different types of reality shows where reality is prevalent. And we want reality, which leaves emotions in us. In recent years, journalism has changed to cruelty, parasitizing on the misfortunes of others. But understand that you are the ones who support it. If you are not part of the solution, you're part of the problem. None of these media would exist without you - without spectators. I am not saying you should boycott all commercial media; just know that you have a choice. First of all, note what grounds this is built on and, especially, stop taking it seriously! It's all just a nasty game with your subconscious.

Playfulness is the nature of every human being; however, we should set the rules ourselves. We see that the direction in which it is moving is not correct and in fact never has been. Therefore we'd better learn to use these "tools" positively. We could help ourselves in many ways by using the media. Also you have to realize that unless something is being publicized, no one will take it seriously. The media has tremendous power, so let's begin using it to our advantage and to keep us entertained without leeching off of others.

Each participant on a TV show is inspired by the opportunity to win, profit, or attract attention. **Try to win your ordinary life instead and start by learning how to love yourself, without the need to impress others with some artificial values. If you respect yourself, you will also be appreciated by others.**

START TO CREATE! If your effort is sincere then you will surely meet someone who will notice it and you will "last" much longer. No one who has actually achieved something got it on the first try. On the contrary, if you want to contribute to the world, you must first know yourself; otherwise it can lead to a disastrous faux pas. The most important thing in this respect is humility, and that you will not develop overnight, but through experience. Just do not make the media your target. Create for your own pleasure! **Media attention is only a secondary effect of your efforts, and they are above all the most illusionary "ego trip" in the world.**

"We will not understand how we could benefit from the diseases and misfortunes of our fellow human beings. We will not be able to explain to our children and grandchildren how we could permit that. We will try not to think about what fools we looked up to and considered celebrities. We will be ashamed of the time when the gelled clowns and smiling buffoon monkeys, who hated having a larger series of orgasms with the same partner, made the front pages every day. We will say that they are to blame, some kind of unidentified `they`, and they will be among us and will point the finger at someone who does not even exist. But we are accomplices to this disgusting behavior, not only those who write, publish and broadcast. We gladly collaborate with them by looking at it, listening to it, reading it and buying it."

B. Filan

EDUCATION

"Learn for life, not for school."
Seneca

The educational system desperately needs reform. Although it undergoes reforms all the time, the nature of education does not change. It is based on memorization. All tests only test the memory. No one teaches us how to think, how to be creative, critical…

The current education system forces us to learn and repeat "facts". We are full of information that many times we do not even know how to use in real life. This system does not take the internet into account. Although they are trying to integrate it into education these days, the internet is certainly not used as much as it could be. Today it is absolutely pointless to "torture" children with facts they will never need. And if they do need them, they can get to them within seconds on the internet. You might argue that what they do in school is about the development of children's brains, but there are thousands of other undoubtedly more creative ways to train the brain. Wisdom is applied knowledge, but we ignore wisdom in favor of knowledge. You will forget knowledge – you will never forget wisdom. **We teach children what to think instead of teaching them how to think.**

The main problem lies in the fact that we support the intellect, not intelligence. Intellect is only a substitute for intelligence. It originates from ego; it needs to accumulate information that would impress society. What do you need so many different facts for? Is your life better? Do you have better relationships? Or is it just that you need to show how much you are able to remember? We have created intellect so we would not have to go beyond the boundaries of knowledge. Intellect lives in logic, which is mathematical in its nature, which means it is actually "dead". But life is not logical. Life is constant change, a process. Intelligence is creative. It wants something new, unknown; it needs experience. Then it grows. Intellect is based on the past experiences of others. Intelligence forces you to be yourself. Our professors do not have to be intelligent; it is enough if they have a well-trained memory. They are obsessed with the past, with the thoughts and experiences of other people. They are like mechanical machines which only produce more machines. Intellect produces – it is in the head. Intelligence creates – it is the vigilance of the heart. If you have fond memories of some of your professors, it is just because they put their heart into it. Those who "do not have heart" can pretend to be serious as much as they want, but no one will ever remember them. And if by any chance they do, it certainly won't be a good memory.

"A man with a lot of knowledge is the most sightless man in the world. Because his deeds come from knowledge, he does not see how things really are. He acts mechanically. He learned something and it created a stereotyped mechanism by which he acts."
Osho

All children are naturally playful and creative. As soon as a child goes to school we try to make a "proper citizen" out of him. We want to make him a reflection of our own selves. That's what our egos enjoy the most. If the child draws, for example, and is inattentive during the lesson, the teacher rebukes him and assumes he has trouble with concentration. He sends him to a psychologist instead of supporting the child's creativity. This is caused by our unconscious effort to divert the attention from the right hemisphere to the left. Due to the failure to develop the right hemisphere, many (especially young people) in the West have fallen for drugs, alcohol, and inappropriate attitudes to sex. The attraction to these compensations lies in the immediate shift of attention from the left to the right hemisphere. And then it (the right hemisphere) works only if you drink or "dream". Somehow, the natural human values such as love, beauty, and poetry have disappeared from life and everyone is just chasing after money, fame, and power. Our education supports this. It's not about creating an original personality, but about producing a competitive, ambitious careerist.

NASA scientists did one very interesting study where they evaluated children's creative genius. Children's "genius", however, gradually disappears once they enter the education system. The numbers are very shocking in this case. Scientists tested 1,600 children between the ages of 4 and 5. It was a test that evaluated the ability to come up with new, different and innovative ideas to solve problems. At this age, 98% of the children were considered to be geniuses of imagination. The same test was carried out by the scientists five years later, at approximately the age of 10, and found, surprisingly, that only 30% of the children were in this category. At the age of 15 it was only 12%, and in adulthood only 2%! This education system has not been set up by chance.

> *"People care a thousand times more about the way to acquire material wealth than they do about reaching the education of sense and heart, even though what a person is, is undoubtedly more important for our happiness than what a person owns."*
>
> A. Schopenhauer

Our society requires something from us all the time. It wants us to be "someone". But we are already what we are. Why do we still have to adapt to someone? Why should we become another copy of some insecure teacher? How many of them live exemplary lives so they can be an example for us? Teachers actually just copy the information and they want us to repeat it back to them in the test. Even if we do not understand it completely… Who cares? The main thing is we can give them what they require. It's similar to buying goods, except that we buy scores and grades. The school system is based on memorization. You can come out of school with a red diploma, but you'll be stupider than before because the only thing you have reached is an overflow of information which you will not even know how to use it in practice. Of course, I'm generalizing a bit here. But the point is, we do not feel joy at school, there is no happiness or beauty. We look for them outside, during the evenings, weekends, with friends… Anywhere, just not in school and yet - how much time a child spends there! There are exceptions, like art schools. But if someone out there decides not to accept you, you're out of luck. So, finally, you cannot study what you really wanted to. And then you will start escaping to your fictional world. You will feel uneasy, but you will have no idea why. There is no one to tell us: forget money, do what you enjoy doing! However, the system doesn't allow this. We have to survive, and thus we try to survive, not living, just existing. Most people only survive and they feel it is "normal" because almost everyone lives like that, and some people are doing even worse. Instead of revolting, we just pity ourselves for a while and then we continue down the beaten track. Till when?!

"We may receive education from others, but
wisdom is reached only in ourselves."
M. E. de Montaigne

Paradoxically, today's teachers and professors suffer more than the students. The natural authority and respect are gone. The students have more money than they do, better cars, better lives. Teachers are no longer "honored". It is due to the system that does not value their work. And so they often compensate for their frustration by demonstrating their power. The technological boom, which they were not prepared for, also led to this situation. The fact is that today students are often better informed than their teachers. Thanks to the internet, they even have broader awareness and diametrically different views on life. Their parents grew up in post-war countries where there were no media, brands, advertising, pervasive sex, internet, mobile phones, etc. All of this appeared in the last fifteen years. People were not prepared for such rapid technological development and heightened materialism. We are unable to stop it, and we do not even know what to do about it. We prefer turning to the past and saying that everything was better before. However, we should not condemn this progress. We should enjoy it and benefit from it! It makes everyday life easier, we just have to adopt a positive attitude towards it. Instead of applying it to the system, especially to education, we stick to the old rules and the established conventions. Young people naturally rebel, but eventually they give up because they do not have the power to convince everyone. They adapt and become part of the group of "good citizens" who were here before them. You have to be a strong personality with natural intelligence to rebel against the system. But then you run the risk of being considered a freak because you do not walk with the crowd.

"Education is an admirable thing, but it is well to remember that nothing that is worth knowing was not taught in school."
Anonymous

For example, Einstein did not even finish high school because he was not able to adapt to the stupidity that surrounded him. Leonardo da Vinci, George Washington, Benjamin Franklin, Thomas Jefferson, and Abraham Lincoln were also not products of the school system. Someone taught them of course, but none of them completed a typical high school education. Nowadays, for example, even the greatest businessmen do not have a proper education. Because paradoxically, if you understand the system, you will find that you are a one-eyed king in the kingdom of the blind. The other extreme is to succumb to alcohol or drugs because you need to escape somewhere and you feel that the outside world will not allow it. You do not have the resources or the power to get out of the system, so you look for the easiest escape.

"School failed me, and I failed the school. It bored me. The teachers behaved like Feldwebel (sergeants). I wanted to learn what I wanted to know, but they wanted me to learn for the exam. What I hated most was the competitive system there, and especially sports. Because of this, I wasn't worth anything, and several times they suggested I leave. This was a Catholic School in Munich. I felt that my thirst for knowledge was being strangled by my teachers, grades were they only measurement. How can a teacher understand youth with such a system? From the age of twelve I began to suspect authority and distrust teachers."

A. Einstein

Man, as such, does not even know how to breathe properly, sit, or stand. He doesn't even know what he wants to do because his own interests were repressed by his parents, teachers, society... Even if he knows, there is no one who would support the idea in him. This system does not support creativity - in anything! Our system only pretends that it is terribly rational and yet it is totally sick. We need to bring more fun into it, more pleasure, relaxation, and creativity. We all earn money just to be able to have fun. We need to bring fun into everything and most of all into the school system. Those are the most important years when the human personality develops. Games are not just for kids. Stop acting so terribly serious and let's bring more joy into the world, please!

"A teacher must be an artist, sincerely loving his job."
A. P. Chekhov

General education should be about human beings as such, as a whole. After this everyone can develop according to their own individuality, their own needs. We underestimate children, but we should learn from them. They are the most enthusiastic and most natural teachers, but instead of accepting it, you still think you are something more. Even our parents were actually "children" when they educated us. Children have had children for many centuries now. You can argument with the biological clock, but that too is changing, just as is life expectancy. There are so many unhappy or abandoned children, simply because the mother did not have affordable health care (or contraceptives) or because she consciously decided she didn't want to be labeled a spinster by society. Men also make rational decisions and then leave the family because they are unprepared, irresponsible, and self-centered. What is it good for?! If people lived in communities, the children would be cared for by the elders – the more experienced people who would have the patience and the necessary information for life. Parents would not be so intimately connected to their children, and from the beginning they would see their children as individuals and independent personalities. They could continue to devote their lives to their interests and enjoy life and freedom. It is a fact that for old people the greatest fulfillment comes from taking care of their grandchildren, i.e., children. They are not interested in their careers anymore, but in transmitting their knowledge and experience.

"Those who educate children should be appreciated more than those who gave life to them. The parents gave them life, but the educators taught them the art of living."
Aristotle

Today, parents are connected to their children so strongly that they are afraid of the day when the child will leave home or, paradoxically, from a certain age they wait for them to leave. So they are either afraid of loneliness, because they have been with someone their whole lives and they cannot live alone. (This means they never had time to get to know themselves.) Or, they may feel like "the best years of life have passed them by" and they sometimes blame the child and try to let them know how much they sacrificed for them. Only very few parents have healthy relationships with their children. Often they just project their own problems and needs onto them. In spite of this, they do not even realize that their child is actually educating them. And so it goes, round and round.

"Why do you think that an obedient child is a good child? No obedient child has been a great statesman or a great mystic or a great poet. Only the disobedient have become great inventors and creators of new things. Just the rebellious spirit transforms old and reaches the new realm of the unknown. A real father does not force his child to do anything. On the contrary, he helps her to be herself. He gives freedom to the child, because he understands that the inner self flourishes only in freedom. The more freedom, the more experience."
Osho

I believe that we have a lot of professionals in education who will lead this system to what we really need based on their experience and expertise. And we will finally be able to learn anything we want at any time. Some beautiful contemporary examples are the Waldorf School, Sudbury Valley, and even the Finnish education system. I wish education was actually available to anyone who is interested in it. This world is so materially secure that we do not need to pay for such basic needs. We have the internet, and although it's not going to replace personal contact and relationships, it can substitute for a huge amount of learning. If only the race for the greatest profit would disappear. And again, globally, 65 millions girls are not in school.

Out the 774 million people who are illiterate around the world 2/3 are woman. **Online courses could solve a large part of free access to education for all.** While note, first we must realize that if we do not provide adequate education to all, we should not be surprised by the kind of people walking around. Because they could not be different or elsewhere, even if they wanted to, because our current system simply does not allow it. Indeed, if we look, for example, at the Middle East, we encounter the absolute programming of children. They grow up following a blind faith that is introjected by their violent fathers. They teach them to fight instead of to think. And their fathers were educated in the same way. This is a huge problem now. **We forget the essentials - the children - worldwide. Give children the opportunity to grow creatively and to think critically, and you will see them joyfully grow.** Do not fight with them, rather teach them genuine accountability, which is the gateway to freedom. Listen to them; they really like to invent creative projects that will encourage not only their education but also their mental development. **Let us involve them in the process of this development and both parties will be satisfied.**

> "*One can hardly believe that a reasonable man can cling so tenaciously to such prejudice. And there is sure to come a time in which school-children in their history lessons will laught about the fact that something like this did once exist.*"
> A. Einstein

Today's education, let's be honest, unless we talk about vocational school, has the value of a paper that is basically unusable in practice. Thanks to omnipresent corruption and arrogance anyone can study anything, even if they have no talent at all. If a parent pays, everyone is very helpful, because whether it's the educational system or professors, they all need money. Never before have Labor Offices dealt with so many "economists" and "lawyers". Paradoxically, the system requires young people with some years of work experience, which is virtually impossible. However, if you have the proper connections everything is possible. Basically, people study for five years to eventually find out that they're unemployed. And that is one in four young people in Europe. Have a look at politics, for example. You do not even need to study political science to become a government minister or to lead a state! I am not condemning it; I am just pointing it out. This world is led by people who officially are educated, but they are mostly unusable as human beings. The system they support enables them to play their games and we tolerate it. Is it really okay?! Even Hitler was a scholar. He was even a vegetarian and a teetotaler. According to our moral codex, he was actually a "super citizen".

"Educating the mind without educating
the heart is no education at all."
Aristoteles

Our current education system is totally hypocritical and impractical. The irony of this situation is that this planet is actually overgrown with unpromising lives, although it sounds cruel. Paradoxically, the highest birthrates are in the countries with the least developed educational systems and cultures, where they cannot even get their basic needs met to fully live. A new generation is growing up, but what will they be like? Every single person/child has an inherent natural sensation which forces them to grow in all directions. And if it is not supported, destruction comes inevitably. Again, **we (all of society) are responsible for understanding the importance of making education available to everyone without exception, with freedom of choice. There is no better investment than that in the development of the next generation, which will later pay for itself many times over.** Today's society is educated according to the usual conventions and it understands neither what natural intelligence is, nor how it develops. It condemns you if you did not study at University without understanding the essence of it. I did not study at university. It does not make sense to me in this form. I cannot accept the injustice with which I was confronted in education from infancy and the eternal struggle of insecure teachers for power and attention. I believe there are those who do their job with the intelligence of the heart, the wisdom of the whole, and creativity. I would be happy if they were not afraid to go for what they believe in and to concretize their new vision of education. I wish you success.

"It is more helpful to know a few rules that can
help you than to study lots of useless things."
Seneca

EGO

"The cause of all misery and evil in the world is egoism. We know about it, and yet it does not prevent us from growing our own egoism."
E. Hemingway

Ego is a part of our nature, but at the same time it is only an illusion. Ego is not you, it is society, or should I say – a social program that is embedded in us. But it is not our true nature. At first sight it may seem to be weird, but it's a fact. During our lives, ego identifies itself mostly with fear and power. **Ego is inherently schizophrenic.** It is also the only "hell" that exists. It forms a duality in which we have to find unity and harmony.

When a child is born, he doesn't have ego as we know it. He does not use it consciously, he is not aware of himself; he uses it only for his own needs - automatically. When he needs to eat - he cries. If he had no ego, he would only be aware of the fact that hunger is present, but he wouldn't do anything to satisfy his needs. He uses it unconsciously, and that is easily demonstrated by the fact that the child first begins to refer to himself in the third person. He does not say: *"I'm hungry"*, but *"Teo is hungry"*. He knows that everyone calls him that, so it's probably him. But then parents and society come and begin to explain to him that it is normal and natural to say "**I** am hungry." And this is the basic pillar of the illusory ego that causes us more problems than joy. And so **the game with the name "I"** officially begins.

And from that moment, only information from outside is being put into us. No one asks a child: Who are you? You might ask him that, but you will only laugh at his response and then just start to put your own programs into him. First, there are the parents' programs, then those of teachers, professors, friends... everyone. The child has no time to find his own identity, and in fact, he is not even supposed to because he is still "just a child who has no idea about life". The most popular question is: What do you want to be? Since childhood we have been struggling with the fact that we should become somebody. Nobody tells us that we are perfect as we are. They demanded this from you, and you naturally require it from your children as well, despite the fact that you still do not know who you are. You float through your life and force your innocent children to fulfill your unfulfilled dreams and desires. You want them to become the person you were never able to become. You want to see them achieve everything that you were not able to achieve. You are trying to insert your program and imprint your warped ego onto them, and to justify this process, you call it love. And, of course, you are giving them the facts! Your imparting so-called artificial intellect. There is no support for the development of their own intelligence, which is naturally a part of every child and is reflected in playfulness, creativity, spontaneity. Because you are so terribly "adult", and you also require it from your children without even realizing it. *"Do not do this, do not do that, stop it!"* is most probably more common than: *"Just play, think, create!"* Explain to your child why he should not do something. Give him a sensible reason and believe me, he will accept it much faster than he would have accepted your screaming. A child has inborn natural intelligence from which we should all learn. Everyone is a real person from the very beginning, and everyone is unique! You are the only reason he is again and again faced with being compared to someone. He must constantly adapt to someone and has no chance to be really natural. You would be very surprised how naturally your children would develop if you gave them freedom. Because the child is close to the source, he is so pure and innocent and we all should return to that point once again - but on a conscious level.

"Identity is the foundation of slavery: identify with something and it imprisons you. If you do not identify with anything and you remain yourself, you are free. The ego is nothing more than identification with something that you are not. Ego is a bond, a life without ego means freedom."
Osho

We have created a society where we are not accepted as we are, and so we force ourselves to become someone else. We are even able to identify ourselves with anything. Actually, from the beginning we are forced to identify ourselves with a name we didn't choose. And with that our own illusions about ourselves start to grow. **Ego** (the mind) is always in the past or in the future. When it occurs in the present moment, it is dissolved and it disappears. **In the present, it is in fact used exactly as it should be, if we wanted to use it consciously.** It is dissolved in love, creativity, in life-threatening situations, or in the perception of beauty. Otherwise, it is very destructive. Ego provokes fear, and that exists only in connection to the past. Ego is the accumulation of the past - it is the condensed and crystallized mass of your thoughts. If you didn't have all those negative programs in your head which constantly warn you about what could happen, you would not have any reason to be worried. Therefore, the child is not afraid of anything, because these experiences are not yet a part of he/she. They are the parents who are really afraid of what can happen - they are creating fear in you. They can warn you, but anyway, the most important is your personal experience. Also, if you weren't crippled by the feeling of inferiority – a feeling created in you by others, there would be no reason for you to seek constant attention or desire for power. If ego wasn't society, you would have no problem staying happy on your own, regardless of the circumstances, because it is your natural state. If you did not compare yourself with somebody all the time, you would not need to have more and more of anything. If you were allowed to be yourself, you would not feel all those artificial ambitions, but you would do things for fun! Like children do! Without special reasons - unconditionally. A child does not suffer from depression because his/our nature is absolute bliss. Ego in its present form is a problem in all areas. Paradoxically, it is really necessary to go through it, to cross its peak to understand it.

So-called character is the Mount Everest of your ego. You need to dissolve it, slowly. You have to descend from this imaginary peak to re-discover yourself. Everyone goes through that step, and everyone experiences his "peak" in a different period, through a different situation. For some, it is a career or sport, motherhood for some women, or new breasts for others, or maybe a relationship, a new car, etc. Our ego really can create "quasi-perfection" out of anything. But it is also the point in a person's life when it gradually begins to crumble. It is a natural dichotomy of life, and if your life is not based on humility, a fall always comes. As they say – pride goes before a fall – and that's it. Humility, as such, is generally understood by most people as late as on their way "back". You simply repeat the same patterns of behavior and you expect that the outcome will be different... and that is logically impossible. Yes, so simple and yet so difficult...

"People can get into the higher world only if they experience the lower one. You can achieve a higher world, if you have gone through the agony and ecstasy of the lower one. Before the lotus became a lotus, it had to push through the mud – and that mud is our contemporary world."

Osho

Your subconscious knows very well that the everyday facades are not your nature. And then you defend the use of the most accessible ways of escape because you need to escape, particularly from yourself. To turn off the head – ego, the left hemisphere. Simply, and many times in an unhealthy way, you forcefully switch to the right side and do whatever you want to do using the excuse: I was drunk. The right hemisphere is also where we can find our emotional memory, i.e., suppressed feelings. That's why with the help of narcotics everything is released. You can make as many excuses as you want, but it is your real self and it presents only the things which you are fighting inside yourself. Maybe it is sadness, aggression, sovereignty, repressed sexuality - suddenly it all comes out. For example, artists use mainly their right hemispheres (the female principle) and therefore are much more prone to addiction than people whose left hemisphere is normally dominant. And if you cannot face reality with all its consequences, there is one more common way to escape - disease. You can find a lot of people, and they may not even realize it, who are happy with their disease. They have an excuse for not doing something because they are sick, and actually it suits them and they like it. Again, this is mainly a game of ego and attention seeking. Whether it's a doctor's care or attention from the family, your ego finally feels important! If man cannot face reality, then he is not responsible for it. It's the way ego protects itself because it's easier than getting rid of it. Ego is very primitive, like our current existence which is based on it.

"If your strategy is a disease, there is no way you can be cured. And it is likewise with madness, which is a last shelter. If everything fails - cancer, alcohol, marijuana, stroke - madness becomes the last shelter."
Osho

More and more people suffer from mental disorders. Unfortunately, you have to realize that you create them yourself. **If you don't spend at least one hour a day just with yourself – meditating or playing sports – you are fully responsible for your own neuroses.** You would rather go to a psychologist and you enjoy his attention. You can even become addicted to him, because nobody understands you as much as he does. Sadly, many times not even he is able to understand. He recites a number of memorized phrases to give you a feeling of importance. They visit colleagues when they have no idea what to do. It is a professional deformation, as is being a teacher. You are still at work, even if you do not want to be, you cannot help yourself. Psychologists are constantly analyzing something, just as teachers always need to educate someone. They cannot depersonalize, they cannot turn off that program in their heads. How can they possibly help you? They only give you some phrases, procedures, and facts which are based on the experience of others. If everyone is an absolutely original individual how is it possible to have one recipe for everyone?

"Managing the lives of others seems to be easy for you. After all, if your management is wrong, it is not you, but them who is going to get hurt."
L. N. Tolstoy

Psychologists mainly categorize people and assign them to groups according to their problems and, as a universal cure, they often prescribe some drugs. You are relieved that someone has given you the attention you were longing for, and ultimately, the problem in itself will be suppressed by some pills to calm down (the head/mind). Psychoanalysis does not examine the nature of a man and the real cause of the problem from holistic point of view, it only deals with the consequences. If they really wanted to help you, they would help you get to know yourself first. They would have to take into account particularly the past, in a general sense. Psychoanalysis should take into account an understanding of the irrational aspects of life and put it together with existence on a whole new level. Freud was an expert in the human mind, but he could not even help himself – he suffered from frequent depression. So then what is the purpose? Psychoanalysts nowadays are only professional providers of attention. They are absolute supporters of your ego. In particular, they want you to be included in the crowd/system as soon as possible, or on the contrary, to become addicted to them because they need regular clients. It's not a real solution, just a way that can only help if you want it. However, avoid new addiction, which is literally psychological in this case. (With all respect to doctors, because once again there are those who take into account knowledge from other fields and approach clients individually - holistically. But they are still by far the minority.)

"A man creates and educates the world, but
man is educated by the woman."
M. de Cervantes

Moreover, since ancient times, ego has been a bigger problem for men than for women. Women are more emotional, more natural; they are, after all, mothers - creators of life. And here comes the starting point for that never-ending conflict which has been around for ages. Women are closer to bare existence, and that's a fact. Men have always felt that big desire to prove their power. Therefore, various leaders and saints in the past tried to suppress women's natural development – because they were very aware of feminine power. It is obvious why there is a proverb saying that behind every successful man is a woman. In the past, women gave birth to children one after another. How much time did they have left to prove who they really were? Men achieved their status just because no pregnancy could stop them. A woman had to sacrifice her desire to "become somebody". Man doesn't even think about it, he feels that it is natural to become someone. After all, "it has always been so." And at the same time, surprisingly, women are twice as resistant to everything - that is a simple medical fact. Her body was just not adapted to hard work because, genetically, her musculature was never forced to work in that way. Fifty percent more men than women end up in the psychiatric ward, and twice as many men commit suicide. And these guys rule our world?

"A mother tries for 25 years to make her son cleverer, and then another woman comes and in two minutes she can easily make a fool out of him."
Osho

Of course, women also abuse their power (ego). Its source is in attractiveness and manipulation. If they suffer from mental illnesses, there is primarily only one reason – the desire for love and understanding. Nowadays it's not possible to say that women are in harmony too. They have only moved their ego to another level of power. However, this is the better case, because if a woman is loved, she basically has no problems. But for the man this is not enough. For him it is quite the opposite: certainty is more important to him in relationships. He tries to shield his ego from harm, and he may also support it by cheating. He never feels his integrity and there is always a conflict going on inside of him. He listens to his mind/ego more often than do women who would rather act intuitively and emotionally. From childhood, a man is told by society not to show his weaknesses - boys do not cry! That's why most of them become insensitive, self-centered people longing especially for power (of any kind), which would allow them to fill their egos with some kind of love. It is false, and so they always want something more than what they have.

"If men were more satisfied with themselves, they would be much happier with their wives." Voltaire

And if they accidentally fall in love, they usually try to escape because they are afraid of it and do not know what to do about it. They hate that helpless feeling when they don't have things/feelings under control. Because love means death for ego. They cannot coexist together. And in these cases, women are more ready to die than men. They know that this is the only real feeling. They know this instinctively because they are mothers, and even if they are not, this program is still in them. They are able to sacrifice half of their lives to someone else. On the other hand, of course, they should create healthy relationships and not project their egos onto the upbringing of their children and their marriage – here they have problems. This is their "battlefield", their opportunity to use their power (ego). However, it is an especially bad game which has been given the name Family. Even in a family there should be freedom, because freedom is the foundation of love. Nobody belongs to you - neither your child, nor your spouse. Nobody. **Love is the most beautiful opportunity to get rid of the ego.**

"The way of the heart is beautiful, but dangerous. The way of the senses is ordinary, but safe. The man has chosen the safest shortcut through life. The woman has chosen the most beautiful, but the most mountainous and dangerous path of emotions, sentiments and moods. And because up to now the world has been ruled by men, women have suffered immensely. They have not been able to fit into the society that man has created because it is created according to reason and logic. The woman wants the world of the heart but in a man's world there is no place for the heart. Man has to learn to be heartier, because the mind is leading all of humanity towards a global suicide." Osho

Nowadays, however, souls have become so twisted and unbalanced that somehow women become men and men become women. This is especially due to the lifelong suppression of our nature. Just as a woman wants to develop in a creative way, a man feels the need to express emotions. Female ego started to get sick of the stereotype that women belong in the kitchen, and the male ego does not want to fight every day for power when there are so many simple pleasures and such beauty in the world.

"If a woman wants to rule, she must pretend
to be doing what a man wants."
H. de Balzac

If a man exchanged places with his wife for twenty-four hours, he would see that in fact she has to bear all the responsibility, and it suits him. If the woman exchanged places with her husband for a day, she would find out how "tiring" that urgent need is to impress someone all the time, to prove his authority while still carrying in his head: I have to provide for my family. Then the woman is automatically the bad one - ever-caring and responsible; and when the man "shuts himself down", then he is really shut down and she can go insane doing everything alone. A man does not use both of his hemispheres at the same time - it's a fact (although obviously, medically speaking both are working all the time). He uses the left one - rational/work/facts - or the right one - when he is acting crazy, when he is "playing" with friends and goofing around. Work or play – nothing in between. A woman cannot understand it because she knows how to do ten things at once and he can do only one. Yes, please accept it - it's a fact. It's exactly the same as when a woman can't decide which side is left or right when she is at an intersection because she uses both hemispheres simultaneously. This is, of course, in many cases an advantage, but in some specific situations (e.g., when they need to make a quick decision) it can be a disadvantage. If we respect each other, there might not be so many conflicts in which the two different egos are fighting, trying to achieve the same goal - themselves. But we have to get to know ourselves first, and mainly start with ourselves. That's also the only way to understand others.

Each of us have male and female principles in us, one pole being more dominant than the other one. Thus, for example there are women with male nature and men who have female nature. But there are men with male nature (their actions being purely rational) whose challenge is to discover the feminine equivalent of the energy in themselves, i.e., to understand the world of emotions. And there are women who should become more grounded, that is, they should act more logically and rationally. In a sense, it is an analogy of the above mentioned hemispheres. If a male begins to discover the "female world" in himself (the principle of the right hemisphere, irrational sphere, intuition, emotions), he will understand that it is much more difficult than he ever thought. For females it will not be any easier when they learn how not to let their emotions overwhelm them. They should begin to train their left hemispheres – logic. And if we can link these two worlds in ourselves, we are on a direct path to the unity. In practice, this can be understood by using their relationship as an example - if you are a woman with a man's character, automatically attracting men who are more feminine (and vice versa). We attract just what we are missing. Even though we actually want the opposite, it does not happen. Everything has its deeper meaning.

The goal of unification on this planet means primarily unification in ourselves. This is currently the greatest challenge for both genders. Males should discover full-fledged males in themselves, and females should find real women in themselves, with all the qualities that our beings offer. In any case, this requires that we equalize the worlds within us. It will not happen overnight, it is a journey – a process. But as soon as after this step, we will begin to act like fully-fledged human beings with all the qualities that are contained in our potential.

Today, ego is mentioned almost everywhere without actually being understood. I'll make it simpler: **the ego represents all behavioral patterns that are not your own. This means any characteristics that cause you problems most of the time and which mainly cause unwanted emotional responses are things that you have to work on. You should begin to gradually consciously remove the pattern of behavior or, on the contrary, if you realize that you are comfortable with it, learn to love this characteristic accepting it as your own in this way.** Since childhood you have accumulated incredibly many characteristics of this sort. When you gradually begin to remove them, you are dissolving your imaginary ego. Until the day comes when you realize that you are "empty", like a Buddha. Empty only in terms of the characteristics that were not beneficial for you, because then you will act purely as yourself – joyful, natural, playful, loving, free - as children, but on the conscious level, i.e., being aware of all the experiences that were provided to you by your life path. In any case, you will neither suffer thereby anymore, nor will anything have personal impact on you. But this means neither stopping in a kind of a delirium, nor losing your emotions – you will just "use them consciously". Joy naturally sometimes alternates with sadness/melancholy, but if you're aware of what it causes with maximum sincerity towards yourself, it will be neither good nor bad for you anymore. You can enjoy even your sadness. After all, it is the language of the soul. Just do not fall into depression, because that's a matter for the head/ego. The more you devote yourself to that effect, the more you will expand your awareness, enhance your natural intelligence, and improve your intuition. It will awaken compassion for others in you, as well as empathy, the understanding of many spheres, and a hunger for a new kind of information.

"With your anger, greed and sex you have to fight, because you are weak. Indeed, anger, greed and sex are not the problems, the problem is weakness. Once you strengthen your inside, as soon as you get a sense of inner presence – a sense that you, your energy is concentrated, crystallized in a single point, the true self will be born. Remember that I was born, and not ego. Ego is a false sense of self. Without ever having any 'I', you believe that you have it - that's ego."

Osho

Realize it or not, most different (motivational) courses in recent years have been focused mainly on increasing self-confidence. Already when we are children our parents either try to teach us how to be confident or they try to ruin our self-esteem because they suffer from insecurity themselves. And so we grow up to become completely shambolic figures who suffer under any criticism from the others;

or we become people with unrealistic ideas about ourselves, ideas which were planted in us by our parents or society. In any case, it is again only a game of ego, the false ideas about ourselves that adapt to anything but ourselves. Therefore, you should not seek or support your self-confidence, but **self-awareness** (although everyone needs to go through its "highest peak"). There's a huge difference. Self-confidence gives power, but only an illusory one. **High self-esteem (a so-called ego trip) is built on very fragile foundations and is always dependent on other people's opinions. Self-awareness, however, provides true inner power which is not dependent on other people, so it's something no one can take away or destroy.** While in the first example, any social failure or awkward accident can be an essential problem. Or alternatively, you believe in your ego so much that you do not accept anyone else and you live in an illusion of their complete perfection - and this is real separateness. Then, most likely, a shocking situation (injury, illness) will come to "wake you up".

So in short – **addressing yourself on the conscious level is the most important now. In practice, this means that using the "mirror" procedure (or various therapies) you will begin to observe and gradually remove programs inserted by your parents, teachers, friends, et al. with which you had been identified during your life. In addition to this, try to be aware whether the masculine or feminine principle prevails in your life and try to start working to settle the energies. Basically, by simply deciding to undergo this course, you will begin to attract people who will automatically "test" you through their nature. Don't address them – they are your teachers. Address yourself. Remove one characteristic and you will remove that kind of person from your life. You will stop cycling in the same problems, yet you'll receive further challenges to overcome, to rise on the imaginary ladder of self-respect/love. This is currently the direct path to "enlightenment". Just you should decide.** After succeeding, you will fit into the absolute flow of synchronicity where you will not have to make an effort to make things happen in your favor, and at the same time, everything will have perfect timing. The joyful perfection of being is now fully accessible to all, notwithstanding the reality that we are taking for real now.

"Know thyself."
Socrates

If I say that the ego is not you, it is especially true in this context. However, if you start using excuses like: *"It was not me, it was my ego"*, then I will ask you: *"And who is your ego?"*. In this case it is you, but it is not a natural part of you. To learn to see the difference, you need to learn to depersonalize from yourself and take real responsibility for your actions. You can try to find excuses and those who will tell you what you want to hear. You can postpone it, no one will prevent you from doing so, but in the end, it will be only you who shall bear the consequences of momentary pleasure. **Ego will never go away completely, the same as the mind. We must learn to consciously use them to our advantage.**

"Apologizing does not always mean that you were wrong and the other person was right. It just means that you value your relationship more than your ego!"
Anonymous

First, try to look honestly at your life, step by step. If you can be really honest with yourself, you will realize the absurdity of the situations you got into in the past and that they were created by you. Or you will realize what kind of things you have tolerated and how it felt good for a while, how you got into variety of unexpected situations, relationships, work, be honest and then you will have no courage to judge others. Look at yourself - critically. Always start with yourself. Meditation techniques can teach you to keep that distance. You just want to be yourself again, but society will never support you. It needs ego because it is ego. It will not fight for its own murder! It's supremely dangerous for ego because if you go back to your nature, you will never let yourself be led like a lamb. But do not be mistaken - self-love does not mean narcissism. Loss of ego "hurts". It is a ferocious fight, but it is just an illusion which you identified with. When it disappears, you begin to perceive who you really are; you will feel true joy! Awareness of yourself actually causes nirvana.

The word Nirvana is not as strongly positive as it seems to be. Literally, in translation, it means – to blow out the candle. The term for this state was chosen by Buddha. He could have picked any other word, because in India there are really lots of them, but he chose this one. He purposely did not choose a positive expression because he knew people and he knew that a positive word would only support their human egos. A negative word doesn't have such power, it cannot get dirty. Buddha said that the so-called "I" is merely a flame maintained by our desires. Once all desires disappear, the candle also disappears and the flame is blown out.

"All the words that awaken desire in you do not help you, because desire is the main cause of your suffering. Longing for something raises tension in you. Nirvana will get rid of tension; there is nothing more to desire. On the other hand, be ready to be dissolved. Once you are dissolved, ego will disappear and the world will remain unpolluted."
Buddha

"Enlightenment" is nothing other than the psychological suicide of your social ego. You cannot force yourself to do it and you cannot even try too hard to achieve it. If you follow the way of self-recognition, it just happens and you suddenly feel tremendous bliss – coming from nowhere, without particular cause. It's not a short trip because you have been sleeping for so long, but if you decide to walk this way, all the doors to a higher truth will start opening. Your heart knows very well what to believe in and what not to believe in. You just have to pay attention and beware of the very sophisticated games that your ego likes to play if you decide to go this way. The game is called "spirituality" and it can be very dangerous for you and for your surroundings as well. Nowadays, many spiritual posers walk this world. It's just a new game of social ego. It found out how to be even more interesting. It exploits knowledge which it can't put into practice, but the speaker's talent makes it seem glamorous. There is a big demand for these goods. There are opportunities to earn money and to get people's full attention. Be careful - pay attention to the spiritual posers and to yourself as well. It's very thin ice which you can dance pirouettes on or fall through. Everything is up to you. A true teacher never comes to you; you have to look for him, to finally understand that he was with you all that time - hidden inside.

> *"The mind is logical. Life is dialectical. You create something and life tells you: Destroy it! You are born and life says: Die! You achieve something and it responds: Get rid of it! You become the peak, the Mount Everest of your ego, and then you transform it into an ego-less abyss. Then you will know both - the illusory and the real, maya and brahma."* Osho

It is our nature to be joyful, do not forget that. Everything else is just a game of ego. Forget what other people think about you. Dance! Laugh! Play, be creative and get back your innocence! Use ego only to fulfill your basic needs. Live in the moment! What is your problem now? Nothing! There will come situations you will have to deal with, maybe they have already come, but they are not here and now. You're only in this moment, for now. Do not let anything draw you in again. Become the only master of yourself, but with full responsibility for your commitments. That's the paradox. Nobody knows you and will not even know who you in fact are. And it is just because you are constantly hiding behind something.

Come out! Awaken your true self because your soul roars with gladness when it is focused. Do not be afraid of it – fear is also just a game of ego. It does not exist. It's up to you how far it is released. Immediately switch to another program - like on TV. Do you want to watch your own program called fear? Switch! Immediately employ your mind with something else, preferably new and unexpected. Feel the present in its entirety. Find your center of being and no longer will you be manipulated by anyone or anything. If you blow out that unquenchable flame of your ego, that does not mean that you will suddenly become very humble or simple. A person who reaches this state is neither modest nor arrogant, he is simply truly himself… in all that beauty which he has been carrying with him the whole time.

"Remember that there are two kinds of selfish goals: material and spiritual. Some people want money and power. Some people are looking for God, nirvana or enlightenment - in any case, all are searching for something. And who is searching? Their egos. Once you stop looking for something, you will get rid of your ego. Once this searching is finished, the seeker will no longer exist."

Osho

MIND

"The intuitive mind is a sacred gift and the rational mind is a faithful servant. We have created a society that honors the servant and has forgotten the gift."
A.Einstein

Apart from the previous information, the most important thing today is to understand how the mind actually works. Despite the fact that almost everyone seeks freedom in some way, people are completely unaware of how much they are actually slaves to their own heads – their minds. Only when we are freed from all those programs and beliefs that create our bonds, only then can we can talk about freedom. The mind is the greatest gift we have received, but we need to learn how to use it.

The mind is just a tool. It will think only what we allow it to think. Everything is only as important as we make it.

Start "working hard" and learn how to use your mind so that it obeys you rather than you obeying your mind. That's the whole secret.

If you can control your mind, you're on your way to the state of no mind. That doesn't mean that the mind will disappear. It will be still there, but it will be still. And if the mind can become quiet, new possibilities are revealed, which will open a new channel full of creativity, because that is the essence of existence - creativity. In the beginning, you have to strive for silence, but then it starts to become more and more natural. This state is meditation - silence - where there is no longer anything but your true being, i.e., the true and boundless love. It sounds so easy just like an advertising slogan or a "teaser to man". And you immediately start thinking: "…but after all, who else can control my mind if not me?"

"A regular person has 12-16,000 thoughts a day. Of these, 80% are negative and 95% are identical to what you had yesterday." National Science Foundation

So how often are you really "quiet"?

Doesn't that voice that always says something really bother you? That eternal turmoil which, paradoxically, always whispers the same thing. Because the mind is not creative - the mind is mechanical. It is your ego and not your essence, rather it is a social program which has been inserted into you. It is an illusion which you can easily believe in, and right now the whole world is built on it because each of us is influenced by our education, school, and environment. All of this is something that is not naturally a part of you. So far, few have decided to consciously remove these deposits from their pasts. On the contrary, we have excuses for everything - it's easier.

"Nothing is either good or bad, only thinking makes it so."
W. Shakespeare

How can we then "dominate" our own minds? Every day we encounter a huge number of sensations, and therefore, the mind many times finds itself where it shouldn't be. We are continually confronted with different facts and points of view, whether we like it or not. Unfortunately, they are mostly negative. But please note that

the more negative thinking there is, the more negative events will become reality.

We create our own reality. We do it with our thoughts. It sounds a bit strange, but it's true. The universe is actually a huge photocopier. All that we send into the universe tends to become real. If you do not master your mind, you cannot focus your thoughts on only one thing. (Many ideas – nonsense – goes through your head daily. Do not be surprised what comes out of the copier.) So therefore**, the most important thing you can do for yourself is to learn how to consciously stop and manage your mind.** Unfortunately, there is one small problem – our ego that is not interested in voluntarily "disappearing". It struggles with the idea that it should get rid of what is most valuable – our mind, because without it, it simply cannot exist as is customary. The mind is exactly the learned programs and repeated knowledge which help him amaze society. Neither your compassion nor your love can amaze society – just the opposite. Your ego needs to control everything. Otherwise, your ego with the help of the mind quickly finds a story in its memory which covers the first one, to eliminate the idea that there could be something ego is not capable of. Egotists do not know the phrase "I don't know." The more egotistical you are, the longer it will take you to admit to a change in consciousness – your thinking.

Nowadays, we all find ourselves in a period in which time is accelerated (ceases to exist in the same sense as before). Everything vibrates at much higher principles and the force is unstoppable. The same happens with our thoughts, which are beginning to materialize much faster. All the "smart books" are merely about a way of thinking. Do you want money? Then you should imagine yourself living in abundance! Do you want love? Then surround yourself with love of any kind in any form! Do you want to be healthy? Then first and foremost you should heal the mind.

Every thought carries energy. And the emotion that accompanies this thought supports it the most strongly. That`s why, for example, you feel very bad if someone attacks you. Their negative energy is transferred to you, and if you cannot defend yourself, you will absorb all of it. It's just a game of energies. The exchange of energy. It has always been so, whether you realize it or not.

!Thought = Energy!

Write it down, please, anywhere - now! Because just a few minutes after reading this text you will return to your old way of thinking. Remember that anything you think about has a tendency to become real. Because there is a lot of truth in the saying: Be careful what you wish for, it may soon come true.

> *"Intelligence is never born from the mind. Intelligence only comes when the mind is thrown away. When you throw away the mind, there comes intelligence. The mind sits on the source of intelligence as a rock. The mind is always stupid and unintelligent. Breaking away from the mind means to be intelligent. Intelligence is not a feature of the mind."*
>
> Osho

We always judge things using our rational minds. You look at something and your mind instantly starts to talk. It's the principle of the computer. We enter a word into Google and we immediately get thousands of relevant links that someone has already put there. That's the way the mind works. We look at something and in that moment we are attacked by hundreds of unnecessary associations based on the past.

In today's "modern" society, alcohol, drugs, and licentious sex are commonly used to turn the head off. All these external resources have a common goal - to get rid of that incessant voice in your head for a while and to perceive presence like never before. Yes, they are quick ways to get good feelings, to perceive the imperceptible, to let your naturalness loose and enjoy the present in all its glory! It is all possible this way, and therefore there are so many people addicted to these "drugs". But it is destructive. It does not come from the inside but from the outside. We have only changed the boss. It is not the head but a kind of "drug" that gets us where we feel more natural, where we are confronted with glimpses of ourselves. That is also why we go on vacation, because we want to "turn off". Again, however, it is caused by something that comes from the outside. We, however, need to trigger this "holiday" from the inside. That is the "magic" that no one can ever take from you.

The mind is just a biocomputer. It works well with all its functions, but it does not have consciousness. It's a robot programmed with memories and knowledge - facts. Do you want to be led by a machine in which there is not and even cannot be anything original? The mind just constantly repeats things. Notice it and realize it. Whenever your mind starts to speak, it takes you to the tracks of the established. Try to do something different and it will lose its power over you. You will reach awareness/presence this way, since that is the only real "meditation".

Every day do something new! Surprise your mind and it will lose dominance over you.

Our main goal is to learn to consciously turn off our minds. All our lives we have been learning how to use them, but no one has ever told us how to stop. Our minds work even when we sleep. They never rest, and because we have the feeling that the mind is us, it will easily dominate us without our being aware of it. If we can turn off the mind (thoughts) and use it only when appropriate, it will obtain tremendous power.

"Lots of research has been done lately. Your mind does not allow 98 percent of messages that come to you to enter - 98 percent! Only 2 percent can enter, and those two percent are interpreted by the mind. I tell you something; you hear something else. I will say something else and you interpret it so as not to disrupt your sleep. The mind immediately provides you with an explanation."
Osho

Get rid of society. I do not mean that you necessarily have to go somewhere in the mountains. You will only find the silence of the mountains, but you yourself will not be silent. Get rid of the society inside you. You have inside yourself an incredible number of programs (behavioral patterns) that are not yours at all, but you identify yourself with them. We constantly identify with something, comparing, judging, so there is a completely fragmented personality inside of us. Meditation techniques can be used to discover these "programs", bring understanding, allow them to be enlightened, and then they can disappear. So you can easily get rid of everything that you do not need for your further development. If you throw away all that is not truly part of you, you will remain "empty", but for the first time you will meet your true self.

"Watching the mind means to look at it with deep love, with deep respect, reverence - the mind is a gift of God. There is nothing wrong with thinking; it's a wonderful process, like any other. Do not be a fighter, be a lover."
Osho

Because, if you cannot eat quietly, sit quietly, or walk quietly, everything is just your learned reaction, not a conscious act. Therefore, you cannot react calmly. That`s why you feel affected by everything. You are easily offended and sensitive to everything. For example, if someone knows you well, he knows exactly how to push that "button" which provokes the reaction he wants to get. And all this is just because you are not anchored.

You are like a ship at sea which doesn't have a port. The waves throw you about as they please, carry you from one side to the other. You think that you are able to control this boat, but the truth is that you are tossed by even the slightest (emotional) breeze. Because you do not know where your port is, you do not have a place to relax. You just sail and sail and it makes you more and more tired and weary. Sometimes you even feel like it's not you at the helm. You blame the wind or bad weather, water quality, birds… everything and everyone because you cannot see that you are alone in this boat. You need company, so you identify yourself with everything you have ever seen. But the others are simply not in your boat. You just imagine that they are part of your boat, but it's your ego that takes each new initiative and identifies with it. Suddenly you will begin to feel that it is actually you or at least part of you! Suddenly you start to feel it, you can even see it, that the reason why you crashed was that stupid wave that took you away, or that it was caused by that bird that tore the sail, or by the rock at the bottom of the ocean… anything except you! But in fact, it was you who crashed… but you were too tired to notice because you were asleep… After all, you hadn't taken a rest for how many years?

"Man is not known by his ideas, but by his deeds."
J. W. Goethe

When someone tries to offend you, you need to become a receiver; you must first accept what is being said. That is the only way you can change the subconscious reaction to a conscious act. But first, you need to stop fighting everything and you need to become "silent and open". If you do not accept this fact, you will always stagger in a vicious circle of conflict mode.

"If you throw a red-hot torch into the water, it will continue to burn until it touches the surface. The moment it falls into the river, the fire is gone - it is extinguished by the river. I become a river. When you try to insult me - it burns when it's thrown, but the moment it touches me, it is dissolved by my calmness. You can throw thorns at me – but they will become flowers in my silence. My actions come from my true nature."
Buddha

Buddha also described this in one story. He sent his disciple to the lake for water. Before he arrived at the lake, a carriage crossed the water and it was all stirred up. The more he tried to calm the surface and draw clean water, the murkier the water became. So he returned to the Buddha without water explaining it was dirty. But Buddha sent him for water again. The disciple didn't understand but he obeyed. When he returned to the lake, it was clear again. Everything that was stirred and swirling before was now calm and stabilized and he could safely draw clean water. What follows from the lesson is that we can do nothing with turbid water; we just have to wait until it calms down. Watch it, take a step back, and wait for a while... This is the principle on which our minds work too. If you step back, calm down, and just observe, it will happen by itself. It's not going to help if you stir up the water (add more thoughts). It will just complicate the whole situation. To achieve genuine consciousness, you have to be quiet and peaceful. You're not the mind; all of this confusion is happening outside you. You just believed it for a while.

"If someone corrects you, and you feel offended then you have an ego problem."
M.McConaughey

Ideas are also co-creators of emotions. It is mostly not situations that make you crazy, but your thoughts regarding situations. Since you cannot stop the flow, you take it to your dreams where your mind finishes the dream with its (paranoid) version – and in the morning you wake up in a bad mood and exhausted. Therefore, it is very important to understand your emotions. **This is the main mission of every human being – to become free on an emotional level.** As soon as you see that your mood is starting to get worse, ask yourself what caused it. **We now ignore emotions in favor of any action.** Stop for a while. What was the actual trigger? Do not be afraid to go deep into the past – whether it's a few hours, or even years. Be honest with yourself and try to remember a similar situation because it is always something that repeats. The reason - the trigger - is certainly there. And if you identify it, then you can say goodbye to it - but it is only up to you and your behavior. Do not repeat patterns of behavior if you do not like them (emotionally exhaust you).

There is a very subtle, yet very important difference between feelings and emotions. Emotions always have something dramatic in them, very intense and essentially theatrical. Although they often take you over, they come from the outside – they are not a natural part of you. Therefore, they throw you off your center of being (your absolutely natural state of being) that you have to get back to in order to get anchored. Nevertheless, they are very valuable and are the best way to get to know yourself. In comparison with emotions, feelings come from our center; they are part of our deepest intuitions. **Feelings bring the highest kind of understanding that goes beyond the emotions and the mind.** This can be seen as a sort of internal leadership (consciousness), the source of which you have no idea about. Then comes the mind to rationalize it all, and it will try to convince you of the contrary from the perspective of the ego (social conventions). Never give supremacy to the mind, if you feel otherwise. Feelings are indeed the language of our soul. On the other hand, misunderstood emotions only tend to hurt, especially you. If you do not believe that you have a "higher self", just take an interest in your feelings (but do not confuse them with emotions). And this is probably the only thing we should actually teach children.

Nevertheless, it is not possible – until you can control yourself, it is difficult to teach it to others. Because if children are allowed to have too much emotional freedom, they start to realize exactly which emotional explosions they can use to manipulate you and they may turn into little tyrants.

"Feel the feeling but don't become the emotion.
Witness it. Allow it. Release it." C.Andrus

Part of spiritual growth is that you do not suppress anything, but you bear full responsibility for everything. To become whole and free on an emotional level is one of the most important aims that we have to achieve. (And if we succeed, we will come back to the emotions again, but on a conscious level - otherwise life would be quite boring.)

Become an observer of yourself.

If you meet someone who is not in a good mood or is angry, or when it happens to you, try to depersonalize yourself in that moment. Watch yourself. Whenever we meet an angry person, we begin to feel uncomfortable. Angry people have a tendency to get rid of this energy because they don't feel comfortable/natural. (To experience primarily pleasure is natural for human nature.) So there are two possibilities:

1. He will tell you why he is so angry, which will make you feel bad too because you will start to experience and share in his story / you will absorb part of his energy.

2. If he is angry with you, he will start to scream at you.

But in both cases, he will feel relief and you will feel uncomfortable. Or it is the other way around. Your situation (your anger) will be passed on to someone else. And then they pass it to someone else… and so it goes, on and on.

"What hurts you so much that you feel that you need to hurt others in order to be healed?"
N.D. Walsch (Conversations with God)

Each attack is ultimately just a call for help.

The best thing you can do is to learn to consciously observe yourself. Depersonalize yourself from your mind. Become an observer of the situation, despite the fact that it involves you. Use your mind as a tool – as a computer. Make your own analysis, but start with yourself. Everything is just your mirror, even if it is difficult to believe it. However, if you feel angry for any reason, I am not saying that you should suppress that emotion. Express it freely, but do not try to get other people involved. Go somewhere and shout your fill, punch the pillows, do some sport etc., you can release your emotions in many different ways. Just do not pass them on to other people. Passing on your emotions is the simplest but at the same time the most selfish solution.

"An idiot is a man who lives in a private world. An idiot has his private idiom. He has his own ways. Always goes his own way. He does not follow anything universal, existential. Only promotes his own ideas. The mind is an idiot… no matter how smart. An idiot can be very smart, can become a great expert, can accumulate vast knowledge, can have many special degrees and diplomas, etc., but always remains an idiot. And the more his mind knows, the more dangerous he is. The highest reality exists outside of the realm of the mind."
Osho

It is necessary to express our feelings rather than stifle them – otherwise, they will always turn against us and come out at the worst possible moment. In our society we are used to the exact opposite. From childhood we are told that we should not cry or scream, we should behave "normally". We are brought up in a society that is constantly deceived, and therefore makes us hide our real feelings, afraid of being hurt by others. We are afraid to be ourselves, and that`s why we continually adapt to some established conventions. We wear an impressive number of masks - at home, at work, with friends, in the shop, and we drive our minds crazy. Actually, they are already crazy. Daily, the infinite number of mental illnesses is increasing. Health care is divided into Western and Eastern medicine, too. Both worlds are needed. However, we should find harmony, indeed, in everything. Western medicine deals with the consequences and brings a solution based on principles from the outside. Eastern medicine goes inside, heals the real causes of the situation. Because as it is often said: Everything is in your mind. Yes, it is.

Idea - thought - emotion – word – energy - reality.

Each disease has its origin in the head. Everything is energy. Just try to write down everything you think about during one day, and think about what you absorb from others, from television, and from the newspaper, etc. How many thoughts have their origin in love or in humor? In nature, everything has its importance and diseases have their importance too. Every psychological problem - negative thinking, unresolved problems, negative behavior, negative attitudes, etc. - is also reflected in the physical world. We are souls whose home on planet Earth is the body. When the universe wants to tell us that we have strayed from our way, that this pattern of behavior is not correct, it sends a signal. Illness, injury, an unpleasant experience, a meeting… it's always just a reflection of our thinking, or karma, but this is an exceptional case. It could be a complicated and fatal disease, and in this case the real cause remains unknown.

Nevertheless, it can easily be detected by regression or by similar kinds of practices. Man is highly creative and invented chemistry - medicine that destroys viruses without having to find the real nature of the problem. Therefore, we have more and more new viruses and recent mutations of various diseases. Nature cannot fight chemistry. We are deceiving nature, but we don't realize that we are just lying to ourselves, in everything. However, I am not condemning "chemistry" at all, because in some cases it is more than necessary. But keep in mind that this should be the last resort to ensure your health. We are natural beings, whether we like it or not. Therefore, the truth is that for every disease we can find the right medicine in nature. The Western world feels the absence of alternative medicine. As a result, the demand for alternative medicine is more intense than it was in the past. Just as sophisticated Western medicine is gradually penetrating the East. (I recommend the book *Health of God's Pharmacy by* Maria Treben.)

"Analysis is a way of thinking; embrace is a manifestation of heart. The mind is a manifestation of all diseases and the heart is the source of healing."
Osho

Our only real possessions in the world are our thoughts and our bodies. Deeds are our speech.

Long story short: If you are angry and you constantly suppress it – it damages you, because suppressed negative emotions cause disease. If you scold the person who caused them, you will relieve yourself. So you throw the boiling energy to someone else (selfish, easiest solution). But note that if you are really angry, you are guilty as well, whether you want to be or not. If you feel that it is not your fault, you have no reason to get angry at all. Or you can still talk about it to everyone who will listen so that you pass that energy on to several more people. Try to stop it. **Take five deep breaths. Try to get**

your being into neutral. And then just use the mind as a tool. If it was caused by human stupidity (that is most often the case) how will it help you if you let yourself be flooded by negative thoughts? Suffering and being miserable because of something out of your control doesn't really make sense. The best thing you can do is to let it go, although that is also a bit of an art form… It involves personal power and self-awareness – how relevant is the situation to me and how can I REALLY affect it? Finally, you will find that everything will actually resolve itself without you. However, if you have to do something about it, try to act like a reasonable person. You will make things much easier, not only for others, but especially for yourself. Problematic situations and meetings repeat themselves just because you repeat the same patterns of behavior which you should get rid of – otherwise, it would not make you angry. Fortunately, nature/ existence has its strict rules and everything always comes back to us. Every negative action, thought, and emotion. So once again we return to the fact that the best way to deal with such energy is to "switch off" our heads, at least for a while.

Do not try to "control" yourself. It comes from the mind, from experience, from the past. If you control yourself, you calculate and therefore you cannot be natural. Let's take a child as an example. He does not calculate; he only exists in his innocence. Everything else is learned from others. It does not come from him. We should not teach our children, but we should be taught by them. That's the innocence from which we come and to which we return (but on a conscious level). Everything else was invented by us - everything. Watch yourself at all times - and be aware. Try to be constantly in the present moment and realize yourself in every situation. Are you walking? Be aware of every step; be aware of the present, of all that is happening at the moment around you. But do not stay there. Be like a river which flows continuously, adapts to every stone, every cleft, but is still aware of its power. Thanks to its nature and simplicity, a river can do everything just by flowing. It does not want anything from anyone, a river just IS. Water is able to save your life as well as it can kill you. If water had ego, we would not survive one single day on Earth.

> *"At all times, we always oppose ourselves. Our actions are going in one direction, thinking in another and feelings are somewhere else as well. We fall apart; we are becoming more and more fragmented. And that is suffering – the loss of integrity, the loss of unity."*
> Osho

If you asked a murderer if he remembers all the details of his deed, he would say no. Because if he had acted with his full consciousness, he would not have done something like that. All of them say that in that moment they weren't there, that in the critical moment they were somehow not present – as if they were dominated by something. They were dominated by the frenzy within themselves which was nothing other than their accumulated past. It was not the present moment which caused such a reaction. Maybe you think that it was, but if it were not for the past, on what basis would this madness occur? If you do not have a program from your past in yourself, you respond innocently, consciously, purely, you are in the present. In the present moment you cannot become a mad person. Once a mad person realizes he is mad, it is the first step towards a pure consciousness. This is the path that leads out – to total self-awareness. But you are constantly comparing something with something; you are suffering from the past and you are still worried about the future. It is your fear that is controlling you. But your fear is based on the past. This means that you have learned nothing from the past, you only create panic. Alertness and consciousness exist in the present. Be aware of yourself at all times. If you are awake and aware, you will not do stupid things - quite the contrary. For the first time in your life you will accept complete responsibility for yourself.

"The entire Eastern methodology can be reduced to a single word: observation. The whole Western methodology can be reduced to one thing: analysis. If you analyze, you walk in circles. If you observe, you have stepped out of the circle."
Osho

Observation is a technique which gets you into the center of being. It teaches you to center your being inside of you. Ego is outside, you need to go inside - that is where your source of endless energy potential is, which you unfortunately do not know at all. If you find your center, you will find the correct distance. Everything that happens, will remain on the edge, it will not touch you inside. Someone can insult you, but you will not be personally affected by it. If you're really in the middle of full consciousness, you realize that it's not your problem as much as it is the problem of the other person who wants to manipulate you. Because if you act in total awareness of yourself, you will act based on your real inner feelings, there will be nothing more to throw you off. Act with full consciousness, always be totally present. If you do everything one hundred percent, you cannot fail. That kind of deed has its beauty and moves from moment to moment. It does not carry the past and does not take the future into account. It is here and now.

"The past is only a dream and tomorrow is only a vision. But the well-lived today changes yesterday into a beautiful dream and tomorrow into a vision full of hope."
D. Carnegie

But it is a big deal for your head to accept it. It still has doubts about some things. Actually, about everything. Indeed, only the present moment exists. If you start to understand this truth, a huge burden will fall off your shoulders. Because all problems exist only in the past or in the future. Only your head makes them alive. Everything is just a situation that needs to be solved. The mind calls it "a problem". And you are taking this problem with you wherever you go - to your home, to work, to friends - everywhere. You cannot just enjoy the magic of the present moment; you still need something to worry about. But that's not you – it is your mind.

> *"The primary cause of unhappiness is never the situation but your thoughts about it."* E. Tolle

In any case, before mastering this art at least a bit, positive thinking is very important. "Positive thinking" is being heard of more and more often these days, but it is still in its infancy. It's like an advertising slogan which roars at you from all sides, and therefore, you will not even think about it, quite the contrary – it bothers you. It is important to remember that so-called "positive thinking" does not mean that you have to put on rose-colored glasses, be terribly good, and tell everyone you love them. It also does not mean that you will always be in an amazingly positive mood. It means that if you think about anything, you should view it in a positive light. Speak positively – do not complain, do not judge or gossip! Simply, just avoid negative programming, skepticism, pessimism, etc., all the things people call "realism" nowadays. If you remove these subconscious programs, you will not have to worry about positive thinking, as it will come naturally, without any effort. If you act "consciously", i.e., you start observing yourself, you will see your negative thoughts very plainly. Then it depends on your intelligence, whether you want to go ahead and give these ideas more attention and energy (which will cause emotional distress), or you will simply see yourself and stop that. And even if something does not work out according to your expectations, believe me, it had its purpose, which will be certainly made clear to you over time. Do not give up right away when something does not work on the first or even the second attempt (even if you thought only positively about it). If you act based on your real feelings and do not condemn yourself, all that is happening is just what you want to achieve in the bigger picture, even if at that point you may not see it at all. Learn to see synchronicity (coincidences in events that are apparently unrelated, but have perfect timing and reason) in the little things that are going on thanks to such an approach.

And if, for some reason, you are sad, do not confuse it with depression. When you are depressed, your head is caught up in negative thinking, even, in a way, indulging in it. It's much easier to be depressed than to learn how to control your head. Otherwise, sorrow is natural; it is a perception of a situation. Just because you're sad, it does not have to mean that you are caught up in negative thoughts. Sadness has its own charm, and it is natural that sometimes it is substituted for ecstatic states, which should be our nature. Learn to enjoy your moments of melancholy; they are just the ones that move us further. **Natural sadness takes place in silence – depression is "talkative"**. In silence you will find the answers you are looking for. Do not fall from sadness into depression. Even in sorrow, you can think positively. It is exactly the period when you can balance life, relationships, and situations - learn from them. But do not succumb to fear. All negative thoughts are only materialized unspoken emotions.

Once you "have to" think - think positively and reasonably - do not make drama.

Is it possible? In this day and age? Just go and watch the news on TV! With all the things going on! How can I think positively in this world? We witness so many tragedies every day! But how much does it affect you personally? If you feel that this somehow matters to you, do something with it! Or do not deal with it – let it go.

Homework: How many positive items of news are on TV News?

The answer is simple and clear - only those cute animals at the end. The stupidity of media is another topic (although it is already approaching the critical level), but your subconscious mind is suffering because of it. You, completely "unconsciously", receive incredible amounts of negative energy. Of course, I don't expect all people to sabotage television and newspaper now (although that would be nice), but at least do not take it so seriously. Don't give it your energy - listen to it, or watch it, but learn to forget it, delete it, clear all the unnecessary information out of your mind. And most importantly: do not spread panic! That is even worse, because the fear and panic that you absorbed is passed on to someone else, although you feel relieved. As we have already mentioned, you are just passing energy on, in this case anger or fear, to another person. Do you really have nothing else to do?!

How often do you wish someone something good just like that, from pure love, without expecting anything in return? Yes, there are a few holidays and occasions when people often wish others "all the best". But what do you actually want for the other? All the best of what? What is "all the best" to me? We need health, love, and abundance, or there are some specific wishes if you know the person personally. You have the power to wish others something more meaningful than the empty phrase, because if you mean it sincerely and honestly, you should know that you are really doing a lot for the other person. We have already learned how to wish others something (unconditionally?), more or less. But how often do you wish yourself something and for yourself? Every day you wish the people you meet a "good morning" or "good afternoon". How often do you wish yourself a "beautiful morning"? Just like that, in the mirror. Let's begin with you first. Think about yourself with love. Let's wish only the best for you! And let's start right now! A busy day might be ahead of you, or you may have had a difficult night. That is something you probably can't change. But the thing you can change is your attitude towards these situations. Change your present moment. Because it is the only thing which is real. And it is made by your thoughts – you are a creator.

So, if you really want to help yourself, begin by being fully aware of yourself in every situation. Observe your reactions and in the moment when you are not happy with them, try to remember whose pattern of behavior that is. Is it truly yours? If you are really aware of yourself, no one will ever throw you off balance. You will not be dependent on what people think about you anymore. Thanks to this, you will achieve peace that nothing and no one will ever disturb. In this state you remain the same, whether you are accepted or rejected, whether you are successful or not. Only people suffering from inferiority complexes always long for recognition. If you recognize your true self, you will understand the worthlessness of ambitions. And most importantly, please remember that we are all unique. There has never been and will never be anyone exactly the same as you. There will never be anyone who thinks the same as you, and therefore, the only place where we can really meet is the silence…

"Silence is the language of God, all else is poor translation."
Rumi

Speech is also only a program that we have invented. Once you enter the world of words, you become distanced from the real being. "In the beginning was the Word." There was. And this is also the reason why we were separated from each other. This is the allegory of Adam, Eve, and the snake. It is the tree of knowledge - knowledge is what moved us on, but also separated us from the essence of existence. Thoughts are the language of the head. Speech is needed for communication, thanks to speech – the head – thoughts - we are creating a world which contains abundance for all people in these times. You need not condemn it – just learn to work with all those things in our favor. We have forgotten ourselves in the head and we are absolutely ignoring our hearts - being. Just take the language out of life and what remains? Therefore, the most effective and the only way to get back to yourself is to reach the silence. Watch, perceive, but do not judge.

If you "must comment", focus on the present. Describe in your head all that's happening now. The past will usually needlessly consume your energy and the future - if you are not specific, concentrating on one thing - will cause even more chaos. Do not force anything, ever. **The mind cannot be stopped completely. It's impossible. Do not fight – only observe.** You will find that every thought is followed by a gap, and it will grow over time, until one day you will find that you are completely calm, centered, balanced, and peaceful. You will no longer struggle with your emotions, but you will understand them.

"The biggest communication problem is that we do not listen to people to understand them. We listen to them to answer them."
Anonymous

Here is a beautiful example. The principle of photography and the mirror. Most people work on the principle of photography, which means projections. The mirror is alive, clean, and reflects only the present moment. Photography is basically dead. It works as well as our minds, because we are full of information. You just feel like you are creating something, but you are only hiding behind a camera which, ironically, you do not even have firmly in your hands. If you are not totally present in the moment, the photos are blurred. In each situation, in every relationship, man simply projects his own views, and yet he thinks that his ideas are the best in the world. You do not realize what you're doing. You are only creating dead moments and burying them at the same time. You are so terribly convinced of yourself that you would not even consider the possibility that maybe you do not know yourself and that most things in your life are just "unconscious responses". You do not respond spontaneously - you have an opinion at the moment. On the other hand, a meditative mind is like a mirror. It is empty of the views of the others, it is cleared of the past, it is itself in each moment. Unless something or someone is reflected in it, then it is just a mirror. However, when reflecting a bird, the mind becomes a bird itself, because it is the only thing that is present. It does not judge, it sees its beauty. When the bird disappears, its reflection disappears too. There is no need to deal with the bird any further. This is the only way you can stay totally present. As soon as you leave the situation, forget about it – it no longer exists. The photographer carries his own collection of pictures in his device and he is constantly comparing them. Which one is the best?

But nothing in life repeats itself and it can't be exactly the same! You repeat some patterns of behavior because you're blind to yourself – you are sleeping with your eyes open. Because it hasn't even crossed your mind that you should think about it, not at all. Nothing is exactly as it was. As it is said, no man ever steps into the same river twice. Again, this proverb has become a phrase without any deeper reflection. But let's think about it for a while. It is not possible to enter the same river a second time because it is no longer the same river as it was when you first stepped into it. The river flow is completely different, the stones are arranged in a completely different way (you hopefully grow up, changed). That's why it is not possible to enter the exact same river. Patterns are repeated just because you are constantly acting while asleep. you stagnate on the spot, you are afraid of changes and just think you are perfect.

"People are just as forgetful and inattentive to what
is going on around them at times when they are
awake as they are when they are asleep."
Heraclitus

Human perfection does not exist. If a person wants to be a real human, then he should act spontaneously - from moment to moment! This is the perfection of the present moment. And if you are one hundred percent conscious in the present moment, fully aware of yourself and your deeds - you are perfect.

"The mind cannot give you happiness, and it's not given by anyone else either. It is hidden in you, and when the mind is in a state without suffering, bliss will begin to flow. It doesn't come from the mind, it comes without it."

Osho

MEDITATION

"Meditation is an adventure into the unknown, the greatest adventure the human mind can take. Meditation is just to be, not doing anything - no action, no thought, no emotion. You just are and it is sheer delight. From where does this delight come when you are not doing anything? It comes from nowhere, or it comes from everywhere. It is uncaused because the existence is made of the stuff called joy."
Osho

Unfortunately, the word "meditation" has now reached a point where the meaning of the word itself is almost completely lost. Few people know what this word actually means, but others have an answer prepared already: "*Only nature freaks do that! Oh yeah, you need something to earn more money! Sure darling, you were in India, so now everyone will meditate? Meditation, it is not for me, it's a cult...*" These are the most common associations of our most creative minds which have already seen and experienced it all. This word "meditation" will be repeated so many times here, and not only here – everywhere. So now I'd really like to replace it with some new, different words instead. Eventually, perhaps it will come to that. Our possibilities are, after all, limitless.

"Meditation is not what you think..."
Anonymous

Meditation is something absolutely beyond the mind. We could say, where the mind ends, meditation begins. However, we exist in a world of the mind. Everything in life is achieved through our minds. Meditation cannot be achieved, it just is. It is our innermost essence, our being.

> *"Meditation is something innate. To launch it, we only need to create a space for it, to give it a chance."* Osho

The mind is constantly talking. If you can stop the internal dialogue for just a moment, you will experience a glimpse of meditation - the state of no mind. In every sentence, in every thought, there are gaps. Silence. It is present everywhere and in everything. We have just stopped perceiving it. We have focused our lives on logic, rationality, knowledge, simply any kind of "sound". We have forgotten about the absolute essence of being. We have forgotten about the natural state of bliss and pure joy which we last experienced as children.

Without even realizing it, we subconsciously look for ways to stop our mind. It's exhausting to constantly think about something. A man who lives in the Western world, even if he doesn't realize it, solves this problem by playing sports. For a person living in the East, it is meditation. The most common denominator is, of course, alcohol and sex. We lose a lot of energy and we do not know how to replace it. These days, the television is a certainly a strange phenomenon. You may think you are relaxing, while at the same time you are receiving an impressive amount of information which neither contributes to your well-being nor is important for your life. Your mind is tired because you keep it busy all the time. You want to "turn off", but you have no idea how. The mind draws our attention to new input and stimuli at all times.

> *"Whims of our minds are even weirder than the vagaries of fate."*
> La Rochefoucauld

In the sixties, the hippies were trying to return to the essence of man. The energy of war was felt by everyone and the desire for peace was much stronger than ever before. The idea was good, but it got out of control. People were trying to reach their being in untrue ways - through drugs, alcohol and free sex. Basically, they were close, but it was still the wrong way since it came from the outside, not the inside. Some may have started to go the way of meditation, but the outside world steamrollered most of them. (The system will sooner or later force you to adapt to the majority.)

All experiences are affected by chemicals. These are divided into two groups. One consists of chemicals which are received from the outside (drugs, alcohol). The other is substances our body creates through fasting and breathing. Essentially, in terms of the reactions of the body, they induce the same experience. If we fast for a long time, we'll have the same hallucinations as if we were taking LSD. When we take deep breaths, a lot of oxygen gets into our bodies and nitrogen levels drop. All yogis do this. If you experience this "path" once, everything else will suddenly become boring. It is difficult to explain to a drug abuser who sees the world as a much nicer place due to chemical changes that drugs are harmful. However, if you would like to test your body, choose the better path of yoga. Just keep in mind that too much of anything is harmful and people can indeed be addicted to anything. Even through yoga you can create a new reality that is far from the common one. So do everything in moderation, including exercises that influence consciousness, which can be very dangerous. However, if you choose the first path (the easier one), you will receive substances from the outside. Getting rid of them will become more and more difficult, and ultimately you will lose yourself. Any addiction IS dangerous.

India experimented with all kind of drugs and then tried yoga. However, you need to leave yoga eventually to get to know the real meditation. Yoga is the body, meditation is the soul. Nevertheless, they are part of one whole. They are not two things but one. Therefore, there should be a term for the body-mind. The words, however, in this case are very limited - just like writing about meditation. The desire for experience is natural, but the essence of meditation goes further. In meditation, you will reach a point where there is no longer anything, only being, in which there is only watchful observation, conscious awareness. That is when you approach the genuine spirituality. If you learn to observe yourself – **be fully aware of yourself.**

Since we are currently having a yoga boom, let us look at it closer.

"Many people have tried to destroy the mind through yoga. That is not the correct way to use yoga. Many people have tried to destroy it through special body positions, different breathing - it also produces great chemical changes inside of you. For example, if you stand on your head in the position Sirs asana, you can easily destroy your mind. If in the head, flooded by blood, it happens. The mechanism of the brain is very delicate. If it is constantly flooded with blood, soft tissues die. Their bodies are healthy, strong, that is true, but their minds are just dead. You will see a beautiful body, but the man has, somehow, disappeared."

Osho

Yoga is a wonderful exercise, but it supports the ego, and that's a fact. It is very important to realize because it is an area where there is a very thin line between real being, giving up, and fighting. Especially recently, you can see that yoga and meditation are often being connected. Both methods are ways to achieve the same goal of man, but with yoga it will take much longer.

"Yoga is not a system that can improve your ongoing life with all its cares. It is an independent lifestyle with strict rules requiring a huge amount of time to perform all the practices.

It was created thousands of years ago. Consequently, it is hardly compatible with today's accelerated rhythm of life, because its genuine integration with daily work or family life is very difficult. It is of course possible to use some of its elements (asanas, pranayama) in our free time. But then we can hardly talk about using the techniques of work with higher bodies because different steps of yoga are to be performed gradually. Additionally, at some degrees of Pratyahara you must renounce all earthly wishes, because they are sources of negative emotions. Such a requirement would hardly satisfy most people who live ordinary lives and are not headed to blend with God any time soon. Perhaps such an objective would be dazzling for many people, but the renunciation of all worldly wishes is currently hardly possible. In conclusion, we can say that it is a remarkable system of physical and spiritual development of man. But ***it is not a system for mass use, because it has its specific objectives and corresponding tools.****"*
A. Svijaš (from the book: *Health is in the head, not in the pharmacy*)

Yoga is a methodology and technique which depends on actions, methods, and techniques. It is based on duality, and so it believes in conflict. It is based on the will. The more egoistic you are, the more it affects you. Achieving perfection in yoga requires infinite effort, so it is a challenge for man because it supports ego. It works very effectively because everyone is egoistic. It gives you the feeling that you are stronger thanks to it, you can really control your feelings, your instincts and eventually you will become a master of yourself - but you created it by conflict, internal struggle. It doesn't wake up life in you, so then what happens is that the yogi comes to a point where his existence becomes monotonous, pointless, joyless... because the more his ego is satisfied, the more useless the yogi's way forward seems to be. Therefore, yogis tend to focus on meditation or tantra in the later stages. Because meditation - the pure being - is missing from yoga. You can choose the way of pure yoga, the goal is ultimately the same, but that way will be longer. In any case, I do not condemn yoga, quite the contrary. Its health effects are immense, both in terms of body and spirit. But if you, as a strict scholar of yoga, feel in any way affected or hurt by these words, you are only proving my previous statement right. Try to understand the whole, do not take anything personally. You are just used to taking it that way, but take distance from yourself. I am just trying to explain to you that in most cases when modern man attends yoga classes, it does not mean that it improves the condition of his conscious being or that he becomes a "better man". No, today it has acquired the same meaning as when one goes to the gym. Also, first of all, it creates endorphins in your body which promote a better sense of yourself. After all, just look at all the Indian names of the positions – that is exactly the same as when doctors write a diagnosis in Latin. Although you do not understand, it sounds so professional that you believe it. Choose the best from everything – if yoga is good for you, then do it! But abide on earth, please.

It is human nature to want to grow. That's why celebrities who have reached everything in the material world begin to search for spirituality. It's a natural human desire to fulfill both essences of human nature. There is no one poorer than billionaires who spend their time making money and nothing else interests them. In other words, they are the richest paupers. Meditation immensely enriches man by providing him with the world of his innermost being. It frees the mind and generates wonderful creativity. Because nature is creative - still changing - **everyone has the ability to change and to create something - something joyful.** Because real is just a change. Do you want to be "stubborn like a rock" or "as smart as a river"? Even the rock changes over time, but it is either a very long process or a very violent one. Be like a water, because it can do everything through its energy, adaptability, strength and purity. Do not be afraid of change - the only thing it brings you is life itself... Why would you be here on Earth, if not for your maximum potential?!

> *"The West needs a spiritual view of the world so that the man who comes to the end of his journey does not feel that this is the very end, but that there is a door to a new life opening. Life is eternal."* Osho

Meditation, or meditation techniques, is the way. Meditation is a state of being. Meditation should be the only "religion" – the religion of human individuality. The religious individuality of man. In meditation there is no one to tell you what to do or what not to do. Just be. That's all.

In the West, however, it is considered a waste of time. The West does not appreciate being, but action. In the East, on the contrary, being is honored. Buddha just sat and did nothing. He just meditated. In spite of this, he is considered the most noble and most reputable man, who was worshiped even by kings. In the East, to be yourself is the highest level of creativity, and people like this are honored. This may be a result of their belief in reincarnation. They are not in a hurry. In the West, however, we have a vision of one life only, in which we have to manage everything. The mind constantly asks for some work, and if it does not have any, it will create a sense of guilt in us: "*Why are you not doing anything? You are wasting time!*"

The sense of guilt and the sense of fear are our only and at the same time our greatest enemies. Remember that. We create them ourselves – they do not exist. Only our thoughts and emotions give them force. If we can tame them, we win. When we manage to calm our minds and use them only when necessary, we awaken their tremendous strength. Meditation is silence. The mind only knows words. You need to shift the focus from words to silence. However, we should not push it. It's not that simple, but one day it will come quietly on its own.

> *"Meditation is like sex, without sex."*
> Osho

Basically, the point is that we should be able to start using the right hemisphere again. The brain consists of two hemispheres. Although they work together, one of them suffers more and more. The left hemisphere is mechanical, totally uncreative. It needs information to exist. The explicit memory, which is not even developed until one and a half years of age, is located there. That is why we can remember hardly anything from this period of life. Nevertheless, we live - still in beautiful purity and ignorance. Implicit memory (emotional memory) is still present and forming us - even if we do not realize it, it is happening. It is located in the right hemisphere, which is creative. It has a sense of beauty, love, originality, simply put - irrationality. Parents, educators, teachers... all these people help children develop mostly the left hemisphere from the time when they are approximately one and a half years old. In practice, this means that from early childhood we are confronted with fiction. Because we learn "facts", instead of our nature. We are full of knowledge and mistake it for intelligence. Natural intelligence is located in the right hemisphere which needs to be re-started. Meditation can do this too. It brings the right hemisphere to life – it is that "miracle".

"Intelligence has been defined from a human perspective. If intelligence was defined in plants, it would be a problem to prove that people are intelligent."
F. Baluska, plant neurobiologist

So if you realize it in its complexity, you will find that you have completely unnecessarily crowded one hemisphere while the other is still missing something. That is the reason why you are depressed or, paradoxically, you do not even know what life passion is, and so you are always reaching for some of your favorite escapes. We cannot control ourselves because a pre-programmed mind does it for us. We, however, do not want to "destroy" the left hemisphere, but rather revive the right one and learn to use the left one. Imagine you have a boss who is an everlasting intellectual, absolutely boring, uncreative, mechanical, and unfeeling. On the other hand, if you are an artist or you're under the influence of drugs, you only replace the boss, but this one is happier, crazier, more natural and creative. But he does not get along with the first boss who is still present there. A conflict arises (schizophrenia). In order to reach harmony, both halves must be balanced. And when there is harmony, then you really begin to live and act like a human being.

It is interesting that our left hand is connected with the right hemisphere and our right hand with the left one. Therefore, we push children to use the right hand for writing. Left-handed people will always be more poetic. They will have more creative ideas and dreams. Such a person will never be a general or an engineer. That is why they are not so useful to society, and that is why we claim that to be right-handed is correct. Also, reading from left to right has the same reasoning. (For example, that is also the reason why are Arabs so emotional.) The left hemisphere has the male principle - yang. While the right side has the feminine principle - a yin. (As for science, that is a very simplified way of expressing it, but it is sufficient for our momentary needs and knowledge.) It is therefore very suitable to occasionally perform ordinary activities using the left hand - if you are right-handed, and vice versa. A good exercise is to do different things with each hand - if you can, you successfully connected your hemispheres.

"What lies behind us and what lies ahead of us are tiny matters compared to what lies within us. And when we bring what is within out into the world, miracles happen."
H. D. Thoreau

Meditation is not concentration though. Concentration is when you focus on one point, which means that it is a state of mind. Centered consciousness. It is necessary for science, but not for spirituality. If you have a look at, for example, scientists, you will see that their lives are concentrated only on a specific problem, but as "humans" they are essentially useless. Also, meditation is not contemplation. This is only enhanced concentration. However, they have a common base. In contemplation you think about some topic, so the mind is still present. It is good for philosophers. In both cases, however, you must lose sanity. You do not accept anything new, you spin around in your "own world". Consciousness acts as a mirror. For example, in concentration if you stand in front of the mirror and focus on your eyes, after a while you will see only your eyes and nothing else. In contemplation you will find out that you are not only your eyes but also your lips, ears, and around you are a few items, but you do not go further than your reflection in the mirror. In meditation, however, it is as if you placed a mirror in front of a mirror. It cannot reflect itself. There is nothing in it. It is empty, as you should empty yourself. Empty of everything. This is the essence of meditation and being itself. That is the easiest way for you to stay in the absolute presence. Try to find some time and simply just be. Leave all the work. If there is a fleeting moment when you are not doing anything, when you're just in yourself completely relaxed, without thoughts - it is meditation. If you can do it once, the next time will be longer, and then gradually you will be able to stay in this state for as long as you wish and it will become a natural part of your being. Then you can perform any action and your being won't be affected at all.

Meditation is not an escape from life. On the contrary, it brings alertness to everything. You become a conscious observer. If you can remain in your center, nothing will put you off balance. Your life will go on, but much brighter, more intense, joyful, and creative. Whether you are washing the floor or chopping wood, do not lose awareness, feel the presence, be watchful and stay in your center. That means shifting the focus from the head to the belly, and this wakes up the heart. We are born in the belly of the mother, we are connected by an umbilical cord, all important feelings we always feel in the belly. The belly is the source of life. (In Eastern cultures it is called *chi/qi*). It is the center which should remain in harmony. The unconscious, intuition, love… they live in our bellies. This is not a Freudian unconscious; that is nothing more than repressed consciousness. "Unconsciousness", to which we must return, is a completely new kind of consciousness. Our consciousness will become intuitive, not intellectual; synthetic, not analytic. The head is outside; the belly is inside. The head needs work, information, knowledge, but the belly simply is, and still we feel all the important feelings through it. It is a bridge between the head and the heart, it is our being, it contains all truth (just now you are still allowing it to be outvoted by your head). **You don't need a special position or a special time for meditation. We come from different parts of the world. There is no one way which would be natural and normal for everyone.** Do not fight with this fact, just try to feel natural. For example, for people from the West it is not natural to sit in the lotus position, just as for the people from the East it is not natural to sit on a chair. Just be relaxed and playful. Meditation is not a serious matter, which also can be said about life itself. It's just we who perceive it as serious. If your approach is playful, you will see how much it changes your existence. You will awaken a child in you, who has been suppressed for a long time. And I know nothing more beautiful than the joy of a child. Try to maintain a sense of humor both in meditation and in life as well.

> *"You have to find your own position. There is no need to look for some teachers and learn from them. Your feelings are your own best teacher."*
>
> Osho

You do not have to leave your home and go somewhere in the Himalayas or Ashrams. It would be just a game of the mind which, in this case, makes us rather dull, but does not disappear. You can find a lot of spiritual people who are very stupid there. But you cannot see it because you have pre-created a certain idea about them.

India is suffering tremendously because of such people. They have deadened their minds and believe they are enlightened. It is not our intention to be like this. We need our heads, it's just we do not know how to use them. If we should give up all worldly gifts, why have we been incarnated here on Earth? The aim of meditation is to make you a much more vital and sensitive person, to enrich you, not to make a poor simpleton out of you. It's just a misunderstood expression - a condition that cannot be described by this word, but still, we have to name it somehow.

"Many spiritual teachers from the East who went to work in the West are more focused on the material than you. They do it for money. They are just ordinary salespeople who have found merchandise that is in demand."
Osho

Creative people can more easily enter into a state of meditation than, for example, businesspeople who live in a totally uncreative way. When you stand in front of two choices, choose the new and tougher way. You will become more creative, livelier, and you will create a favorable environment for meditation. Also, ambitious people cannot meditate because meditation is about discarding ambitions and efforts to control others. We have not come to this world to become a product of society. We have come here to enjoy ourselves. Our mind, however, is trying to prevent us from feeling like this, together with our society which keeps creating the feeling of guilt within us. And if you get rid of ambitions and desires, that does not mean you stop living. On the contrary, for the first time you will totally enjoy the presence! Clarify your intention, but establish short-term targets only. Surrender to what is - accept everything that comes. If an opportunity to get involved in a new project comes, and if it resonates with you, go for it. If not, then not - regardless of your ideas and plans. Goals can be as numerous as days in the year; the only fact that remains is that you need to enjoy every step. With each climax still coming to an end, to be able to start something new, and we are all on this trip, every day.

"Innocence is not a state of unconsciousness; it is a state without ego. Get rid of all ideas, goals, and ambitions. Innocence is to live in the present."
Osho

With meditation we are trying to find innocence because that is our natural state. We're innocent when we are born and when we die. An innocent man does not recognize any ideology, has no prejudice. He is as pure as a child. He looks at everything with childlike curiosity and experiences joy as if he were seeing things for the first time. Pure love and humor are innocent. Everyone looks for love, and everyone likes to laugh. Love and humor keep us awake and present. When you laugh, you do not think. If you're in love, you do not think (although this can change rather abruptly). Also, if you find yourself in danger, you act instinctively. Therefore, **if you are not looking for a relationship (love), you are looking for "God" or adrenaline.**

"We should tackle reality in a slightly jokey way, otherwise we miss its point"
L. Durrel

If you are not naturally joyful, the real cause lies in your past, and it is individual, but trust me it's there. The biggest criminals, psychopaths, and most people addicted to drugs (here it is more individual) were abused or abandoned in their childhood. They were lacking in love, which is always manifested later in the form of various deviations. That is why successful businessmen have found their love in money or in controlling others. Most of them are just deformed souls, which we should treat as such and try to heal them instead of condemning them. But what does our society do with a man like that? Shut him in jail where he becomes a much bigger criminal, or his psychiatrist prescribes the strongest medicines which completely numb him. If he is addicted to drugs, they send him somewhere to a farm where he is no longer confronted with the reality to which he will have to return, sooner or later. Ninety-eight percent of people like this will just find another addiction, whether it's exercise, a relationship, food, or something else… but it is still an addiction. These people are not being helped (in terms of addiction). The consequences are being suppressed, while the real reasons remain unresolved. Unfortunately, different systems, ideologies, educational methods, etc. have defaced many more souls than we are able to admit. Today we can say that our whole society is sick. The greatest medicine, of course, is to throw everything out like garbage, empty the container, pour out all the accumulated emotions, raw emotions, everything that prevents you from living life joyfully. Many times we do not even realize it, but "early experiences" are the things which cause us an emotional exhaustion, inappropriate reactions, or many different "deviations". They are inscribed in the implicit memory - in the emotional memory. We usually do not have any idea about them, but our soul remembers them very well. They create in us the perception that the world is not a good place, and we subconsciously start to fight and defend ourselves. Abuse, adoption, parental depression, separation, and even so called proximal neglect, when a parent is present physically but not emotionally. These are major problems with many ambitious parents today. Just ten minutes a day of touching supports brain development, not to mention expresses the sincere loving emotions that a child truly needs to feel. Then there are the experiences of later childhood or adolescence, which you even (un)consciously forget because you do not want to think about them, and so you simply "turn them off", as if they never happened. You forget, but they remain in you and cause many problems. Therefore, it is important to be cleaned on a conscious level. (To do this, you can find a variety of meditation courses which are already targeted at specific areas of life. Find the one that resonates most with you. You can unlock your childhood or your relationships with your parents, with work, money, etc. Today they are different female and male circles, which are practiced in many places. There is now a vast range of possibilities.)

"If you never heal from what hurt you, you'll bleed
on people who didn't cut you." Anonymous

Meditation is a life, not a livelihood. Everyone has to do something; otherwise our energy would gradually come to a standstill. Meditation means a jump from the head to the heart, and finally from the heart to the being. Most of our lives, thanks to this system, we spend at work, and we feel that there is definitely no space for meditation. The opposite is true. Work will not harm you. On the contrary, if you find work which you want to do, work which makes your soul sing, through it you will achieve the coveted meditative subconscious absolutely naturally. However, you should be able to "leave" your job even if you love it very much. **Be vigilant when you are at work, and do everything completely - fully, but when you get home, be at home. Learn to be present wherever you are, one hundred percent. Then you will learn to postpone any action and at any time enter into your being - that is meditation. Be yourself, immerse deeper into your being, but do not confuse it with an escape. On the contrary, learn to be alert at all times. If you come back to yourself, to your true being, you will start to appreciate yourself much more and that is the way people around you will perceive you as well.**

Jesus first became a meditating man and only later became the Christ - Buddha (Buddha and Christ are only two different words for enlightenment). First, however, he was merely the son of a carpenter who worked with his father. **If a carpenter can become a Buddha, why not you?** In the name of religion we indoctrinate innocent children with horrendous nonsense, totally destroying the natural intelligence of the child by telling them, for example, that Jesus was born of a virgin. And these kinds of "holy truths" are abundant in every religion. However, if you teach a child to meditate, you do not want him to believe in something. You just want him to experience a state without thinking. It is an experience, not a doctrine. Learn as soon as possible to spend a few minutes a day in silence - without any action (it will be very helpful in the future). Even children shut themselves off naturally, without knowing that they are doing it. They simply turn off. They are natural mystics because they are close to the source, and they have not yet been influenced by society. Small children are naturally meditative. They live in absolute presence. They do not think "uselessly", do not analyze, do not judge, do not know depression. They are obviously sincere, joyful, playful, and creative. And that's where we should return. Children are our greatest teachers. The best meditation for them can also be any creative or sports activity. At approximately the age of fourteen, a space is created for that noisy and eternally doubting voice in their heads - the child "officially" enters the world of duality. All the programs which the youngster absorbed during childhood begin to activate themselves. Puberty comes, closes the heart, and the child suddenly wakes up in "reality". Thus begins the well-known "fooling around" and rebellion, because the young person cannot grasp what is happening to them. If they perceive meditation as part of their nature, they will be able to cope. The voice in their heads will not be so loud and intense. The child will remain much calmer, more balanced and united.

"I tell you the truth, unless you change and become like little children, you will never enter the kingdom of heaven."
Jesus

Again, we should become children, but this time on the conscious level. This is the allegory of Jesus. It is necessary to awaken the quality in ourselves which is characteristic of children. We should return playfulness and spontaneity to our lives. We should wonder, discover, and enjoy the little things again! This brings us to meditation. You can recognize an "Enlightened person", respectively an enlightened consciousness by them having the energy of a child. Although it's a fact that only an enlightened consciousness can recognize itself. However, don't forget that there isn't really anything to be achieved - just issues to get rid of. No serious person (philosopher, priest, politician, intellectual…) evokes the joy in us, which is the essence of being. And if he cannot live out his joy, his life becomes only an item to speak about and to generate philosophical considerations about. But real "teachers" live out their joy.

Bliss is the goal, but meditation is the way. Without meditation no one recognizes permanent bliss.

Meditation cannot be defined the same way as love, however, in our verbal perception it is mainly a process of getting rid of the dominating mind. **If someone offers you meditation, it's basically impossible. Because it is your most natural state of being. Nobody can give it or take it away from you. You should know that it is actually the meditation technique that will bring you closer to the silence.** All the original meditation techniques were born in the East – in India. They did not take Western man - the Western mind - into account. Our minds are indeed different (depending on their respective programming). Today the situation is critical, and the East has found itself where the West was about 300 years ago. Of course, this has happened, paradoxically, because of the British occupation of the East and their subsequent exploitation and the strong influence of Western religions. Today the Eastern mind is in complete contradiction. It cannot grasp the material world which currently prevails there. In the Western world, we have reached material abundance, so it is necessary to set the mind free. If we do not, if we do not clear our minds, the mind will act destructively. (Today's reality is obvious evidence.) We need to activate positive creativity, the irrational part of our being - bring to the world the female principle. If you notice the so-called "enlightened" masters (Jesus, Buddha, Osho, and so on), you will find that they have something feminine in them. Man must understand his feminine part (emotions and heart) to understand the whole. However, woman has nothing easier, since she lives in a world of emotions and moods every day and it is often much more difficult to cope with it. Women lack logic and men lack understanding. Everyone carries both the feminine and the masculine principles, but the female was suppressed by the millennium. So it is gradually happening that women are becoming men and men women. We truly need to harmonize it all.

"If we taught each eight-year-old child to meditate, we would eliminate violence in the world within a generation."
Dalai Lama

Osho examined these two worlds (minds) his whole life, which is why he felt the need to create new meditation techniques that would be effective for both types of minds. They're called catharsis techniques. Our minds are constantly working, and so the techniques that originated thousands of years ago and were applicable to a completely different kind of man cannot be used in the present day. Today we are flooded with large quantities of information, so it is almost impossible to just sit "quietly". A long time ago our lives made reaching catharsis natural, especially while doing handicraft work. The hands are connected to the deepest parts of the brain, which is why people who work with their hands live with much less stress than those using only the head. Paradoxically, however, in today's society those whose mind is moving towards insanity are more appreciated than those who work with their hands and are much balanced and calmer. That is why a businessperson/manager needs to do a sport, or he works in the garden. He unconsciously starts doing anything that will distract his mind (alcohol, drugs). Even at night we are unable to turn off our minds, so they actually work without rest. Even dreaming is an activity of the mind. Alertness can be achieved even in dreaming (lucid dreams), but first you must learn to be vigilant, especially during the day. It is said that a man should be clean enough to be able to get rid of his dreams and to be able to be "silent" at night. At today's level of perception, however, we should realize that dreams are the best means of communication with our subconscious. To "delete" dreams should be the last step we want to experience. Now, try to hang out more with yourself and learn to communicate with your subconscious, which always knows the truth. Before falling asleep, concentrate on the question that bothers you and also ask for the ability to remember the dream in the morning. You do not need to consult a dream book. Your feelings upon waking will tell you everything you need to know. And then gradually you will begin to awaken vigilance in dreaming too. If you feel that you did not dream, in most cases it means that you just don't remember your dreams and that you deeply suppress your subconscious. Once you start to work with it, even subconscious astral traveling will start to open up for you.

"Meditation means that a person is relaxed, as in a deep sleep, but still awake at the same time. Keep your consciousness - let the thoughts disappear, but you have to maintain consciousness. And that is not difficult. We just haven't tried it, that's all."
Osho

Osho's techniques are the most effective techniques ever invented. They are even used in many clinics worldwide. They are used to empty the mind in a chaotic way. Our minds are organized, like order, and are content when "all is as it should be". However, if we get into a situation which we are experiencing for the first time and there is no system in it, only chaos, the mind will not be able to respond. It will have to shut down because it has no program for something like this. **Following a twenty-one-day process can lead us to a point**

where we are able to maintain this condition permanently. That is, this number constitutes the time in which a neuron track is formed in the human brain, i.e., a new habit. Therefore, it is also the amount of time necessary to remove any vice - addiction. That means that if you meditate for twenty-one days, the brain gets used to the "silence in your head" and it becomes a natural part of you. However, because you have not practiced it before, the head is much more dominant and after a time it will fill the silence with noise again. Therefore, it is recommended to repeat this process until your consciousness becomes naturally meditative. Then you will not need any techniques because this state will become your absolute nature. (Another option is to swap three days of meditation – three days off, or seven/seven, and thus accumulate 21 days.)

As it says, life is a dance. **Dance is the best and most accessible meditation**. Do not dance mechanically, become a dancer. And then leave the dancer as well, and let only pure dance remain. Dance any way you like - crazily, out of control, and full of joy! Try a daily half-hour dance and then sit quietly for half an hour - it's the most accessible technique, anyone can afford it. All rituals have always been associated with dance. It is pure joy and can transform even the deepest grief. Whether untouched Pygmies or the ancient Greeks, the "original civilizations" settled everything with dance.

"Dance, as much as you can… sing! And do not take things so seriously, it's fun to be alive, it's fun to pray, it's fun to meditate!"
Osho

The principle of all Osho meditation is to surprise the mind and engage it in new, uncontrollable catharsis techniques, after which comes the silence. And that silence is meditation. The sauna is one of the oldest meditation techniques, if we do it the right way. First, we experience great heat, which we are not accustomed to at all. If we stay there long enough, the mind will start having big problems. It will use its last strength to start persuading us that it has had enough, despite the fact that the body could have lasted a bit longer. Then we should get into ice-cold water, to which we are not accustomed to either. In this way, you cause absolute (physical) catharsis. If you just lie down and wrap yourself in something warm, then comes the real silence - meditation.

Our being subconsciously seeks "meditation". We do not have any other word for this state of being. That is why it seems to us like something unknown, something that does not concern us. The opposite is true, and **if you understand what condition is described by the word meditation, you realize that this is something we experience normally, it is just that we do not do it consciously. In essence, everything you do with love and full attention is meditative.** And you will gradually learn to bring this quality of simple being into everyday life. However, we must first get rid of all the junk we all carry and then it will come spontaneously. Then you will become a meditative person in everything that you do. There is no joy more permanent than this. Everything else is temporary.

> *"Death, love, meditation - they all occur in the present. If you are afraid of death, you cannot love. If you're afraid of love, you cannot meditate. If you are afraid of meditation, your life will be to no avail - in terms of fulfilling its merits. You will never find the true happiness in it."*
> Osho

Within the limitations of language, the word meditation also has a dual meaning. Meditation, as we have said, is when the "mind is off". It happens, however, that someone tells you to meditate on something. In this case, the meaning is getting into conflict. Because if you meditate on something, of course you feel that you are creating something, particularly a stream of thoughts. But it is not meditation, it is thinking. It's a very subtle difference, and yet the most essential. That is why to be able to meditate on something; you must achieve silence first. In this case, it is about understanding - deeply feeling the situation through the heart - not thinking. First, you must be able to turn off the flow of ideas in your head. Only then can you turn your attention to your being – your center - and connect with your innermost feelings. If you can do this, higher consciousness will begin to flow to you. You will naturally connect to the source of virtually all information. Maybe it sounds like science fiction to you, but trust me, it works and it brings happiness and the pleasure of being back "home". Of course, it will be difficult in the beginning, but only because you have totally forgotten how to use your cognizance - consciousness. It's as if you have been lying down for years - sleeping. Of course, it will take a while for you to walk alone again. But you know how to walk! The body has just forgotten about it because it was sleeping for years, that's all. Today there is a great need to wake up and start being yourself - for yourself. There is no magic in it, no control, no restrictions. Then comes the real freedom that you will not find in today's world. This is true freedom - to be yourself. But it must come from you, not from the outside. **Your self-consciousness will bring you true freedom**, which everyone subconsciously desires. Because now you are a slave to your own head, as if it were a system.

This does not mean you will become a so-called "good person." There are many "good" people, but they have suppressed many problems within themselves. Such as priests, for example. They can almost be considered saints, but they are actually dead to real life. There is no intelligence in them, only ideology. Just look at them! Have you ever seen a happy and joyful priest who evoked in you a sense of how amazing it is to have a union with God? No. They are completely lifeless. It is some kind of act which has nothing to do with real life. Try listening to their words, they have just been reiterating themselves for the last 2,000 years. Confession is a beautiful example of how it should not work. (By the way, confession was created only as an "official" way for the church to control its "sheep" – nothing more.) If we tell someone else about our "sin", it is going to relieve us, but that does not mean that we have accepted it in ourselves. We have fooled ourselves. It is just a game of ego. If it really worked, there would be lots of good people walking around! Confessing something doesn't mean accepting and understanding it. It will remain in us. That`s why, for example, so many priests have problems with sexual deviations. **Repressing sexuality is the worst sin committed against humanity.** Priests would like to feel alright about their condition and approach, but they do not. Their ideology convinces them that this is the correct way. They do not have a healthy attitude to sex. Even though they have given it up voluntarily, it is against human nature. Most of them did not come to it naturally; they were lured into it like sheep chasing the dream of heaven. It's just exactly the same "ego trip" that politicians, philosophers, and professors take. For sure, we can find those who can truly transform this energy and feel that it is their destiny to serve others, but there are not many. If there are some, they will soon be suppressed or expelled as has been the practice for centuries. If some priest reads these lines and gets angry, it just confirms what has just been said. You are full of ego which is massaging the feeling of being needed. There is nothing more to it. If you really examined history, you would not be able to "believe" anything that has been repeated over and over for centuries, but the opposite is true. A "good person" in today's society is mainly a hypocrite, a robot implementing moral principles that were invented thousands of years ago. It has nothing to do with the higher consciousness, and especially with real life. He is constantly judging, condemning, still giving advice on how to be better, and would like to conform everyone to his image. He minds everybody else's business but not his own. He cannot accept things as they are. Everyone is a sinner to him.

On the other hand, if we become conscious - indeed pious - we will stop passing judgment. We will begin to accept everyone and everything as it comes. Otherwise, if we are not alert, we are not free, we're just slaves to our minds. We need to remain in the pure presence, without all the programs of the past. That is why it is very important to get rid of the past. I do not mean, however, you should forget it. Just cast some light on it, call it what it is, and don't be afraid to re-feel specific situations again (for the last time), to understand them, to say farewell to them. Then they will disappear on their own. And most importantly, start to do things differently. **It is not enough to talk - act!**

"Everything you do - your love, sex, friendship - all is unfinished. If during the day there is something unfinished, you will be dreaming about it at night, because the mind tends to complete everything. From the moment it is finished, the mind is free."
Osho

The mind needs to complete things. So complete everything and move on! When you become conscious, things will never be bad or good anymore. Everything will be just as it is. Because if you are in a state of full consciousness - self-awareness - you can no longer do anything that would not be in harmony with you. You will never have to regret anything because if you act with full awareness, you cannot do anything wrong. And even if you sometimes look to the past, you'll know why you acted the way you did. If you acted with full awareness, you will have nothing to regret because it was, at that moment, the best solution. Because if you act consciously, your acts are based on your innermost feelings. Wake up the true intelligence in yourself - the intelligence of the heart. However, you are always controlled by your thoughts and baffling emotions that throw you from side to side. What is more, you make other people suffer under your feelings. In your case, it's just a game of ego that thinks especially of itself. *I feel like this now; so accept it, all of you! I'm not going to change! If you do not like it, go away! Me, me, me...* WHO? You just have to understand your nature and awaken compassion. WHO AM I??

"Once you have reached full consciousness, there is no question of choice - you just do everything right. You are doing it innocently, just as innocently as your own shadow follows you around."
Osho

Who is really inside of me? Sit in front of a mirror and look for the answers to these questions, please. Repeat this until you can really honestly answer from within - WHO AM I?

(I recommend doing this exercise in the third person. You need to create distance from yourself, which is important if you really want "to see" yourself - as it is much easier to see others than it is to see yourself. In practice this means: Who is in me? – In me is somebody who is sad, disappointed, cheerful, etc. Name everything you can, go deep, find out what caused these feelings, and then break free from them. Depersonalize from yourself and don't take yourself too seriously. That is the only way you can become an observer of the games of your mind.)

Whatever you do, never forget that you are an observer. You will forget again and again. You will be overwhelmed by some thought, emotion, mood. Something will always distract you. Realize it and come back again into the midst of observation. Let it become part of you, and you will be surprised how it changes the quality of your life. The aim of meditation is not to make a "priest" out of you, but a man with all the qualities of being - someone who is spontaneous, cheerful, creative, playful, loving, and compassionate. Osho called that man the Zorba-Buddha and it's the most beautiful expression. **Live in such a way that you enjoy life as did Zorba the Greek, but remain as meditative as the Buddha. Do not lose your life passion at the expense of yourself.**

"First I am a Zorba, and then I am a Buddha. And remember, if I have to choose between the two, I will choose Zorba, not

Buddha… because the Zorba can always become the Buddha, but the Buddha becomes confined to his own holiness. He can not go to the disco and become the Zorba. And to me, freedom is the highest value; there is nothing greater, more precious, than freedom."
Osho

As the cycle of life is a circle, try to imagine a man standing in a circle. You walk around the edge, sometimes many times again and again. And all you need to do is just to move to the center. Move your attention to your middle. That is where your real being is. If you can do it the first time, you can repeat it again and again. You will learn that it is natural for you to feel your center – your true feelings. You will forget, you'll still come back to the edge sometimes. You will feel uncomfortable, sad, or silly there. But slowly you'll gain the ability to go back to the center and then go out to the edge and back again. This will become natural to you as soon as you realize that it's okay. Because no one wants you to just remain quietly in your middle. You have to come out to the edge. But if you can remain with your feelings in your center, the "edge" becomes only your playground, but you will remain in your center under any circumstances.

"The whole science of meditation lies in nothing other than moving to the middle, taking root in it and staying in it. And from there the whole view changes."
Osho

Extrovert and introvert characteristics are present in everyone, that is the harmony of it. Only you do not know how to work with them, so it is necessary to anchor yourself to avoid flying from one extreme of your emotions and thoughts to the other. Hypersensitive people live on the edge of the circle. Even if they feel that they are acting sensually (because they are so sensitive!), it's just a game of ego (for example, people who are born under the water signs are in extreme).

It's also a problem for many artistic souls. Despite the fact that they are closer to meditation because they live much more intense and creative lives, they paradoxically stay on the surface oftentimes. They go into their middle (meditation) only when they are dealing with art; otherwise, their emotions take hold of them. Even these "terribly sensitive" people can behave absolutely heartlessly. They oscillate between extremes much more frequently, precisely because they are not anchored. Therefore, they have problems in relationships or in different life situations more often than, for example, a village farmer who is in harmony with his being as such. Artists fight against society, but they do not realize that the real problem lies within them. They live in a world of emotions, but those emotions often overwhelm them sooner than they would anybody else. Their right hemispheres are more dominant, so they should exercise their logic thinking and learn to ground themselves. However, in such cases, meditation techniques can be very helpful. These techniques can also help them take this quality of meditation - their being - which they live out mostly only during their creative moments, with them into their everyday lives. Actors are the closest to reaching this understanding because they are their own lifelong "tools". Even many theatrical exercises are used as meditation techniques, such as when clients consciously observe their learned behavior patterns, whether emotional or physical. Questions and introspection gradually lead you to become aware of everything you do, but consciously.

> *"Once you get to the center, anything that happens on the surface will cheer you up. It is not a matter of fighting on the surface, but a process of sliding to the center. Then comes the takeover, and not the forced control. It's a state which arises spontaneously."* Osho

You will try and you will strive for a long time and you will have no idea what state you're actually in. You will be seeking and constantly returning. Even Buddha - Siddhartha Gautama – undertook a six-year-long pilgrimage looking for "the truth" with many teachers, doing everything they said, but nothing happened, no substantial change. He did everything so perfectly that he could not even be blamed for anything. He was just sent from one master to another because after a while they had nothing to teach him. After all he had gone through, he felt so exhausted that one day he could not cross a small river. Then he stopped. He knew that he was doing something wrong. He sat down under a tree that night and realized that all efforts are useless. He understood that there is nothing to achieve, that the very notion of achievement is nonsense. He had done everything – he cut his ties with the world, gave up the kingdom of which he was the prince, he experienced all desires. There was nothing more to achieve which would be worth trying. For six years he refused everything, he meditated, practiced yoga, fasted, and engaged in many other practices, but nothing made him truly happy. Until that evening when he understood. He was sitting under a tree, completely relaxed with no desire or goal. There was nowhere to go, nothing to endeavor, because there was nothing worth any further effort. That night he even slept properly for the first time. When he woke up in the morning, he saw the last star disappearing from the sky. His eyes were like mirrors, there was nothing in them. The last star disappeared and the Buddha said: *"With this star I disappear too. The star has disappeared and I have also disappeared."* Because the ego can exist only if you are striving for something, your efforts are food for the ego. *"The moment I broke away from striving, I reached it, I understood."*

This does not mean you have to give up everything and go sit under a tree somewhere. There is still the six years which preceded that disappearance. For some it may be a year, for others a whole lifetime. "The problem" is that without effort no one can achieve anything, but at the same time you cannot achieve something only with effort. With effort you get to a place where every effort disappears, and then you can understand - surrender to, what is... and be grateful for it. Buddha added a whole new dimension to meditation.

"Meditation you do an hour in the morning and an hour in the evening does not make much sense, even if you did it four or five times a day. Meditation is not something that you will engage in for an hour or fifteen minutes a day. Meditation should become synonymous with life, like breathing. You cannot breathe only an hour in the morning and an hour in the evening, because you would not live to see the evening. Meditation is like breathing. You breathe while you sleep. You breathe, even if you fall into a coma."
Buddha

Therefore, there are so many meditation techniques and so few meditative people. Because the goal of everyone should be to transform their ego into existence, not to go to meditation classes twice a week. Therefore, if you happen to be interested in Osho meditation techniques it is important to remember that they are just a way. They are part of that six-year-long journey. But you do not have to go and look for different teachers, because **the whole secret lies in you – nowhere else.**

Buddha created the oldest meditation technique he called **Vipassana.** The literal meaning of this word is "to watch". In a metaphorical sense, it means "to observe, to be a witness." All other meditation techniques are just different forms of observation, and observation is the basis of each meditation. It begins with the body, because it can be observed most easily. The way we move and walk, the way we sit, the way we eat... Try to be totally present in the moment which is observed. Walk as if you were walking for the first time; watch every move, as if it should also be the last. It is not a problem to observe the body because it is material. Therefore, that is the first step in Vipassana, because it is the easiest.

The second step is to observe the mind. With this you will get to a much finer world - observing your thoughts. They are very gentle, but very powerful. They are like radio waves – they cannot be seen, but they are just as physical as the body. The only requirement is not to judge anything. Once you start judging, observation disappears. Just a thought - "this is a good idea" is a judgment based on the mind. Do not take a stand. Watch your thoughts just as you would watch the clouds sailing across the sky. They are neither good nor bad. It is the same with ideas – they only sail through your mind. Just watch them and you will be surprised. Once you get used to observing, there will be fewer and fewer thoughts and the gaps of silence will become bigger. When you are one hundred percent observant and do not judge anything, it means you have become a mirror. It never judges; it is still the same. Either it reflects something or it does not reflect anything – it does not judge. If you succeed, you will achieve great success and you will have handled the hardest part.

In the third step, you'll go from thoughts to emotions, feelings, and moods. From the mind to the heart, but still with the same condition - no judging, observation only. You will be surprised by the extent to which you have been a captive to your emotions, feelings, and moods. You might find it more difficult than the second level, but that's only because you cannot control your thoughts. Your feelings are now at the same level as your thoughts. Therefore, it is important to first "tame" your head, and then you will be able to identify your feelings using your heart, not your mind. Once you become an observer at the third level, you'll become your own master. There will be nothing to disturb you, nothing to control you. When you complete these three steps, the fourth will come all by itself - as a reward.

"You cannot push it. You cannot keep trying more. It will just happen one day. You take three steps to prepare, and the fourth is the reward from the existence: it is a kind of quantum leap. Suddenly, your life force, your observation comes into the center of your being. You return home. Feel free to call it self-awareness, enlightenment or liberation top, but it will always be so. You have arrived at the very end of your search. You have found the truth of existence which is accompanied by an immense ecstasy like a shadow." Osho

Remember - observe. First the body, then the thoughts, and emotions at the end. Observe them from a distance, as if it was all happening to someone else. Forget everyone else for a moment to find you, but paradoxically, don't forget that through others we recognize ourselves. Direct your attention inside. Then the change can come. But do not try to awaken your consciousness with willpower. This is also a kind of mind game. Try to achieve an understanding of it – acceptance. When anger is being expressed, learn to understand it. Do not suppress it, do not try to control it, because it will return to you in the worst possible situation because it stayed in you. This is the space where you can use a rational mind and try to understand your reaction as an observer without any condemnation. You should try to understand it, but participate only as an observer without any contempt. Try to take a neutral point of view when looking at yourself. Then you will be able to keep that same point of view towards everything, and there will be nothing that can possibly dominate or disturb you. With awareness, you will find yourself; you will find your center of being. You do not have to hurry because we're here and that's enough. First, learn how "to be", and then your life will become much easier. Our problems are created by our minds, so they actually do not exist - everything can be solved and everything is finally solved, so do not make drama. If you act from your consciousness and alertness, it starts waking up an inner natural intelligence in you. Nevertheless, observing is only the way to move forward, so be careful and don't make a target out of it. It should become a conscious act at the present moment, not just a delayed reaction. So far you have been accustomed to observing others. That is your greatest hobby! Start to observe yourself. Be really conscious. Observing should bring new activities into your life, spontaneity and playfulness. This does not mean that observation should be your main activity. It's just a way to learn how to be awake, alert, and conscious at the moment. Look at yourself critically. Alertness without judgment expands consciousness and breaks down the ego. That's the point, identified by many outstanding teachers.

They were, however, always standing alone. **You will experience enlightenment in solitude, but the real challenge for now is to apply it to everyday life, especially to your partnership, and later to child-rearing. This is the real challenge of our time, when this state is accessible to everyone.**

"This is the secret: stop acting automatically. If you can get rid of your automatic activities, then life becomes meditation. Then every small action like showering, drinking or talking becomes meditation. Meditation is a quality that you can bring into anything. It is not some strange activity. People believe that – they think that meditation is something special where you sit face to face with the sunrise, repeat a mantra, burn incense, and do this or that at certain times with certain movements. Meditation has nothing to do with anything like that. Those are just more automatic operations, and meditation is against automatic actions. If you are alert, receptive, then any activity becomes meditation; any movement will help tremendously."

Osho

Practical advice:

"Every morning just after waking up, before you open your eyes, be like a cat and stretch properly. Stretch every part of your body. And after three or four minutes, still with your eyes closed, start laughing. For a whole five minutes just laugh. First you will do it intentionally, you will be acting, but soon the initial sound will change into a real laugh. Dive into laughter and get lost in it. Maybe it will take a few days because we are not used to something like that. But after a while it will be spontaneous and it will change your whole day." Osho

(Recommended literature on the topic: Osho – The Orange Book / Osho – Meditation: The First and Last Freedom)

LOVE

"Of all that is eternal, love is the most beautiful!"
Moliere

Writing about love - is it even possible? We can describe relationships, situations, people… everyone tries to do it. Love is a part of everything, but has anyone ever defined love so that we can truly understand it?

Love is the only real feeling that exists. All the other feelings are based on love. Although it seems incredible, it is true. Every feeling is based on love. Fear, hatred, jealousy, anger… All those feelings are created just because we do not have enough love, and they are only an opposition of love, which means that love is present everywhere. If we are afraid, we are afraid for ourselves or for someone else. In any case, the fear is based on love, whether for yourself or for someone else.

"Love goes through all, no, love is everything. How can you say that there is no love, when it is nothing but love? Everything you see, emerged out of love. Everything shines with love. Everything pulsates with love. Everything springs from love. No, I repeat, everything is Love."
F. Araqi

Hatred and love (although they are opposites) are paradoxically divided by the thinnest border. If you harbor hatred for someone it is based on emotions and feelings which are based on love and, unfortunately, if you "hate" something or someone that means that you condemn it/them. That means they are a part of you and you have to learn to like them (understand them). Anger exists only because there is something which is not as you wish it to be. It is not in agreement with your ideas, with your ego. So it's just something you create in yourself, something that can be controlled if you become conscious. Maybe I have confused you a bit, but I am sure you will find your way.

We create all feelings/emotions ourselves. Only love cannot be controlled or even defined. In spite of that, everything revolves around it. Because it is the only feeling that is real. Everyone looks for love, all people desire to be loved, and everything contains love. It was us who deformed it. Love, as we know it today, is just some chemical reaction or property. It is not the essence of life. We think that it is a relationship, marriage, children, friends… to each of these people we are bound by a particular kind of love. Yes, we can even feel that there are several kinds of love. It is like ice cream: you love strawberry ice cream today and tomorrow it will be chocolate ice cream, but when you discover "any different flavor of ice cream" then you will really love it! That is the easiest way to explain love. And everyone's favorite is to wait for love. People say: *Everyone has love, but I do not. Life is so unfair. Love disappears after marriage! Love does not exist! Love hurts! Love will only hurt you - just look around: everyone is getting divorced! Love is blind and naive! Love is an illusion of the artists! Love is food for the poor! Love is death…*

"Love - it is the only door through which you can leave time. That is why everyone wants to be loved and everyone wants to love. Nobody knows why so much importance is attributed to love, why there is such a desire for love. If you do not know it, you cannot truly love or be loved indeed. Love is one of the biggest phenomena on earth." Osho

Love is the most unusual death – the death of the ego as we know it in relationships with others. Because love itself is infinite. When the body dies, it's clear to all. However, when the ego dies, it produces fear. The body remains, but something in you doesn't know how to deal with it. Something is different. We are not sure how to control it; we do not know what to do, so we have defined it with the following sentence: Love is blind. Love is not blind, but at that moment we cease to exist in our minds. The mind is struggling to survive, not us. We are happy, but scared at the same time. We are scared of losing that feeling. Maybe you would rather not accept this feeling, and you would rather stay with your mind. This game of certainty does not like change. You'd rather give up this feeling, in order to avoid losing yourself, in order to avoid having to worry about losing the feeling. It is cowardly and almost all men act like this because their existence is, for most of their lives, in their minds. Therefore, they have a problem with women – personalities: ego simply discovers in their presence that it is far from being as perfect as it thought. It is a very depressing feeling for them, so they prefer to prove their egos where they can succeed, i.e., in the presence of weaker personalities. Women act mostly with the heart. That`s why they are able to sacrifice their whole lives for love (kids). As a matter of fact, love is the simplest way to dissolve the ego. It's another reason why an egoist cannot really love. He can talk about love, sing, write, but he never truly loves.

"To fear love means to fear life, and those who fear life are already three parts dead." B. Russel

Nothing makes you happy, you are not able to enjoy anything. Because love is happiness! You cannot live without love. That`s why we have created some kind of fake love in which we feel that we're in love, but our egos live on. Almost all people live like that; it is "normal". Relationships have been transformed into investments and business. We calculate everything. Who cares if the relationships are blighted by quarrels, conflicts, and misunderstandings! Who cares if every day we search for something that would replace love! Why do people have lovers and mistresses? Because they played it safe – they obeyed their minds, not love. But love will still find you. We will keep looking for love and it will always come. Whether it is in the form of lovers, whether we run to different things, or to work, to alcohol or other addictions. We run to anything that provides us with the feeling of being happy - that we are truly alive. Nevertheless, true love can be experienced only at the cost of losing yourself. Paradoxically, however, you will find your true self. Until we find love, we just float through life, but suddenly everything is brighter. However, there is fear and your ego which remind you that you are "losing yourself". But if you ignore them, you will discover something inside yourself that you have been vainly seeking the whole time. It is the biggest test of your courage. There is nothing that can test us more thoroughly than love. Do not worry, be brave! Nothing in life is worth more than love! Because nothing else exists and we are not looking for anything else anyway. Even the worst criminals would not be where they are, were they not missing love. Although it may sound a bit naive, everyone longs for love. Even if it is unconsciously.

"All you need is love."
J. Lennon

Everything is hidden in our past. When a child is born, an unconditional love naturally radiates from him. When we begin to form him, other feelings come. How much attention and how much love did you have when you were a child? How can a child who grew up in an orphanage, who no one ever embraced or loved, grow into a man who "believes in love"? Or a child who had a babysitter because the parents did not have time… or maybe they did have the time but kept arguing all the time, insulting each other, or even involved their child in their conflicts. We have grown up in a time when it is hard to believe in love because we do not see it anywhere around us. How can we believe in it? How can we believe in something that no one has ever seen, that no one can define, that everyone damns just because everyone was "disappointed by love"?

We are not being deceived by love, but by people.

It's like a vicious circle that starts with our parents and ends with our children. If you do not resolve to say goodbye to old patterns of behavior, you will not change anything. Love has always been and always will be. First you need to discover it in yourself. You must first love yourself before you can love everything and everyone else. You are still dissatisfied with something. You have a big belly, protruding ears, thin hair, short legs, small breasts, etc. The mind constantly forces you to doubt that you are a perfect human being. Why? Because no one ever told you that you are? We keep struggling with some doubts. We look through a magazine or we watch a movie and we feel that we should look exactly the same as someone in the movie. There has never been a time when the appearance mattered so much. This illusion is created by the media. Our world has never been so connected as it is today, and instead of taking advantage of it, we more or less do not know what to do. We just feel that there is some pressure on us. Children look up to desperate pop-singers and actors who don't even know who they are with their countless masks. How can you love yourself when you have a constant need to look like someone else? A need to be like someone else? Parents hold other people up as examples of behavior their children should strive for. They do not teach them to find their own individuality. They do not let them grow up the way the children feel is the best. No, they want them to become a "somebody". The child does not have time to discover his own self and then comes school where he is confronted with teachers who require something of him every day. Then comes high school and everyone treats him along the lines of: *Yeah teenager, of course! You are crazy, we cannot even take you seriously.* And so parents either shackle the young person, which naturally leads to rebellion, or he suddenly has complete freedom because nobody has the time for him. The young person realizes that the world is not nearly as good as it seemed to be in childhood, that people are bad, that they want something from him all the time, and if he does what he enjoys, they will say: *Do not waste time with nonsense! Do something normal!* And so the youngster really starts to "waste time" with something society requires of him. Because that is "how it should be". Society kills his identity, kills his feelings. The young person feels misunderstood, but everyone tells him that it's okay. After all, it is just puberty. And if the natural character and creativity in him are not supported, then comes destruction. At a time when we need the most attention and understanding, we are confronted with ridicule and rejection. Then suddenly comes adulthood. We chase after work, after relationships, after money... We are kept busy worrying about many different things but forgetting the most important – our own selves. **How can you love someone you do not really know at all?** How can you love someone else if you do not love yourself? In every relationship we look for, and find, just our own reflection.

"What is love? When we can see an idealized
being in the eyes of the other."
L. Pirandello

Subconsciously we love ourselves, but we go about it through the outside world. We do not know how to discover the inner world, and so we always search for ourselves in someone else. At any time, in any relationship, we just discover another part of ourselves. If we look at our past relationships, we will find that each of them has brought us something. They have helped us discover something new or gotten rid of a part that we did not need anymore. The thing we love most in others is in reality just a reflection of ourselves. It's actually a quite peculiar paradox, but it is the best school for us, even if we do not see it as such at that moment. When the initial infatuation disappears, the chemistry and hormones calm down, then comes the real test of courage. What are you willing to tolerate? What didn't you see before? What didn't you want to see? Can you really live with this person or would you rather run away? And the worst thing is that most of the time it is your own self you are not able to tolerate. You are actually not able to live with yourself. If you have not accepted yourself, you are in a vicious circle. It's hard to look in your own mirror and see the fact that this is primarily fear – of yourself. Because you may even know who you "really" are, which is why you will not tolerate it in others. Ultimately, you get scared of yourself because you know how you would behave in certain circumstances… and you are not going to tolerate another "psychopath", the one in you is sufficient after all! Do you feel like you are losing yourself? Why? Or to whom? Our egos shout: I'm not going to change! And you do not realize that even you do not know who you are. And so you will continue to find partners with whom you will encounter the same problematic situation until you realize that it is not their problem, but yours. And those problems can be countless, as can be our relationships. Not to mention that kids have kids. There is nothing more irresponsible. There are so many forms of contraception. If we have the free will to create a new life, we should have that option when we are not in a good enough situation to take care of a new life. In this case, there is nothing worse than making excuses based on religion, society, or the notion of using the child as an object of extortion. What kind of a person will the child grow up to be without normal conditions for life? If you do not have love, a harmonic home, if you have a mother who didn't want you in the first place and lets you feel it very intensely? Will the Christians take care of you? They can build a million orphanages, but they will never give you what you really need - love.

"Love needs two things: it has to be rooted in freedom and it has to know the art of trust." Osho

Everyone needs and looks for love. However, you must first begin by loving yourself. Only then can you truly love others without the danger of becoming dependent on them - love unconditionally. Because that is what you do, you always depend on others! You do not know how to live with yourself, and so you constantly search for someone. You do not love people as they are, you have hundreds of comments on each of them. In fact, you only need to realize that you're really alone. Everyone is alone – and at the same time we are part of the whole. Discover yourself, learn to live with yourself, and then there'll be nothing greater than sharing the joy either with a partner or with a child. Therefore, there is no need to go to the mountains or to the monasteries to understand love. Try to discover it in your daily life - this is the real challenge. It's not the easiest path, but if you decide to follow it, know that the whole universe will be encouraging you and the more precious outcome will be reached. Others only help you see yourself. Realize it and go through all the demons acquired over the years. Everything is just a mirror whether you like it or not. Look into the past, but do not suffer because of it. Do not relive it, just try to see it as something you need to learn from. Nothing will ever be as it was, do not be sentimental or bitter. Learn from it.

> *"The cause of every suicide is unrequited love, sometimes for a woman and always for life."* F. M. Dostoevsky

First of all, resolve the problems in your relationships with your parents. This is the greatest and most important task in our lives. You are also the most affected by these relationships. It is up to you if you want to try some therapy, of which there are many kinds, or use regression, or simply observe yourself according to the principle of the mirror as an uninvolved witness. It is very important to understand these relationships. How many times have you acted as they would - it does not matter if your behavior resembles the behavior of your father or your mother. Both are present in you. Please try to answer these questions:

How often do you react just exactly like your mother or father?

How many patterns of behavior have you unconsciously adopted?

Which of your opinions are really your own (experienced) and which come from your parents?

What were all the things you did because they wanted it, not you?

How well did they prepare you for life? (not materially)

How did they really support you in what you really wanted?

Was their relationship an example for you?

How many times have you found yourself in a similar relationship?

What problems did your parents have? Have many times have you dealt with them? Are these problems yours or theirs?

Did you condemn them for something? If so, you will experience it too.

This last question is the most important one. Surely answer it – and try to see yourself as you really are. In spite of being sometimes quite minor, these issues set our relationships. Everything that we do not understand – we condemn – will return. Try to go into detail with various patterns of behavior of yours and yours parents, and try to be (self)critical.

Therefore, it is extremely important to sort out the relationship with your parents. They are not going to change. You can try to change them, but it is better if you try to understand them. Find out about the real reasons why they acted the way they did. Maybe you are not in touch with them, or maybe they have left, so you think that there is no way to find out. In this case, it is important to allow the idea into your consciousness that there are past lives and nothing happens by chance. Using the above-mentioned practices there is a way to easily determine the actual cause of your past misunderstandings. If you become compassionate, it will open many doors to you. Do not forget - **the only thing you can really change is how you relate to them.** You cannot change anything else. You can try, but it's the most naive idea ever – to change someone else. Always and in everything begin with yourself. If you stop fighting, you'll win. (As a "shortcut" I recommend e.g. the weekly intensive program Osho Primal Rebirth or therapies which focus on your parents from the beginning of yours creation. There is also the possibility of prenatal regression.)

> *"There are people who are less ashamed of their most powerful display of hatred than of the smallest acts of love."* J. Paul

Our soul, before entering this world, chooses what she wants to learn in this life. And even though it sometimes does not look that way, **ALL of us are on this planet voluntarily. What more do you have than yourself?**

Even "love at first sight" is just a karmic meeting. Souls already know each other from past lives, and so they recognize each other. Maybe both have been humbled and they will stay together for the rest of their lives. However, in most cases they only have something unresolved. Again, this can easily be detected using regression or intuition. It's up to you which path you choose, but if you cannot move from a place, regression is the easiest solution (if you go through your heart). If you identify a problem, it will "disappear", and again it's up to you if you want to go further in some behavioral pattern or if you decide you have done all that you could and it is time to go in another direction. Do not be afraid and do not fight it. **If you follow your feelings and don't reprobate yourself, there is always something better prepared for you. That is the law of the universe.**

"When a man knows why he loves, he does not love."
J. Jesensky

Love is unconditional. Love has no conditions, it simply is. Awaken it in yourself and you will never again "need love" because you will understand that love has always been here, and it always will be. It is just that you forgot about it for a while. We search for love everywhere, but rarely in ourselves. Love yourself as you are, but remember that only a fool does not want to change. Life is a process. Love is life. Only the ego feels that it is perfect, it does not want to change anything. It lives in an eternal illusion of fear. When you're in love, you feel like you were flying. You do not feel fear, you live every moment of your day, you are in the present more than ever, enjoying that, you even feel beautiful like never before! Do not depend on others to awaken this feeling in you! No one will give you more confidence than you when you begin to believe in yourself. At the same time, understand that nothing is forever. Everything is constantly changing, so you shouldn't get stuck in one place either. Become love and become naturally joyful! You can share only the things you have. If you do not have something, you just want to get it and that is not the right way. That is why we become slaves to our partners in all kinds of relationships, because we do not quite know how to love and live without "owning" someone. Every relationship is individual; there is no formula for all. But it is something we have to experience to the fullest. Only in love there is no golden mean. *"After some time you will get used to it…"* This is stupid, but it is possible to get used to everything. In every relationship you should be 100% present, give the other your full attention and respect, and be his/her support in good times as well as bad. It's not a phrase, if you want to have a fulfilling relationship. **Love**, in this case, **is** actually **the only "fight" where both sides can be winners.**

If you decide to fully follow this path of sincere self-love, each relationship will be helpful to you in your real understanding

of who you genuinely are. And when you succeed, you naturally attract your dual soul who will fulfill you for a lifetime. Each person has one somewhere, it is just very hard to find that person when you are constantly confronted with meaningless relationships that are based only on the fact that you do not want to/cannot be alone. If you want to approach this issue seriously, you must begin to act like it. As late as then, the universe will "play" in your favor. It is difficult to attract true love if you are constantly surrounded by lovers and you secretly hope that someone will cut in. Maybe he will, but you will hardly notice it through all those insincere games. First of all, all our relationships are our teachers. Therefore, do not reject them while waiting for the right "prince/princess". First of all, all our relationships are our teachers. Therefore, do not reject them while waiting for the right "prince/princess". These are the so-called transient relationships that always move us forward, teach us something new. Enjoy what comes to you here and now. Don't worry if it does not work out how you wanted. If you follow your heart and you do not consciously hurt anyone, your next relationship will be a bit better. And if your problems return repeatedly, then solve yourself (your parents' relationship), because in that case you are "unteachable" and entangled in something that only you can free yourself from. Above all, do not be afraid to leave relationships that do not work - be free, but be responsible. Manage yourself with others as you would like them to behave towards you.

"If I accept the fact that my relationships are here to make me conscious, instead of happy, then my relationships become a wonderful self mastery tool that keeps realigning me with my higher purpose for living."
E. Tolle

Once you find yourself, you'll never be irresponsible again. If you understand that we are all linked together, you will stop behaving selfishly. Do not let anyone take advantage of you though. Say "no" whenever you feel like it. In particular, women are the ones who tolerate extremes in their partners, even it is not beneficial for them over the long term. Observe the signs. Sometimes listen to others who care about you and who you know do not want to manipulate you but rather wish you only good. Also, do not go to extremes when it hurts you and, most importantly, do not lie to yourself. If you have the strength to leave the relationship because of your self-love/self-esteem, you will send the message to the Universe that you value your soul and want only the best for it. As a result, it ultimately comes. Be bold - for yourself. If you are staying in a relationship only because of your children, I can tell you from personal experience that it is not the solution. Children are very sensitive to the environment in which they grow up, and if they do not have a harmonious environment, you will only create problems for them in their future relationships with others. You can bring happiness to others only if you yourself are happy. Cooperate with your inner world, listen to your feelings which are in the abdomen and in the heart, and you will never regret anything. If you go down the road of your feelings, you can always say: I felt that way at that moment and I did all I could. If something did not work out, do not worry, you can feel good that you followed your feelings, your being, your love… then you really won't regret anything! Be happy about the fact that you have made contact with your inside, your true self, that you have acted according to "your" truth. Giving preference to our own interests does not make us selfish - it just means we are aware of ourselves. When we betray ourselves in order to avoid betraying others – that is also treachery, ironically the worst one. **Appreciate your true self, listen to it, do everything possible to keep your soul shouting: That`s me!** Love can become a deep meditation, the deepest. Lovers know something that the so-called saints don't know. They touch the center which many scholars missed. Love is silence. Love is completely outside the mind, that`s why it is of meditative character. We cannot describe it, it simply is. It is in silence, because the silence is real. Everything else is just thoughts and words. Silence is - it is impossible for it not to be. Therefore, even if we are in love, the greatest "tides of love" are experienced in silence. We choose a partner with whom we do not mind being quiet. We even enjoy silence for the first time. No words can describe the feeling when we look into the eyes of our loved one, when a mother looks at her child at night while he is asleep... Everything beautiful is in silence, in love. And meditation can create this feeling in us without having to become dependent on the love of others. But remember that **everything becomes really beautiful only if it is shared.**

"The essence of love is not to love a human being, but to be filled with love."
Osho

Sex should not remain sex - it's the tantric teaching. It should be transformed into love. Love also should not remain love – it should be transformed into light, into meditative experience, into the peak of the mystical. If you love, simply lose yourself in love, forget yourself, become love! Let it fill every cell of your body... Then it will not be your love or my love - it will simply be love! In its purity and innocence.

With all my heart, I wish you the discovery of endless love for yourself. Love yourself and you will love everything and everyone - absolutely. Be an example to the others - in the name of love.

"Through meditation you look for your own self, your being, your existence. Through love, through the heart, you share your happiness. And that's the way love is: sharing in bliss, sharing in joy, dancing and experiencing ecstasy."
Osho

SEX

"The love of two people lacking erotic is only a game of words and falsehood."
J. Cocteau

Sex is nowadays one of the most overestimated and most underrated issues.

We are sexual beings (here on earth). This fact should be accepted without any prejudices. **Creation happens through sex.** We came into this world thanks to sex and we continue to create new life with the help of sex. One of the highlights of every love relationship is sex. Each of us thinks about sex. Sex is an absolutely natural part of us, whether you admit it or not.

Although sex is a kind of challenge for everyone (even if you do not want to admit it), nobody wants to talk about it publicly. As a phenomenon, sex has been distorted for more than two thousand years, and now people can't find the right attitude towards it. Ironically, it can nowadays be seen everywhere and in everything. Sex has been repressed for centuries as something immoral, although it has always been practiced. The only difference was that nobody wanted to discuss it openly. The fact is that our relationship with sex has been distorted by Western religions. In India, where the Kama Sutra and tantra were born, the relationship with sex was very natural. It was considered to be the art of the body and souls. Sex was part of everything and it was a very powerful inspiration for many artists as well. As we mixed East and West, sex was also affected by these two opposite poles. Therefore, today in the West sex is everywhere and in everything, and in the East it has become a strongly repressed instinct.

Sex is one of many ways to express our energy. There has always been just one energy, although it can be seen in various forms. Sex is a vent for a particular kind of energy which you can choose yourself. Different theories have plugged this vent and forced this energy to circulate over and over. This causes unnecessary pressure upwards, to the head, and that's the reason why we become so neurotic sometimes too. **The energy itself is neutral. If this energy is expressed in a biological way, we call it sex.** The same energy can be expressed and used on our spiritual journey, and then it's called divine energy. If you use it for something creative, you also allow it to flow freely because creativity is the principle of existence. However, if the energy in you is stagnating, it manifests itself destructively. So it's up to you to choose how you use - transform - your energy.

"Sex is just a beginning, not an end. But if you miss the beginning, you will miss the end. Sexuality and spirituality are two ends of the same energy."

Osho

Western psychology has come to the conclusion that basic human "disease" is close to sex. People are extremely distant from their own nature, and the reason is not the sex itself, but their attitude towards it. Actually, the biggest sex organ is the brain, as it was said. That is because we live in the world of the mind, not in the world of existence and nature. Sex transferred to our heads is simply called sexuality. Thinking about sex is sexuality as well. Sex is not bad, only sexuality can lead to perversion. Experiencing sex is something totally different. If you are simply experiencing it, you can go further and you are able to transform it. However, if you have it mostly in your head - mind, you'll become obsessed with it, or, on the contrary, you will become totally bored.

Sex is a kind of natural biological flow of vital energy which forms only the base, not the top of being. When sex becomes your only aim, you will waste your life. It's the same as if you wanted to build a house, but you spent all your time only on the foundation. That is why this sexual energy - or instinct - is disappearing over the years. Sex is a possible path, not a goal. Do not give it a spiritual or anti-spiritual meaning; take it as your own part, simply as a fact. Only death is certain. Therefore, sex has become an obsession. Nobody will stay here forever, so it is necessary to replace your body with a new body – some kind of a replica. Sex is so important because the whole existence depends on it.

"The sex inside man, his libido, is even more vital than electricity. A minute atom of matter killed hundreds of thousands of people in the city of Hiroshima, but an atom of man's energy can create a new life, a new person! Sex is more powerful than an atomic bomb. Have you ever thought about the infinite possibilities of this force, about how we can turn it to our advantage?"

Osho

We start to perceive sex (consciously) in approximately the 12th year of life and the loss of interest in it comes after the 45th year (this can vary and the numbers can be different – everything is changing and we still haven't discovered our true potential yet). If you want to discuss the topic of sex with your child, you may find out that he is not interested in it yet. Kids just have many questions because they love them so much, but basically, when you are explaining something they don't understand what you are saying. The human body is set according to some kind of breeding cycle, which can be represented, for example, by the natural arrival of a girl's first menstruation and boy's first (night) pollutant. In every phase of our lives we feel this kind of energy in a different way, as it is very individual. The most important thing is not to suppress it. The so-called religious attitude towards sex has created perverse sexuality and a culture which is obsessed with sex. Sex is healthy and if it is suppressed, it can get twisted. Religion is focused on death, not on life, and therefore, it has created a man who is sexually oriented. Although they have shown you a golden peak of celibacy, they haven't even tried to give you a guide to the first step - to understanding the basis of sex. Without an understanding of the basic power of life in all its forms, any further attempt to limit or suppress sex will only be another step towards the further degeneration of man. We can't keep fighting nature if we are part of it. Our society is sick because the foundation of our relationship with Mother Nature is sick. The fact that almost all swear words refer to sex in some way is also interesting. We have invented all kinds of words, just to avoid saying the words penis and vagina. The suppression of sex creates all sorts of deviations, which in extreme cases can even cause death.

"Human beings can never be separated from sex. Sex is the primary point of one's life; one is born out of it. Existence has accepted the energy of sex as the starting point of creation. And your holy men call it sinful, something that existence itself does not consider a sin! If God considers sex a sin, then there is no greater sinner than God in the universe."

Osho

Sex represents the death of our ego again. If we experience sex in totality, we exist in the present moment, which makes us unable to think. That is why we like it so much. We return to our nature, and it makes us subconsciously happy. Nevertheless, it is only an illusion. It's "only" a moment in our lives. Experiencing orgasm is an indescribable feeling of satisfaction - bliss, but only for a while.

However, in the awakening moment, kind of sadness and distress is hidden - that`s why most people fall asleep after making love. If you observe animals and their expressions after copulation, you'll see sadness or disappointment, as if they were cheated by someone. Indeed, this is a trick of nature. It wants to reproduce itself, and therefore, it invented a very good way – the feeling of an orgasm, pleasure - a feeling which we would like to experience as often as possible, and we would do anything to get it again. Without this sensation, sex would be only gymnastics.

Basically, a man as such is not complete, and a woman is not complete either. They are simply two parts of a whole. In sex, harmony occurs between these two poles – they join to create unity. For a moment, we connect with this universal energy which is naturally joyful. The female principle is actually stronger than the male one. The soft is stronger than the hard, because its passivity and adaptability let things flow freely, which is actually the principle of the whole existence – the act of letting go - real faith in the fact that everything is as it should be. But if there is no harmony between the partners, it is always the woman who receives the man's energy. Therefore, if a man is aggressive, the woman can not do anything, she only absorbs the energy. So the man is relieved and the woman suffers - that's fact. That is why we should begin to understand this energy exchange. For example, scientists have found that even the DNA of every male with whom they have sex remains in them.

The woman is a mother - creator. When a woman becomes a mother, her interest in sex automatically decreases. For nine months she was living with a new life inside of her which throbbed in every cell of her body. Then the role of the woman becomes absolute. That`s why she is suddenly so beautiful and happy. A woman will never be completely satisfied until she becomes a mother, until she recognizes that deep spiritual relationship that can exist only between her and the child. (However, if she can't be a mother, it must have its own reason which can be discovered. By all means, it is a kind of test for this woman, which happens for her own good. She experiences it because she needs to learn something by going through this. She planned it in the higher realms, whether you believe it or not. If you have a problem getting pregnant, it is always first and foremost related to a mental block which may also be in the partner.) Motherhood changes and affects primarily women; it is not such a substantive change for men. A man can't even give her a feeling like the one she feels when she becomes a mother. He, however, can get very close to this energy while being present at the birth. In the West, women are losing interest in motherhood because they have experienced sex. They subconsciously feel, even though they can't define it, that motherhood is going to change their sex drive. It will not have as high of a priority as before. On the other hand, in the East they are more aware of this fact, and that`s why there are a lot of so-called child marriages. If a girl or a woman experiences the greatest pleasure in motherhood so she will not be attracted to sex. She will never really get to know sex, and therefore, she will not create any particular attitude towards it, only that one she can see from the outside. Her husband will automatically be looking for some other lovers because he is not satisfied by his own woman. But that's his own fault as he has a huge desire to own. For example, in India these child marriages have gone to such an extreme that if they marry a girl at an early age and her husband accidentally dies, she automatically becomes a widow for her whole life and she is sent to a shelter for widows. She will live there all her life because she is "unclean". According to Indian law (of which widows have no idea if it is in force) she officially becomes a lover ("whore") of various high-ranking men. These days, in India there are an estimated 34 million widows! (See the movie *Water* by the Indian film director Deepa Mehta.) Unfortunately, even in these cases we can go to the extreme - even today there are villages in India where such young widows are burned alive (!) with their deceased husbands.

"On the 23rd of January 2014, police in the Indian state of West Bengal announced that a young woman was gang raped on order of the municipal council because she fell in love with a man professing another religion. The information was issued by the AP news agency. Police officer C. Sudhakar said that in relation to the case they had arrested 13 men. The wave of rapes that have occurred in India within the last year have provoked the general public to anger as the country suffers from chronic sexual violence and the government is unable to protect women. The case in West Bengal is particularly worrying because the rape was allegedly approved by the Municipal Board consisting of the village elders. Neither such boards nor their decisions are legally binding in India, but they are perceived as an expression of the will of the local community. People who ignore this advice risk being excluded on the margins of the society".
TASR (the Press agency of Slovakia)

This is the contemporary image of the country of origin of the Kama Sutra, and many "seekers" look up to it as a holy land. Today it is really important to be able to see all countries holistically and with their errors. Pedophilia is part of all "holy texts". There is also discussion in the Muslim world as to whether people may have sex with corpses. Bulk rape perpetrated by immigrants in Europe is merely a consequence of our sex war. Do you still have the feeling that today's humans are okay - healthy?

Sex is our basic energy, and it should therefore be understood as a whole, whether you are male or female. The woman is the heart, the man is the mind. Both are equally important, but still, they should be in harmony. It is only our minds which always create some problems – by searching for differences, comparing, and assessing. So once more: **Sex is a transformation of our energy, which needs to be released**. This energy is continuously flowing out – through the eyes, fingers, feet… and that's why after sexual intercourse everyone feels so exhausted. This energy escapes from our bodies. It can't escape when the circle is closed. Therefore, women tend to be less tired than men. The shape of the vagina is curved, so the energy is absorbed faster. The shape of the penis causes the man to give out much more energy, so that's why men are more exhausted and tired than women. Paradoxically, the activity of women, compared to men, in sex is minimal. However, it was suppressed because of men's fear. Because if a woman's body is ready, it is very difficult to satisfy her. A woman can experience several orgasms in a row; she can experience a multiple orgasm. A man (now) simply can't experience that. And so it happened that needs of women were repressed. In fact, up to eighty percent of them have never experienced the feeling of an orgasm. They can give birth to a child, satisfy a man, but they remain unsatisfied. On the other hand, it would be quite unbalanced if the woman had such a possibility and the man did not. (This topic is dealt with in detail, for example, by Mantak Chia, the author of numerous publications, in his books *Multiorgasmic Man; Multiorgasmic Woman.*) According to statistics, about sixty percent of men have premature ejaculation. This means that before they really merge, it's the end. The irony of this situation is the fact that only in recent years has the female prostate been discovered. For this discovery, we should thank the Slovak professor MUDr. Milan Zaviacic, DrSc. In 2001, he gave a name to the recently discovered part of the female body – a prostate (prostata femina, lat.) which serves the same function as the male prostate. The only difference is that the ejaculate doesn't contain sperm. We can say that this is a new erogenous point in a woman's body that has nothing to do with the G-spot or the clitoris. With this discovery, more than seventy percent of women could reach orgasm! (One is even capable of experiencing an anal orgasm, which is still taboo.) This is the main reason why women are so irritated or vicious. No philosophy or religion can help them as much as men can. Tantra and science agree that if a woman is not satisfied in bed, she will stay in conflict mode. So please, admit to the possibility that in this case the problem doesn't lie with the woman but with the man. If a woman can't reach orgasm, she will become anti-sexual, and therefore, she will start to seek satisfaction in other things. She will shift her focus in an entirely different direction and her man will later on accuse her of indifference. He will find a lover just to make himself feel unique, despite the fact that, ultimately, the other woman will start to feel like she is being "used" too. And so it goes, over and over, because it's been "normal". That is actually also the reason why a woman becomes frigid.

This kind of attitude has recently appeared in some men as well. In this case, I would recommend looking into the past - whether the recent past or past lives using regression - the reason is there. Either it was caused by some bad experience (or maybe more of them) which caused mental block, or it may be caused by the unceasing mind, hence the inability to relax and find themselves fully in a given situation. I suggest you look for some tantric course for men in your neighborhood. It is focused on a specific area and men appreciate it immensely, even if they initially have a big problem with their ego. After overcoming it and recognizing the unexpected opportunities, for example, of the so-called men's rings in which you interact with other males in an entirely new way, you will open yourself to the higher principle of sex and will never see it as superficially as before – in the best sense of the word. Another reason for sexual disgust is based on the fact that recently men have also been awakening their feminine (emotional) energy which they certainly need in order to function fully. They are more sensitive than ever before and they do not know how to deal with it. It simply happens on its own because our relationships (man – woman; but also with ourselves) are totally unbalanced. This sick condition can be observed in the simplest example that we all know so well. If a woman makes love to one hundred men, she is considered to be a whore. However, if a man does exactly the same thing, he is "macho". This is not about emancipation. It came about only because of the suppressed nature of women – suppressed, paradoxically, by men. In the last century, men "allowed" this to happen by leaving their women alone because they had to fight in wars. The woman was the one who had to take all the responsibility, substitute for her man, and start to fulfill his duties on her own. It is up to men to take responsibility for what is currently happening to women. For it is in particular a reflection of what is happening to them. (By the way, the so-called emancipation was "officially" created as some kind of men's game. International Women's Day and the related activities started based on the initiative of the Rockefellers who wanted to tax the other half of the citizens and get children into schools as soon as possible to be able to influence their thinking. Also note that women's goods are always more expensive than men's, and women earn incomparably less money.)

We live in a male world, and that's a fact. An excellent example is the fact that women have to pay for hygienic pads when they menstruate, although each one of them gets their period naturally whether they want to or not. I guess no man has really thought about that, ever. We have to pay health insurance whether we want to or not. When someone is bleeding for almost a whole week every month, isn't that considered a health problem by any chance? (If this happened to men, they would probably be hospitalized each month ☺). In any case, women should change their attitudes to menstruation, too. It is a sacred process involving the blood of life from our bodies (which can be used for various rituals, fertilizing plants, etc.). If a woman was 100% adapted to the timing of nature, she would menstruate during the new moon, and during these days she should be given at least three days off work. It is the time when a woman should dive into her inner world because she has endless possibilities for communication within herself - with her intuition. During the full moon, which is a time of celebration and sharing, we should have our energy at the highest level. But we, in this society, ignore such an undoubtedly natural part of us as menstruation; we make it into something negative. Nowadays, women suffer from what should be taken as a celebration of themselves. Of course she is irritated when others treat her in ways such as: *"Oh God, she has her period! Run away from her!"* instead of being accepting and having time to understand what is happening to her. Again, if we look into the past and even now – even today there are several countries where menstruating women (and pregnant ones, too) are considered unclean, and during this time they are simply isolated from everyday life – literally. The family does not want to have her at home and they behave accordingly towards her. Again, this is mainly an example of how the original habit, when women had to relax, got out of the control and changed into the absolutely inhuman treatment of women by men. But the fact remains that a menstruating woman is incomparably more sensitive, and the man, even if he unconsciously feels this imbalance, it is he - his energy - which raises a very raw and aggressive response from the woman during this period. If we accepted each other on the conscious level - knew ourselves - we would avoid a number of problems. Nevertheless, it is an interesting fact that men also have "their days". It just isn't visible. Every man would have to observe it, which would help not only him, but also his surroundings. **These hormonal fluctuations also happen to them regularly, once a month, and even much more intensively.**

We could also have very long discussions about how to treat pregnant women who work almost until they go into labor, and then they try hard to be accepted back into the system as soon as possible – that's nonsense! The mother's body alone needs at least nine months to recover, not to mention her psyche. How can some "highly developed" countries have three-month maternity leaves?! The separation of mothers from their children is consciously being created. How can a child fully grow up with a nanny? Without ever knowing real motherly love? After all, this has to be the most beautiful period which a woman may ever experience! Of course, this requires strength and patience, but those are virtues that we should teach our children, too. But it is difficult to teach them something that you do not know. And if you're focused on your career and you do not have a real relationship with your children, why are you having them?! Do you want to have a small human at home who will unconditionally love you? Somebody who you can boss around? Whose childhood will be destroyed by you because you can pay for it? Were you educated by your parents in this way? Did you have a happy childhood? Every single day, even every single moment in the life of your child is shaping him more than you even realize. The emotional memory, which affects the whole life the most, will have a huge deficit with a tremendous number of problems later (especially in relationships). Mothers have such strong bonds with their children that they are even responsible for their illnesses before they are twelve. If a child has any serious disease, first begin to address the psyche of the mother – and the child will start to be healed automatically. On the other hand, especially if you are a single mother, you can hardly afford to buy diapers for the baby with the poor financial support from the state, and it is really impossible to support yourself. The "hardest" and most responsible role is also the most under-appreciated. Why? Because those (men) who make the decisions do not have the slightest chance to fully understand it. Regarding childbirth, our usual attitude towards it is that it is very painful and "scary." Nevertheless, it should be the most beautiful experience because a new life is coming into this world! Giving birth in a natural way and, especially in a natural environment, can be changed into the most beautiful sexual experience, without any doubts. Women should scream with pleasure, not from pain. (On this subject, an excellent documentary called *Orgasmic Birth* was made by Debra Pascali-Bonaro.)

Very serious are the forever-discussed topics of abortion and contraception. Again, however, note that those who make the decisions regarding these topics, paradoxically, are mainly men. What becomes of a child who is born to a mother who has no real interest in him? If she doesn't have the right conditions, she cannot provide the best care, she will never love him as much as he needs, etc. What kind of life awaits him? There is an excellent video on this subject by Teal Swan (Scott) – *"Should I Get an Abortion or Keep the Baby?"* – I will not explain it further, so please check it out. But, unfortunately, again we can challenge the profanity of this time. Due to the fact that people are opening and perceiving their consciences, many perversions are gradually coming to light. The admission of Ms. Carol Everett who managed several abortion clinics in the United States is an example. She admits that in this case it was purely business that led them to go so far as to manipulate children's attitudes to sex as soon as they were in kindergarten. Later, with cards, they lectured at schools and knowingly prescribed pills that failed and distributed condoms of poor quality. As she mentioned, if you teach a girl that abortion should be her natural contraception, you will gain a long-term client. In this system, as many as 42% of the girls returned to them! But that's not all, as this perversion is growing - a global business with embryos and aborted fetus is thriving. These are actually used in the cosmetics, food and especially pharmaceutical industries. In the US, it's ironically the *Planned Parenthood Federation of America* (PPFA) which is at the forefront of this disgusting business. And who originally funded this organization? "Surprisingly", Mr. John D. Rockefeller Jr. Hormonal contraception is also a pharmaceutical business that originated in the 1960s to increase female employment. In the nineties, there were few women who did not have the contraceptive prescribed. However, the hormonal changes that these drugs cause affect women at the comprehensive level, and paradoxically men also. And this is the new real threat to change the essence of man - through the hormones - because we can not control them ourselves.

> *"I feel we have reached such a level of gender equality that it has begun to cure hormonal systems. Men are feminine, they have little testosterone because of this poor sperm, and women, on the contrary, have inactive female hormones, have higher cortisol and testosterone,*

and it looks like as if there is unification even at the hormonal level. And that is completely fatal in terms of reproduction."
H.Maslova, psychogynecologist

The latest example of this sick relationship between "women and sex" could be the life story of Waris Dirie. In her book *Desert Flower*, she clearly describes unsavory practices which she, unfortunately, had to experience as a young girl. To this day, more than 2 million women around the world suffer or die annually because of absurd female genital circumcision, which amounts to about 6,000 women/girls per day. Presently there are approximately 140 million women alive that have been mutilated this way worldwide. On the contrary, the male circumcision may have its health benefits without endangering one's "manhood". However, for women it represents an absolute deformation of their genitalia's natural condition, which results in a lifelong physical and psychological trauma. **None of the Western religions** (Christianity, Islam, Judaism) **recognize woman as a whole, and certainly not as a sexual being.**

However, there was a time before, when women abused their power - the power of emotion, intuition and manipulation - to control men. So from a holistic point of view, this is mainly the offset of energies. Therefore, now we need to find the true harmony between men and women.

Sex is nature itself. Do not suppress it, otherwise it will result in something much worse than you'd expect. According to statistics, ninety-eight percent of mental illnesses and neuroses are caused by suppressed sexual desires. If you decide in your mind that you are going to avoid sex in the future, suddenly you see it everywhere, in everything, and most of all, it will take place in your dreams as well. If you're not in love (when you are incomparably closer to meditative sex), you should learn to use sex as meditation – give it a whole new dimension, fully enjoy the presence of your partner, do not just wait for your orgasm. The more you meditate with the help of sex, the less impact it will have on you. When sex becomes meditative, you will feel love. Love is a combination of gratitude, friendship, and compassion. If you're feeling these, you can make love, transform sex into lovemaking. Do not be afraid that you will lose something. On the contrary, you'll gain much more. You've probably experienced momentary glimpses of meditative sex, but you just did not know it. In fact, it is a very profound experience to such an extent that if you get to know it, you will not want to go back to the superficial gymnastics.

Meditation is nothing serious, meditation is pure joy! It is the only way you can transform sex. Without meditative consciousness, sex will only repeat itself. It is vulgarized and eventually it becomes boring for you. You feel cheated and you seek sexual excitement elsewhere. You will begin to search for new ideas, toys, people... and all this just because you didn't find "meditation" in sex. You have become a slave to sex, it has become your master. And you can't be friends with someone who controls you. Blaming "natural instinct", which is true in a way, but the difference between us and animals is in the consciousness. You can consciously decide how you will act. It can be controlled, but excuses suit you better. It is pleasing for our ego, not for our soul. Therefore, after this "one night stand" you prefer to leave. You simply satisfied your "lust", which in this case is comparable to animals in heat, nothing more - nothing less. Of course, it is only up to you which kind of life you choose. You are satisfied with it just because you have not seen anything that went beyond. Be vigilant, alert, become an observer of your own self. Begin to want more and explore all the possibilities we have. But do not make it a priority. This is just one component of the whole. If you are awake and conscious during sex, sensitive and attentive, you're on your way to transformation.

> *"Life is a constant movement towards a state of no ego, no time, whether you realize it or not. The deep desire of every human is to know his true self, to know the truth, know the original, timeless source, unite with what is outside of time, to achieve a clean state without ego. The world revolves around sex in order to satisfy the inner longing of the soul."* Osho

Nowadays, love usually comes before sex. Actually, it should be the other way around. What you feel at first is nothing other than attraction - a chemical reaction in your body that leads to sex. Each meeting is karmic, whether it's for a day or for a few years, it should happen. In any case, it is about sex. If not, you are on the level of friendship. (You are afraid of friendships between men and women and that is why you say that they do not exist. That means only one thing - you don't have a natural attitude towards sex). If you are strongly attracted to someone, you need to overcome this initial tension to really get to know the person well. Therefore, it is typical that the whole passion - so-called love - disappears after sex. Love, in fact, comes after sex. Then you really get to know the person who you chose according to chemistry. It's just unnecessary suppression of nature. Even if you have met someone, and walked and talked for hours so you could be persuaded that you fell in love. It was, unfortunately, mainly your ego which felt so understood, heard, related... But if your sexual appetites are completely different, infatuation will quickly grow into friendship after some time. Of course, you may feel otherwise, it all depends on your centre - heart and feelings – as always. I'm just trying to describe what is a healthy approach to sex. Do not underestimate it, but at the same time do not overestimate it.

If you are closer to sex, enjoy sex. If you are closer to love, enjoy love. It is only society that keeps you from enjoying your natural sexuality. For example, in Polynesia people make love in public. They are not familiar with this suppression, and so no rape or murder exists there. And which is worse: sex or murder? **Try to be interested in sex as if it was some kind of art.** After all, it's the most beautiful art that we have distorted. Try to learn more about tantra. It's not something you should worry about, exactly the opposite. It is a way to transform sex. For example, in tantra you should satisfy yourself first, and then you can make love for hours. Isn't that a better, more enjoyable idea than ten minutes of exercise? "Lust" is the one that makes pervert sexuality, not love. **Make sex a celebration, not a custom.**

Tantra says: accept yourself as you are. Only then can transformation be possible, transformation in which you must use yourself in particular. The basic point of tantra is sex – the basic energy through which we were born. All the cells in our body are sexual, that`s why our minds constantly revolve around sex. Tantra is based on the inherent power of sex, and it doesn't fight against it. It converts it and advises you to be friendly to it. It is our energy, it is not a sin. It can be used against you and it can be used in your favor. It is pure, your attitude is up to you. The moment you get excited and you are full of energy which is going to be released - forget that you are going to have an orgasm for a while. Stay in this beautiful flow of energy… merge with your partner, try to create unity, enjoy the warmth, excitement, become one, create a circle and surrender to the present moment.

According to old alchemical images that you surely know, you can choose from three states. It's a picture of a naked woman and man standing inside geometric shapes – a circle, a triangle, and a square. This is the basis of tantra.

During normal sexual intercourse there are actually four people present, not two – that`s why there is a square. That is because each of the partners is divided into a thinking part and a feeling part. This means that there is an absolute split into four corners. It's an encounter, but it is not fusion. This happens, unfortunately, most often.

The second type of encounter looks like a triangle. Two people are present – with two bases. For a brief moment they become one - but only for a while. It's better than a quadrangular encounter. In fact, it gives you more joy and vitality because you, at least for a brief moment, join the existence - merge into one. You broke a quadrilateral separation - but only for a while.

The third option is the best – it is represented by the circle. This encounter is tantric, timeless. You become a circle. There is no time present, no desire, only fusion, unity, and infinity. This can happen only if you do not seek ejaculation. If you have a problem with it, satisfy yourself beforehand and then just take the orgasm already present in every cell of your body. Don't hurry, you have a lot of time.

Relax and take it all as a game. This is not about control - that would be contradictory. You need to relax completely. Close your eyes, feel the energy of the other, dissolve yourself, lose yourself, but do not push it - relax. And if you look into your partner's eyes, you will feel even greater depth; there is a true meeting of souls. Old habits will reverberate from the beginning. Do not fight them. Watch them, accept them, and stay in the present. Initially, you may feel like you're a bit lost, but it's just an old habit - nothing more, nothing less. After some time, however, the peak will transform into a valley and you will understand that no peak was worth it. Just be patient, relaxed, meditative.

> *"Sex is more than an act of pleasure, it's the ability to be able to feel so close to a person, so connected, so comfortable that it is almost breathtaking to the point you feel you can't take it. And at this moment you are a part of them."*
>
> T. York

There are also "channelings" available (receiving information from higher consciousnesses, other entities, angels, and masters), in which Mary Magdalene (Jesus' lover) explains the natural sexuality that was deliberately suppressed by the Church 2000 years ago because it is the strongest form of energy. She calls it the sex magic of Isis, which is part of the alchemical practices of Hora, through which she and Jesus reached ecstatic states of consciousness. (But for this understanding you must first go through the basic knowledge this book contains. Only then can you get beyond the boundaries of it. Otherwise, it might sound to you more like some science fiction right now.) Thanks to sexual energy, we can activate the greatest potential in ourselves to create the strongest magnetic field, use our full potential here on Earth. The strength of this magical exercise is comparable to an atomic bomb. However, it is necessary to practice it with your soul mate and the basic emotion must be love, otherwise it will only be an exercise which won't lead to the expected results. Once you succeed, it will be a huge leap towards understanding yourself and the universe as well. For this to happen, you have to know the alchemy of the light body, Mer-ka-ba. The sex which is practiced today has nothing to do with its real potential.

> *"For nearly two thousand years one of the strongest and fastest ways to the knowledge of God has been described as bad. It's ironic that the church has denounced it as a sin - to intimidate all those who would come to it by chance..."*
> Mary Magdalene

Tantra gives us higher energy to release, which is positive. When our energy moves in a circle, no energy is being lost, quite the contrary. Both partners give life to each other - they extend their lives. If you are able to delve into such excitement that will not only lead to climax but to life itself, you will understand sex. Your partner represents just the doors to existence, to the feeling of the whole. Once you experience it, you can use this technique alone and it will give you new freedom - independence from the other. What will happen is that the whole existence will become your lover. Later on, a morning walk or sunset can give you this feeling. You can really be in a sexual liaison with the entire universe. If you learn to create this circle in yourself, you will feel true freedom. Therefore, tantra says that sex is the strongest bond. It can be used as a way of absolute relief, but it may also "destroy" you. It's the same as poison - it can be used as medicine, if you know something about it.

First, learn to give, to make receiving more enjoyable. Do not be selfish. If you want to share, you must first have. Therefore, it is also very important that we change our attitude towards masturbation. It is natural and everyone has been doing it since childhood. We all experiment with our bodies daily, so let us learn to accept it. It's your body, you really own it, and you should treat it with respect. The more you indulge yourself, the more you can give. Again, it's just society under the influence of morality, deeply influenced by religion, who are simply trying to make us feel guilty. Nothing like that exists! It's your body, your temple. Take care of it, do good to it. Only in this case, using stimuli from the outside (e.g. porno) means that you satisfy your body with outside influences. That`s why masturbation does not lead to a feeling of fulfillment. You just satisfy your body. It's okay, but it has no depth, that's all. However, we have released a stream of energy that would otherwise stagnate (it could later turn out as destructive, as we can use it creatively). But even masturbation can be upgraded to meditation in the event that you enjoy yourself totally in the present. You can experiment with it as you please, it's up to you. If you acquire a real awareness and consciousness, everything can become completely different.

The most sensitive topic concerning sex is fidelity. In today's terms, maybe it would be better if we called it property.

"Marriage as such is neither good nor bad,
success or failure is only in us."
A. Maurois

It's just a game of ego, that feeling that someone is yours. Nobody can be yours or will ever be able to be. In this world, we are actually alone – everyone is alone. Cheating, as we know it, appears only because our relationships are based on poor foundations. Most relationships continue just because of reason, children, prejudice... Whenever there is a "because", the relationship is not complete. Therefore, you start looking for somebody who has something that your partner does not have. If your relationship is based on true love, understanding, friendship, compassion, and you are sexually satisfied, you have no reason to look for another partner. But you're afraid to come out of the certainty, and you are rather cowardly searching for satisfaction somewhere else while at home you play a game of perfection. It's your stupidity and especially your fear. It suits you to remain in a relationship that doesn't satisfy you, particularly because you're afraid of being alone. If you learn to live on your own, you will never need this "certainty". If your ego disappears, you will never have any need to own someone ever again. However, if the "cheating" happens "by accident" (karmic attraction), there is no reason to make a huge scene about it. It's "just" sex. But it is very difficult to accept this position after so many years of distorted attitudes. However, no encounter is accidental and it is all happening for some reason. (Maybe you just have to go through the feeling of forgiveness because you did the same thing in past lives.) But if stronger feelings for someone else come into it, then be honest, first and foremost with yourself. Only then can you be sincere with others.

"When you are faithful to yourself, you
cannot be unfaithful to anyone."
W. Shakespeare

Today's "spiritual posers" have found a detour in this direction as well. They can't bear the responsibility which comes with the relationship, and so they use so-called freedom as excuse. This is again, however, mainly for ego fulfillment. You can't go in depth of relationship if you are changing partners like socks. And if it happens that they have a long-term partner, they feel free to cheat on them with the feeling that if their partner does not know about it and they don't feel any remorse, then it's okay – all that matters is that they feel good - because after all, it is about freedom! Wrong. There are a myriad of different relationships, and lately mostly those based on sex, but if you do not live in totality, the feeling of emptiness will always hit you. And honestly, would you tolerate that from your partner? I doubt it. It is important to realize that with such an approach you are actually taking away the liberty of another - stealing his life. The second thing is that there are a lot of women who know about their husbands' infidelity, but they are satisfied with their standard of living or they make excuses saying that they have to hold their family together - maybe their mothers or grandmothers lived like that, so it's probably normal… But listen to your heart - does this relationship really fulfill you? Is this what you dreamt of as a little girl? You have given up your self-esteem in exchange for money and property. You are living in a dead relationship. Of course, it's up to you - what really satisfies you. If you are intentionally hurting someone, it will return to you, always. Whether you want it to or not. In the end, it depends only on your understanding and agreement. The second fact is that **if you are completely conscious, if you are truly awake and aware of yourself, you do not do to others what you do not want done to you**. This means that if we realize that we are part of each other, that we are mostly a mirror, we have respect for others (the same respect we feel for ourselves), we will not do it. Men have a bigger problem with it, because presently they act mostly unconsciously – subconsciously. Note that if a man is very excited, he transfers all the energy to his genitals. In fact, it could be compared to the state of a trance. If you give him some information while in this state, he certainly will not remember it. However, if he focuses on it (if you gave him this example), he will remember, because he will already be acting consciously. That's the difference.

If we look at this issue from a historical point of view, there are indisputable facts as to why this kind of property was established. When the world was not so technically developed, people had to take care of themselves as well as they could. In the north, they had to be coherent and resourceful. The most important thing for women was to become "economically" sufficient to take care of their families - and therefore, they needed a man. That's why the institution of marriage was established – to ensure security - property. You wouldn't find anything deeper in it, regardless of our nature, and in particular, regardless of the opinion of women. So there was a feeling created in the woman - that she "must" have a man, otherwise she will not survive - as was many times true in the past. In the southern countries, you will notice that this need for fidelity is not so strongly rooted. That's because in areas where it was warm, women could easily take care of their families. They did not have such a problem with housing or food which, in this case, grew everywhere. They did not, and still do not, have the same approach as women who have to fight for their existence. Of course, in the south this led to extremes, such as polygamy, but again, this cult was created by man. It is definitely not suitable for women, but unfortunately nobody asked them about it. Therefore, the question of loyalty is particularly a female problem, and for men it is typical to make excuses - by bringing up nature and history. This approach naturally led to the need to "own" someone - from both sides.

"In a hunting society where birthrates are low and death rates are high, both the female and the male must protect, provide for and treasure each child. In Africa where men were driven more by sexual coupling than the love of family, and where the most honored are those with the greatest number of sexual conquests, an

individual child or its mother meant little to those males who had many. When human life is too abundant it tends to lose value. On the other hand, in a struggling small band that faces the severest challenges of survival, each life becomes precious. In its rarity comes the appreciation of life's beauty. Our ancestors had that appreciation. A man who has many sexual partners is not as selective about his mate as one who must choose for a lifetime. And, in the hard climes, women and their families had to select men for their loyalty and responsibility. So evolved our race and so arose the nuclear family."

D. Duke: My Awakening

It is not at all about monogamy, bigamy, or polygamy. These are just words to justify the fact that we act unconsciously. This can be likened to a state of drunkenness or even to a murderer - he can't remember his offense, he was acting unconsciously. That`s why he will say in court that he did not do it. Actually, he was not present in his own reality for a while. It is unfortunately the same with our so-called instincts. It is all just because your actions are based on your past and it simply suits to you shield yourself with apologies which allow you to act any way you chose. If you are lacking something in the relationship, you are only deceiving yourself if you are looking for it somewhere else and at home you are pretending that everything is okay. **Look at the situation holistically and not selfishly - that is the difference in the perception of consciousness**, which is currently still at the level of phrases. An interesting thing is that it is mostly women who are able to forgive in cases of cheating. The male ego cannot bear the image of somebody else in his place. However, if he is unfaithful, he asks for forgiveness. If women should come to hate men based on all their experiences with them, it would mean the end of all relationships. A disappointed man is much worse than a disappointed woman and he suffers for a long time. Sometimes his ego cannot get over it at all, and he chooses to stay alone rather than risk another aggravation. Excuse me, gentlemen but you are incomparably weaker in this.

Homosexuality.

Although I was looking for some specific information, I found nothing more than assumptions. With confidence I can say only one thing: homosexuality is a result of our war with sex. It can't be found anywhere outside civilized society. Natives who live in isolated areas can't even imagine it. It is very strange that in this day and age of "highly modern society" no one knows exactly what homosexuality actually means.

Homosexuality was, as a medical diagnosis, excluded from the tenth edition of the International Classification of Diseases on January 1, 1993. Until then, it was usually explained as a mental disorder - as "*an exclusive or predominant affection towards people of the same sex, with or without sexual intercourse.*" This was decided by doctors from the American Psychiatric Association (APA), who in 1973 removed the diagnosis of homosexuality from the diagnostic manual of diseases. Many APA leaders who were behind that step now admit that the decision was not correct and acknowledge the political background. The "unpathologizing" of homosexuality happened after gay movement activists forcibly stopped several APA meetings in the early '70s. This step was not preceded by any serious scientific debate. In an effort to present homosexuality as normal, their arguments were as follows:

Homosexuality is inborn – although there is still absolutely no proof of that.

1. *It is determined genetically* – there has been genetic analysis performed on several homosexual couples and the conclusion was: "*The research evidence has not produced a 'gay gene'.* ***If we discover the gene of homosexual orientation, then we can begin to identify what causes the gene.***"
2. *Homosexuality can be found in some animals, so it's natural.* Animals are not "conscious" species, so once again, we

should note that comparing humans with animals borders on absolute unawareness of self. Homosexuality is a rare exception among animals, the same goes for the example of cannibalism. Nature and Wildlife Magazine notes on these topics: *"It occurs because the animals get confused and by mistake, they recognize their own kind as a prey. Exceptional situations occur in animals because of the lack of other means of expression, such as speech. Their absence can be replaced by other affective states, expressed by aggression, fear or sociability. Often, they change their sensations or objects. Animals can adapt to external stimuli faster and behave beyond the norms, since they are not bound with any rules like people - such as public opinion, the conscience and so on."* So experiments indicating that homosexual behavior is in harmony with nature on the basis that it occurs between animals are only fabricated. Biologists and psychologists do not share this view. Logically, if there were purely homosexual species, they would have died out long ago. The fact that animals of the same gender have sex can be attributed to the natural attitude of animals towards sex. They have no prejudices as people do. Only prejudices push homosexuals into the position of outsiders. Again, the problem is only in the human mind - judgement, morality, and religion. You are able to totally condemn a man just because of a few minutes of "gymnastics".

"Religion has tried to poison sex, but sex has survived, it is still alive and full of poison." Nietzsche

Homosexuality is a phenomenon typical only for human beings. This does not mean we should denounce it, exactly the opposite. It just has to be understood. Every single person is unique, and any "categorization" in this case does not make sense. The causes may have occurred in past lives, in the prenatal period, during childhood… One of the possible causes could even be the absence of the father or mother's dominance, etc. It might be due to the spiritual growth of their parents, who need to go through such a relationship, although their gay child is paradoxically very balanced. There may be many other reasons indeed, but we all should take responsibility and move forward from this point. The soul itself chose this incarnation – this body, because it needs to go through this, regardless of the reasons. (From the higher perspective, we live in a special age that many souls simply wanted to experience, and they did not care in what kind of body.)

"A person who suffers from gay affection, lacking friendship with his father, and in his adult life is experiencing "reparatory urgency": he wants to gain his share of masculinity that has not developed in relation to his father from his sexual partner. A critical period for gender identification is the period before the third year of life. If the father does not confirm the boy's initiative, he does not notice him or even openly rejects him, the boy is internally injured and defrauds his father to defend himself from further injuries in the future. On the other hand, his father remains a mystery to him and masculinity remains a fascinating territory. The disorder of sexual identity is the foundation of later homosexual attraction. The mechanism of psychological causes of lesbianism is similar to that of male homosexuality. But the girl must go only one way, away from her mother, to create her personal and feminine identity - unlike the two phases of separation in the boy: when a boy as an individual separates from a father, he must still confirm his distinction from him as a man (while the girl does not have to do the second step)." J. Nicolos (www.narth.com)

No matter how much I like gays and lesbians, I must say that they more often suffer from various mental disorders. They are more labile, more prone to addiction and hypersensitivity. In general, they seem to be more unstable than heterosexuals. On the other hand, they are much more open minded (to other opinions) as they are a part of a minority. So, in reality, a transsexual may have a much more "sober view" about this world than some eternally frightened heterosexual. Paradoxically, fidelity does not have so much value for homosexuals and this is also proof that this is really only "a problem", which is manifested through sexuality. I'm not saying that homosexuality is a problem. What I am saying is that homosexuality is fundamentally a problem of our approach to sex in general, and every personal "trigger" is actually in the past. Nothing more, nothing less. The proof of this claim is the fact that in homosexual relationships there are always two opposite poles - one female and one male. So the relationship still needs two units - we really do not glaze nature. Not to mention the relationships in which partners (male and female) are together just for the sake of society, while each of them has a different sexual orientation. We live in incredibly hypocritical times. We have to look at it and try to see it with all the nonsense that we have created. At present, there are paradoxically even "heterosexual" men who see homosexuality as something attractive. They do not know how to live their sex lives, so they actually experiment with everything. The irony of the situation is that they have begun to cheat on their wives with men because it is much more convenient for them - when they are out with a male friend, women do not suspect anything. Today there are even gyms full of gay men, which means that they are no longer confused sensitive boys, but at first glance real men. This is very backwards, and indeed there is a big gender problem that is fully reflected through sexuality. In fact, we are losing our identities as men and women. Identifying as LGBTI (lesbian, gay, bisexual, transgender and intersexual) is also being greatly supported by our elites, who have the biggest problems with their sexuality themselves in the first place. Presently it is even contemplated that letter "P" for pedophiles would be added to this acronym. They even go as far as to compare pedophilia to heterosexuality. It is really going overboard. If you are gay, please note that this is again just a "label" that is not an essential part of who you are; you may have identified with it, but it is not who you are in the first place. I understand the need for registered partnerships, but this is happening mainly due to capitalism and health policy. Everyone should have equal rights, but this form of "LGBTI marketing" is not proper and it actually affects many children, who in their purity and innocence, absorb all these sick attributes of the society. In Brussels, for the fourth time (2018), a trade show of children for gay couples was held! Babies offered as goods?! How did it come to this?! There isn't anyone who would really defend children's rights around the world anymore! These days we should rather have marches supporting real men and real women.

"Homosexuality is not a problem. We should start to be interested in real problems and not drown in unreal ones. Here lies the trap of our mind: creating unreal problems, which you need to deal with, while the real problematic issues are still increasing. It's an old strategy: politicians, priests and so-called spiritual leaders offer false problems to solve to keep you busy with this falsehood." Osho

In the end, from a higher perspective, we are even heading for so-called neuter (but it should not be of a physical nature). In the future, gender will not have the weight it has today. Unfortunately, we are again on the road to extremism, even with regard to this issue. This "neuter", if grasped correctly, would represent unity among the sexes, which means full understanding of the masculine and feminine principles in ourselves. But all over the world we can see confused children who cannot "grasp" their sex today. When you think of your childhood, each of us was dominant in one principle (man or woman), despite our sex. This means that there were girls with boys' character and boys with girls'. It was normal, and with time everyone found themselves (or did not find themselves, and that is still reflected in their relationships). Today, however, much more sensitive children are born, in relation to existence and to themselves, and therefore they often have problems understanding themselves in early childhood. As these "problems" have never been defined, instead of seeking for themselves what is missing, they are supported by a system of radical solutions to change their sex. The fact is that the souls who have chosen a body that contrasts with what they feel are exceptional, but it is definitely not as extreme as what we see today in direct transmission. Knowingly, a "cult of neuter" has been created so that we are getting worse at returning to ourselves. We are losing our identity. It is not an accident that these neuter models will be offered jobs in the fashion business. However, this approach is again only an extreme example of human abuse as such. **Each of us has one dominant principle - male or female. Our task is to discover the other half in ourselves and to unite them. The soul is "unisex"**, but with such a low level of consciousness, we are heading towards the extinction of the human race, and it is not right. (And again, we can find a connection with religion where the word "Shekhinah" is abused a word originally from the Kabbalah which represents the female equivalent of God. So we have an allegorical name for this connection, but, again, it is misunderstood.)

What happened to man? Who is responsible for this? Everyone. Although you may think it has nothing to do with you, this program circulates in you too, the program which has, over the centuries, been creating this perversion - struggle with nature. Now it is very important to recognize that **sexual energy is divine** and interest in sex should be religious (though we must first understand the true meaning of religious). So in any case, **enjoy your sexuality, try to understand it, and whatever you feel, let it flow freely.** What is this global hypocrisy and judging good for? **It is again particularly our school - part of our development as a human race.**

"Man is incurably religious..."
C. G. Jung

The first step towards the liberation of sexuality should start with children. Allow them to be naked as much as possible so they can naturally accept their own bodies as well as the bodies of others. Start to promote this approach, talk with them openly and frankly, and do not insult their natural intelligence. If everything is properly explained to them, their bodies becomes a natural part of them. If they are surrounded by love, in the future, they will not succumb to unnecessary perverse deviations. They will not have any reason to! An hour of silence during the day will help them keep this energy. At approximately the age of fourteen, the gate of meditation is opened – a meditative state. For the first time they start to realize their true souls and their desires. Awakening this moment before the first sexual experience will stop the mad hunt for sex. Energy finds its noble use. This is the first phase of the transformation of sex. It is precisely the period when children, respectively young people, should feel our love – teach them to love. It is a paradox that exactly in this period they usually lack love so much, and therefore, they have to search for it everywhere. Children from harmonious families tend to have sex later, when they are ready, as they are much more aware. Conversely, children of disharmonic families crave sex because they lack love. People who "do not know" love are usually filled with sexual desires and they remain obsessed with sex. Their happiness is directly proportional to how much love they receive. Therefore, love is the basic energy - even in sex.

There are two ways to reach a higher consciousness, to reach your inner essence: sex and meditation. Sex is in our nature, so it is natural for all of us and we all practice it - including animals and plants. It is available to everyone. However, if one wants to get over this most basic instinct, he will go on, he will add a whole new dimension to sex. This will be the birth of a new man. If not, we are still equal to the animals. Although we dress like humans, eat like humans, talk like humans, but we are like animals inside. That's why that animal in you screams, and mostly at the worst possible moments.

Sex should represent the understanding of souls, harmony, and pure joy! Life itself… But one day we will have to let it go too. In sexual intercourse we seek unity, a fusion. However, this experience depends on someone else. One needs to unite with the whole universe. An encounter between two people is only temporary, while a connection with the universe is eternal. This understanding will set you free. No human relationship is eternal, so many times ecstasy turns into loneliness because we can't merge forever. This is that fictitious internal conflict which can never be solved in relation to someone. However, when you unite with the whole universe, you will experience bliss which you can't even imagine now. If you stop depending on others, you will be flooded with a feeling of love and infinite freedom. Only then, will you be able to give it to others, and then your relationship will start to make real sense. Your love relationship may last your whole life so you can go more in depth and enjoy it like never before! However, again we return to the same: Watch yourself and be aware of yourself even during sex. Be really honest with yourself and it will open the door to higher understanding. **The difference is in quality, not in quantity.**

To conclude this topic, I would like to clarify the two oldest questions: penis size and the size of a woman's breasts. As it is often said: Even with a little clown you can play a great performance. It's true. Every man has a different penis size, and so every woman's vagina is a different size. This means that we should find a partner with whom we are in absolute harmony in this area as well. Even so, the vast majority of men with large penises only try to satisfy themselves during sex and it is painful for most women. However, men with small penises are much more sedulous and they can be incomparably better lovers. The same goes for breast size - a lot of men do not like big boobs at all, quite the contrary. Again, if you find your true soul mate, you will merge physically too. So in the end, the size really does not matter. Everything is individual and depends only on us and our approach, nothing more - nothing less.

"In God sex becomes sensuality. God is sensual. Sex is life, sex becomes fun, joy, play. Emotions become sensitivity, compassion, love. A sense becomes understanding, conscious, meditation." Osho

THE MIRROR

"The mirror cannot reflect the gods if monkeys are looking in it."
E. Hemingway

The most important thing of all is to know yourself - only then are you able to deal with everything else that comes from the outside – from others.

Everything that annoys you about others (i.e., that evokes any unnatural emotional reaction in you), you do as well.

It's the most wonderful paradox, a great challenge, and most of all, it is a super game of finding out what you are able to think about yourself. It is often the most difficult self-confession. Really, anything that bothers you about others, you actually carry in yourself. But at least for a while, you have to give up on your ego. If you realize it, face it, and accept it as a natural part of you, you will forgive yourself and also others. After some time, you can rise above it and with a little self-irony you can maybe even laugh at it. Life can be very amusing if you have the right attitude towards it.

Your own reflection can be found in others. You can recognize yourself through others.

Out of all these chapters, this is the one that will cause your ego to get the most rebellious - *this cannot possibly be true! I know so many simpletons, I simply cannot be compared to them?!* Or can I? If it truly set you off, if you are really angry, if you cannot reconcile yourself to it, and you are "fighting" (condemn) it on any level, then you can be sure it's true. You have at least a part of it in you. The part which has to be removed. And the sooner you deal with it, the better it will be for you.

The character trait that bothers you the most in another person is somehow a part of you and you often behave the same way towards someone else yourself. Quite often do other people reflect it to us to an extreme, which helps us to get to know ourselves and it should make it easier for us to notice it and work with it. It is a character trait that is taken from the past and is not an essential part of us. However, this may also be a reflection of a trait that we are lacking, respectively one that we have suppressed. In its essence, we envy it in others, so it also causes a disproportionate emotional reaction in us. (For example, it irritates you how spontaneous and crazy someone can be because of how you always plan and rationalize everything yourself. It is a signal for you to introduce more spontaneity into your life and to give up those strict plans. So even the "mirroring" technique has two sides to the same coin.)

"A relationship is undoubtedly a mirror in
which you discover yourself."
Krishnamurti

Exercise:

Think about the person who annoys you the most. How does he do it? Analyze precisely the exact cause. Try to get into the details, define the exact characteristics. Or just the opposite – generalize the feature. Now, think and honestly admit when you have behaved very similarly, if not the same way. Usually not towards the same person, but paradoxically to someone else. But the pattern of behavior remains the same. When you admit it and realize it, you are doing the best possible thing for yourself.

In practice this means, for instance, this: I am angry about how stubborn some man is. Question: How often have you been stubborn? The pattern of behavior is what matter, not the situation. Be self-critical. Or here is another example regarding general characteristics: I'm angry that people do not care about the world, that they are so ignorant! (So, I feel that I can do nothing about it, "they" are the culprits, not me!) How often do you ignore your true feelings towards yourself? How can you save the world if you still have not saved yourself? It is impossible, and every person you meet only reminds you of that fact. Or, for example, many people do not actually listen. You get angry because you are trying to say something to that person, but he continues to do the same thing so that you feel that you have no influence. Are you sure you listen to others? Do you listen to the person who is doing this? Perhaps he answered your question several times, but you are so wrapped up in yourself or imagine he gave some kind of "expected response" which you would like to hear that you feel like he is not listening to you, while it is just that his answers differ from those you would like to hear. So who's actually angry – him or you? Thus, is it his problem or yours? If only you are angry, then address yourself. Why do you have these expectations? Why do you want to change someone else instead of just changing your approach or opinion? If the other neither solves the issue nor emotionally responds, then it is you who is not listening. He is setting up a subconscious mirror for you. If he is your partner, first note whether he also really wants what you want from him or whether it is only what you want. And if it happens so much that it is harmful to you, then find another solution rather than voluntarily remaining in a situation that is not beneficial for you. Mainly, do not worry about things that you cannot change. You really cannot change others, you can only change yourself. In this way, your surroundings will begin to change as well and you will become open to people you meet rather than fighting them. The more you ignore this fact, the greater the extremes of their unnatural nature you will encounter. It intensifies proportionally to your ignorance, so you should really be able to see and understand that it is not "their" problem, but yours. Accept it, start to work on it = you will stop meeting those kind of people. It is as simple as that. All of these are just our tests.

Also, you may see yourself in another person in a good way, but it tends to be mostly misleading, unless you really know yourself. You create an idealized version of yourself and you begin to feel that the person is your soul mate! (until the first problem comes). In any case, if it is not reciprocated, then such person is there just to teach you something. Overcome your ego and work on yourself through this relationship. We do not always need to be lovers to have a good relationship. Friendship between a man and a woman is the most beautiful school because we are passing exactly the counterpart which we should balance in ourselves. Do not be angry at your partner, try to understand him, and in particular, always try to learn from the situation.

"People have a constant tendency to blame others for their misfortunes. Once you say that X, Y, Z are the culprits of my suffering, then you will never be able to change the situation. Apologies, always only apologies… If you cannot say: I am responsible for everything that happens in my life – if you do not accept responsibility for yourselves – nothing will change. Anything/anyone I am – it is my own creation.
I AM RESPONSIBLE FOR EVERYTHING
THAT TAKES PLACE IN MY LIFE.
Focus all your blaming on one point…
and that point is YOU."
Osho

Next time you find yourself in a similar situation – when you are angry and feel like attacking, take a deep breath and tell yourself to

STOP! Think about yourself – how often is your reaction exactly the same? So, are you angry at yourself when you do this? I highly doubt it. So just smile to yourself and try to forgive the person who doesn't know what he is doing (but forgive yourself as well). He is living in ignorance, but you are not, not anymore! Do not play this game of false ego importance again. If you want to climb the ladder of your own self-esteem, first you should start by respecting yourself, only then can you truly respect others. Be an inspiration for others, but try to avoid searching for fake respect. Of course, try to point it out to the other person - and you can safely guess if it is their ego or humility responding. It is also important not to become haughty, feeling that "I know how it works," and suddenly, without any self-reflection, holding a mirror up to others. If the person on the other side is not open enough to your opinions, you will not be able to do anything about it. You can only change yourself and your attitude. Please don't forget that. Everything in life should be accepted with humility. But do not confuse humility with weakness. Everything and everyone is connected and you are just starting to understand how it works.

Understanding "the mirror" is the most important thing you can do for yourself in practice. So mind your own business, forget about the rest.

"If you try to understand the universe, you will never succeed. However, when you understand yourself, you'll understand the whole universe."
Buddha

Begin to watch yourself, try to depersonalize from yourself for a while. Look at your reactions from a distance. Presently you are watching everything and everyone, but not yourself. This is a current phenomenon, as if you had nothing else to do. It is much easier to deal with others. We have created an almost perfect environment for this phenomenon. Actors, singers, politicians, athletes… you know everything about them! What for? Just to kill time, to avoid dealing with ourselves. You run away from yourself whenever it is possible. Because there is still something going on, there is always someone you can talk about. And it's actually very pathetic that we spend so much time doing that, but this age is fully accustomed to it. It's also a game of power which the media controls. The powerful and rich have turned the media into their toy - to deceive our senses, and especially to distract us from what is really going on, and especially from what is truly natural. What will my neighbor say about it? What will my mama say? And what about my colleagues, what will they say? Wherever you are, you are just changing masks, pretending you're someone else. You are afraid to be yourself; you can't find anybody who would truly be himself. You have learned how to take advantage of these masks. You have found out that you can work with them quite successfully, and what's more, they quite suit you. Of course, when you are standing on a stage which is full of actors who are wearing the most beautiful costumes, delivering the smartest monologues, and wearing the best make-up, and you are the only one naked there – you will not feel comfortable at all. You will quickly put your good old mask back on and stop sticking out from the crowd. It's easier to adapt to this popular game.

You are afraid of your own mirror, so instead of looking in it, you hold it up to others. Who cares if you do not see yourself. Using the game of energies you will push someone into a corner with your arguments and you will be satisfied with how successfully you "struck him out". Instead, you should realize that it is you who has the problem. You're the one who needs help. It is you who you should be interested in, no one else.

Older people and our parents are the worst. They suffer from some kind of a complex: "*I cannot help myself anymore at this age… for what should I change?!*" Or: "*I'm older - I'm right*", without ever looking at themselves critically. They have lost the motivation to change anything. However, they not living, just surviving. Indeed, is the opportunity to lead a happy life poor motivation?! It is never too late to understand yourself, and if you avoid it in your present life, you will meet it in the next. It's only up to you how long it will take. Really, you all are just the mirrors, and especially children.

> *"You are avoiding the mirror! But as long as you avoid it, you cannot become beautiful."* Osho

If you don't manage to truly understand that first and foremost you have to get to know yourself, your life will not have any deeper meaning. How much time do you waste dealing with issues of others? Even if you feel you want to help them, it's just your ego's desire to remake them according to the image you have, to make them different according to your own truth. Every person is an individual. And although we are all linked, and this can be seen in the principle of the mirror, we are all different. You cannot impose your truth on anyone else. It is yours, feel free to hold on to it, but do not force others to accept it as well. Others will always only be able to understand it in their own way. They are not even able to receive it in the form you were trying to pass it on to them. It is impossible for two people to think exactly the same way, so it is absolutely pointless to waste your energy on someone who doesn't even require anything from you in the first place. It's just an attempt to satisfy your desires. Therefore, first of all, deal with yourself and solve your own problems. However, others can help you a lot, thanks to you being able to recognize yourself in the other person. However, you may be fighting this idea, just observe yourself. It's the most you can do for yourself. Stop judging, no one has this right. Neither God nor priests, nor mothers – no one! Everyone is on a completely different level of development and was incarnated to Earth with a completely different, personalized mission. You will never be able to understand this all, and the only thing you can do is to learn to understand yourself. If you recognize yourself, you get rid of everything you no longer need, and you will learn to live meditatively (i.e., fully at any time, without routine or automation).

"Be unprincipled, unscrupulous, and live in the present moment! As a mirror reflects what is in front of it, your consciousness reflects the moment you encounter, and you are acting in accordance with this reflection. This kind of awareness is meditative, it is samadhi, it is innocence, it is divinity-thus Buddhahood."

Osho

JUDGMENT AND DENIAL

"Everything that irritates us about others can lead us to an understanding of ourselves."
C. G. Jung

Everything you condemn – you attract.

It's a fixed law of the universe thanks to which you can see very well that our lives have their own unwritten rules. Another piece of evidence is the old proverb "never say never".

There are some things which you cannot internally reconcile with, and you only fight with them, usually for your whole life, and therefore you condemn them. Whether you want it or not (respectively certainly not), you will attract them. For example, a woman who condemns rudeness, insults, and scolding will eventually marry the greatest cad. If you are strictly against alcohol, it is very likely that you will eventually start with it. You hate people who are hypocrites - but have you always told the truth to others to their face? Do you condemn how your neighbors educate their children? Later you may struggle with exactly the same problem while raising your child. Do you condemn cheating or corruption? Do you think you would never "do this" in your life? Do not worry, you'll get the chance and you'll see how easy it is to succumb to it. Do you condemn your parents for how they treated you in the past?

You will have the opportunity to experience the same thing, just to understand, to learn to accept everything that comes to you. **We do not know all the circumstances that lead to a person's behavior. Only when we open our hearts can we accept everything that comes to us without needing to judge it.**

"It is only with the heart that one can see clearly."
A. de S. Exupéry (The Little Prince)

A great example of how today's society works is definitely our attitude towards sex. At some point, it seems like man is being chased by a campaign promoting sex. It is everywhere and in everything, and at the same time, it is a totally suppressed and deprecated phenomenon. It was "frowned upon" for thousands of years, and thus it has recently been revealed in a very liberal, uncontrolled way. We suppressed it before and now it hits us in its most extreme forms. And it is the same with all the other things.

"The mind of an ordinary man is controlled by the law of contradiction. ***We are crashing into what we want to escape, because the object of fear finds itself at the center of our consciousness.****"*
E. Coue

Morality is the way which leads directly to condemnation. It should show us how the ideal man should be, according to some idea - but whose idea is it? We can never be "ideal", and this only leads to condemnation or even feelings of guilt. Condemnation is hypocritical, and like morality, it just creates more hypocrites. You will never be ideal in a sense that will suit everyone. Therefore, remain nothing more than a fake. It's also one of the reasons why man is schizoid. A child is in unity. He has no moral principles or codes, he lives in his nature, spontaneously and in the presence of the whole. Therefore, children are so beautiful. They are neither moral nor immoral - they are pure as they are. You can forgive your children for any stupidity, but when you are an adult, you have regrets regarding almost everything. It is you who set up the programs inside of them, how they should and shouldn't behave, what is right and what is wrong. You teach them what to condemn according to your own opinions. While at the same time, it is you who is wearing such an impressive number of masks. In front of your children you pretend to be the ideal role model, while you are hiding an enormous amount of information and many situations from them. It seems like a paradox, but moralists are always the first ones to fight against and condemn hypocrisy although they themselves are the ones who created it.

"Since ever we are meeting things we are supposed to learn to accept. So let's meet them – and turn them out into our own advantage."
R. Frost

Each judgment is made on the basis of the past and memorized programs. Education, meetings, your experiences, and also those of other people, all of this creates a certain kind of behavior that is the basis for your later condemnation. But be aware that everything repeats itself just to make you reconcile with it. Racism is the most visible program from outside – clear proof that you judge based on experiences that are not your own. No child is born as a racist, it is not his opinion, but yours. And even if it was your own experience, one meeting with a prat encourages condemnation of all the others?! Most frequently, men and women generalize the opposite sex in a similar way. *"All women are chickens and all men are swine"* - how often do we hear it?! So in practice, it seems that if a woman says over and over again that "all men are primitive", then those are exactly the ones she meets over and again. For example, if a man condemns "whores", then it is precisely the whores who excite him the most. And why do you have this program in yourself? Based on your past! Be aware of the situation or the person that caused this and then move on. The more you wander in the same pattern of behavior, the more you will attract exactly what you are rejecting.

Nobody has the right to judge you, and so you should not judge either. Are you perfect? Definitely not. Look at your life honestly and especially, critically. Could you be a role model for others? If you judge, you actually condemn. Each thought full of judgment will come back to you sooner or later. Do not waste your energy this way, it is absolutely not necessary. Look at yourself instead - and clean up the mess in your own house first.

"Nothing ever goes away until it teaches us what we need to know."
P. Chordon

IDEALIZATION

"Freedom we can idealize, but when it comes to our habits, we are completely enslaved."
Lama Ole Nydahl

Many times we come across the attitude: It will be this way, period! However, this approach is very dangerous, although only for ourselves. Do not idealize anything or anybody in your life, otherwise, the universe will show you that everything "can" be completely different from the way you want it.

You idealize your partner, job, kids, family, anything. You have some specific idea and you fiercely stick to it - you simply want it to be your way. You may not even know why, but you still insist on it and it is still not happening according to your wishes. Or maybe it is, but there is still something missing. The best way to illustrate this phenomenon is with a relationship. In the beginning, you see your partner with completely different eyes. Yes, it's love. Yes, it is "chemistry", but the essence is somewhere else. You idealize your partner and you create your own projection that you fall in love with. You have always wanted someone like him/her; that`s why you believe that he/she is really like that. Through the veil of chemistry and love euphoria you are overlooking those thousand and one little things. Or even "better" - you believe that your partner will change. In your mind, you have your own picture of them. You believe that they will change because of you, and you will not accept any other option. You think you can change them - you can manage it, no question about that! In that case, be aware that the opposite will happen. Everything will crystallize in a completely different way because you are obstinately sticking to your fixed ideas. Then the universe, through your partner who will be acting totally unconsciously, will show you that it can be, and therefore will be, completely otherwise. You start blaming everyone around you instead of taking responsibility for your own decision. You were the one who believed that your partner was going to change, no one else, not even they themselves. Maybe they promised you they would, but probably only under pressure from you - to save your relationship. If they had wanted to change - they would have done it based on their own decision. If they did not honestly intend to change, it will never happen. It was you who idealized them in your thoughts. You attributed qualities to them, qualities that you would like to see in them and you, unfortunately, somehow overlooked the reality. The first conflict will show you their true face, and believe me, this face will be much more natural than any of the idealized ideas or beliefs you had about them.

"Anger is authentic and true. There is no shorter route which would lead to harmony than anger. But negative anger hurts. An injury cannot cure another injury."
Osho

You idealize your children. You are literally putting your ideals into them. And mostly those which you didn't manage to fulfill. There is nothing worse than imprinting your past dreams and desires onto your child hoping they can fulfill them. But the fact is that, ultimately, fate will "screw" you over. The child will unconsciously - subconsciously - ruin all your ideas about them. For instance: You had always wanted to study law, but you did not. So now you're convinced that your child "should" become a lawyer. But your child is interested in the arts, and he wants to study something that you find totally irrational. You don't take it seriously and you tell him that he can do it after school in his free time. You fiercely insist that he study law. For his own good, of course.

There are three possibilities:

1. The child will do everything possible to show you that it is your idea, not his. The more you insist on something he does not want, the more you force him to do exactly the opposite. It doesn't matter how persuasive you are. If the child has a strong personality, he will go his own way, regardless of your ideas and obsessions - and he will even subconsciously ruin and destroy all of those conceptions of yours - idealizations.

2. You have a strong personality and you support him financially, so he should be thankful for that. So you force him to study what you want. Now you have achieved what you wanted, but the child will feel happy only when he does what he really enjoys. It could take years, but eventually he will leave law because he will feel he can become fulfilled with something completely different. He may not even understand why it took him so long to recognize it and find himself. If he has enough power, he will eventually return to what he was originally drawn to. It's a pity that he wasted so much time in his life chasing something he never wanted to do just because he wanted to have "peace at home".

3. He will never come back to his passion and he will find satisfaction in the most affordable substitutes such as sex and money.

"When there is nothing you idealize, it is impossible to provoke you. Nothing can touch you, because everything is important or unimportant to you on the same level. However, ***if your opponent finds a way to provoke you, you should be***

grateful to him, because he has found exactly the value to which you assign too much importance. " A. Svijaš

The point is that it is simply worthless to idealize something. Always admit that there are also other options, not only the one which you most wish for. Always. Do not project your unrealized ideas, problems, complexes, or past onto anything or anyone else! Whatever it may concern - whether it's work, relationships, sports, things, situations. It's natural that you want things to happen your way, even to imagine that everything is already happening the way you want it to, but always admit there are also other possibilities. Be open to more alternative results, because then in the case of failure at least it will not hurt so much. **Try to set an intention, not a goal. If you do not reach the goal, you will be disappointed. But the intention is always the way for what fills you.** Because if you have an "open heart", then you trust the existence and you know that "failure" does not exist. It's just our school – just another test that should move us forward. Do not be influenced by the opinions of others because they have no idea what is actually your way. Do not get drawn into their reality. Be aware of yourself and especially trust what you really feel. And if the situation caused sadness in you, enjoy it and don't be depressed. Something better always comes if you follow your heart. Oftentimes, however, different lessons are more important to us at that moment. It could also be a quite different way that will lead to what we really want in the long run, a way that we cannot even imagine today. And maybe over time we will even change the target, and we'll find something new - better. Because as we grow, the desires of our souls change as well.This means that you can achieve everything you want, if you can accept that it very well may turn out differently. Incriminate neither yourself nor others. It's a game, and if you are open to this game, everything will happen in your favor and will be beneficial for you, even if it sometimes may seem otherwise. With time, everything has its own greater sense - that is the law of the universe. Also, regarding people – rid yourself of any prejudices – everyone is your teacher, whether you want them to be or not. Trust your vision, just do not idealize it. Open yourself up to anything that comes. Whatever it is - accept it, and it will open new doors for you. **Trust the existence and do not look for ideals - create them!**

"If you put the responsibility upon the others, you will remain slaves forever, because no one can change anyone else. How can you change someone? Has anyone ever changed someone else? The desire to change someone else is the most unfulfilled desire in the world."
Osho

MATERIALIZATION

"You can rule the whole world, the whole universe. But if you cannot control your mind and senses, you lose."
H. H. Radhanath Swami

If you've ever read or heard about the book *The Secret*, then you can easily imagine what the concept of materializing is about (i. the law of attraction). Every thought is a form of energy which we send into the universe. It will be reflected there, and in a materialized form, it will return. This is probably the simplest way to explain it.

Every single thought IS material. If you do not believe it, you can begin your research in quantum physics. As radios broadcast, so do all the people in the world. (We just don't know how to tune in to the right frequency.) Every day we change our frequencies according to the feelings, emotions and mood we are going through. On this basis, we attract specific types of people or situations. As they say "like attracts like" and "birds of a feather flock together" - these old sayings only confirm this fact. We increase our frequencies through the paths of meditation, introspection, and in particular, self-perception. The higher you ascend on this imaginary ladder, the higher frequencies you broadcast. The lower ones become less and less attractive for you. This creates big differences between us - people, but on the level of consciousness that is psychological.

As we cannot keep our minds clean (we are not even able to think about one thing at a time), thoughts very often come back to us in different malformations. One idea overlaps another and we do not want to believe what we are actually thinking about… and that's the reason why our various desires are often garbled. Imagine that the universe is a giant copy machine and you want your image to be red, for example, but you are constantly thinking about the black one. Then you find out that it can also be yellow, but if it is not yellow, then the green is also very good. Although most of all, you would love to have it purple, but then you feel that you are asking for too much after all, so you think that you will never be able to get purple! What do you think, which color will be created from this mixture of thoughts?

"Many people spoil their lives only with the ideas of the unhappiness that may come."
A. Maurois

Thoughts will be materialized more and more quickly in the near future, so now it is extremely important that you learn to keep your mind clear. Use your thoughts consciously. Everything you can think of has a tendency to become real. You have already read about this in the chapter Mind, so I will just review it a little bit. **All the books which are supposed to help you achieve something are only about a way of thinking.** Be aware of this and stop attributing to them the magical powers which are inherent in every single person (rather than the thousands of motivational books). Mostly, the point is that you should write down various affirmations in the present tense as if you already had what you desire. Affirmations are actually little prayers that should be chanted every day.

I'm healthy and happy.

I live in wealth and abundance.

I have a job that I like and it fills me with joy.

I have a partner who loves me and I love him/her.

You can affirm absolutely anything. **First, however, define what you really want.** The best is to write down these affirmations on a piece of paper, hang them around your house, and read them daily. And you will give them even bigger power if you chant them aloud. Be aware of the fact that to make it work, you have to determine exactly what you want - and very specifically, because the universe is extremely creative. And, of course, you should not idealize. It may seem like materialization has lots of rules, but don't worry, it's very easy and simple. Basically, you only need to become a master of your mind. You can really achieve anything you want.

Often, however, these affirmations do not work. This is mainly because visualization is the most helpful in materialization, and mainly of the feelings of the heart. That is, the heart is the strongest source of electrical and magnetic fields in the human body. Thus far, we have been used to giving the brain preference in everything, and all those "motivational books" are based on it, too. Because if you have enough willpower and imagination (such as people born under the sign of the scorpion usually have), you will also achieve the expected results, and relatively quickly. However, compared to the heart, these waves emanating from the brain are weak. The heart is electrically a hundred times and magnetically up to five thousand (!) times stronger than the brain. As we know it, the physical world consists of these two fields. It can be proven on the basis of physics (not esotericism) that if we can change the magnetic or electric fields of an atom, we can change the matter. **Therefore, our beliefs are most important.**

Emotions are equally important in this process. In this case, apart from the fact that the emotions in us are always created by external events, you should realize that they come from the heart. Insults are the simplest example. They are "only" words. However, their real power is given to them by the emotions that accompany them. I can absolutely destroy and offend a person using a single word, but the same word can be used to aptly and humorously gloss a situation, or to say the same thing to someone with a smile which would have vastly different effects. The vibration of the word is thus conditional on a particular emotion. The dialogue is, of course, an issue for both sides, and I am not saying that we should insult each other peacefully and with a smile. Words should be valued – they are materialized vibrations - and it is up to us whether we use a particular word as a medicine or as poison. There is always a choice.

Regarding thus, materialization, it means that in practice you should imagine (feel) that you live as you wish. Try to see the situation that you're materializing. Try to feel like it has already become real. The more you believe, the sooner you will begin to see glimpses of your desires in reality. Believe and proceed step by step to fulfill your desires. However, be aware of the fact that it doesn't work when you are just sitting around doing nothing while waiting for the miracle. **The universe needs to see your effort to achieve the desired goal (purpose).** Every day, take one little step towards making it real. If this is not possible yet, then at least think about it how it would have come true. However, it is also possible that you will not get it right away. Then just trust in a "higher truth" and know that the situation is good how it is and there is a hidden reason behind it.

In retrospect you can see that everything has its higher purpose (if you listen to your inner truth and you are in harmony with your feelings).

And most of all, please, do not worry too much about things that don't exist yet. Because that is actually our minds' favorite "sport", all the time dealing with what would happen if... It steals our attention and gives it to everything we still do not have, instead of doing exactly the opposite. Therefore, we often attract it. It's even easier to deal with the negative aspects because we have to more or less get accustomed to them. We all have thousands of reasons why "it will not work" prepared in advance. They did not believe them, you do not believe yourself, so you do not believe others. Therefore, it is most important to start believing mainly in yourself, otherwise you will find yourself once again in a vicious circle. Permanently enjoy your presence, whatever it brings you. Learn to receive everything that comes to you with an open heart, because sometimes even the things you reject determine what you secretly really want. Each step determines the next one. Therefore, we must know the darkness so that we can see the light. Live in the present and be there in totality – 100% present at any one time and spend only a set amount of time on materialization, otherwise break free from it! It is extremely important not to remain in your imagination, not to live in an illusion, in a vision of something better. Presence is what you have created with your past thoughts and deeds. And now try to primarily control your thoughts to create a future which can make you happy. You are responsible for your thoughts, for your reality – no one else is. Take full responsibility for them (for yourself).

"The gift of mental power comes from God, a Divine Being,
and if we concentrate our minds on that truth, we begin to
vibrate with the same great force as the entire universe."
N. Tesla

Create an environment that is comfortable for you. Meet with people who fill you with joy and happiness. Consciously choose higher vibrations. If you desire to address the above frequencies, you can start through music, which also has its vibration. Even music is manipulated, and it has begun to be formed differently than it was originally. For nearly a century ago, the Austrian philosopher and reformer Rudolf Steiner began to alert humanity while warning it against negative tones that may cause greed and aggression. The "original music" has the fundamental frequency of 432 Hz, but current "Western music" has a frequency of 440 Hz. This negligible difference has a great impact on human perception and consciousness. It was officially approved in 1955 by the International Organization for Standardization (ISO) at the prior recommendation of the Nazi party. The reason is perhaps obvious to everyone. (Try listening to death metal or techno vs. Mozart and Beethoven, and you will feel the difference even without measuring instruments.) **The whole universe has its rhythm and consists of vibrations and sounds** – begin to sense this.

"In one experiment, laboratory mice were exposed to heavy metal music, and subsequently instead of going through a maze they became aggressive and killed each other." Fakty.cz.sk

"Since you are a musician, I would recommend you work with the tone F# on the level of 1.0 to 1.618. This way you will benefit from the vibration which directly connects to the Central Being. You will be inspired. From that moment you will attract all the modalities – to such an extent as you can express it, because the subliminal value of F# is the subliminal form of all that exists in nature."
Bashar (channeling through D. Anka)

"Beethoven's Symphony No. 7 is the expression of this vibration, the second movement, the first three minutes. This tonality allows you to find the exact vibration field of everything that you want to attract, whether it is people, situations, information, opportunities, etc. You can also use it to work with your health status and learn to let things flow themselves, letting them go and releasing anything that is not necessary for your subsequent development, and to forgive yourself and others."
Bashar (channeling through D. Anka)

Maybe you are saying to yourself now - if it were so simple (materialization), somebody would have "invented" this a long time ago, and he/she would have used it to create his/her own happiness. You can be sure that it has always worked like this and will continue to work the same way in future, and nowadays, maybe even more intensively. But if you have doubts already now and you do not believe it, you will again entangle yourself in that circle of negative thoughts - forever doubting and full of fear. It can be difficult to keep your mind alert and clear without unnecessary things, as the mind is always trying to resist anything new. It is programmed that way. It's up to you whether or not you decide to change your thinking, and more importantly, learn how to turn it off sometimes. No one else can do it for you. Every person who has achieved something in his/her life has been focused on a goal and didn't stop believing in it even five minutes before the finale. It's just a test of your patience. And if it does not work according to your plans, there is certainly a good reason, and it will bring you something quite different which may be much better for you, something that you previously could not have even imagined. Existence always has something ready for you! If you follow your true feelings, then something even bigger will come. Just test it yourself and you will see. Believe that you are able to do miracles.

> *"Clearly, patience is power; with time and patience the mulberry leaf becomes a silk gown."* Chinese proverb

So why wasn't this "discovered" by anyone before? To tell you the truth, it was, but before, there was nothing as powerful as the media we have nowadays. We've never been able to share so much information as fast as we do now. We just did not have the opportunity to hear about it and, mainly, there is/was always a struggle for power. In the Middle Ages (and later) we would have been burned at the stake for heresy with such thoughts. In Russia there have been many institutes (founded many years ago) that have been investigating these things – just without informing the public. **Because can you imagine what happens when one actually realizes that he is responsible for everything in his own life, and that even he is capable of creating anything he wants, and so easily?**

The idea of the changing of our consciousness was never fully admitted, and liberation from the old ways of thinking has always been suppressed at some point. All of this was simply considered to be something supernatural. And which generation is here today? The one which suffered wars, communism, exile? Only today's youth are growing up in so-called freedom. Let's take the internet, for example. What would it have been called in some prophecy from the past? After all, if somebody had predicted something like that, he probably would have only been laughed at and then hanged. What do you think, which verse in Nostradamus' prophecies refers to the internet? If you want, you can find it there. After all, just because of the small-mindedness of people of that time, he had to hide everything behind verses. Today, he would be worshiped as a holistic doctor – a visionary, while then he was persecuted as a heretic. Our consciousness is changing our level of perception. Indeed, our minds will adapt to anything which fits us at the moment, whatever even for a short while will ripple the imagination. **With this awareness of ourselves we could safely change the current state of the world. And everybody has that power.**

Indeed, we also have something which is called collective consciousness. The more people are afraid and think negatively, the worse the situation in our world will become. Therefore, collective prayer and meditation are practiced widely in the world nowadays. The more people pray (i.e., speaking, feeling, thinking) for something together, the more quickly it will have a tendency to materialize. A US study was conducted in 1993 which attracted the attention of scientists around the world. In Washington, 4,000 people attended a mass meditation to reduce crime. The result amazed everyone, from that time crime demonstrably fell by 20%! This study was carried out again later in Seattle, with a higher number of participants, and the crime rate dropped again – by 40%. This is reality. So, meditation/prayer in this case refers mainly to the feelings of the heart and the subsequent materialization of thoughts/feelings/intentions.

Prayers have always represented a kind of meditation. Essentially, they are part of everyone because everyone asks for something and is thankful. Special, even mystical significance has been given to prayer, again mainly by religions and the fact that they have just turned those "general requests to the most famous". Real prayer should be filled with **gratitude** and **compassion**, because these two virtues come directly from the heart. If you are thankful for something, in this way you manifest the fact that you already have it. So-called materialization is confirmed by the common denominator of almost all prayers, which is the final word Amen - the so-called declaration of affirmation: "so be it". In general, however, prayers have been turned into empty phrases about God without a deeper understanding of their meaning. It is better to create your own prayers, and if any of it resonates strongly with you, forward it. And if you get the opportunity to participate in collective meditation which includes a higher purpose, do not hesitate to do it. This is another way we can significantly help mankind. Regarding visualization meditation, it is also very effective because it works with **the attention of consciousness** which **has the power to strengthen its target**. You can purify the aura, to help your body, as well as others, send a color energy to Earth, etc. (However, this meditation does not address the state of consciousness of our personal growth.)

"Therefore I tell you, whatever you ask for in prayer, believe that you have received it, and it will be yours." Jesus

You can even call anyone from the spirit world to help you in the materialization. Whether you need Masters (spiritual beings who lived on earth before and were enlightened), Angels and Archangels, or other beings. There is even an elemental realm from which you can call elves and fairies to help. (Remember your childhood. Where do children get these visions from? Why did the movie Avatar resonate with so many people?) When you go out into nature, try to feel the presence of these gentle creatures. Ask them for anything, give them all your fears and worries and they will gladly help you. If you have any problems or you are in a negative environment, call on Archangel Michael and he will immediately help you. Archangel Chamuel can help with love, Archangel Gabriel helps with communication and career, Archangel Raphael will heal you with his emerald light, or you can simply visualize this light… the list goes on. For them, there is no such concept of time as we understand it, they can be present everywhere at once. Try it and see for yourself. However silly it may sound, just admit that there is something such as an irrational side of life. There are loads of literature on these topics, so I have decided not to dig very deep into the details. (I specifically recommend the literature from Doreen Virtue.)

In combination with materialization, phases of the moon can also help. Try to materialize things as the moon waxes, which reaches its climax during the full moon, and as the moon wanes, try to break free from all you wanted.

Materialize your luck! Trust the alchemy of life. Miracles happen, just do not stop believing in them.

"There is no miracle that would be contrary to natural laws. Miracles are only contrary to our ideas." St. Augustine

KARMA

"If more people reflected on the fact that cognition is salvation, there would not be so much suffering. All human suffering comes from ignorance."
Agni Yoga

Karma is action. Any action.

Each of us carries a so-called karmic container. This container is filled or emptied. Filled with evil deeds or emptied by good ones. This is probably the simplest way to explain it. **Karma is actually the educational system of our existence. If we were looking for perfect justice, it could be defined as karma.**

To understand karma as a complex topic, you have to accept the idea of reincarnation. Each one of us comes to this world with a specific mission which our soul chooses before being born here. In the "intermediate space" there is no ego, we have nothing to struggle with there and no one to fight with. All that is there is the so-called higher truth – pure intelligence. Based on our previous lives we can easily determine what we "need" to experience. Although it may sound a bit sci-fi, it's true. It's only a game, but because of artificially created ignorance, we take it very seriously. Of course, everything would be much easier if we knew our nature and our mission all the time, but then this game would lose its charm as would the educational principle that we voluntarily experience to further our personal growth. Therefore, regression techniques should be an absolute part of psychology and medicine. Thanks to our pasts, it is easier for us to understand the present, whether those pasts are quite recent or far behind us. (Interestingly, they banned regression techniques in Israel!)

Karma is a part of our relationships, our illnesses, our existence. Karma is in everything, everywhere, always. It's like we have our own personal guide or teacher with us all the time, and he knows exactly what we need to experience at the moment. Of course, almost everyone starts to think about "these things" after they experience some kind of critical moment or break-through in their lives which affects them emotionally or physically. Trying to find justice in that, but without the ability to see it. Why did this and that happen to me?! Why did God take my loved one away from me?! Why should I have this disease, what did I do wrong?! Everything, thanks to universal truth, has its own meaning. Although, it can look absolutely absurd at some points. We do not know all the context surrounding the scenarios involving other people, and we often don't even understand it regarding ourselves. If you learn to take life as a game, and it is a game for sure, then you can relieve yourself from many unnecessary doubts.

The most common educational system is a disease. Of course, I don't mean the one where you are running naked through the snow and suddenly you have got pneumonia - that is stupidity, and most of all, a conscious choice. But if you have no idea what could have caused your illness, then it is karma. However, at present there are more and more drugs and tools to cure various diseases, which is why different mutations appear, because we have learned to "outmaneuver" the nature. Nobody tries to find out the real cause of the illness. The doctor only prescribes some medications, and that is the most help we can get from him. And if a medicine he has prescribed does not work well, we invent a new one. And we let them feed us all of that. It is a solution that comes from the outside, not the inside. We must learn how to understand a person completely. We have to take more than just the body into consideration, and consider the soul. **Diseases appear repeatedly because we repeat the same behavioral patterns. It is not about genetics. Every disease has its spiritual - psychological cause.** (You can find those definitions on the Internet today.) And it is true also with regard to surgery - if any part of the body is removed, "the problem" is only transferred to another part of the body (will not disappear unless we change the pattern of behavior which caused it). Every organ has its spiritual significance, and thanks to that, we can identify the area of life we need to treat. It's also possible to diagnose the area even based on a rash on the face. It's all connected and basically very simple, if we begin to perceive themselves as spiritual beings. Because as we already know - the last thing the pharmaceutical industry wants is healthy people. Absorb this information and try to dig deeper into the topic, please. This does not mean that you should ignore all doctors now and search for some witch doctors or shamans instead. Medical science is entitled to some respect as it has undergone incredible progress. However, until now it has been focused mainly on the body. But nowadays, it is necessary to admit the mystical aspect of life.

Each person has four karmic tasks:

1. Do not gain any new "sins" in your present life.
2. Fulfill your mission in life. (Sometimes it's quite simple, it depends on your heart and what you really feel that you should do, or you always felt like you wanted to do… whatever that is!)
3. Detect and eliminate your karmic problems (based on the situations which constantly repeat themselves in your life).
4. Untie your karmic knots. (You can find them by analyzing your relationships – regarding the type of people you meet.)

Lots of exercises can be found in literature specifically written on the subject to help you diagnose your karmic container. However, the easiest way to get to the point is to honestly look at your life at this moment, where you actually are at present. Take some distance from yourself and describe your current situation.

Be really honest with yourself. Ask yourself: How did I get into this situation?

But do not close your eyes to anything, be really honest with yourself. Your mind will provide you with thousands of buck-passing attitudes towards why this was how it was. That is why it is important to depersonalize from it and simply accept the facts. One step always encourages further steps. However, if you do not solve the problem in the beginning, you will certainly get caught in an infinite loop, and you will not want to deal with it, despite feeling uncomfortable in the situation. And so it goes with all the "knots". They are repetitive just because you repeat certain behaviors, thus attracting the same type of people. (Analyze your relationships; they usually have something in common with your relationship with your parents.) However, if you realize this, you can easily leave it. It is of course difficult in relationships, but it is the best school for us. You can experience "love at first sight", i.e., a karmic meeting. With this soul, you owe each other something, you should learn something. As soon as this happens, it is time to go further, thus untie the karmic knot (if you are not hurting each other). You decided so at the highest level when you were planning this incarnation so that you could get to a higher level of awareness. Men are mostly scared (even if they would never say it that way) because it subconsciously dissolves the ego. But if you do not want to encounter it again, perhaps with much worse circumstances (since you've already sabotaged it once), go for it! Only time will show us how it will all develop.

We usually call these relationships fatal relationships, and oftentimes we can hardly call them "positive". But they only last until the moment when we decide to leave them. This is also the case when we have to start thinking rationally. It is a mostly imbalanced relationship where one party exploits the other (in any sense), it is a relationship where one doesn't respect the other, but on the contrary constantly humiliates and emotionally blackmails them. Yet it is "love like hell", and therefore it is very difficult to leave it. However, if you can see what this relationship needs to show you, it will be much easier. You need to figure out whether the relationship fills you in all aspects, or you just have to learn something. You are the one who needs to respect yourself first. If you don't respect yourself, you will not be able to respect others and it will be very easy for others to manipulate you. Everyone's cup overflows one day, and then it's time to go. If you obey yourself, out of all due respect and love for yourself, but also with responsibility towards others (if you have any obligations), there is certainly something better prepared for you. Do not worry about the old dogmas that say you should stay with one partner for a lifetime, that it is immoral to get a divorce, etc. If at this point everyone ended the relationships which do not work, it would also "release" an enormous number of people who would then be given the opportunity to experience what they want, and especially with whom they want. Of course, if someone has managed to have children in a dysfunctional relationship, it is much more difficult. But it is better for a child to grow up in a harmonious environment, not in a family where parents argue and disrespect one another. Sometimes the souls just owe it to each other. (We would find an answer in regression.) Many single mothers and fathers with their children find partners who do a lot more for them than the "biological" parent did. Do not be afraid to leave a dysfunctional relationship, because if you do not do it, it will come back to you.

Another example is that kind of person who really likes to help a lot – always helps everyone. Despite this fact, they fail to help themselves in their own lives. It very often happens that their good will is misused by others because they do not know how or, more accurately, they do not want to say "no". In their case, however, it is only a strange game of ego. They do all those good things at their own expense, but they expect something in return. They simply love to feel needed. Paradoxically, they are usually the ones who often neglect their own relatives or those who deserve their attention the most. Never do anything at your own expense. It's a much bigger sin than to disappoint others. Your programs are just badly tuned. Change them to gain some advantage for yourself. I'm not saying that you should stop helping. No, only do not do it at the expense of your life - everyone is responsible for himself/herself. It may evoke in you imaginary feelings of guilt, but it does not really exist. It's just a game played by others. If you're completely aware of yourself, recognize which feelings are truly yours, and then no one will ever get you into such a trap again. It is not egoism but self-esteem.

There can be one more exception. You live exactly "according to the books". Higher truth and love are also part of your daily routine and despite all of that, things are not happening the way you want them to. Then, let it be so. Be aware that the universe (yourself - your subconscious) has other plans for you. It knows exactly what you need to experience and it will arrange everything in the way which will bring you the biggest benefit. It was actually us who "planned" it for ourselves, but meanwhile we fell into unconsciousness. **Our soul knows exactly what is best for us at the moment.** So even if you have planned something, or you have a particular intention, even from the point of view of the heart, it may not be the best for you at that moment. Accept that it is otherwise - for your own good. Because the more a human "fights", the more stubborn he is, and the more closed his heart is. **"The path of the heart" means that you open up to reality although at the moment it is not what we would like.** We are often led to our desired goal in a way that we could not have even imagined. This is the so-called principle of surrendering - letting go. Only then can you live in the present moment. If you get rid of "unnecessary plans", i.e., desires, you will start to feel real freedom. And when you finally actually get released, you get into the flow of synchronicity where everything is linked with everything and mainly, everything happens only for your additional benefit – that is the perfection of time – perfection of lively intelligence that has the ability to adapt to circumstances exactly according to our karma. That is the most wonderful miracle for me. We are all one and everyone should want only the best for themselves, but he should also have the ability to wish it for other people as well, because it will return to you through them. In the past, it was a little slower with karma, but now it has rapidly accelerated so that after a while you will see it in reality without having to have any specific belief. But this does not mean that everything is predetermined. You can just "plan" your highest potential (some experiences and meetings) which is designed to bring you to your real target here on Earth, meaning your existential fulfillment – your life mission. However, through your deeds you change and customize your reality exactly in such a way that it brings you to the very place you need to be at the given moment for the sake of your understanding. You have free will, always and in everything. But you exist in the world of duality rather than in unity, i.e., the harmony of your heart with your head, so you often go against yourself – and this creates the problems that occur repeatedly. If you can unite, every step you take will be correct and you will never regret anything. Our "great plan" is in absolute harmony with our heart, so do not worry about it – it will not lead you somewhere where you will feel uncomfortable or like you are being controlled by something, quite the contrary. In any case, everything is interlinked, and there are always several potential scenarios for our lives that are being developed solely on the basis of our thoughts and particular acts/karma. You are solely responsible for your life. If any situation is affected by other people, then surrender to what is – they are just your "educators" on the path of life. If you can accept the situation without your ego fighting it, know that you will be the winner. Trust the existence and lose yourself in the flow of life from moment to moment - with the passage of time, everything has its meaning, indeed. Believe that everything happens only for our highest good.

Live your truth and you have nothing to lose. Truth makes us free! Do not be afraid to take real responsibility for yourself.

Be honest with everyone, and especially
with yourself. Believe in yourself.

"Karma is not a restriction, your activity is not a restriction. If you are limited by something, it is just because you wanted to be limited by it, otherwise there are no restrictions. Just as you naturally stop being governor when you leave office; you can get rid of every past life you have had exactly the same way. The dream has ended, whether it was good or bad. You are awake. This is exactly what a person who meditates does. At any time he is leaving his past. It stops existing for him and he is free. Then there is no karma anymore."
Osho

(*Recommended literature on the topic: Alexander Svijaš – Karma I, II, III*)

ESOTERICISM

"In thousands of new outfits we meet again and again on the road of life."
C. G. Jung

Divination, palmistry, numerology, astrology, various human designs, etc., obviously, there is a growing interest in all these topics lately, just because **we spend our whole lives simply trying to discover our own true selves.** Everything has its own nature, but we cannot take anything definitively. However, they may help us discover our own ways of understanding ourselves – nothing more, nothing less.

A soul chooses its destiny and its path before incarnation. When it gets an opportunity to live its life here on earth, its own free will and the opportunity to choose are given to it – regarding everything. Due to our intuition being repressed rather than naturally developed, human beings forget why they came into this world. A child can naturally feel this connection with the whole existence because he is pure and innocent. It often happens that he can see ghosts, angels, old souls, or has imaginary friends… Unfortunately, from the very beginning he is confronted only with denial and accusations that he is lying. We all start to push him to use his left hemisphere, to develop facts, inserting our opinions into him, and the right hemisphere only gets a chance when the child is playing. Parents want to load into their children as much information as possible, and as time goes by, even the child himself feels a sudden desire "to become big". Nobody has ever told him: *It does not matter that you can't count to ten if you can draw so beautifully, and that is something that matters!* No. He must instead face his parents' criticism because for them what matters is that the neighbor's kid can already count to twenty! You "kill" children because when you were a child, you were killed by adults as well, and it doesn't make sense because even you yourself, when you are doing something crazy, you can feel that joy of doing something which is beyond the control of your boring, logical, structured mind.

When a person is born, at that very moment, the world is being influenced by many different constellations, whether those are planets, numbers, circumstances, family, name, etc. All these things affect us and everything has its own meaning. Regarding planets, these affects are described with the help of astrology. Their position in the universe at the time of our birth is significant. The position of each planet defined our character – it's like a "given" program which we should recognize during our lifetimes. If it causes problems, we should slowly get rid of it. Otherwise, we should begin to love it, and thus, gradually, we will begin to return to the innocence which exists only in the present. Put simply, this means that it is the patterns of behavior that are given to us beyond the "genetic" ones – i.e., the so-called inherited behavioral patterns that were given to us by our parents. We are mostly only aware of the signs of zodiac, which represent the positions of the sun and its status at that time. The sun is the most powerful planet in our system, and despite the fact that affects us the most as well, it's not definitive. That day, also Venus and Mercury were in specific positions, for example. Venus affects love and our relationships. Mercury affects our senses. So in practice, it may look like you were born under the sign of Pisces, but Venus was in Scorpio and Mercury was in the sign of Libra. This means that even though you are a Pisces, in love you usually behave like a Scorpio, and when it comes to some decisions, you behave just like a Libra. Of course, there are more of these planets and each one influences us in a different way. This was just an example - it should encourage you to move forward in search of your own true self. We are also influenced by the time of our birth, i.e., ascendant, which again may be found to be in a completely different sign. That especially affects us after our 30th year of life. If you put together the day, month, and year of your birth, a numerological number from 1 to 9 will come out as a result. Using this method, you can very easily understand the direction you are moving in, and thus, the things you should cope with in this life. We can add the Chinese horoscope, which is determined by the year of your birth, and some elements as well, and you can go crazy trying to find out who you really are. These are only facts and you should take them only as **a user manual**. They contain a lot of information that may help you to understand yourself better, but they are just definitions which we have to understand, accept or overcome in the first place. Man is always developing himself. Everything changes, nothing is permanent, and it would be silly to think that you do not need to change as well. It suits you to use it as an excuse, that your current situation or status is simply "given", that you basically can't do anything with it. However, **you have free will - in everything. It's up to you who you really want to be, respectively who you already are. You decide which of your predetermined characteristics provide dominance, or on the contrary, what you should strengthen in your life to be in harmony with yourself. You are responsible for who you are in the present moment. Everything is changing from day to day, and man can change as well, if he really wants to.**

"As soon as you believe in yourself, you will know how to live."
J. W. Goethe

Thanks to numerology, you can even find out the year in which you are right now. If you calculate your date of birth to the current year, the number that comes out is the year in which you currently live. It also has 9 cycles, and each has a certain energy. This can help you make certain decisions or understand why things happen as they do. You can also wait for a better moment in the next year or month. You are also placed somewhere by the position of the planets. This can allow you to make some astrological predictions. All elders and leaders of the past understood the importance of these elements and they always used them as the basis for determining the dates of major events – unfortunately, mainly wars.

"All human life has its cycles and periods and no one's personal turmoil can be permanent. Winter still retreating before the spring and summer, though sometimes when branches are dark and the earth cracks with ice, one would think that will never come, that spring and the summer, however they will come, always come."
T. Capote

Divination is mainly a psychological game. Each card has its own energy and your subconscious will choose one based on your feelings, past, thoughts, ideas… Based on these life facts that you have experienced, there is always one the most likely potential scenario of your future direction, but what the reality will be is exclusively up to you. It is very individual and only a kind of navigation. It is up to you how much you will succumb to the prophecy. You always have the freedom of choice. After all, what would it be all about if everything were strictly designed in advance? There are some roads, people, situations that are predetermined (based on past lives, i.e., karma), but you can affect the overall progress based on your current karma, i.e., your recent actions. In practice, it may look like it is your so-called fate to be in an accident. If you live a decent and proper life, you haven't hurt anyone, and on the contrary, you are a very caring and kindhearted person, you can change your predetermined future.

You are not going to avoid the accident, but it will happen only in the form of a small crash, not very serious, in which no one will get hurt. If, however, you don't behave so well, it will have a much worse impact. Basically, you can affect everything that happens to you. If you succumb to the prophecy and it ends up exactly as the psychic told you, it is mainly because it happened according to the principle of materialization. You materialized it because you started to believe it. That's all the "magic" hidden in it.

As I have said before, man has always been seeking certainties in his life, and any kind of fortune-telling simply chases after these certainties, only in a bit more refined form. We want to ensure that we are doing right things and making the right decisions. We want to be sure that we are following the path which is best for us, that the best partner is waiting for us somewhere, that our current job is the most suitable for us, etc. However, we forget that the only real thing in life is simply constant change - nothing is stable and nothing is guaranteed. The more intensely you start to believe in some sure things in your life, the more painful it will be when you lose them. Trust your heart completely, it is the only accurate counselor you will ever have. And if you keep on following it, I am pretty sure you will find yourself in the right spot on your life journey. You have always known what's best for you and where you are willing go. Don't let others manipulate or fool you, all the correct answers have always been hidden within you. So-called *dejá vú*, which literally means *already seen*, is perfect proof that you are exactly in the spot where you are supposed to be. This moment or picture has been planned by your soul in higher spheres (it is part of another reality), and when you experience it, it proves with certainty that you are at the right place. Since there is only presence, everything in the cosmos exists simultaneously - time is just an illusion.

"Time does not exist. What we refer to as the `past` or the `future` has no real basis and is only a part of our mental constructions.

The idea of time is a convention of thought and language, a social agreement. In fact, we only have this moment."
D. Millman

Our minds hardly understand that time does not exist, it is only an illusion. Werich said it very nicely: *"Time was invented by people only to know since when, for how long and for how much."* That's true. Time in eternity can be compared to the situation in the morning, before getting up, when we fall asleep again for a moment. We dream and experience the whole story, very long… We wake up and surprisingly discover that it lasted only five minutes. People who have experienced clinical death have been able to feel this "eternity" as well in the moment when they came out of the body. They felt like they were never going to return again. They felt like they were gone for a long time and they experienced something ineffable. Some of them saw angels or Jesus, even spoke to them… while according to our understanding, they were unconscious for only a few seconds. They agree that they have been flooded by endless love and peace. So what are we really afraid of?

"If everything ended with death, life would be meaningless and suicide would be the only right solution." Osho

Death does not exist. Everything is eternal. Now it is simply beyond the borders of our understanding here on the Earth. Death expresses a kind of a new beginning - the transition into eternity. We are one. Everyone. The one infinite energy fragmented into millions of particles. However, we have the gifts of the mind, freedom of decision, but unfortunately, we are still living in duality. Since we all have free will, it sometimes happens that a person takes his own life out of despair. One always has a choice – therein lies his infinite schism. However, if someone commits suicide, his soul often remains chained to the ground, and it will be released and sent "back" when the right time comes for him or when he resolves his outstanding issues here. When people talk about surviving suicide, they first got into an area which they describe as "hell", and from there they were transferred to the higher, much more pleasant realms. This hell is simply created by mental images of ourselves in the moment of death, because if someone wants to die, he probably doesn't gain any pleasure from it. On the contrary, he experiences indescribable anguish, which in this case materializes on the given level of his consciousness. That is nothing pleasant and at last, the soul will in any case be forced (will wish) to return to the level where she gave up. Otherwise, she will be charged with karma. Whether we realize it or not, all of us are going through incarnation on Earth and we are headed towards the so-called eternal cleansing (enlightenment). So, endurance is definitely worth it.

Many times we can also feel the presence of someone deceased. Sometimes their energy comes back to "check" on us, to revive our love and shared experiences. If you, however, feel pain or discomfort, it means that you have something outstanding between you, and that soul wants to deal with it. Try to remember what it could be and forgive her. Literally, help her release this world. Again, you can get help from some radionic experts or regression therapists, or you can address your challenges yourselves if you feel them genuinely and apply your common sense. If you do not want to deal with people, angels can help you as well as archangels and ascended masters, whose streams of consciousness still exist in this "eternity". They are very happy to help you whenever you ask, and you do not even have to do any special rituals.

If you can accept that death does not really exist and that only we - humans – have attributed such depressive energy to it, everything will change! Because that is the magic of the moment, trust the existence! What are you more afraid of than death? That is the fundamental problem with our minds – the illusion of death. And the people "on top" of the hierarchy in this world know it very well. Get rid of all unnecessary fears! It's not good if someone close to you has left (died). But it is unpleasant mainly because we have given such pathos to it. If we realized that this man is at this moment somewhere else and he is much better off than we are, we would not waste our tears. There are many cultures that understand this "transition," and every funeral is especially a celebration for them. It is necessary to change our consciousnesses, our real awareness. Of course, before it happens, do not suppress your feelings, let them out, do not flow in them. It is very healthy to cry everything out this way, and it is very natural to grieve for someone who we have loved and lost. Take a week off, "enjoy" your sadness, feel it to the fullest, talk to the soul of the deceased. Just do not blame anyone and do not dwell unnecessarily in the sense of despair. Although it seems completely unfair sometimes, it was planned to happen that way. The soul itself before entering our Earth chose its time to pass. It needed to learn something and to teach the others as well. We cry just for ourselves, and it is ultimately only our "school" – for those who are still here…

Here on Earth, everything is simply one big game and you have to learn to play it as well as you can - here and now - there is no later! If you're playing a game, you're fully involved in it. You don't think you are going to continue later, because you know that if you stop, someone else will win. In this game, the winners are everyone who understands the rules, because we are one body and one soul.

Recently, the term "purification" has been used very frequently in esotericism. But note that in this case it is mainly the conscious purification of oneself using the above-mentioned methods, i.e., the mindful removal of any parts of you that are not genuine. But of course, purifications on the astral level exist as well, which are also very helpful. Another very simple method you can use is the visualization of light (conscious attention). Sit or lie down in a comfortable position, close your eyes, and imagine yourself breathing in sunny golden light. Imagine it; feel it to the tips of your toes. But exhale (feel what should leave) dark black light, which is the universe (or silver for the moon). Repeat this whenever you want and you will regain beautiful energy. Before falling asleep you will soothe yourself, and after waking you will regain your strength, or, throughout the day, you can stop for a moment. There are plenty of such techniques today. Just select the one you feel comfortable with. Angels and archangels will gladly help you with all as well if you ask them and open yourself to their guidance. Crystals are also very helpful. Each one of them has a different energy. We can use them to heal not only ourselves but also others. They can be used to accumulate new power, and you don't even need to do any special rituals for that. Another very efficient healing technique comes from Hawaii - *Ho`ponopono* - which has become very popular recently. Discover the unconventional temptations of life, that variegation is endless! Just do not become addicted to anything, because then it loses its meaning.

It's time to wake up from this unpleasant dream where the one-eyed man is king. You could open both eyes and then it'll be only a short step to awakening the proverbial third eye - your true intuition, your "higher self". Imagine that you have three eyes but you are still looking with only one. You are missing so many things... I already mentioned at the beginning that this third eye is purposely systematically closed (by our way of living), so, again, it's up to you if you want to open it or not. Concentrate your attention between the eyebrows whenever it is possible. **True intuition is always in harmony with your feelings; it is never based on fear.** If you act on that basis, the solution will always be nice for you. If not, you have succumbed to a rational solution – the mind. There are many techniques for opening the third eye, so if you come across any, they will be very beneficial for you.

Explore what you wish and, most importantly, see everything around you! Learn to be an observer of yourself. Try to see synchronicity in everyday trifles. All these philosophies can only help you. Numerology and astrology are only instructions to be used. Learn consciously to apply them to help yourself. Find out why you behave the way you behave. There is nothing supernatural about it. If you understand the facts, you will see them as they truly are - it will be much easier to work on change. Everything is changing, nothing remains still. There is always something to improve. But do not confuse it with the fact that you are going to change your nature, that you are going to be completely different. No. Just get rid of the acquired patterns of your own behavior which are no longer required, which were only creating unnecessary problems. It does not seem so now, but if it happens, you will be really happy. Your behavioral patterns do not help you in everyday life. On the contrary, you can be impacted by anything negative. It is not about "producing" new people, but about waking up happy people, because that is your true nature - unconditional joy. Therefore, you are searching for esoteric advice because subconsciously you suspect that you are something more than only a body. Maybe you just weren't supported by anyone ever in esotericism. **People tend to ridicule what they do not understand**, but don't worry about it. All of us want to be happy and satisfied, so start today.

Life is really not rational, and the sooner you admit it, the better for you.

If you know yourself, you will become truly yourself and you will learn how to live in the total presence - here and now - you will become unpredictable and not even a fortune-teller will have an impact on you. This is the principle of the mirror. If you are clean - innocent - you are unpredictable. I know what I'm saying. No psychic ever "saw me", although I have met many of them on my way.

All those widely discussed topics like angels and enlightened masters may sound a bit weird to you, simply because our consciousnesses have been manipulated for many centuries. Actually, the most manipulative fact that we have been told is that we are alone in this whole universe. No, we are not. Some extraterrestrial civilizations have already tried to contact us several times, and moreover, they have already been cooperating with some of the governments here on Earth. In Russia, in US, and not only there, we can find multiple institutions dealing with these facts. Also, many perceptions have come from these higher spheres which have guided us, and thanks to which a technological boom started here on Earth. Unfortunately, we have been infected by many lies and negative depictions of these astral nations, so that we feel separate. All those UFO dramas contrived by world governance were simply created to invoke fear in us. These "astral people" from other galaxies are in touch with us, nonstop. They love us, and they are guiding us and controlling our awakening so it can proceed in harmony. They are trying to help us, using their technologies, mostly regarding freely available energy. However, it is definitely not in the interest of our elite so be careful how this information will be presented to us nowadays.

"We know that extraterrestrial beings visited our planet. Ships were found as well as bodies."
Dr. E. Mitchell, Apollo 14 astronaut

"There is evidence that we have been contacted by another civilization that had watched us for a long time beforehand. The appearance of these aliens is very special. They use very advanced technologies."
Dr. B. Oleary, former NASA astronaut and professor of physics

"I think they were afraid to disclose such information because of what it would do to the public and thus they invented one lie, they had to support it with other lies, and now they do not know how to get out of it. There are a lot of spaceships circling around our planet."
G. Cooper, a former NASA astronaut

Socrates, Tesla, and Einstein admitted publicly that they received information through communication with extraterrestrial beings in deep meditation.

There are also many dark forces in the Universe that exist around us as well. They have been incarnated here on Earth, and they are responsible for many of the crimes which are happening now. Many people are connecting with these energies (souls) through their thoughts, and later on they are surprised when they become fully controlled by them. The truth is that it's all about our conscious decisions, which you do not have to realize (because it became your "norm", most likely from childhood). It is advisable to look for an expert then, but you can help yourself again. If you don't give any power to this negativity, no energy at all, it won't be able to nourish itself with your thoughts and it will be forced to leave. It's not part of your nature. You simply need to start to vibrate on higher frequencies - meditation or being surrounded by nature can help you a lot with it. In the universe, there is a so-called black hole present as well - where all the negativity from Earth is being concentrated. Obviously, it's possible to create "heaven on earth" as we have heard about it so many times, and peace and unity, as negativity can coexist in parallel, but at another place.

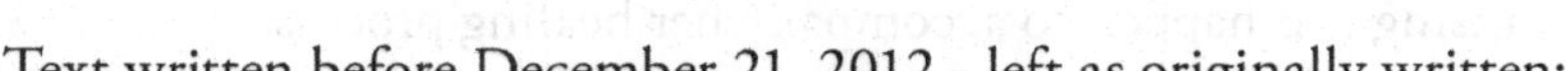

Text written before December 21, 2012 - left as originally written:

Fortunately, this period of change is just starting. So, the much anticipated 2012 is really a breakthrough, whether you realize it or not. For a long time, the ancient Mayans kept us in darkness, although also thanks to them, many facts have been explained to us. In any case, they were neither the first nor the last ones: as a matter of fact, there are very many predictions of this kind worldwide (for example, the Indian Vedas talk of the age of Kali Yuga based on the same principle). Also in this case, I select a particular point.

Earth has its own energies, exactly as every human being does. This time, it is awakening its Kundalini energy which is being moved from India to the Andes for a longer period of time. (That`s why the so-called "seekers" have also shifted their attention to South America.) This stream was launched in the sixties when the Dalai Lama left Tibet and gradually wandered across the earth. Kundalini energy can be experienced as a sexual energy, but it gradually increases moving up the spine. Unlike sexual energy, which is more creative, Kundalini energy has a spiritual nature. The shift of this energy will be felt by everyone, even if they are not particularly aware of it. Kundalini has a feminine equivalent.

As for earth cycles, we are right in the period when, after about 13,000 years, we will move to the forefront of feminine energy, therefore to the heart. Until now, mostly male energy has occurred, which was obviously necessary in many ways (and still is). However, currently it is more than destructive, so it is very positive that this will change (harmonize). It is also the time when we begin to realize deeply that our mother Earth needs more of our attention. For a long time we have not taken care of her. On the contrary, we have been destroying her. Therefore, in some places on Earth, various so-called cleansing can happen to accompany her healing process.

If you ask scientists what is happening, they have to admit that the Earth's magnetic field is getting weaker. That is probably the only tangible evidence of change. Mother Earth has decided to take "off" a few kilos and to lose a bit of the force of gravity. At the end of 2012, everyone should weigh 0.001 mg less, and things should be 6 mg lighter. It seems like a negligible difference, but the effect is primarily psychological. Gradually, we will have to admit that thoughts are material. Part of our ideas will abandon us allowing our internal space to increase and giving us the freedom and consciousness to use our thoughts in a much more creative way. For people who are meditative and do not live only in their so-called heads, it will be a very nice change, they will appreciate it. They will be able to materialize anything quickly. For them, matters of the practical and material world will be a bigger deal as it is something that is a part of them (with which they are unnecessarily "fighting" today). For those who "live in the head" (the male equivalent), it may be a bit difficult and there is a high probability that they will fall into depression because they do not understand what is happening. Every negative thought will materialize itself much faster and attract more similar situations. It will also "forcibly" open their emotional (female) part to learn to understand the whole. So it's up to you which path you consciously choose and if you want to further develop or you want to stay only in one extreme. In practice, this also means that if today you need a hundred ideas for a simple operation, in 2013 you will need only 70 of them. It's definitely not anything to be afraid of, quite the contrary.

In fact, our thoughts will actually start to materialize much faster. This means that it is really necessary to learn how to control your head and be able to manage your thoughts. The path of meditation is therefore necessary for everyone, without distinction.

On the universal level, we will move from the third to the fifth dimension. This is the essence of the Mayan calendar. The phenomenon of dimensions is as follows:

1D, i.e., the first dimension - the first circle in the calendar: shows a primitive society, where one sees only himself, does not deal with anything except for his own being (survival) - I.

In this age, we cannot rely on any myths or legends because man cared only about survival. Even then, however, he got the most important thing - free will.

2D, i.e., the second dimension - the second circle: one begins to perceive polarity, others (good - evil, day - night, yin - yang) - YOU and ME.

He can also perceive a space around him and start to wonder how it was all created. As these questions have no answers in this space, he creates the idea of someone else who created everything. But he does not know how to name or understand him, and so to "some forces" unearthly power is assigned and he provides them with different victims. This creates myths and legends based on the information which he receives, but he does not know to process them.

3D, i.e., the third dimension - the third circle: one begins to perceive that there is indeed "something" greater than he is, some higher power, but he doesn't know how to identify it, he is separated from it – ME, YOU, and GOD. Past, present, future.

Man becomes aware of his free will, but he doesn't know how to work with it. Now he is convinced that there is something more above what he called God, and on the basis of this knowledge he creates a dialogue with him. The low level of consciousness interprets many messages judging on its own experience, which gets into a trap. He trades with God - I'll obey your commands if you give me eternal life.

We are here at this time.

However, we are going through the third to the fifth dimension. So where is the fourth dimension?

4D, i.e., the fourth dimension - the fourth intermediate ring: it's time, the presence.

We should realize that we have created time as we know it. What really exists is only the presence, the ungraspable moment - now. In space everything exists at the same time. In this period, we may find that we are so-called "lost in time". It will run quite differently than we are used to. If you can pay attention to your existence right now, then you're smart enough to open. Now you should understand the fact that it is not a God who creates our reality, but we who do it ourselves. Everything that has happened in our lives was projected by our own thoughts. Just as time here on Earth is only our projection. **There are regular cycles, but not time itself.**

> *"Space-time is four-dimensional space uniting the three-dimensional physical space and time. The perception of time and space as an independent concept is dependent on the observer, but space-time is independent of the observer and forms the basic framework for the feasibility of physical laws independent of the reference frame in the universe. Herman Minskowski introduced space-time in the years 1907-1908 (Einstein Professor of Mathematics)."* Wikipedia

5D, i.e., the fifth dimension – the last circle: man realizes that he is God, and always has been.

In this dimension, time will no longer exist as we know it now. When one realizes his true potential, he can materialize anything he thinks of without time limits. His consciousness becomes consistent with the whole universe. He will be no longer separated from the source, but will be the source itself. This dimension also changes the structure of our DNA. When entering the fifth dimension, more DNA chains will be activated, allowing us to open wider consciousness and use new abilities that we still do not use. New souls – kids - will be born with this expanded DNA and supernatural abilities such as clairvoyance, telepathy, etc. will be natural for them. **The vibration level of each person will increase individually because everyone is at a different level of development.**

"What happens in your heavenly kingdom?
***Jesus**: There will not be any time."*

Now it is very difficult to even imagine it, but this is the main reason why it is so important to follow the path of meditation. It is necessary to learn how to control our thoughts and how to switch all our attention from our heads to our hearts. Indeed, you will keep creating your reality for yourself - this time consciously. Therefore, what you believe in right now will be very important. Everything you take as your own personal truth will become your personal reality as well. Therefore, focus mainly on positive things, please. Try to do not accept anything negative emotionally, even if you observe it, do not take it personally – it is not you, in this case it is happening outside of you. Watch everything like a movie, but try to watch positive movies. If there is a fire on a canvas, it does not mean it has to burn that canvas.

We have a real opportunity to create an enlightened society. Therefore, many souls have returned to earth to experience this wonderful event. However, there is still a risk that not all of them will pass through this gate - figuratively speaking. Not that it was badly planned before or something like that. The thing is that everything always depends on individual free will. Just by reading these lines your consciousness expands and opens, although this is no longer a "holy scripture", nothing more than your own signature. Unfortunately, lots of people will not want to hear about that option, not even to experience it. They will remain "trapped" in 3D (in duality), in ignorance, without a life passion, dependent on everything that comes from the outside, and possibly in depression. However, the worst is that they can still (for a while) influence events happening on earth. Therefore, it is more than likely that many reckless disasters caused by man will occur. These ignorant people will never understand what they are going to lose. They will laugh about the date December 21, 2012 because from their perspective, nothing really happened. However, you should not be intimidated by this time. On the contrary, only when you experience the darkness, can you see the light. Therefore, everything that was going on had its own meaning. Do not be afraid and try to believe that we can feel/live like never before!

In practice, there is only a one-way ticket: to consciously decide to follow the path of light – the path of good (and act accordingly). Then, everything else will be attracted to you by itself.

5D is a new consciousness.

Our consciousnesses will vibrate on much higher principles than they have been till now - **on the basis of unconditional love**, which will become a part of our everyday lives, not just a moment. We are becoming love. We are going to feel and see true unity - harmony. We will see beyond the veil of reality that we know today. Every day will become a celebration for us and we will not understand the people who willingly remain in so-called 3D. **The differences which will arise between us will be mainly psychological, yet very significant.**

Despite these wonderful predictions, first we have to let go of everything that is not working for us anymore, and it could hurt a little. However, this is more about how much you are willing to admit to yourself. The number 13 (2013) is in fact the number of death, but it also means a new beginning. Do not be afraid to get rid of everything you do not need for your further development - relationships, situations, work… anything that is not in harmony with you. It can also be applied to the situation on Earth and to everything that is happening to her. **First, we have to eliminate dysfunctional systems and patterns of behavior, and then we can begin to function "normally"- as a human beings.**

Text written in 2018: Although I am currently editing and more so supplementing the text that arose few years ago, I deliberately left the previous text here. As a matter of fact, the people who had perceived these changes were really looking forward to the "new world", but they somehow still cannot see it. Many people expected miracles and today they are disappointed because it did not happen according to their expectations. In terms of space cycles, it is indeed a historic moment, but in our view, that moment may still take several years. Understand that it is just about us – each one of us. As all the "informed" people were waiting for miracles, they somehow forgot that first of all, they must be the "miracle" for themselves. You can skip neither the level of perception nor all the challenges that await us here on Earth. This "game" would become absolutely meaningless if we had awoken on December 22, 2012 and everything had been supposedly "reset". After all, it is impossible and nobody promised you anything like that. It is just that you have believed the simplest version and misunderstood the issue. You have purified everything, just not yourself on the conscious level. Everything changed and nothing changed. It is up to each of us to understand that this 5D perception is an individual matter of the level of vibration of our consciousnesses – and it exists indeed. I am saying this based on my own experience. It did not happen overnight, but it happened gradually. After the pre-announced date, it just dramatically accelerated and finally stabilized. However, 2013 was exactly the main test of whether we are really able to endure, even in difficult times, to be as conscious, powerful, and inspiring as we say we are. In any case, today it is completely visible in reality that many more people have begun to naturally open up to this consciousness than ever in human history. This human burnout has never occurred before, with a mirror set directly by the media. Never before have we really been interconnected via the internet. You can watch live how much we opened after 2012. That is simply a fact rather than a kind of science fiction. This means that if you had actually been ready in that period (purified on the level of your consciousness) you would have been flooded by infinite bliss and understanding. Because you did not address it, virtually nothing visible happened. **YOU have to become the change you expect from others.** It is not possible to make it happen otherwise. Also, if you solve all these esoteric conjunctions of space and connections, return to Earth first. No, supernatural abilities will not make you a better person. It is imperative to begin to consciously perceive your tests and relationships. Start addressing yourself rather than others. What have you changed in your life to make things happen differently? You always have a choice. Stop making yourself a victim – you are a strong and wonderful human being, who has come an incredibly long way. Do not give up five minutes before the end, please. Change yourself and you will change your entire environment. Know yourself and you will know the universe – it is a direct correlation. No other way is possible. **By provoking you at least a bit, every single person becomes your teacher and has a message for you that is the most important one for you at the moment. Now we all need each other. We all are interconnected and this global change can take place only through us.**

"If you are in a hurry, you will never arrive. You can even arrive just by sitting, but in a hurry you can never arrive. The very impatience is a barrier."
Zen proverb

According angel predictions, we should soon be able to start functioning on completely different principles, i.e., those of light and love. Without money, without politics (as we know it today), without wars or exploitation. The only thing necessary is to start to believe. To create a new world, we simply need to believe that we can operate quite differently and incomparably, in a more beautiful way - which means fully and more blessed. **One candle can really light up a room, but the same amount of darkness cannot beat the light.**

Therefore, let's begin to cooperate, on behalf of all of us.

I am looking forward to a new, enlightened society very much and I hope you will join us.

"Cripples, beggars and the beaten passed a praying hermit. Seeing them, the holy man knelt in deep prayer and said: 'Great God, how is it possible that as a loving creator you can look at such things while doing nothing about it?' After a long silence, God said: 'I did something. I made you.'
Sufi school story

SUMMARY

"Just give people the key, they can unlock their own locks."
R. McCammon

Life is an endless process. Human life is very short compared to the existence. However, we do not know how to live. We have in our hands **the most beautiful gift**, but we do not know how to use it. We are playing a game which we do not know the rules for. Actually, we know some rules that are thousands of years old and we follow them. When we look back into history, we find that if a man was wise, he would realize that those rules don't work, and they even fail every time. And we, instead of learning from it, we just complain and feel that it is "normal" because it has all been going on for several thousand years. The whole thing is in its essence and splendor very simple (it is just the mind is unable to accept it so easily). If only the present moment exists, why should we worry about the past or the future? Would that solve anything or do you think that it would somehow help you if you heard this moment how Jesus, Krishna, Buddha, Mohammed, Moses, or Osho meant it all? Your mind is convinced that it would help, but the fact is that at this point it is all completely useless information for you. Nevertheless, it does not guarantee any significant change in your consciousness. You just get some new information and **your understanding is not directly dependent on it. It is about the awakening of the reality that you**

must first experience. But HERE and NOW, you do not need it, indeed. The only one who is important at this point is YOU.

"A really mature personality does not transfer his responsibility to someone else; he is responsible for his own existence. Germany, a country full of scientists, philosophers, professors, poets and intellectuals became a major victim of quite an ordinary average man. And this man ruled them. This example should help everyone understand the stupidity of intellect. Intellect is superficial."
Osho

At the moments of birth and death we have nothing. We are translucent, and it is also the only time we are actually visible. **What if we were visible our whole lives?** You are afraid, you feel guilty for everything, and you do not realize that fear is created by a past that no longer exists, and guilt is generated by society and your mind - it is not you - it's not here and now.

Fear and guilt are our only and greatest enemies.

Try to get rid of them whenever you feel them - consciously switch to another program. Because if you think about the future with fear and worries, you will attract those things. If others are still making you feel guilty, it's just proof that you are acting unconsciously. Both of these feelings (emotions) are always dependent on the external stimulus. If you were alone, you would not even think of feeling guilty - for anything. If you have done something stupid, take full responsibility for the whole situation and behave as a reasonable person. All religions (and behavioral patterns based on them) are absolute experts in inducing guilt and fears, because then we can be controlled. Thus, politics are based on the fundamental principles of religion. Everything is just about power. Whether it is a parent, friend, priest, politician, teacher etc., all they want is to control us! Despite this fact, they cannot even manage themselves.

"When the power of love overcomes the love of power, the world will recognize peace." Jimmy Hendrix or Sri Chinmoy Ghose :)

Look in detail at the lives of each of them and you will find that none of them have **the right to judge you**. No one. Not even the so-called God. He/She is part of you, why would he/she condemn him/herself?! He/She does not judge, just as you never place yourself in the role of a judge. Everyone has their own truth, because everyone is influenced by other surroundings, experiences, people, situations, etc. And if you act on the basis of your inner truth and love, you cannot make mistakes and regret your deeds. Always act based on real feelings, which come from your middle. Each of us has a center (hara), which is about 2-3 cm below the navel. That is the source of all of our genuine feelings (thus we can feel the "butterflies" when we fall in love, or we can feel fear). There is an essential connection with the mother as well as with our inner truth. **Listen to yourself**, perceive and, in particular, consciously observe yourself. Only then can you rise above yourself and become a master of yourself.

"You can consider yourself lucky if every one of your joys is born within you."
Seneca

Be yourself, but never at the expense of others. After all, you already know that everything (deed, and judgment) will come back to you sooner or later anyway, and everyone is just your mirror. **If you do not like the reflection, first change yourself.** Get rid of that part of yourself. If you understand this game and put it into practice, you will be able to accept everyone. This does not mean that you have to be friends with everyone. **Everyone is at a different developmental stage and you have met them in your life for some reason. If the reason – the point of the encounter – is fulfilled, it is necessary to go on.** Our souls, before entering this world, agreed that they would help each other. Accept it, understand it, and only then can you turn a negative encounter into a positive encounter. No encounter is random, and they are all needed for our growth. Just the ego fights endlessly, or just the opposite because it wants to always look the best at all times! Actually, functioning in this way is not even possible, but you convince yourself that it is possible because you want to see it like that. You never even really see inside the heads of other people, so ultimately it is just your hypocritical game. Be honest with yourself in the first place, then you can be honest with others. If you can see yourself and the whole situation holistically, with the necessary distance, and you understand the point, then you will be able to move further. If not, you will repeat the situation or meet similar people with similar problems until you actually accept/ understand that the "problem" is not with them, but with you.

"If you can trust yourself when all men doubt you,
but make allowance for their doubting too."
R. Kipling

Discover yourself - that **silences your mind**. Learn how to consciously switch it off. Find at least an hour a day for yourself. It's your investment not only in yourself but in all your relationships. And our lives are, after all, based on relationships and cooperation. Therefore, we continue to be internally driven to be better. Because life is changeable! No moment is the same. That's why you should try not to stay the same, want to be a better person. And if you can calm the mind, you will feel a great influx of new energy. If you throw out all the "mess" in you, which has accumulated over the years, then there will be silence. And silence is love, silence is the universe, silence is creativity. Every thought contains a space - silence, and if you can perceive it, you are on the best way to yourself. Then just start to lengthen these gaps. Perceive the presence fully. Be like a sculptor who removes the clay to form a beautiful statue. **You are crowded with a lot of useless things - get rid of them!**

"It seems that perfection is not achieved when nothing can be added, but when there is nothing to remove."
A. de S. Exupéry

Head for perfection, but do not make it your destination. Perfection is static, it cannot grow any more, is essentially dead. **The way is** actually **the destination, every single step** of it. Tomorrow you will get run over by a car and then what?! What will you have from all of those plans for how you are going to be different and elsewhere, but now you cannot be?! You do not have to be perfect, just be yourself. That is the perfection of creation. Each rose is different, although at first sight they all seem the same, yet they are all perfectly beautiful. But we have a mind and free will. We can develop; it is our duty - at least to ourselves. **There is no perfection of man, there is only perfection of the moment,** and therefore, in particular, give one hundred percent.

"Strange! Man is concerned about the evil that comes from the outside, from other people, thus about what can be removed. But he does not struggle with his own evil that is in his heart."
M. Aurelius

Do not be afraid of the truth, do not close your eyes to it, it will always backfire. Unfortunately, after countless experiences, I regret to say that people generally do not want to see the truth. Often, they do not even want to hear it. They are able to force you to lie to them for their "own good" – because in some cases they are really not interested in listening to it. Paradoxically, even then, even though they do not know the whole truth, they do not have a problem with judging you. A minimum number of people has the power to proceed to confrontation. I personally do not understand that. Truth makes us free. But your ego is afraid that it will hurt, it is concerned that it will have to leave something comfortable which it has become accustomed to, and so you prefer to live in lies and secrecy. Today's man is an incredible hypocrite. That is sad, especially for him. After all, you cannot live like that for long. Well, you can, but when you watch the film that will run in front of your eyes at the end of your life, it will be only you who will regret it all (and will repeat it in the next incarnation). **Speak the clear, bare truth and do not dramatize unnecessarily. Rather, enrich your daily life and do not make thinks up just to make your life look more interesting.**

"The truth is usually simple and short. Lies and nonsense tend to be more colorful and fantastic. Therefore, lies suit the poor head better than the truth."
J. Thomayer

The truth will always, sooner or later, come to light. And then it hurts because it came too late. You've gotten used to the fact that it hurts, and so you prefer to avoid it. Then you live your life full of empty hypocritical masks and wonder why you are not happy. You look for happiness wherever possible because you have been taught to do it like that. No one has told you that this so-called happiness is your absolutely natural state that does not depend on any external perceptions. On the contrary, society creates the illusion that all happiness comes from the outside - from people, situations, things, work, money, etc. Happiness is not something separate or something you can get. If it depends on outside circumstances, it is always very transient. It is also the ultimate reason why people have children – so they can shift their responsibility for their happiness to someone else. And then your happiness is just a reflection of your relationships, whether with your child or partner. Again, it is not the inner sense which is our absolute part. After all, look at children: they are happy every day until you start to burden them with your learned "truths" and until you teach them about the "reward for something" system. In fact, all you need to be happy is "only" the removal of all those lies (programs) under which you grew up, which are the basis of your actions, and thinking. And it is a step back that nobody can take for you. Try to accept the fact that **the truth is your best friend.** It is important to realize that the truth is variable, not static. What is true today may not be true tomorrow. This fact is beautifully demonstrated by the principle on which science works. There are always different circumstances in which we find ourselves. Nothing is static; therefore, the **truth is also relative in parallel with the present moment.** But in that certain moment it is very necessary. However, it is very delicate and you have to learn to handle it. So try not to hurt anyone just because you need to prove the truth to yourself – treat others as you would treat yourself. **Any teacher can show you a direction, path, technique, but action must be taken by you.**

> ***"There is only one truth, but it has thousands of levels. Whoever is on the higher level understands the truth of those who are on the lower level. The one on the lower level does not, however, understand the truth of those on the higher level.*** *Everyone has, therefore, their own truth, which corresponds to the degree of their development."* Film - Powder

Communicate - ask questions and learn how to really listen. The more ways to communicate we have, the less we communicate. Unfortunately, telepathy is still in its infancy, so it is very important to start normally communicate with each other again. Nothing creates more space for your imagination than the fear of confrontation, if you do not feel comfortable in a relationship or in some situation. It is impossible to understand those who choose to remain mute. Also, you calculate in your communication - do not do it, you are lying mainly to yourself. We tend to say only part of the whole truth and we want to hear the opinions of others. But we tell it to them in such a way which will only make them confirm our feelings and say what we want to hear. We are even able to present our "transformed truth" as "facts". **Learn to see the whole and speak the whole truth**, it will help you - because it is not about anyone else in this case. You condemn others without knowing the real reasons for their actions. I know it from my own experience. If you meet a hundred people who "know" me, you will hear a hundred different opinions about me. But out of a hundred people, only one will be really interested in getting to know me, in hearing the facts or the reasons for my actions. And even so, he will be able to perceive only through his eyes and experiences. In the end, nobody sees inside our heads and hearts. Therefore, forget about what others think about you. If you act in harmony with yourself, you have no reason to feel "guilty". **It is always the unsolved complexes of the others which lead to the problematic relationships they have with you.**

"I hate the truth, which says that it is infallible.
If in doubt - tell the truth!"
M. Twain

The things that annoy you about others are only your mirror. The more you fight it - the more you attract it. **All you condemn – you attract**. Do not idealize anything or anyone. Trust, but don't be blind. Dream, but stay down-to-earth. And particularly: have compassion. Do not pity. Have compassion. Pity is just a game of ego, compassion comes from the heart. Try to understand others, but do not accept their views as yours. We wear masks of all kinds - parent, child, brother, friend, lover… UNITE! A beautiful example is the English word "personality". As the Greeks would say that everything comes from them, so this word has its origin in Greek drama. "Sona" means voice, sound, and "Per" means through the mask. So our personality as we know it, is only a voice emanating from under the mask.

"Only if we have faith in ourselves, can we be faithful to others."
E. Fromm

We all long for love. We look for it every day without realizing that it is still with us. It did not go anywhere. We just feel that it is something that we can only receive from others. This is not the right approach. **Love is the only true feeling.** Everything else is based on love, from which arises fear, respectively the illusion of fear. Feelings of insignificance, inferiority complexes - everything is just a manifestation of the lack of love. But first you have to love yourself, accept yourself as you really are. Fall in love with yourself! But be aware, once again therein lies the rub. There is a big difference between unconditional love, with which you receive yourself in your entirety, and selfish love, in which you believe no one is better than you. This is a very fine distinction and very treacherous. It is really easy to succumb to so-called spiritual pride because it is very sophisticated in its "pretense of modesty". Especially if you're not confronted with your direct mirror (e.g. your partner relationship), because you don't accept it, or you consciously avoid it. All of them are our teachers, on whatever stage of development. Everyone is. Begin to eliminate your ego (all those meaningless programs that are not a natural part of you) and start to use your heart again. This is the only way. Love has not got many forms, love just is, just as we should learn to just be.

Fall in love with yourself, but do not go nuts about yourself!

"Endless love is an unbeatable weapon. Is the `summum bonum` of life. A coward is incapable of exhibiting love; it is the prerogative of the brave. It is no wooden or lifeless dogma, but a living and life giving force. It is a special feature of the heart." Gandhi

If everyone started seeking their nature, we would understand that we need neither religion nor any other group to belong to. Nobody and nothing can make us happier than ourselves. Everything is temporary, even we are. Happiness that depends on external circumstances is food for the ego. Of course, certain things or situations make us happy, and that is good! But try to keep this feeling just like that… You will not be able to because you are still confronted by your own mind (and therefore it is important to learn how to consciously switch it off). **Learn to be with yourself.** Do not be afraid of solitude. Then nothing will surprise you in old age. Loneliness brings us only ourselves. So what are you afraid of? Of yourself?! Be a friend to yourself, otherwise you will be constantly dependent on someone. Again, you will find yourself in a vicious circle full of mistrust and unauthorized judgments. And if you do not trust yourself, how can you trust others?!

"When you live with people, do not forget what you learned in solitude. And in solitude think about what you learned among people."
L. N. Tolstoy

Loneliness is not the same as isolation. A lot of people get it wrong and in that case loneliness becomes food for the ego and not for the heart. Even in solitude you need to be creative. You should gain new energy – from the silence of meditation. This does not mean that you have to give up the world. A lot of people do it, but they are not happy. They just have not met anyone who has told them how unhappy they are. That is why they are lying to themselves, claiming that they do not need anyone. They grow numb towards everything, whether it is the intelligence of the mind or the heart. This happens to great egoists, spiritual posers and then especially in old age, when people feel that they have no choice. Until then they had constantly surrounded themselves with people. They "did not have time" to solve the problems with themselves because they were dealing with others their whole lives. Then comes disease, which is merely the last scream of their bodies in response to their lives. Just imagine: your family members, friends, and acquaintances are slowly but surely leaving you, and even if you wanted to enjoy your life anyhow, you do not actually know how, and even if you knew how, you would not have money for it. For this state, you become absolutely unpromising citizens. It's just a pity that those who govern it forget that they too will be old one day. But paradoxically, those who make decisions regarding this situation will be able to steal enough for their retirement, so this problem is not relevant to them. That is the reason why they cannot be trusted. Most of them fall victim to some serious illness, and only when it's too late, they begin to realize the importance of true values. Learn to be alone and you'll never "need" anyone and will never have to emotionally abuse anyone. The sooner you do it, the less it will surprise you later. Everyone is alone. Today's retirement homes should become beautiful resorts with **communities**, where one can truly enjoy his retirement. He will be surrounded by like-minded people with similar hobbies, will not feel abandoned but quite the contrary. Again, it is just a game of the mind and ego, which gives you the feeling that your family wants to "discard" you. Change your thinking and do not emotionally extort those who still have a whole life ahead of them, please. There are so many old people who basically haven't understood anything. Disease keeps them alive and they still do not understand the meaning of life, so they "abuse" all those who love them, bitch about life, and they want to die, but cannot...They cannot because they are still fighting with something. Relax, surrender to what it is, open your heart and be good to others, and to your own thoughts - this is your ticket to the other world. The cause of your disease is only in your past and in your patterns of behavior.

"People get older but do not mature."
A. Daudet

Our **age** can be divided into **horizontal and vertical aging**. Almost everyone gets older horizontally. The timeline of life is straight and you just count your years. You get old, but you do not mature. However, vertical age (development of our soul) is equally important. In practice, this means for instance that on paper you can be 30 years old, but in terms of maturity, experience, or thinking, you have the energy of a sixty-year old person (and vice versa). And believe me, it's just a convenience, as we are often faced with the fact that people become aware of their genuine priorities as late as when they are sixty or seventy. You are no longer dependent on useless things, you have different values, and you can see everything much more easily (of course, if you do not turn sour). There is nothing you would rather have than a young body! Therefore, work on yourself now.

"It is never too late for us to be what we could be."
G. Eliot

Once you start looking for the truth, it will come to you. Just as when you start looking for yourself, you will find it. Inside, you know very well what no longer makes sense, what you artificially keep just because you're afraid of change. Discover yourself and go back to what you've always wanted to do. There is no man happier than the one who actually does what he enjoys, and he does it with his heart and joy – it cannot be done otherwise. Feel free to leave a job that does not suit you. The universe always has something ready for you when you obey your heart. Maybe it will not be so easy at the beginning, but the universe also wants proof that you are serious about this change. Find yourself in creativity and use it to your advantage. Creativity is really in everything! It is in your whole life, every day – introduce it to all your actions, start to play again. Even in the case of quite common activities such as cleaning, shopping, etc. – always do something differently, playfully. Because now it is only your repressed creativity that gets transformed into destructive energy. That is why there are so many quarrels, conflicts, and wars. One needs to use his right hemisphere playfully and creatively. It is only this day and age that makes people depressed and destructive. Therefore, a change in our **thinking and the expansion of our consciousnesses** are more important today than ever. **The world is changing – we are changing.**

"Let all your actions, speech and thoughts be as if at this moment you had to let go of your life, like the time that was given to you was an unexpected gift!"
M. Aurelius

Fortunately, new children are born - new souls - pearl and diamond children. In the mid-eighties and early nineties it was the indigo or crystal children. Indigo because their aura contains predominantly this color. They are much more receptive, sensitive, and precognitive. They have understood the principles of life since childhood and seek the truth everywhere. Often, they have a problem with authority and with systems that do not work, and they know it internally. Due to the ignorance of parents and teachers, however, they are often sent to psychologists who often label them as problematic or hyperactive. Nevertheless, they just need attention and understanding. They are here to be an inspiration and to change dysfunctional patterns. New souls (pearls and diamonds) are completely clean. Unlike indigo children, they are not burdened with karma, so they look at everything with new eyes. They do not have programs of suffering, deprivation, and injustice in them. They love life, the earth, and all living things. They are even already born with extended DNA. Consequently, they have many genuine properties that now seem supernatural (clairvoyance, telepathy, channeling, etc.). Pearl children carry the feminine principle, and diamond children represent the male principle. They have been born to show us how to live properly, in harmony with the whole being. They carry an age-old wisdom in them, the knowledge, truth, and pure creativity. They have strong personalities; they realize they are on a great spiritual mission. The oldest were born circa 2000, but most of them were born in 2013 (we can see this also thanks to the fact that very many genuine personalities died that in that year - everything is in harmony).

Among adults we can currently find the so-called golden children whose souls come from the time of Atlantis, Egypt, or they carry the suffering of the Christ. They are old souls who have gone through many incarnations and are aware that they do not want to experience the fall of civilization again, as they have already experienced it many times before. They currently suffer from an aversion to life, depression stemming from the current state of society, dissatisfaction and overall apathy to the fact that things are not as they wish them to be. Their typical trait is that despite their many talents they are mostly unappreciated. Paradoxically, they often abuse their power, which is in this case mainly psychological. However, it is very important to realize that these souls were those who dominated others in ancient societies and now have found themselves on the "other side" as they are the so-called victims. Again, it is mainly a compensation of energy. These souls have the task at this moment to raise the level of society and change dysfunctional rules. They carry a very ancient wisdom. It needs to be discovered behind the veil of karmic suffering that must be removed with awareness of the present and with the awakening of compassion. Golden souls are the most appropriate parents for pearl and diamond children. (If you feel that you have such a sensitive child at home, seek out relevant literature to make it easier for you to cooperate with him. He will be thankful.)

"Respect everyone, but respect children a hundred times more and beware not to ruin their childlike purity."
L. N. Tolstoy

Children are the greatest treasure that we have - the greatest teachers. Always respect them, give them the freedom to develop, encourage them to do sports, the arts, and to be creative. Do not be afraid of them, and do not get angry at them if they shatter all the ideas that you had about them. They are your school, as their children will be for them. Feel unconditional love for them, but let them be free. Try to give your children as much freedom as possible until they are seven years old. It is the most important period in their development, when they take in all that will influence them in future. If you let them "just be", their inner wisdom will take them in the proper direction. It is the exact opposite of what is happening, so you again will find it difficult to accept it. Anyway, obedient children have never made it "far". Let them be bad sometimes. That is what we were prohibited from doing, and it is always reflected later in the most inappropriate situations. There is nothing better than firsthand experience. Remind them of the risks, and if they get burnt, they will really learn from it. Feel free to communicate with them as if they were your equals (in important moments). Children have natural intelligence, do not repress it with your infantile behavior. Take them as an example in terms of sincerity, spontaneity, joy, and unconditional love! **Discover the curiosity of the child in you and start asking questions.** Children constantly ask questions, and you should start asking them again, too. Ask questions about anything, the universe will always give you the answer. Children are particularly our educators - never forget that please. But even children need some boundaries, so again, there are two sides of the coin with this approach. You cannot let others extort you emotionally, on the other hand. You need to create authority through your exemplary behavior, not by screaming. In the end, their education is a reflection of your intelligence and patience. The child learns everything he sees, and therefore, it is important to handle him with care and not underestimate the most important period of his development. We are all in the circle of eternity and that is not just a phrase. With regard to **education**, deal with your children individually. **Each child is a personality** and needs something different and even at different times in their development. And they always tell you - listen to them and trust them. There is nothing worse than not believing your own child and talking up the quality of teachers if it is directed against the children. There is always the possibility of dialogue, and the child has innate intelligence, so you can reasonably explain many things. Society kills their nature and the search for truth. After all, do you know enough about life to be able to educate someone? Can your relationships be an example?

Can you admit to mistakes and apologize to the child? How many times have you behaved the way you swore you would never behave again? How often do you just switch to your parents' programs? Are you truly happy with yourself, enough to create, to shape a new life?

The educational system desperately needs reform. Nowadays, we have computers we use to find facts. We do not need to "stuff" so much information into children – they will forget most of it anyway. The result of this approach is pressure on children who are many times unnecessarily traumatized and humiliated by teachers. Not only is the child not interested in the subject matter which he is being exposed to stress for, he does not even understand it in its entirety, and in many cases, he will not ever even need it. Everyone has their own mission in life, their own way, everyone is interested in something different. We feel it most purely in childhood. At this time we see glimpses of where we should go in our lives because our souls are strongly connected to the "source" – the existence. Of course, the child would prefer to play; therefore, learning must be devised through play and creativity in particular. There may be general guidelines, but a substantial part of that should be handled individually. Otherwise, we just create new slaves: *make them get used to being "from – to" in some institution as soon as possible, to obey orders and become obedient - they will live like that their whole lives!* Unfortunately, this is the main principle of today's schools. There are people who deal with it on a professional level, I'm not here to invent that system. I only want you to open your eyes, to make you understand that the present system is not working. **Whether it is education, morality, politics, health, interpersonal relationships, etc. Unfortunately, whenever we look at anything more closely, we find that, essentially, it does not work. There are experts and studies that can provide us with solutions based on the real needs of people. They are just consciously combated by those who are in power and who want to thrive in this immature system.**

We all should have one common goal - to live a full and joyful life.

There is only **one true instinct: SURVIVE!** Even **sex is** just another form of the same **energy**. When you make love, you feel that you live. Sex is the gate to creation - an unconscious way of creating a new life - reproducing. Here on earth we are sexual beings, do not suppress this fact, but do not abuse it either. Our body is programmed to feel a natural desire to create, therefore to create a new life is the greatest event for everyone. Is there a nicer sense of fulfillment? All who have had children have only then understood that they have something to live for. Because you are the Creator, like everyone else. We are one fragmented being - energy. **You are God.** And when you realize that she/he is in everyone, you will have no need to hurt anyone. If you understand the alchemy of life, karma, reincarnation, the eternal circle which also always returns everything to you, you will no longer be separate, but quite the contrary. Understand that we are all linked and it is much better to cooperate than to fight. **Religion** in the form in which we have it today is a fraud and a lie. It is only **about power. With the money of the Vatican (Christians), Saudi Arabia (Muslims), and Israel (Jews) we could feed the whole planet. So who really cares about people here?!** It is not a religion, it's not politics, it is not morality, it is not an educational system, it is not even health care… **the only thing you can begin to trust is YOU.** Nobody else can do it for you. Search for your truth and it will lead you to a higher truth. You can be wrong, but do not be afraid to admit it.

"Peace begins with a smile."
Mother Teresa

All religions and similar groups fail because they do not accept people in their entirety. They consciously divide us in the illusion that they want to unite us. They create a feeling in us that our happiness is dependent on them, and it is absolute nonsense. We have the entire splendor in ourselves all the time! It is not separate! It's nice to be the so-called Buddha, but what does it actually matter if you sit locked up in some monastery? We need to know and **enjoy life as Zorba the Greek**, but as not to let it overcome us, we must **discover the simplicity of the Buddha**. Try to find harmony living between passion and humility. Let the **present moment become your kingdom**! Learn to accept life with all its beauties, but do not become dependent on anyone or anything, that is the miracle. Have a glass of wine, enjoy sex (if it is in harmony with your feelings), but do not abuse them, and particularly - do not hurt anyone. Learn to enjoy everything like a child, as if you were seeing and experiencing it for the first time. Do it with innocent joy, not with the intention to have and to control. Wine has always been the so-called drink of the gods; there is an ancient truth in it. There is no quicker way to see what you do not have balanced than to drink alcohol. (However, hard liquor has a very low and destructive energy.) But do not add an illusory strength to it and do not hide behind it. Take responsibility for every action, for all your words. Find your nature and merriment in everyday life. **Buddha is a status exactly like Christ**. Only people have personified these words. Otherwise, it is our greatest nature - a state of being. Absolute consciousness, permanent bliss and understanding. A state that goes beyond our minds. The mind is a good servant, but a very bad master. Try to understand it, learn to be an observer of its constant games. And when you learn to consciously observe it, it will become quiet, although it will not disappear. You will continue to use it, but only as a tool – just for the purpose it is created for. It will just happen one day and you will be flooded by the surreal feeling of pure joy and humility. Forget any categorization - Buddhism, Christianity, Islam, Judaism, Hinduism, Zen, or Tao. Take the best from everything! But go your own way.

"Of all the animals in the world only man knows how to laugh, although he has the fewest reasons for it." E. Hemingway

Laugh whenever possible. Children laugh incomparably more than adults - those statistics are tragic. There is no better medicine than humor and love, and paradoxically, these are the two things that people fear most. Duality is in everything, and it's up to you which pole you choose until you understand the unity. Laughter invokes joy, but it can also hurt someone severely. You fear love and you know that nothing hurts as love does. At the same time, we search for love and fun our whole lives. Always choose the better side of the coin. The choice is really up to you. Laugh! Every morning just after waking up, just start laughing for a while and see how it starts your day. Smile at yourself in the mirror and wish yourself a good day! Smile just like that, at any time, without a specific reason. If you actually start to "see", you will just laugh…

> *"Every morning when I wake up, I can choose to be happy or unhappy, and I decide to be happy. How is it possible that the majority choose to be unhappy? Why do you not see that you have a choice? If you like being unhappy, then stay unhappy, but remember that you have chosen it for yourself and do not complain. No one else is responsible for it. It is your drama. When you want it so, when you like to suffer so much and want to spend your life in misery, then it is your will, your drama. You're playing it and play it well!"* Osho

A smile melts the ice. It relieves the situation, entertains us, and makes us well. So why don't we do more activities that make us laugh?! **Laughter is the best meditation.** Laughter leaves us in the present. If we sincerely laugh - we do not think. People love comedy, they love to have fun and to laugh. It's our nature - to be joyful. That is why sitcoms are very popular. It's mainly because we subconsciously seek out the present and the gaiety. Sitcoms are based on situational humor. It means humor set in the present, based on the present, described by the present.

"The robbed that smiles steals something from the thief."
W. Shakespeare

Go through life with humor, there's no better cure! Everything can be taken with humor. But it is not the same as mockery. Do not take life seriously, although it may sound absurd. Look at everything from a detached perspective and add the humor. You really can lighten any situation. It's up to you; it's just a game of your mind.

"The mind can give you bread, but it cannot bring you joy, bliss. It is very serious, it doesn't even tolerate laughter. Life without laughter is below the human level. Animals and trees cannot laugh. Laughter is an expression of consciousness at its highest degree. People who are intellectually busy - saints, scientists, great leaders, they all cannot laugh either. They all tend to be very serious and that state is actually a disease. It is a cancer of the soul, a destructive state."
Osho

Dance, sing, and pray. Your body only reflects your soul! They are not separate as the words for them are. Body and soul are, in this incarnation, one. Learn how to take care of your body, give it the respect it deserves for bearing you. The body is your temple. Heal your soul and you will have a healthy body, it is a direct correlation. All diseases are only the programs in your head. I recommend reading the book by Alexander Svijaš - *Health Is in the Head, Not at the Pharmacy.* Health is the most important thing for us, so that is why I will not attempt to summarize the truths that are contained in many books. This is the only topic which I do not pay closer attention to in this book because it is easily available. But certainly, the truth is that if you cure the psyche, which means that you do not harm yourself with your own wrong attitudes to yourself or to others – you will be physically healthy. This means that if you can change your thinking (attitudes), you change everything. Our bodies are like smart computers (but not artificial intelligence, they are alive, which actual computers will never be), which always tells us what area of life it is necessary to cure. Stay calm and communicate with it, the answer is within you. If you are in an early stage of any health problem, try to give that place your full attention. **Our consciousnesses have truly miraculous powers, and if you target something, it automatically strengthens** (which you can apply to everything). How many times have you given your attention to what is fat, skinny, ugly, or something else? Use the power of consciousness in positive way, also in this case. Also, it is our face that communicates with us through a rash or other signs. It is very simple to determine in which area we are having a problem. (In this case, it is summarized, for example, in a book by Markus Rothkranz called *Heal Your Face.*) But still, I would like to add that the plane of the soul should be added, i.e., the higher understanding of the problem. In practice, this means that if I have a rash on my nose (for example), it means a heart problem, i.e., I will not buy drugs for the heart, but rather I will try to find the cause of the pain in my real life and heal the situation. Many health problems can be identified this way without having to visit a doctor. Everyone is able to heal himself and also has the all the right medicine in nature. The prospects for an enlightened society are perfect health for everyone (who understands the alchemy of life).

"Health is the only wealth, of which we are robbing ourselves."
M. Mamcic

In any case, try to live as healthy as possible. Drink mainly water, because **water is life**! The human body is seventy percent water. Water is able to bind to any emotion or idea. The Japanese scientist Masaru Emoto did some research in which he examined water from different parts of the world and also the impact of words and ideas on it. Under the microscope, it was beautifully shown how strongly words and ideas influence the crystalline composition of water. Again, it was confirmed that what we think creates our reality not only emotionally but also physically. If we had a healthy psyche, almost every (serious) disease can be defeated by a 40-day fast during which you drink only (pure alkaline) water. Rather clean your body before disease sets in. But again, beware, please. Today we have even encountered the new concept of an "aquaholic". Well-known corporations seek to do business selling water. As a result, people are instructed by the media as to how many liters of water they are "required" to drink. (Circa 90 billion liters of water are sold annually worldwide in plastic bottles, requiring circa 50 million barrels of oil for their production.) Doctors and scientists again agree that this is mainly an issue of the individual needs of specific people, rather than talking about specific daily requirements. People live in different climate zones and engage in different activities – all these factors should be taken into account. Never before have you seen people who always carry a bottle of water, until today. Water is life, but nothing should be exaggerated. People are again beginning to drink tap water because there is no need to succumb to the spreading panic. If you are in an area where you know that the water is not quality, then create your own. Get yourself a jug (the best is from colored glass because colors also have strong energetic support), put the crystals (charged) or shungit in the bottom, write a mantra or some energy words of blessing on it, and let it sit in the sun for at least an hour. Then you can drink water with your own program and without having to buy expensive filters.

> *"Have you ever wondered why people spend 5 dollars for a tiny bottle of Evian? Try spelling it backwards."* G. Carlin

Try to eat as many raw vegetables as possible, or at least do not do more than steam them to avoid losing a large amount of the necessary vitamins. Vegetarianism awakens a greater sensitivity to the energies within you which we kill by eating meat. But it is not impossible to achieve "enlightenment" with a steak in your mouth (figuratively speaking). Anyway, if you get to a higher frequency, the body itself will begin to ask for new eating habits. The ancient question of whether or not vegetarianism is natural is a question of our development. The consumption of meat has been a part of us for as long as we can remember (in this cycle of humanity), and thanks to that we have gotten to where we are (physically). Today, however, we have achieved almost everything that can be achieved in the physical world, and it is therefore necessary to go further. The fact is, however, that many vegetarians are currently returning to eating meat. If that is your case, do not blame yourself because the body always asks for what it is missing. Today we find ourselves in such dense energies and at such a low vibrational level that people who do not eat meat can be very hypersensitive or "lost" in this reality and therefore need anchor. In most cases, they have to untie karmic knots with people of lower energies and your soul wants to attract them so that you can "leave" him/her or resolve something. For today, personal growth and past cleansing are the most important tasks on earth. Apart from the fact that all of us are gradually moving towards the same goal (leaving meat), there is one unmistakable fact. It does not sound too good, but this consumer society is going to "eat up" the whole planet. We have already mentioned facts about beef and animal extinction, not only on land but also in the oceans. So today, this need is not only about man, but also about the Earth as a whole. That is why it is part of our growth today to stop/abandon this extreme consumption of meat as well as its waste. Vegetarianism is therefore mainly a matter of our development, and whether we can do it in this or another life, our soul will surely pass through this process. It does not happen from day to day, so do not force it if you do not feel it at the moment. It will come only when the time is right. Meanwhile, you can change the energy of every meal by saying to it: I love you / thank you. Enjoy every bite and try to chew as much as possible. **Turn every meal into a celebration, not a habit.**

Recently, healthy "bio" eating has been mentioned more and more often. However, this may be a great gimmick for your ego again.

There are an infinite number of organic foods of which we do not even have any idea where they come from (and for the highest prices). The soul shatters, but the body is perfect. A person very quickly comes to believe that they are living a healthy and exemplary lifestyle despite the fact that their personal life is often in ruins. With this way of eating you will increase the frequency, but if you have not calmed the head, you can more quickly materialize various nonsense. Do not get lured into this game. We have already experienced a similar crash of physically perfect society. Even in this case, there must be harmony. The positive thing is that people who follow this approach (as well as thanks to the internet) have actually become interested in what they eat, because much more food is chemically treated. Read the ingredients and avoid at least the E`s (emulsifiers).

"A healthy person has a thousand wishes,
but a sick person has only one."
Indian proverb

Please exercise. Even if you are not very sporty, try to at least go for a short walk during the day, or at least use the stairs instead of the elevator. Your body will be grateful for every little movement. If you do not like running, swimming, biking, or the gym, try yoga or other Eastern practices (Qigong, Tai-chi, etc.) that will teach you to get to know your own body in harmony with the soul. Simply try anything, except chess. **Sport** has also been brought to "physical perfection" in a way, and today it is a major issue also. However, it is not an important topic for you unless it concerns you. Science and technology have allowed us to have just about everything as far as equipment, footwear, clothing, etc., that means anything that has gradually improved our physical performance. We have gone beyond our means, and therefore, today the top level of sport is mainly about competition between pharmaceutical companies. In this "visual age" we would all like to look our best and we are therefore often willing to sacrifice everything, in this case literally ourselves. Different doping preparations of the worst quality which were originally made for race horses, anabolic steroids, etc. will eventually destroy you. Not only do your muscles grow, but also all the other organs in your body, which can quickly result in death. These different "drugs" also fundamentally affect the individual's psyche and development, which can also lead to brain degeneration. Today it is a serious problem among young people. And again, it is a "vicious circle" where on one hand these preparations are supported, i.e., the development of official doping, and on the other hand a war has been declared on doping. And if it is not about doping, it is about the state budget. Many people have had no chance to become professional athletes because of this crap in top sports which promotes this "fair play". And so there is also only one common denominator – money. Professional sports now have completely different rules, so do not make them your goal, but exercise for pleasure. Competition is merely a need of the ego. It is important to keep your body moving. Not only will this boost your energy, but it will also improve your mood! Every movement produces endorphins - the hormones of happiness - so let us meet them halfway. It is very important to rotate time spent passively and actively. Sport is also a meditation technique that leads us to turn off our heads. If a child learns to play sports regularly, later on he will need to move (to switch off) as part of his nature. And not only that, sport also teaches us discipline, responsibility, patience, cooperation, etc., the meaning of real life values - winning and losing. There is no better foundation for a man than to actively engage in sport. But if you do not know how to have a good relationship with it, walking in nature is equally beneficial.

"A true asylum always available to those suffering mentally is and will always remain - nature." G. A. Lindner

You know very well how comfortable we feel when we are in nature. It's our natural environment. **We are part of nature**, which provides us with endless energy. Do not destroy nature, please. You do not need to be a part of any movement to do something for this world. It is enough if you (for instance) once in a while take a garbage bag out with you and pick up the garbage in the woods. Or at least do not throw your trash on the ground. After all, we are giving the environment a pretty hard time with everyday transportation. It is time to realize that the Earth is our home and to begin acting accordingly. Support environmentally-oriented projects, if you feel inclined to do so. This problem actually affects us all. In any case, we should remember that many "problems" are just unnecessarily inflated. It is so, for example, **with global warming**. If you seek out neutral experts, they will tell you the same thing. The conditions on Earth have always been changing, and they are changing today. It is nothing exceptional., it is a fact. However, **we are accelerating these changes by our own stupidity**. What we breathe and eat today is really unbearable. Just as we have oil for at least 300 years, but then what?! **Let's not destroy the earth just to enable certain corporations to survive.** If we could have electric cars or hydrogen cars (even antigravity ones) which would not release any polluting gases into the atmosphere, why not have them?! Why do we have to pay companies for energy if we have inexhaustible resources?!

We support one percent of the population who does not even know what to do with so much wealth. They buy land in space, on a planet where there are absolutely no conditions for life. They pay incredible amounts of money for ridiculous studies, to be able to create some vacuum in which they could live – but why?! Half the world is starving, and those who could solve it build air castles, buy islands, and build nonsense because they do not know what to do with so much wealth. They lost their common sense and realistic perspective a long time ago.

The world of money no longer works. It will be difficult for your ego to digest it, but only for those who have money. The majority of people are only surviving, not living. The world is controlled by the same family clans that control and are shareholders of all the world's banks and giant corporations. They play their game in a way that makes them prosper. They do not care about you or me, or about those who are starving or do not have an acceptable standard of living for this day and age when there is enough of everything for everyone. It does not matter! Because according to them, this planet is overpopulated, so it really suits them, and on the contrary, they take steps to get rid of most of the population. In any case, they need to create fear in us and at the same time ostensibly provide help in order to create the illusion that they are needed. They divide us... In the next few years, fertility should be controlled, especially in certain specific areas. Because, paradoxically, the most children are born in the areas where there is the greatest poverty. No wonder they say that sex is the entertainment of the poor. After all, what would you do if you do not have education, could not do any cultural activities or travel!? The system does not give them a choice. Isn't that sick?! Take advantage of technology, chemistry - here's a possibility. If all people had access to health care and access to contraception, we would eliminate many problems. Forget the "religious" approach, we created it. It is not possible to not be where we are now. Young Europeans would like to set up functioning families if they had the right conditions, but they do not have. The financial crisis was created for whom? For ourselves! Money is now just an invented debt.

"If you want to feel rich count the things money can't buy."
Anonymous

Paradoxically, also in this example we can find a spiritual dimension. The whole world collapses and who is prospering? The East. Again, it only compensates the duality that is present in everything. In the West we have gone through materialism, which did not fulfill our desires and expectations, and now we tend increasingly towards

Eastern cultures. The East, however, has discovered the power of money, but again in a very unhealthy way. Therefore, at present China and India are prospering. (Were it not for the disaster in Japan, it would have joined them as well.) But if you look more closely at them, you will find that humanity has vanished from these countries (in terms of functioning). China, for example, has emerged from poverty only over the last 30 years. This was preceded by the great "cultural revolution" when one dictator decided he would take over all the industrial states. So he ordered that all the steel in the country be melted and that everyone must work. However, few people today remember that as a result of this idea about 30 million people died in 3 years. Many left their homes and families rather then to work in absolutely appalling conditions. The people had become machines and worked in conditions which common people in the West couldn't even imagine. (It has been a long time since I have seen a product on which it was not written *"Made in China"*.) They tend to escape, because the conditions created for them in their own country are intolerable. Those who dare to go the way of freedom are persecuted or arrested. Another example for us may be the so-called cultivation method of Falun Gong practiced in China, introduced by Master Li Chung-c`. It relates to everything about the harmony between mind, body, and spirit and includes five simple exercises (on the principle of the Five Tibetans). It currently has about 70 million followers who understand this simple need to find/harmonize themselves. However, this is exactly what "the communist regime" does not like. In 2006, information surfaced that all over China there are concentration camps where they kill these followers and their organs are sold all over the world! It is a plain and current fact. Again, they are not in harmony anymore. Corporations only generate new slaves – in places where the most people are and they need some security. Therefore, the suicide rates in these countries are the highest in the world. And how do they "motivate" them more? All these societies have officially "forbidden" sex - everywhere and in everything. You will not find a sex shop there, or even a single porn channel. Nevertheless, in these countries they enjoy sex to the fullest but in the most hypocritical ways. Relationships will be fake, but they will be financial superpowers! For whom?! Almost the whole country of India is starving, you cannot even buy toilet paper without corruption (figuratively speaking), but their politicians spend money on the development of deadly missiles. According to their Minister of Defense, they have qualified for the "elite club" with that test. The main thing is the ego remained intact… Therefore, the last thing they really had – spiritualism – has moved to the Andes.

> *"One can exist without ego because the individual is a reality which does not need the ego. However, nation, race, church and state - none can exist without ego. Ego exists as an artificial center that holds everything together. Therefore, there can be Buddha without ego, but not the Buddhists. Fake unity needs a fake center, otherwise it dies. India as a country, as a nation, as a race, desperately needed some way to create some artificial center. No standard alternative was available - money, technology, science or political power. Therefore, the only solution to which it was able to run to was spiritual desire - another world. This country smells and boasts of the past because it has nothing else to boast of. It rants about its falsehood, holiness and spirituality - that is all nonsense. It lacks the basics and talks about the temple. You can build a temple, but first you must lay the foundation."* Osho

And we could go on this way about any country where freedom is suppressed. Unfortunately, in these Eastern countries it is now most visible. We can be thankful that their culture is based on values like humility and modesty, otherwise they would have (with their numbers) swamped the Western world a long time ago. But what do you think will become of the next generation who is living in these nihilistic conditions?! Or let's take a look at benumbed North Korea. People there "do not know" about mobile phones, or even the internet. What information do they have?! If you go there on vacation, they will take these objects away from you. Even you should not be in contact with the outside world. And if you tried to "open their eyes", it would be considered an audacity and the tactlessness of the impolite white world. Democracy, freedom, humanity?! This is a live demonstration of programming!

This world - society - is sick and I do not think that it can be cured in this world of money. There will always be someone who will want more and who will feel a desire for power. Now it would take a lot of money to create a world without money. However, it is possible. But, people who honor the man would have to be able to get "to power". Those whose main interest is humanity and not their bank accounts. After all, statistically 99 percent of the world might wake up (if everyone had access to information channels). We also have a lot of experts who have been held back by their humanity and have stopped working on the project "to take over the world". This desire has always been there. We have experienced enormous progress, especially in the last century. We should be mature enough to be able to live without money because our resources are more than sufficient. Return to nature; celebrate life and not goods. Every country should, first and foremost, create the right conditions for its own people. Not everyone out in the world away from their homes is happy. Maybe it is time for them to return to their own countries and apply their knowledge and experience there.

"For peace of mind it is necessary to resign from the post of director-general of the globe." L. Eisenberg

Education should lead us to it. But what happens in schools is unacceptable. Children present themselves as individuals and teachers are not ready for that. And if our education is based on history, why conceal the facts?! How can be possible that the questioning of some historical event is criminal?! Why apologize for things instead of learning from them?! Let's teach tolerance, humility, compassion, humanity… is it possible? See what's happening in the USA. Children have guns and enter schools through metal detectors. They grow up in absolute arrogance, hypocrisy, and ignorance of the rest of the world. They teach them how to be patriots, while everyone forgets that their roots lie somewhere else entirely. How can USA question the (not-)accepting of immigrants at all, when their whole country - except for the Native Americans - consists of immigrants?! They grow up in blind faith believing that they are the best in the world, and yet they overlook reality because they are being isolated from it. Dazzled by Hollywood glitz and unrealistic dreams, they are not informed about the tragic poverty which is increasing exceedingly. Today, 3.8 million inhabitants are officially homeless there, although reality is much more tragic. Most children nowadays grow up with a nanny or a babysitter, so they never fully experience dedicated and true motherly love as well as other normal human relationships. This separating wedge is knowingly created around the world, but especially in the "highly developed" countries. If children do not experience this most basic proximity, they will not feel the need to cooperate with others, will not be able to perceive others, nor will they be capable of empathy - and that is what our governments need - mindless robots and slaves. Friendships and partnerships have changed into pure business relationships where each person only cares about himself. No cooperation (if money is not involved), no real values, no full-fledged relationships. And that is also a major problem today - because what is forcefully generated is this separation amongst us and support for the artificial ego. And the British are also a problem. They think they are the best and then go and make a "mess" in other countries. Of course, the "mask of a gentleman" must be counterbalanced somewhere. The so-called freest nations have so many restrictions, and especially for young people, that is not possible to fully grow up. Drinking is banned for young people until they are 21 years old. Close the bars around 1 o'clock in the morning and what will you get?! Of course - negative rebellion. However, it is absurd that an 18-year-old American girl can drive a tank in Afghanistan, but at home she cannot even have a beer. Nearly every shopping mall in the US has a permanent branch where they recruit to the army. For young people without work, this is the simplest leak. This is sick. Systematic enslavement exists from childhood. Why is school attendance compulsory for nursery school kids in these countries? Think about it - it is nonsense. Both of these nations have been convinced for generations that they have the manual for the world. **Are these really the countries which should be an example for the world?** Look at them in detail and critically.

The first world, second world, third world. Just these terms make us feel separated from the issues of others. **Problems of the Third World? Don't we have, by the way, just ONE world?!** The so-called primitive cultures are infinitely closer to real life than those who only pretend so, the so-called civilized world.

At present, we are (thanks to the internet) really interconnected for the first time in history. We have the ability to share information with the whole world in one single moment. Such a situation has never existed before, and therefore, please, let's use it in a positive way. Therein lies our greatest hope. Today there are already enough of those of us who want to change it. Search for some of these initiatives on the internet and try to engage in them sometimes if they correspond to what you feel. The force of creation is also a matter of common consciousness, so the more we think (act) on the right intentions, the more they tend to take place. And in particular, we must pay attention to any handling or manipulation. **Today we can only trust our intuition**. Do not succumb to fear, we are able to do it!

"A man who is perfecting himself, is perfecting the world."

S. Smiles

You're the only "God" that exists, you are the Life. Nobody is more or less than you. Forget about all the instructions, systems, and religions; seek your own truth. Which religion today is a celebration of life? Even in the most peaceful form of Buddhism, monks burn themselves to death as a form of protest these days, and the Dalai Lama has nothing against it! I will not kill a fly, but I will kill myself?! Indeed, it almost resembles Islam. For whom did you actually sacrifice yourself? Do you think that this will change anything?! In a world where every day ca. 30,000 people die just because they do not have their vital needs met, do you really think that you will save someone or something with your own death?! There is only one reason. People's natural intelligence is numbed. Whether they are Buddhists or Muslims. Do they have access to real unbiased information?! In the temples or mosques, do they browse the internet or do they live with the information which is provided to them?! Asexual Christians, aggressive Muslims, racist Jews, or frustrated colored minorities... **who will save us?! First of all, it must be MAN! Religions have completed their mission, accept this as a fact.**

"Someday, after mastering the winds, the waves, the tides and gravity, we will enchain the power of love. And then, for a second time in the history of the world, man will have discovered fire."
P. T. de Chardin

Forget separation. More and more differences are created only because we discover our individuality. This world, however, does not support it, quite the contrary. If you find yourself, you will not let them control you and that is what the government fears. They really do not care about anything else. **Asian, Christian, gay, Jewish, black, transsexual... the main thing is that you pay taxes!** In the world of money no one examines your origin. It's all just a protest of our subconscious soul. A huge test of our tolerance. And we fail - in everything.

In fact, everything has been invented! There are communities that already live disconnected from the system. There are teachers who understand the need for change and know well what it should look like. There are also doctors who understand the need to treat the person as a whole. There are scientists who have solutions for almost anything! **These people do exist, they just need to be given space!** Who appoints them? We can go through lots of absurd polls and meaningless elections so we could use this effort a little more constructively. No wonder it is said that if the current elections could change anything, they would have been banned long ago. **Direct democracy in its full extent** (as it has never been applied) **is the way we can move further in many ways.**

If you are in harmony with yourself, you inevitably create harmony in your surroundings. It takes you to the stream of synchronicity when things start to happen without you forcing something. Each timing, meeting, inspiration, and situation will be in harmony with your "higher plan". Do not forget that everything takes time. Every baby is in the womb of his mother for nine months. Do not give up on anything that does not work out on the first attempt. We are like children, and we want everything now. But we are "big" already and then comes **the art of patience**. Eventually, everything will be solved, crystallized, for better or worse - it's mainly about your perception, and even so, everything always happens only for your benefit. Something that today can seem like deterioration may be the best thing that could happen to you in the future. Do not judge people or situation, accept everything with humility - in retrospect it will have its own meaning. **Learn humility**, but remember, that does not mean that you have to become overly modest and obedient. It's mainly about recognizing that there is nothing more and nothing less than you. It is the understanding that the president is just a person exactly the same as a homeless man, and also that you can become one or the other from day to day. However, the greatest humility is if you can apply it to yourself and to your emotions.

Be honest and sincere (especially with yourself), even in the most difficult moments - it is a true act of humility. Do not fight unnecessarily with others, but nor with you. **Find yourself and you will discover the whole world. Go back to real values, and the greatest and common value over all should be LIFE**.

"When will we really learn that we are cells of one body? Until the spirit of love towards our neighbors, untouched by race, color or faith, fills the world and makes our lives realistic. Until our deeds are a true testament to human brotherhood - until a long queue of people are filled with a sense of responsibility for the good lives of others, until we achieve social justice."
H. Keller

Fall in love with life! At every moment. It is you who decides what will follow. Take full responsibility for your life, for your actions and relationships, for this world. It is never too late to start looking for the truth. And the truth is within you. Be thankful for each new day! Be grateful for every smile, for every breath. Love is full of gratitude and compassion. **Gratitude is the most beautiful prayer.**

"Gratitude can really change your life... and the best thing is that the law of attraction will give you more of everything that you feel grateful for and what makes you happy. When you feel frustrated, the law of attraction gives you more reasons to feel frustrated. Start to perceive all the things that you have in the present life for which you are grateful. It does not matter how little they are."
T. Swan

Remember that **everything is meaningless if you cannot share it**. However, if you act only on the basis of your ego, so that you donate to others only because it makes good for you, then it is just your game and not real happiness. These games can be played for a long time but eventually always leave you with an empty feeling.

Happiness dependent on others never lasts long. But without others you cannot enjoy it to the fullest. Again, there is a very fine line and a very important edge of the same coin. Share your joy, but do not become dependent on the recognition of others. Just be aware of the fact that if there was no one with whom you could share something, that it would have exactly the same value which has now - none. Because here and now is only you and this text. There is nothing more to it. And at the same time everything. Accept the paradoxes of life and learn to see unity in them. Share love, it always returns, maybe not from the same person, but it will return. Fill others with joy as you would do for yourself - unconditionally. In your own solitude, get to know the solitude of others and then share it. No one will understand you completely, but try to have compassion for that person. We are all on the same path, just on different levels. **The road IS the goal.**

"Who rules the moment, governs life."
M. Ebnerová-Eschenbach

Learn to live in the present. Be aware of each breath and it will return you to the present moment. **Just breathe... you are exactly where you need to be.**

Make today your new birthday. If you've read this far, you understand the point, and in particular, if you have started to **apply it all to your life**, you have been born again. But this time into the conscious world. Enjoy this moment filled with love. Just like that. Experience an unconditional joy. Smile. Go to the mirror and look into your eyes. Promise yourself that from today you will want to see and know the truth. That you will do everything to be satisfied with yourself, to rediscovered innocence, beauty, and the playfulness of a child in you. Rejoice with each new day. Fall in love with yourself. Whenever you do not know how to act, ask: **what would love do? What would someone who loves himself do? The answer is always so**

easy. We always have a choice to decide from the position of love or ego - always. **Believe in yourself and listen to your heart. It will reward you.**

So do not forget:

"We are not human beings having a spiritual experience. We are spiritual beings having a human experience."
P.T. de Chardin

Love yourself... Believe in YOU... You do not need anything more... You are a "god", believe it or not... You are... Everyone is... You have an opportunity to create... You have the option to create a new life... You create your world - with thoughts... Just understand that everyone is a god, and so everyone is a part of you... So just do not do to others what you do not want them to do to you... And do not judge... Everything you condemn – you attract... Be in harmony with yourself... In everything... And then you will be in harmony with the whole universe... Because you want to be happy... so be happy! Every morning wake up with that feeling... You are a god - creator... You decide what happens next...

GOD = LOVE = LIFE

Do you believe in life? Do you believe in love? You do not have to... They are here even if you don't believe in them... The perfection of man does not exist... It is only the perfection of the moment... So just be who you want to be...

LOVE YOU

"There is no need to search; achievement leads nowhere. It makes no difference at all, so just be happy now! Love is the only reality in the world because it is the beginning and the end of everything. And the only laws are paradox, humor, and change. There is no problem, there never was, and there never will be. Release your struggle, let go of your mind, throw away your concerns, and relax into the world. No need to resist life, just do your best. Open your eyes and see that you are far more than you imagine. You are the world, you are the universe; you are yourself and everyone else, too! It's all the marvelous Game of God. Wake up, regain your humor. Don't worry, just be happy. You are already free!"

(D. Millman - Peaceful Warrior)

P.S.

Well, a slightly emotional conclusion, a lot of information at once, good feelings, and one more question on the tip of your tongue: Okay, but what now?

So let us summarize it one more time:

1. **Read this book again.**
2. **Begin to work on yourself in the sense that you will observe and slowly remove programs from your parents, friends, partners - anyone. You can recognize them based on the principle of the mirror and your emotional reactions - if your reaction to something is too emotional, this is the part where you should work it out. To break away from the bonds of emotion is the main goal of every man - whether you believe it or not. Then comes the ecstasy you have been longing for... excuse me – nirvana...** ☺ (Later, you will use your emotions only to your advantage - consciously, because without them we would die of boredom)
3. **Be bold! Do what you enjoy! Take a chance and the whole existence will reward you! If everyone started doing what he enjoys and what fulfills him, we would fit into the flow of synchronicity like a piece of the puzzle (this is also true for relationships). There is no**

need to save the world (if you do not feel like it); it is necessary to save yourself first. In the beginning it is not easy, but if you succeed, you will be able to respect yourself and others will respect you too. Nobody will come to rescue you this time – it is just up to us - every one of us.

4. **Speak the truth! And do not dramatize things.**
5. **Do not judge anything and do not idealize unnecessarily.**
6. **Forgive others and learn to have compassion. Slowly start opening your heart… melt away all your fears…** ♡
7. **CREATE - anything! And if you have the feeling that you have nothing to do at the moment, just DANCE!**
8. **Smile, please ☺**
9. **The further you get, the higher frequencies you will emit, and the more your physical surroundings will change. We operate on the principle of radio waves - each of us has his own frequency and you resonate with the one that suits you. The more you work on yourself, the more you increase the frequency, and the less the lower frequencies will suit you. It will be natural for you to change your friends. However, do not look down on anyone. Be humble and act according to what you feel.**
10. **Take up some active meditation techniques. They help you silence the mind, to create a distance from it. They expand awareness and teach you to live in the present. And if you can, take part in collective meditations for peace and greater missions. The more people, the greater the force of creation.**
11. **Remain in the present - HERE and NOW. Put a sign (ribbon) on your hand, which when you look at it will remind you that you have to fully return to the ongoing situation.**

12. **Do not do to others what you do not want them to do to you.**
13. **LOVE - everything and everyone, but first learn to love yourself unconditionally.**

May J O Y accompany you every day.

CHAPTER 21. = PRACTICE.

"Tomorrow never comes, it is always TODAY."
Osho

ENJOY ☺

Printed in the United States
By Bookmasters